BRITISH FUNGUS FLORA
AGARICS AND BOLETI

Edited by D. M. Henderson, P. D. Orton and R. Watling

---

2 | Coprinaceae Part 1:
Coprinus

P. D. ORTON AND R. WATLING

EDINBURGH

HER MAJESTY'S STATIONERY OFFICE

1979

ISBN 0 11 491565 2

COPRINACEAE

INTRODUCTION

This part contains the characters of the family Coprinaceae with a key to genera, followed by the genus *Coprinus* in detail. The other genera, *Lacrymaria, Panaeolus* and *Psathyrella* will be dealt with in later parts.

Opportunity has been taken to alter the format as explained in the observations to the genus *Coprinus* on p. 7, which we hope will be accepted as an improvement.

We would like to thank Miss M. Holden, Rothamsted Experimental Station, Harpenden, Herts., for invaluable help with the keys to the stirps and species, and for much helpful advice and discussion, and also Dr. R.O.F. Kemp, Department of Botany, University of Edinburgh for much help and information about cultural details.

Finally we would stress that this can be no more than a preliminary account of the genus *Coprinus* in Britain, for there are many references in the descriptions to taxa as yet undescribed or unnamed or improperly understood, and it is hoped that this work may not only help towards more easy and correct determination of species but also stimulate others to help in clarifying these.

FAMILY DESCRIPTION

Basidia borne on gills (lamellae); gill trama of hyaline or coloured, non-gelatinised hyphae irregularly arranged or parallel to a central strand of similar, slightly paler or slightly darker elements. Development of hymenium in European species enclosed by formation of obvious or scanty velar tissue (bivelangiocarpic to paravelangiocarpic). Basidia often short and broad, usually 4-spored, sometimes 2-spored (Fig. 21) and in one genus, *Coprinus,* frequently of more than one size (Figs. 19 and 20). Basidiospores variable in shape, usually smooth and usually with distinct germ-pore. Spore-print distinctly coloured, fuscous or olivaceous black, sepia, cigar-brown or umber, rarely paler; in one group, *Psathyrella sarcocephala,* the spores are slightly pinkish cinnamon in mass. Flesh homoiomerous with or without laticiferous hyphae, usually thin and at maturity in most members of the genus *Coprinus* reduced to a liquid mass. Clamp-connections present in many species. Cap cuticle of sub-isodiametric cells giving a cellular structure (Fig. 14) which is frequently obscured by the development of a veil, or less frequently of radially arranged inflated, ellipsoid cells (Fig. 17) also frequently obscured by the veil. Marginal cystidia present, usually numerous and in groups; facial cystidia frequently present. Chemistry not well investigated; chemical tests are not used in distinguishing species; physiology of vegetative and fruiting stages of several species very well-documented. Genetics very well known in several species; *Coprinus cinereus* (as *C. lagopus*) is used as teaching material.

1

SYSTEMATIC ARRANGEMENT

COPRINACEAE

    Panaeoloideae

    *Panaeolus (Fries) Quélet

    Coprinoideae

    *Lacrymaria Patouillard

    *Psathyrella (Fries) Quélet

    Coprinus (Persoon ex Fries) S.F. Gray

*Genera to be dealt with in later parts

Coprinus:

Heinemann, P. & Josserand, M. (1941). *Coprinus erythrocephalus* et *Coprinus dilectus. Bull. Soc. Mycol. Fr. 57:* 36-49. Josserand, M. (1933). Importance de l'ornamentation pileique pour la détermination des *Coprinus. Ann. Soc. Linn. Lyon, 77:* 89-95. Josserand, M. (1933). L'étude des Coprins fimicoles. *Ann. Soc. Linn. Lyon, 77:* 96-113. Josserand, M. (1944). Etude sur quelques Coprins. Description de deux espèces nouvelles. *Bull. Soc. Mycol. Fr., 60:* 5-18. Kühner, R. & Josserand, M. (1934). Description de quelque espèces du group de *Coprinus plicatilis* (Curt.) Fr. *Bull. Soc. Mycol. Fr., 50:* 53-63. Kühner, R. & Josserand, M. (1944). Etude de quatre Coprins du groupe *'lagopus'. Bull. Soc. Mycol. Fr., 60:* 19-32. Kühner, R., Josserand, M. & Yen, H.C. (1947). Différences morphologiques entre plusieurs souches de Coprins de la *section Micacei* et confrontation de leurs haplontes. *Bull. Soc. Mycol. Fr., 63:* 171-186. Kühner, R. & Romagnesi, H. (1957). Compléments a la "Flore Analytique" VII. Espèces nouvelles, critiques ou rares de *Naucoriacées, Coprinacées & Lepiotacées. Suppl. Bull. de Soc. Nat. d'Oyonnax, 10-11:* 3-94. Lange, M. (1952). Species concept in the genus *Coprinus. Dansk. Bot. Arkiv., 14:* 1-164. Lange, M. & Smith, A.H. (1953). The *Coprinus ephemerus* group. *Mycologia, 45:* 747-780. Locquin, M. (1947). Etudes sur le genre Coprinus 1. Quelques Coprins fimicoles. *Bull. Soc. Mycol. Fr., 63:* 75-88. Locquin, M. (1949). Un critere nouveau pour la définition de genre *Coprinus. Ann. Soc. Linn. Lyon, 18*(5): 89-92. Locquin, M. (1955). Recherches sur le Coprins. *Bull. Soc. Mycol. Fr., 71:* 5-18. Massee, G. (1896). A revision of the genus *Coprinus. Ann. Bot., 38:* 123-184. Orton, P.D. (1954). Observations on the genus *Coprinus. Trans. Brit. Mycol. Soc., 46:* 263-276. Orton, P.D. (1960). in New Check List of British Agarics and Boleti, Part III. *Trans. Brit. Mycol. Soc., 43:* 198-202. Orton, P.D. (1961-72). Notes on British Agarics in *Notes Roy. Bot. Gdn, Edinburgh.* Pilát, A. & Svrček, M. (1967). Revisio specierum sectionis *Herbicolae* generis *Coprinus. Ceská Mykol., 21:* 136-145. Pinto-Lopes, J. & Almeida, M.G. (1970). *'Coprinus lagopus'* a confusing name as applied to several species. *Portug. Acta Biol.,* Series B, 7: 167-204. Romagnesi, H. (1941). Les Coprins. *Rev. Mycol (Suppl.), 6:* 108-119. Romagnesi, H. (1945). Etude de quelques Coprins (2[e] series) *Rev. Mycol. 10.* (5-6): 73-89. Romagnesi, H. (1951). Etude sur quelques Coprins III. *Rev. Mycol., 16:* 108-128. Watling, R. (1967-72). Notes on British Agarics in *Notes Roy. Bot. Gdn.,* Edinburgh. Waveren, E. Kits van (1968). The 'stercorarius group' of the genus *Coprinus. Persoonia, 5:* 131-176.

Panaeolus:

Hora, F.B. (1957) The genus *Panaeolus* in Britain. *The Naturalist,* Hull. Ola'h, G.M. (1969). Le genre *Panaeolus,* essai taxonomique et physiologique. *Rev. Mycol. Mem. Hors. Series 10:* 1-273.

Psathyrella:

Malençon, G. & Romagnesi, H. (1953). Le complexe *Psathyra corrugis* s. Ricken. *Bull. Soc. Mycol. Fr., 69:* 101-127. Orton, P.D. (1960), in New Check List of British Agarics & Boleti; Part III. *Trans. Brit. Mycol. Soc., 43:* 198-202. Romagnesi, H. (1939). Sur le genre *Drosophila* Quélet. *Rev. Mycol.,* 4(NS): 117-130. Romagnesi, H. (1944). Classification du genre *Drosophila* Quélet. *Bull. Soc. Linn. Lyon, 13:* 51-54. Romagnesi, H. (1952). Species et formae nova ex genre *Drosophila* Quélet. *Bull. Soc. Linn. Lyon, 21:* 151-156. Romagnesi, H. (1966).Description de deux nouvelles espèces du sous genre *Psathyrella. Bull. Soc. Mycol. Fr., 86:* 539-545. Romagnesi, H. (1975). Description de quelques espèces de *Drosophila* Quél. *(Psathyrella* ss. Dilat.), Complément a la contribution a l'étude du genre *Psathyrella* (Fr.) Quel. (Agaricales). *Bull. Soc. Mycol. Fr., 91:* 137-224. Smith, A.H. (1941). Studies of North American Agarics I. *Contr. Univ. Mich. Herb., 5:* 1-73. Smith, A.H. (1972). The North American Species of *Psathyrella. Memoirs of the New York Botanical Garden, 24:* 1-633. Watling, R & Jurand, M. (1971). Two new coprophilous species of *Psathyrella. Notes Roy. Bot. Gdn. Edinburgh, 31*(1): 143-153. Waveren, E. Kits van (1971). Notes on the genus *Psathyrella* I. *Psathyrella gracilis* and *P. micorrhiza. Persoonia, 6(2):* 249-280. Waveren, E. Kits van (1971). Notes on the genus *Psathyrella* II. Three new species of *Psathyrella. Persoonia, 6(3):* 295-312. Waveren, E. Kits van (1972). Notes on the genus *Psathyrella* III. Unorthodox approach and key to section *Atomatae. Persoonia, 7(1):* 23-54.

The following references cover various aspects of the biology of members of the Coprinaceae. (Where *Coprinus lagopus* is mentioned in a reference see remarks under that species in text).

General:

Buller, A.J.H. (1922-24). In *Researches in Fungi 2 & 3,* London. Burnett, J.A. (1968). In *Fundamentals of Mycology,* London. Butler, G.M. (1961). Growth of hyphal branching systems in *Coprinus disseminatus. Ann. Botany. (London)* [N.S.], 25: 341-352. Butler, G.M. (1966). 'Vegetative structures' in *The Fungi* (London) 2: 83-112. Chow, C.H. (1934). Contribution a l'étude du développement des *Coprinus. Le Botaniste, 26:* 89-232. Ikediugwu, F.E.O. & Webster, J. (1970). Antagonism between *Coprinus heptemerus* and other coprophilous fungi. *Trans. Brit. Mycol. Soc., 54:* 181-204. Kühner, R. (1926), in Contribution de l'étude de Hyménomycètes et specialement des Agaricacées. *Le Botaniste, 17:* 5-224. Lange, M. (1952). Species concept in the genus *Coprinus. Dansk. Bot. Arkiv., 14:* 1-164. Locquin, M. (1944). Structure & développement des spores de *Coprinus narcoticus. Bull. Soc. Mycol. Fr., 60:* 43-46. Reinjders, A.F.M. (1963). In *Les problèmes du développement des carpophores des Agaricales et de quelque groupes voisins,* Hague. Taber, W.A. (1966). Morphogenesis in Basidiomycetes in *The Fungi* (London) 2: 387-412.

Biology (Spores):

Pegler, D.N. & Young, T.W.K. (1971). Basidiospore morphology in the Agaricales. *Nova Hedwigia, Beihefte 35:* 1-210.

Chemistry:

Birkenshaw, J.H. (1965). 'Chemical constituents of the fungal cell' in *The Fungi*, (London) *1:* 179-228. Watling, R. (1971). 'Chemical Tests in Agaricology' in *Methods in Microbiology*, London.

Physiology, Genetics & Cultural Studies:

Anderson, G.E. (1971). *The life history and genetics of Coprinus lagopus.A practical introduction to biochemical genetics.* Weston-Super-Mare. Bille-Hansen, E. (1953). Fructification of a coprophilous *Coprinus* on synthetic medium. *Physiol. Plantarum, 6:* 523-528. Bille-Hansen, E. (1953). Fructification of three coprophilous species of *Coprinus* using glucose, sucrose and maltose as carbon source. *Svensk. Bot. Tids, 50:* 81-85. Brunswick, H. (1924). 1. Untersuchungen über die Geschlechts- und Kernverhaltnisse bei der Hymenomyzetengattung *Coprinus. Botan. Abhandl. Herausgeg v. Goebel 5.* Buller, A.H.R. (1924) *Researches on Fungi 3*, London. Casselton, L.A. & Casselton, P.J. (1966). Control of fruiting of *Coprinus lagopus* on certain synthetic media. *Trans. Brit. Mycol. Soc., 49:* 59-81. Day, P.R. (1959). A cytoplasmically controlled abnormality of the tetrads of *Coprinus lagopus. Heredity, 13:* 81-87. Day, P.R. (1960). The structure of the A mating type locus in *Coprinus lagopus. Genetics, 45:* 641-650. Day, P.R. (1963). Mutations of the A mating type factor in *Coprinus lagopus. Genet. Res. Camb., 4:* 55-64. Day, P.R. & Anderson, G. (1961). Two linkage groups in *Coprinus lagopus. Genet. Res. Camb., 2:* 414-423. Fincham, J.R.S. & Day, P.R. (1963). *Fungal Genetics*, Oxford. Fries, L. (1953). Factors promoting growth of *C. fimetarius* L. under high temperature conditions. *Physiologia Pl., 6:* 551-563. Kemp, R.F.O. (1975). Breeding biology of *Coprinus* species in the section Lanatuli. *Trans. Brit. Mycol. Soc., 65:* 375-388. Kemp, R.F.O. (1970). Interspecific sterility in *Coprinus bisporus, C. congregatus* and other basidiomycetes. *Trans. Brit. Mycol. Soc., 54:* 488-489. Lange, M. (1952). Species concept in the genus *Coprinus. Dansk. Bot. Arkiv., 14:* 1-164. Madelin, M.F. (1956). The influence of light and temperature on fruiting of *C. lagopus* in pure culture. *Ann. Bot. (London)* [N.S.], *20:* 467-480. Madelin, M.F. (1956). Studies on the nutrition of *C. lagopus* especially as affecting fruiting. *Ann. Bot.* [N.S.], *20:* 307-330. Quintanilha A. (1944). Le conduite sexuelle de quelques espèces d'Agaricacées. *Bol. Soc. Broteriana*, (2nd series) *19:* 27-65. Quintanilha, A., Quintanilha, L., & Vasermanis, A. (1941). La conduite sexuelle et la systématique des Hyménomycètes. *Rev. Mycol.* (NS), *6:* 3-48. Vandendries, R., (1925). L'hetero-homothallisme dans le genre *Coprinus. Bull. Soc. Roy. Bot. Belgique, 57:* 139-146. Watling, R. (1971). 'Basidiomycetes: Homobasidiomycetidae' in *Methods in Microbiology*, London.

Key to Genera

1	Gills and often also the cap ± deliquescent; gill-faces parallel or subparallel; basidia separated by large inflated sterile cells, often of more than one size	**1 Coprinus**
x	Gills not deliquescent; gill-faces not parallel, so gills ± wedge-shaped in section; basidia of one size, not separated by large inflated sterile cells, though not necessarily developing all at the same time	2
2(1)	Basidiospores ornamented; cap with innate fibrillose layer of coloured hyphae; veil fibrillose, abundant	**2 Lacrymaria**
x	Basidiospores smooth, or if ornamented (a few species only), then cap smooth or radially rugulose and veil none or slight	3
3(2)	Gills spotted when seen from the side, because of patchy development of basidia, olivaceous-black to fuscous-black; spores from slightly to distinctly lentiform, often limoniform but ellipsoid or ovoid in *semi-ovatus,* not bleached or discoloured by concentrated sulphuric acid	**3 Panaeolus**
x	Gills not spotted when seen from side, variously coloured; spores not limoniform, rarely lentiform, variously shaped, sometimes bleached or discoloured by concentrated sulphuric acid	**4 Psathyrella**

1. COPRINUS (Fries) S.F. Gray

A Natural Arrangement of British Plants, I: 632, 1821

Type species (selected): *Coprinus comatus* (Müll. ex Fries) S.F. Gray

DISTINCTIVE CHARACTERS: Fruit-body usually dull coloured; part of or entire fruit-body generally deliquescent (Fig. 10) and gills always parallel or subparallel (Fig. 13). Basidia 2- or 4-spored, less frequently 3-spored, usually 2 or more sizes present on any one gill (Fig. 19); separated by sterile cells (basidioles; Fig. 15).

GENERAL CHARACTERS: Fruit-body minute to medium, less frequently large; cap campanulate, cylindrical or ellipsoid then convex and usually fully expanding, dry to humid, smooth (Fig. 28), setulose (Fig. 27), mealy or fibrillose; stem central. Gill-trama regular or subregular becoming irregular with age (Fig. 16); cap cuticle cellular (Fig. 14) or of radially arranged inflated cells, often over-laid with velar material (Fig. 17). On the ground in woods, pastures, heaths etc., and on dung, and on plant remains and refuse material; usually saprophytes, although one documented case of a species acting as human pathogen. Development where known either bi-, mono or paravelangiocarpic (Fig. 1-10).

The species are separated mainly according to the presence or absence of veil and its characters when present, spore characters, habitat, the number of sterigmata on the basidia, and any characteristic smell. In this genus it is only comparatively rarely that one finds basidia with different numbers of sterigmata on one gill. In such cases either 2-, or 3- or 4-spored basidia should predominate and this should indicate which choice to take in the key. Information on these features is therefore essential before using the key to species. Size of fruit-body is somewhat variable but can be critical, more especially in species consistently producing very small fruit-bodies always less than 10 mm broad, as can details of marginal cystidia and presence or absence of facial cystidia. Some dung-inhabiting species grow from sclerotia which need to be carefully looked for, and some wood-inhabiting members of Stirps *Domesticus* grow from a thick, dense, matted, orange or reddish-brown mycelial tomentum known as *Ozonium.*

Several of the larger species are edible and considered delicacies, some species of the *Coprinus atramentarius* group are toxic if eaten with alcoholic drinks. All species are probably saprophytic; *Coprinus delicatulus* (= *C. cinereus*) has been isolated from man.

The descriptions are not arranged alphabetically but in systematic order in this rather large genus in order to have descriptions of related species on successive pages. They are divided into four paragraphs giving macroscopical, microscopical, cultural and habitat characters in that order, followed by a paragraph of observations as necessary. Distribution is mentioned together with habitat when possible, but much still remains to be learnt on this subject and such information is of necessity incomplete in many cases.

The following characters which are ± constant throughout the genus and are not of taxonomic significance are not given in the descriptions. The gills are mostly free, more rarely slightly adnate, usually lanceolate and only rarely ventricose. They vary from rather distant to fairly crowded; generally speaking, the smaller the fruit-body the more distant the gills, the larger the fruit-body the more crowded the gills. The gill-edge is white or greyish flocculose, denticulate or atomate in young fruit-bodies. The flesh is always thin except at the centre of the cap and mostly coloured like the cap or slightly paler and the hollow stem is white or greyish and sometimes hyaline and only rarely slightly coloured internally. Except in Section *Pseudocoprinus* deliquescence is not mentioned, for all species in Sections *Coprinus* and *Micaceus* deliquesce ± rapidly, those growing on dung perhaps most rapidly.

Size of unexpanded cap given as 35-65/25-46 mm means 35-65 mm high and 25-46 mm broad. In the microscopical characters spore colour as given is in water and aqueous ammoniacal solution unless otherwise stated. The stem-cuticle consists of parallel ± cylindric cells sometimes (eg. in some members of Section *Pseudocoprinus*) giving rise to specialised cells (eg. setules) which are mentioned when critical. Clamp-connections 'present' means that they have been found somewhere in the fruit-body, most often in the hyphae of the veil or the stem-base, but in some cases at the base of the basidia.

92 species of *Coprinus* are admitted to the British List in this work, *C. stellatus* sensu Buller is doubtful although *C. stellatus* sensu M. Lange is British, and some others need more careful study. This is an increase of 33 on the total in the New Check List of British Agarics and Boleti (1960). Of these, 14 are new species, 3 are validations of nomina nuda, 2 are varieties raised to specific rank and 13 are foreign species recently recorded. In addition *C. patouillardii* is used in a different sense, and the taxon in the New Check list under this name is included as *C. cordisporus,* and *C. cineratus* is excluded and replaced by *C. semitalis. C. velox* is also excluded - see obs. on *C. stercoreus.*

Keys to Sections and Stirps are supplementary and are only given to indicate the scheme of classification. Ecological lists, and lists of synonyms, mis-determinations, rejected names, species mentioned in the observations and cultural characters are given at the end. A page index is provided to the species described.

We have found it necessary to modify the more familiar arrangement of Lange (1935-40) based on veil type because in certain groups, notably *Impexi* and *Vestiti,* we consider there are unrelated species grouped together. Some groups do relate directly to Lange's divisions eg. Stirps *Lagopus* ≡ *Lanatuli,* Stirps *Hemerobius* ≡ *Nudi,* and Stirps *Ephemerus* and *Hiascens* ≡ *Setulosi,* but in some areas rather drastic changes have been considered necessary to incorporate recent information. The main divisions have been based on the structure of the cap-cuticle, inflated cells radially arranged in Section *Comatus* (Fig. 17), ellipsoid or subglobose cells in Section *Micaceus* (Fig. 14) and pyriform cells (hymeniderm) in Section *Pseudocoprinus* (Fig. 193).

Kühner's genus *Pseudocoprinus* (1928), with *Coprinus disseminatus* as type, has been used as a section and expanded to include the species complexes about *C. plicatilis, C. ephemerus* and *C. hiascens,* and, although it is larger, we think this is a useful and natural unit. There is some developmental information which

8

supports the divisions adopted. Indeed the section *Pseudocoprinus* may in the future be defined around those species with monovelangiocarpic or paravelangiocarpic development; consequently *Pseudocoprinus* may in this extended form be worthy of recognition at higher rank.

The unit 'Stirps' has been adopted to minimise the nomenclatorial changes necessary in a group which no doubt will alter again as more information is available. However, the following new combination is necessary:-

Section Pseudocoprinus (Kühner) Orton & Watling

Basionym: Pseudocoprinus Kühner in *Le Botaniste 20:* 155, 1928.

SYSTEMATIC ARRANGEMENT

COPRINUS (Persoon ex Fries) S.F. Gray

Section I	Coprinus	
Stirps 1	Coprinus	
	1. comatus	
	2 sterquilinus	
Stirps 2	Atramentarius	
	3 atramentarius	
	4 acuminatus	
	5 romagnesianus	
	6 insignis	
Stirps 3	Erythrocephalus	
	7 erythrocephalus	
Stirps 4	Echinosporus	
	8 echinosporus	
	9 phlyctidosporus	
Stirps 5	Picaceus	
	10 picaceus	
	11 episcopalis	
	12 scobicola	
	13 extinctorius	
Stirps 6	Lagopus	
	14 lagopus	
	15 lagopides	
	16 cinereus	
	17 macrocephalus	
	18 radiatus	
	19 pseudoradiatus	
Stirps 7	Friesii	
	20 friesii	
	21 argenteus	
	22 gonophyllus	
	23 urticaecola	
Stirps 8	Tigrinellus	
	24 tigrinellus	
	25 rhombisporus	
	26 xantholepis	
	27 saichiae	

Stirps 9 Filamentifer
28 filamentifer
29 vermiculifer
30 xenobius

Stirps 10 Utrifer
31 utrifer

Section II Micaceus Fries emend Schroeter in Cohn

Stirps 11 Micaceus
32 micaceus
33 truncorum

Stirps 12 Domesticus
34 domesticus
35 ellisii
36 xanthothrix
37 radians

Stirps 13 Flocculosus
38 flocculosus
39 poliomallus

Stirps 14 Cortinatus
40 cortinatus
41 filiformis
42 luteocephalus

Stirps 15 Niveus
43 niveus
44 latisporus
45 pachyspermus
46 cothurnatus
47 cordisporus
48 ephemeroides
49 patouillardii

9

Stirps 16	Narcoticus s		Stirps 19	Hiascens
	50 narcoticus			75 hiascens
	51 radicans			76 impatiens
	52 laanii			77 callinus
	53 semitalis			78 angulatus
	54 cinereofloccosus			79 plagioporus
	55 triplex			80 subdisseminatus
	56 trisporus			81 subimpatiens
	57 foetidellus			82 bisporiger
	58 tuberosus		Stirps 20	Auricomus
	59 sclerotiger			83 auricomus
	60 stercoreus			
	61 martinii		Stirps 21	Hemerobius
	62 saccharomyces			84 hemerobius
				85 megaspermus
Section III	Pseudocoprinus			86 plicatilis
Stirps 17	Disseminatus			87 galericuliformis
	63 disseminatus			88 leiocephalus
	64 silvaticus			89 nudiceps
	65 hexagonosporus			90 miser
	66 dilectus			
	67 curtus		*additional species	
	68 heptemerus			
Stirps 18	Ephemerus		Stirps	Atramentarius
	69 ephemerus			91 kimurae
	70 bisporus		Stirps	Hiascens
	71 congregatus			92 subpurpureus
	72 pellucidus			
	73 stellatus			
	74 heterosetulosus			

Key to Sections

1	Veil filamentous or consisting at least in part of ± globose cells; setules absent	2
x	Veil absent or cap with setae or setules	**III Pseudocoprinus** p.
2(1)	Veil filamentous, of ± cylindrical cells	**I Coprinus** p.
x	Veil at least in part of ± globose cells	**II Micaceus** p.

Key to Stirps
I Section Coprinus

1	Cap medium to large (except *radiatus* and *pseudoradiatus*)	2
x	Cap small to very small	7
2(1)	Veil not forming distinct layer of separable scales	3
x	Veil forming distinct layer of separable scales	4
3(2)	Cap cuticle splitting into conspicuous reflexed scales; veil forming ± fugacious ring or zone at base of stem; on soil or dung	Stirps **1 Comatus** p.
x	Cap cuticle remaining smooth but veil in the form of minute inseparable scales at least in centre of cap, and also as zone at base of stem; on or associated with wood	Stirps **2 Atramentarius** p.

4(2)	Veil forming reddish scales	Stirps 3 **Erythrocephalus** p.	
x	Veil forming white, whitish or greyish scales		5
5(4)	Spores warted	Stirps 4 **Echinosporus** p.	
x	Spores smooth		6
6(5)	Hyphae of veil of narrow cells 2-10(-12) μm broad, not consistently constricted at septa (Fig. 26)	Stirps 5 **Picaceus** p.	
x	Hyphae of veil of relatively broad cells 8-44(-60) μm broad, often constricted at the septa (Fig. 22)	Stirps 6 **Lagopus** p.	
7(1)	On grass, *Carex* or *Juncus* stems, or other herbaceous debris, or on burnt ground		8
x	On dung		9
8(7)	Veil scales on cap white	Stirps 7 **Friesii** p.	
x	Veil scales on cap coloured at least in part	Stirps 8 **Tigrinellus** p.	
9(7)	Veil entirely filamentous	Stirps 9 **Filamentifer** p.	
x	Veil including some swollen cells	Stirps 10 **Utrifer** p.	

II Section Micaceus

1	Veil atomate, soon fugacious; medium to large; on wood, often caespitose	Stirps 11 **Micaceus** p.	
x	Veil atomate, mealy or floccose, more persistent; sizes and habitats various		2
2(1)	Veil a mixture of cylindrical and globose or swollen cells		3
x	Veil entirely of ± globose cells		5
3(2)	On wood; medium to large; veil with some thick-walled coloured cells (Fig. 25)	Stirps 12 **Domesticus** p.	
x	Habitat otherwise; mostly small or very small; veil usually lacking any evidence of thick-walled coloured cells		4
4(3)	Veil with some cells swollen, but neither thick-walled nor diverticulate	Stirps 13 **Flocculosus** p.	
x	Veil with globose, ellipsoid or cylindric cells, which are often thick-walled or diverticulate	Stirps 14 **Cortinatus** p.	
5(2)	Cells of veil smooth or with crystals dissolving in hydrochloric acid (Fig. 23); spores without visible remains of perisporial sac	Stirps 15 **Niveus** p.	
x	Cells of veil with minute peg-like protuberances, thus appearing minutely warty (Fig. 24); spores often showing remains of perisporial sac	Stirps 16 **Narcoticus** p.	

III Section Pseudocoprinus

1	Cap surface veil absent (Fig. 28)	Stirps 21 **Hemerobius** p.	
x	Cap with long thick-walled setae or thick- or thin-walled setules, sometimes also with sphaerocysts		2

11

2(1)	Cap with long, thick-walled yellow-brown setae; (growing on burnt ground)	Stirps **20 Auricomus** p.
x	Cap with setules; sometimes also with sphaerocysts	3
3(2)	Cap with setules and sphaerocysts	Stirps **17 Disseminatus** p.
x	Cap with setules only (Fig. 27)	4
4(3)	On dung	Stirps **18 Ephemerus** p.
x	On soil, in grass, on wood or other plant debris	Stirps **19 Hiascens** p.

Key to Species

(Those species enclosed within brackets have not yet been recorded for the British Isles)

1	Cap *either* with veil at least when young, *or* with setules	2
x	Cap quite smooth when young, without veil or setules at any time (Fig. 28)	103
2(1)	Cap without setae or setules but with veil at least when young as silky-fibrillose, felty, floccose, mealy, scurfy or granular scales or as atomate meal	3
x	Cap with setae or setules, with or without sphaerocysts (Fig. 27)	72
3(2)	Stem with distinct membranous ring, which may break or remain at base of stem as the cap expands	4
x	Stem without distinct membranous ring, but in *atramentarius* and *domesticus* and their allies, and a few others, there may be veil remnants on the lower part of the stem, which form a volvate or ring-like zone	6
4(3)	On soil or in grass, especially on recently disturbed ground; (large and very tall-stemmed species, at first with very elongate cap with ± recurved felty scales)	**1 comatus**
x	On dung	5
5(4)	Cap medium to large, at first with dense felty or fibrillose scales; spores (16-)17-22(-23)/10-13(-14) μm, ellipsoid with excentric germ-pore in side view, ovoid in face view	**2 sterquilinus**
x	Cap small or very small, at first entirely white mealy-scaly; spores 6-9/5-6/6.5-8μm, lentiform, subglobose or indistinctly 5-angled with central germ-pore in face view	**48 ephemeroides**
6(3)	Veil on cap *either* apricot, coral, brick or reddish rust at first, *or* whitish turning pinkish in places	7
x	Veil on cap white, grey, saffron, fulvous, clay-pinkish, vinaceous buff or sepia	8
7(6)	Veil on cap of globose or broadly ellipsoid hyaline or encrusted cells, forming granular whitish then pinkish or clay-buff scales; spores 11.5-14.5/6-8/7.5-9μm, lentiform, ellipsoid-amygdaliform in side view, broadly ovoid or 6-angled in face view; on dung	**46 cothurnatus**

12

x   Veil on cap of filamentous encrusted hyphae 6-12 μm
broad, forming apricot, coral, brick or reddish-rust
scales; spores 8-10/4.5-5 μm, ellipsoid; on soil   **7 erythrocephalus**

Note: see also § 75 for some species with reddish veil with setules.

8(6)   On or near stumps or buried wood or on soil, solitary
or subcaespitose; cap medium to large, grey or clay-
brownish often with buff or sepia centre, at first with
minute, whitish or brownish scales from veil at least
at centre (but entirely apricot, rust or cinnamon
scaly, or fibrillose in *romagnesianus*) stem often thickened
near sometimes attenuated-rooting base and with basal veil
remnants when fresh; veil filamentous, of narrow hyphae
rarely more than 20 μm broad.   9

x   Not so; if robust and subcaespitose on or near wood, at
least some cells of the veil globose or rounded   12

9(8)   Cap and at least lower half of stem with conspicuous
apricot or rust-coloured scales from veil; spores smooth,
(8-10/4.5-5.5 μm, ellipsoid or slightly amygdaliform in
side view, ellipsoid or cylindric-ellipsoid in face view)   **5 romagnesianus**

x   Veil much less conspicuous, of minute scales often
restricted to cap centre and stem-base only; spores
smooth or rough   10

10(9)   Spores rough with low warts, (10-)11-14.5/(6-)7-8 μm,
limoniform with papillate, hyaline germ-pore in side
view; cap at first minutely adpressed white
fibrillose-scaly then often ± smooth   **6 insignis**

x   Spores smooth, 8-11/4-6 μm, ellipsoid or ellipsoid-
amygdaliform in side view; cap with minute brownish
scales when fresh, often at centre only, often soon
smooth   11

11(10)   Spores 8-11/5-6 μm; cap usually large, 30-65/30-70 mm
before expanding, some scales usually persisting at
centre; on or near dead wood   **3 atramentarius**

x   Spores narrower, 8-10.5/4-5 μm; cap medium,
10-30(-35)/12-23(-30) mm before expanding, scales
very minute often completely disappearing; on or
near wood or on soil (often on paths)   **4 acuminatus**

12(8)   Robust with large cap and tall stem; cap with
adpressed white, clay-pink or vinaceous buff, silky-
fibrillose felty scales which become separated from
each other as cap expands; stem with conspicuous
rounded or marginate bulb, up to 300 mm long;
smell often strong, disagreeable; on soil or in leaves
in woods, especially beech on basic soil; spores
(12-)13-17(-18)/10-12 μm, broadly ellipsoid   **10 picaceus**

x   Not so; if cap large, habitat or other characters different   13

13(12)   Veil consisting predominantly of globose, ovoid, or
broadly ellipsoid cells   14

x   Veil *either* a distinct mixture of globose or vesiculose cells
and filamentous hyphae, *or* entirely of filamentous hyphae   36

14(13)   Cap entirely glistening atomate-mealy at first, later becoming
smooth; caespitose or gregarious on dead wood; veil of
easily collapsing smooth or slightly encrusted globose or
ellipsoid cells with rather thin, hyaline or slightly brownish walls   15

x   Not so; if cap atomate-mealy, habitat or veil characters
otherwise   16

15(14)   Spores distinctly mitriform in face view (broadest near
apex), 7.5-10/4-5.5/5-6 µm (Fig. 100)   **32 micaceus**

x   Spores ovoid in face view (broadest at the middle),
6-9/4-5/5-6 µm (Fig. 101)   **33 truncorum**

16(14)   Cells of veil warty-punctate with small peg-like
protuberances, which are *either* thickenings of the cell-
wall *or* are diverticulae (Fig. 24); spores sometimes with
parts of or the whole of the perisporial sac visible when
mature; sometimes with unpleasant smell   17

x   Cells of veil smooth, or crystalline-punctate becoming
smooth in hydrochloric acid (Fig. 23); spores never with
visible perisporial sac when mature; rarely with unpleasant
smell   30

17(16)   Basidia 3-spored; on dung; smell strong, nauseous   18

x   Basidia 2- or 4-spored; habitats and smell various   19

18(17)   Spores narrower, 8.5-11/5-6.2 µm, ellipsoid or slightly
ovoid in both views, perisporial sac barely visible in
water; stem base characteristically ridged-swollen, stem
rooting or not; cap grey, often with grey or buff tipped
scaly lumps   **55 triplex**

x   Spores broader 9-10.5/(5.5-)6-6.5/6-7 µm, ellipsoid or
ovoid in face view, slightly amygdaliform in side view
with thin perisporial sac; stem base not markedly swollen;
cap coarsely white or whitish mealy scaly, scales at centre
sometimes becoming clay-buff   **56 trisporus**

19(17)   Basidia 2-spored; on soil or in grass   20

Note: if on dung, see obs. on 58 *tuberosus*

x   Basidia 4-spored; habitats various   21

20(19)   Smell none; spores shorter, 11-13(-15)/5.5-7/7-8.5 µm,
with conspicuous perisporial sac and apiculus   **54 cinereofloccosus**

x   Smell of yeast or beer; spores longer, (14-)15-18(-20)/8-10 µm,
without or with incomplete or inconspicuous perisporial
sac, apiculus small and indistinct   **62 saccharomyces**

21(19)   Spores less than 9 µm long (cylindric- ellipsoid lipsoid
or slightly phaseoliform, without perisporial sac and
with indistinct apiculus, (6.5-)7-8/3-4 µm; fruit-bodies
very small to small; on dung)   **60 stercoreus**

x   Spores 9 µm or more long   22

22(21)   On *Carex, Juncus* or *Scirpus* debris, smell none;
         spores relatively broad and large, (12-)13-16(-17)/
         (6.5-)7-8.5 μm, with rather broad germ-pore, rounded
         at base with small apiculus, with or without
         incomplete to ± complete perisporial sac   **61 martinii**
x   Not so; habitat, smell or spores otherwise   23
23(22)   On dung or rotting vegetable matter (e.g., old potatoes);
         spores rounded or narrowed at base, apiculus indistinct
         or conspicuous, perisporial sac from none to complete
         and conspicuous   24
x   On soil, amongst grass, on sawdust, wood chips, or the cut
         surface of logs or stumps; spores narrowed at base, apiculus
         conspicuous, perisporial sac complete and conspicuous   28
24(23)   With sclerotium or distinct long rooting stem-base, spores not
         showing dark lines or dots   25
x   Without sclerotium or distinct rooting stem-base (rarely
         slightly rooting in *narcoticus,* which has spores showing
         dark lines or dots)   27
25(24)   Smell strong, unpleasant, of gas or acetylene; spores
         narrowed at base with conspicuous elongate apiculus
         11.5-14.5 μm long, perisporial sac sometimes becoming
         less conspicuous as spores mature; stem without sclerotium
         but rooting and often joined by mycelial cord to the stems
         of other fruit bodies; on dung or rotting vegetable matter   **51 radicans**
x   Smell none, or pleasant of fried mushrooms; spores
         rounded at base with inconspicuous apiculus, shorter,
         9-11.5 μm long; stem with sclerotium; on dung or dungy straw   26
26(25)   Sclerotium small, up to 5 mm broad; stem with long rooting
         base from sclerotium; spores with thin sometimes indistinct
         perisporial sac, 9-11/5.5-7 μm; fruit bodies very small; smell
         weak, fungussy or none   **58 tuberosus**
x   Sclerotium larger, up to 15 mm broad; stem arising
         directly from sclerotium, not rooting; spores with large
         conspicuous perisporial sac, (9.5-)10-11.5/5.5-6.5 μm;
         fruit bodies small to medium; smell strong, pleasant
         of fried mushrooms   **59 sclerotiger**
27(24)   Smell strong of gas or like *Tricholoma sulphureum;*
         fruit-bodies small to medium; spores narrowed at base
         with conspicuous apiculus, marked with dark lines or dots,
         10.8-13.5/5.4-6.8(-7.2)μm, perisporial sac conspicuous   **50 narcoticus**
x   Smell often strong, stercoraceous; fruit-bodies very
         small to small; spores rounded at base with small
         apiculus, not marked with dark lines or dots,
         9-11/5.5-6μm perisporial sac none or incomplete
         or indistinct   **57 foetidellus**

15

28(23)   Smell strong, unpleasant, stercoraceous; (spores
9.5-13/4.5-6/6.5-9µm with conspicuous perisporial
sac, sometimes marked with dark lines or dots, see obs. on *50 narcoticus*

x   Smell none or indistinct   29

29(28)   On sawdust, wood-chips or the cut surface of logs or stumps;
spores 9-12.5/5-6/6.5-8µm, ellipsoid to slightly elongate-ovoid,
marked with dark lines or dots   **52 laanii**

x   On soil or amongst grass; spores relatively narrow
10.5-13.5/4.5-5.5/6.5-8.5µm, elongate-ellipsoid to
cylindric-ovoid, not marked with lines or dots   **53 semitalis**

30(16)   On dung   31

x   On soil, or on rotting plant matter or decaying
household refuse   35

31(30)   Cap and stem with whitish mealy scales often turning
pinkish or clay-buff; spores lentiform, ellipsoid-
amygdaliform in side view, broadly avoid or ± 6-angled
in face view, 11.5-14.5/6-8/7.5-9µm   **46 cothurnatus**

x   Cap and often also stem with white, grey or brownish
mealy scales which do not change colour; spores
otherwise   32

32(31)   Spores less than 10µm long, lentiform, subglobose-
angular in face view; cap small or very small, less than
10 mm broad   **47 cordisporus**

x   Spores 10µm or more long, ± lentiform but variously
shaped; cap small to medium   33

33(32)   Cap white or grey to clay-buff scaly, scales varying from
minutely mealy to coarsely warty; basidia 2-spored;
(spores markedly lentiform, ellipsoid or ovoid in side view
with broad, central germ-pore, subglobose-limoniform
sometimes indistinctly 4-angled in face view,
14-17/8.5-10/12.5-14µm)   **45 pachyspermus**

x   Cap finely white mealy scaly; basidia 4-spored   34

34(33)   Cap small to medium, thickly covered with persistent
white mealy scales; spores somewhat lentiform, germ-
pore broad and central in side view, 15-19/8.5-10.5/
11-13µm, ellipsoid-amygdaliform in side view, broadly
ellipsoid often indistinctly angled and ± coned towards
the germ-pore in face view   **43 niveus**

x   Cap very small to small, at first white mealy scaly but
soon becoming greyish; spores markedly lentiform,
germ-pore fairly broad and rather excentric in side
view, 14-16/8-9/10-12.5µm, ellipsoid or ovoid in
side view, indistinctly globose-angular in face view   **44 latisporus**

35(30)   On soil; veil on cap entirely scurfy-floccose, forming
fringe at margin and apical ring-zone on stem; spores
ellipsoid or ovoid, 9-11/5-6µm; cap very small to
small   **40 cortinatus**

x   On rotting plant matter or decaying household refuse; veil on cap forming whitish or ochraceous mealy scales, not fringing the margin or forming apical ring-zone on stem; spores lentiform, subglobose-angular in face view, 7-9/5-6/7-8μm; cap small to medium   **49 patouillardii**

36(13)   Veil a mixture of globose or vesiculose cells and distinctly filamentous hyphae, which are often encrusted pigmented (Fig. 25)   37

x   Veil entirely of filamentous hyphae, which sometimes have some of the cells diverticulate or coralloid or with thick, coloured walls but rarely encrusted pigmented   46

37(36)   Cap entirely glistening atomate mealy at first, later becoming smooth; caespitose or gregarious on dead wood   15

x   Cap mealy, floccose, granular or scurfy scaly, but not glistening; rarely subcaespitose but often gregarious in small numbers; habitats various   38

38(37)   On dung; cap very small to small   39

x   On wood, sawdust, straw heaps or on soil; cap very small to large   40

39(38)   Cells of veil hyaline, thin-walled; veil whitish or brownish; spores elongate-ellipsoid or slightly amygdaliform with small germ-pore, 7.5-9/4.5-5.5μm   **31 utrifer**

x   Cells of veil with yellowish or encrusted walls; veil grey; spores cylindric-ellipsoid, with broad germ-pore, 7-9/3.5-5μm   **39 poliomallus**

40(38)   Spores 11.5-16.5/6-9.5μm, ellipsoid with excentric germ-pore; (on wood, sawdust or straw heaps; cap with adpressed floccose-fibrillose scales; cells of veil mostly cylindric 5-20μm broad, but some cells, especially the end-cells, variously swollen and broader)   **38 flocculosus**

x   Spores shorter, variously shaped, germ-pore central   41

41(40)   Cap very small, 2-6 mm broad; stem filiform, not more than 1 mm broad; on soil or wood   42

x   Cap small to medium; stem more than 1 mm broad; on stumps, logs or twigs; (veil of smooth hyaline ± globose cells 20-60μm broad, together with chains of ± thick-walled cylindric or fusiform cells, often with end-cells pyriform or vesiculose, with walls not diverticulate, encrusted or smooth, brownish or hyaline sub micr.)   43

42(41)   On soil (often under *Mercurialis perennis*); cap greyish with whitish mealy scales, centre becoming buff, spores ellipsoid, 8-10/4.7-5.5μm; filamentous constituents of veil diverticulate, thick-walled and hyaline   **41 filiformis**

17

x   On wood; cap brownish or grey, at first with blackish mealy
scales; spores fusiform ellipsoid-amygdaliform, 8-9/4-4.2µm;
(veil of ± globose hyaline cells 20-40(53)µm broad, together
with chains of cylindric, fusiform, clavate or globose, encrusted,
often thick-walled cells, 3-30µm broad)

                           (*coniophorus* Romagnesi, RM 6(1941): 115, fig. 3)

           Note: if on soil and filamentous constituent of veil of thin-
walled, smooth or crystalline covered hyphae   see **40 cortinatus**

43(41)   Spores 6.5-8.5(-9)/3-4.5(-5)µm, cylindric-ellipsoid or
-phaseoliform; stem-base often with marked volva-like
veil-zone   **35 ellisii**

x   Spores broader or longer, phaseoliform or not; stem-base
more rarely with volva-like veil-zone   **44**

44(43)   Spores cylindric-ellipsoid or -phaseoliform, (7-)8-10/
(3.5-)4-5µm   **34 domesticus**

x   Spores broader, phaseoliform or not   **45**

45(44)   Spores ellipsoid-ovoid or slightly amygdaliform, not
or barely phaseoliform in any view, 7.5-10/4.8-5.8µm;
thick-walled cells of veil sparsely encrusted-pigmented;
cap often paler   **36 xanthothrix**

x   Spores ellipsoid-phaseoliform, 8-11.5/5-6.5µm;
thick-walled cells of veil often strongly encrusted-
pigmented; cap often darker   **37 radians**

46(36)   Spores 11.5-16.5/6-9.5µm, ellipsoid with excentric
germ-pore; cells of veil mostly cylindric 5-20µm broad,
but some (especially the end-) cells variously swollen and
broader;   **38 flocculosus**

x   Spores otherwise (if of similar size then germ-pore
central); all cells of veil cylindric or narrowly fusiform   **47**

47(46)   On wood; cap small to medium, at first entirely covered
with whitish veil which splits into small adpressed
fibrillose-floccose scales, those at centre often yellowish
brown and ± reflexed; veil of two kinds of filamentous
hyphae, the broader ones hyaline and constricted at the
septa, 10-36µm broad, the narrower ones with thick
brownish walls, 1-6µm broad; spores broadly amygdaliform
with large truncate germ-pore 8-10/5.5-6.5/6.5-7.5µm   **13 extinctorius**

x   Not so; habitats various; veil entirely of broad, or
entirely of narrow hyphae   **48**

48(47)   Spores warty-rough; cells of veil narrow, 4-12µm broad,
not diverticulate   **49**

x   Spores smooth; cells of veil broad or narrow,
diverticulate in some species   **50**

49(48)   On twigs or sticks, sometimes apparently in leaves or on
soil, but probably attached to buried wood; spores
amygdaliform or limoniform with crowded low warts and
very broad truncate germ-pore (2-3µm broad),
(8-)8.5-10.5/5.5-7 µm   **8 echinosporus**

x   On burnt ground; spores ellipsoid or ovoid with conspicuous
    rounded warts and also pointed hyaline warts near the small
    ± rounded germ-pore, 8-10/6-7.2μm   **9 phlyctidosporus**

50(48) Spores lentiform, ellipsoid-amygdaliform in side view,
        markedly mitriform in face view, 7.5-10/5.5-6.5/7-8.5μm;
        in beech leaves on basic soil; cells of veil (3-)4-8(-9)μm
        broad, hyaline and thin-walled, or brownish and thick-
        walled but not diverticulate; (cap small to medium)   **11 episcopalis**

x   Not so; spores never mitriform in any view; habitats
    various   51

51(50) At least cap-centre and stem-base sulphur to lemon-
        yellow when fresh; on dung; spores 10.5-12.5/5-7.5μm,
        ellipsoid or slightly amygdaliform; veil of narrow filamentous
        hyphae 2-3.5μm broad with yellow vacuolar pigment, and
        also broader non-diverticulate often yellowish encrusted-
        pigmented hyphae 10-12 μm broad   **42 luteocephalus**

x   Not so; if on dung, characters otherwise   52

52(51) Cells of veil on cap relatively broad, 8-44(-60)μm
        broad, often constricted at septa, always thin-walled,
        hyaline and non-diverticulate (Fig. 22)   53

x   Cells of veil on cap relatively narrow, 2-10(-12)μm broad,
    not constricted at septa, thin- or thick-walled, hyaline
    or brownish, in some species diverticulate or coralloid   59

53(52) Cap very small, rarely more than 6 mm high before
        expanding; on dung   54

x   Cap small to fairly large, 10-57 mm high before expanding;
    habitats various, on dung or not   55

54(53) Spores 7-9/4-5(-5.5)μm, ellipsoid or elongate-ellipsoid   **19 pseudoradiatus**

x   Spores 11-14/6-7μm, ellipsoid or cylindric-ellipsoid,
    sometimes slightly phaseoliform in side view   **18 radiatus**

55(53) On sawdust; basidia 2-spored; hyphae of veil on cap
        8-20μm broad; (spores 11.5-14/7-8.5μm, ellipsoid or
        slightly amygdaliform; veil on cap splitting up into
        scattered adpressed scales, those at centre often reflexed)   **12 scobicola**

x   Not so; basidia 4-spored; hyphae on cap broader,
    10-44(-60)μm broad   56

56(55) On dung   57

x   Not on dung   58

57(56) Spores relatively broad, 11-14/7.5-8μm; stem never
        rooting; scales of veil on cap and stem rather lax, of
        rather long fibrils (also see 18 *radiatus*)   **17 macrocephalus**

x   Spores relatively narrow, 9-12/6-7μm; stem rooting
    or not; scales of veil on cap and stem dense at first,
    of shorter fibrils   **16 cinereus**

58(56) On burnt ground; spores lentiform, ellipsoid-amygdaliform
        in side view, ovoid or subglobose in face view, (6-)7-9/
        (4.5-)5-6/(5-)6-7.5μm; cap deliquescing, margin soon
        becoming torn or revolute; often gregarious or
        subcaespitose   **15 lagopides**

19

x   On soil, in leaves or in sawdust, especially in shady places; spores ellipsoid or slightly amygdaliform, (10-)11-13.5(-14)/ 6-7μm; cap often persisting and found entire but thin and papery; often solitary, but sometimes in small groups, rarely subcaespitose   **14 lagopus**

59(52)   On dung   60

x   Not on dung   62

60(59)   Cells of hyphae of veil sometimes diverticulate, 3-12(-14)μm broad, thin-walled; spores (9-)10-13.5(-15)/(5-)5.5-6.5μm, ellipsoid or cylindric-ellipsoid   **30 xenobius**

x   Cells of hyphae of veil not diverticulate, 3-8μm broad, thick-walled in *vermiculifer*; spores shorter, not exceeding 10μm in length   6

     Note: if spores 10.5-12.5/5-7.5μm,   see **42 luteocephalus**

61(60)   Spores 7-8/4-5μm, ellipsoid-ovoid in side view, ovoid or submitriform in face view; hyphae of veil on cap thin-walled, 3-7μm broad   **28 filamentifer**

x   Spores 9.5-10/5.5-6μm, ellipsoid or cylindric-ellipsoid; hyphae of veil on cap of both thin- and thick-walled cells 4-8μm broad   **29 vermiculifer**

62(59)   Cap with setules (often missed) as well as fine white scales of branched thin-or thick-walled non-diverticulate hyphae 2.5-4.5 μm. ellipsoid-ovoid or slightly amygdaliform with slightly excentric germ-pore; on soil in woods)   see **91 (heterothrix)**

x   Cap without setules; cells of veil diverticulate in most species (but not so in *argenteus* and *tigrinellus*)   63

63(62)   On burnt ground or plaster, or on soil or very rotten wood; small to medium, cap 15-40 mm when expanded   64

x   On herbaceous debris; very small to small, cap rarely more than 20 mm when expanded   66

64(63)   On burnt ground or plaster; (spores lentiform, germ-pore broad and truncate, broadly ellipsoid in side view, broadly ovoid or subglobose in face view, 6.5-9/5-6/ 6-8μm; hyphae of veil, thin or thick-walled, 1.5-5μm broad, often diverticulate)   **22 gonophyllus**

x   On soil or very rotten wood   65

65(64)   On soil (?) or refuse; spores subglobose to broadly ovoid 10-13.5/8.5-10 μm; hyphae of veil hyaline thin-walled 3-10 μm broad   **91 kimurae**

     Note: see *C. spilosporus* Romagnesi. (RM16: 112, fig. 2, 1951) with lentiform spores with broad germ-pore and paler areas near the apiculus (7.2-10/6-6.5/ 6.5-8.5 μm).

x   On very rotten wood; spores lentiform, germ-pore broad and truncate, ellipsoid in side view, broadly ovoid in face view, uniformly opaque, 8.5-9.5/6-6.6/6.5-7.6μm; hyphae of veil hyaline, interwoven, not diverticulate, 3-7.5μm broad; (stem often thickened immediately below young cap, this thickening often persisting) (*velatus* Quélet sensu Josserand, BSMF 71: 115, figs.13, 14, 1955)

66(63)   Veil scales on cap persistently white (? sometimes slightly coloured in *saichiae*); walls of hyphae of veil scales hyaline or yellowish brown   67

x   Veil scales on cap distinctly coloured at least at tips (buff, fulvous or sepia); walls of hyphae of veil-scales often brownish   70

67(66)   Spores only slightly lentiform, broadly ellipsoid or ovoid in face view, 6-8.5(-9)/4.5-5.5(-6)μm   **23 urticaecola**

x   Spores more distinctly lentiform, subglobose or globose-triangular in face view   68

68(67)   Spores broader, 7-9(-11)/6-7/7-8μm, mostly distinctly subglobose in face view, longer ones broadly ellipsoid-ovoid   **20 friesii**

x   Spores narrower, within the range of 5-8/4-5/5-7.5μm, ± subglobose-triangular in face view   69

69(68)   Spores subglobose ± triangular in face view (Fig. 66), 6-8/4.5-5/5-7.5μm; cap very small, becoming expanded with revolute margin   **27 saichiae**

x   Spores slightly smaller, more clearly subglobose-triangular (sometimes submitriform) in face view (Fig. 77), 5-7/4-5/5-5.5μm; cap rather larger (up to 15 mm when expanded), sometimes becoming ± acutely umbonate with margin torn or split radially   **21 argenteus**
Note: if spores more rounded with germ-pore barely truncate and often with fragments (? of perispore) attached to the outer wall in places, see obs. to 27 *saichiae*.

70(66)   Scales of veil on cap dark brown (sepia) at least at tips; cells of veil diverticulate; spores rather broad, subglobose or broadly ovoid with small germ-pore in face view, 7.5-9/6-7μm; on *Juncus* or *Carex* debris in wet places   **24 tigrinellus**

x   Scales of veil on cap paler, but coloured (cream, ochraceous, buff or fulvous) at least at tips; cells of veil diverticulate; spores narrower or differently shaped, germ-pore broader; on grass stems   71

71(70)   Spores larger, 7-9/5-5.5/5.6-6.5μm, rhomboid or indistinctly angular-amygdaliform in face view (Fig. 80)   **25 rhombisporus**

x   Spores smaller, 5.5-7/4.5-5/5-5.5μm, submitriform or ellipsoid-rhomboid in face view (Fig. 82)   **26 xantholepis**
Note: *C. solitarius* (Lange) Pilát & Svrček has broadly ovoid spores 8.5-9.5 x 6-6.7μm. see Česká Mykol. 21:137, 1967

72(2)   Cap with long narrow thick-walled yellowish brown
setae, 100-350/3-6(-10)μm, apex 2-3μm broad; stem
without setae or setules; cap rusty tawny or bay when
young, 15-30μm broad when expanded; spores 10-13/
6-7μm, ellipsoid or slightly amygdaliform; on soil or
attached to dead wood   **83 auricomus**

x   Not so; cap with setules but without setae, if setules thick-
walled they are shorter and not so deeply coloured   73

73(72)   Cap with setules and sphaerocysts when fresh (Figs. 177 & 178)   74

x   Cap with setules but without sphaerocysts when fresh (Fig. 193)   82

74(73)   On dung; spores distinctly 6-angled in face view, 10-14/
6-7/7-8.5μm, sometimes with small peg-like projections
near the apiculus; cap when expanding soon purplish
date or brown-vinaceous at or around centre, small to
medium   **65 hexagonosporus**

x   Not so; if on dung, characters otherwise   75

75(74)   Cap with minute coral, apricot, brick, rust or rusty
tawny flocci or scurfy scales when fresh; cap very
small, rarely larger   76

x   Not so; flocci or scales on cap, if present, whitish or brownish   78

76(75)   On dung; setules on cap and stem distinctly capitate; spores
with small ± excentric rather rounded germ-pore, 10-12.5/
5.5-6.6μm, ellipsoid   **67 curtus**

x   On soil or mud; setules on cap and stem not capitate;
spores with central or excentric, rounded or truncate
germ-pore, of similar size or longer   77

77(76)   Spores 11-14/6-6.5μm, ellipsoid, germ-pore ± central,
rather small and rounded; marginal cystidia vesiculose
to broadly lageniform   **66 dilectus**

x   Spores smaller, 10.7-11.2/5.2-5.7μm, ellipsoid or
slightly amygdaliform, germ-pore excentric, large
and truncate; marginal cystidia sphaeropedunculate
(*pyrranthes* Romagnesi, RM 16: 128, fig. 6, 1951)

78(75)   Spores warty-rough (roughness sometimes showing beneath
the perispore), limoniform or amygdaliform in side view,
germ-pore conspicuous and truncate, 11-15/7-10μm;
cap small to medium   79

x   Spores smooth, shape and size various; cap very small to small   80

79(78)   Cap buff, saffron, sienna or cinnamon, margin often greyer,
appearing smooth but minutely pubescent when fresh, soon
deeply plicate-striate to centre (looking like *micaceus* but
without the 'mica'); sphaerocysts often rather sparse and
fugacious; small to medium, cap 10-40mm high before
expanding, stem 3-6mm broad; basidia 4-spored; spores
11-15/7-9.5/8-10μm; solitary or caespitose on soil or in
leaves in shady places, more rarely in woods   **64 silvaticus**

x   Cap clay or clay-buff with slight cinnamon tinge at centre, minutely granular when young, soon smooth and with incised plicate margin; small, cap 6-12mm high before expanding, stem 1-1.5mm broad; basidia 2-spored; spores 13-15/8-9.5μm, warty beneath the perispore; on soil (*verrucispermus* Josserand, BSMF 60: 11, 1944; RM 16: 108, fig 1, 1944)

80(78)   On dung; spores ellipsoid with ± excentric germ-pore, within the range 10-15/5-7.5μm   81

x   On or about old stumps or dead or buried wood; spores ellipsoid-amygdaliform, 7.5-10/4-5μm, germ-pore central, apiculus conspicuous; (densely gregarious; cap always pale, whitish or pale buff then greyish)   **63 disseminatus**

81(80)   Setules on cap with capitate apex 6-9μm broad, neck 3-5μm broad; spores 10-12.5/5.5-6.6μm, ellipsoid; sphaerocysts sometimes visible as minute reddish flocci   **67 curtus**

x   Setules on cap with apex not or hardly swollen, 2-4μm broad; spores 11-14.5/5-7.5μm, cylindric- or elongate-ellipsoid, germ-pore markedly excentric; sphaerocysts with hyaline or brownish walls, hardly visible to the naked eye   **68 heptemerus**

82(73)   On burnt ground; spores mitriform in face view, lentiform, 8.5-10.5/5-6.5/6.5-8.5μm   **78 angulatus**

x   On dung, on soil or in leaves, more rarely on dead wood; spores never mitriform, markedly lentiform only in *eurysporus* (see § 94)   83

83(82)   On dung; rapidly deliquescent; cap small or very small   84

x   On soil, in leaves or on dead wood; tardily or not at all deliquescent; cap mostly small to medium, more rarely very small   90

84(83)   Basidia 2-spored; spores with excentric germ-pore (Fig. 195)   85

x   Basidia 4-spored, spores with germ-pore central or excentric   86

85(84)   Spores smaller, (9.5-)11-13(-14.5)/5.5-7(-7.5)μm; setules on cap (50-)88-130/(8.5-)12.5-22μm broad; cap pale brownish or greyish when expanded   **70 bisporus**

x   Spores larger, (13-)15.5-17.7(-20)/(8-)9-10(-11)μm; setules on cap rather shorter, (30-)53-74(-89)/(4.5-)7-9(-13.5)μm, apex (1.5-)2-3.5(-5)μm broad; cap purplish date or brown-vinaceous at centre when expanded (*sassii* M. Lange & A.H. Smith in Mycologia 45: 755, 1953)

86(84)   Cap with some short thick-walled brownish setules, 23-33/6.5-8.5μm, apex 2.5-3μm broad, as well as longer hyaline ones, 60-73/10.5-13.5μm, apex 4-5μm broad; spores with germ-pore central to slightly excentric, 9.5-11(-12)/5.5-6.5μm, ellipsoid or slightly amygdaliform in side view, ± ovoid in face view; facial cystidia absent   **74 heterosetulosus**

x   Not so; setules on cap thin-walled, hyaline or more rarely brownish at base   87

87(86)	Spores with germ-pore distinctly excentric (Fig. 209), 11-15/6-7.5μm	88
x	Spores with germ-pore ± central (Fig. 198) sometimes shorter or narrower	89
88(87)	Caespitose or gregarious, more rarely solitary; on dungy straw, silage or compost (not on fresh dung); cap on the whole pale, buff, saffron or pale cinnamon	**71 congregatus**
x	Gregarious or solitary, rarely subcaespitose (not in big clumps); on cow or horse dung, especially when old; cap on the whole darker, cinnamon to rusty tawny at least at centre, sometimes becoming sepia	**69 ephemerus**
89(87)	Spores narrower, cylindric- or elongate-ellipsoid, 8-10/4-5μm; facial cystidia absent; setules rather longer and slightly broader, 35-80/10-16μm	**72 pellucidus**
x	Spores broader, ellipsoid or slightly ovoid, (8-)9-12(-13)/(4.5-)5-6(-6.5)μm; facial cystidia present; setules short and slightly narrower, 40-60/ 8.5-12μm, apex acute 3-4μm broad see obs. on *73 stellatus*	
90(83)	Spores warty-rough (roughness sometimes showing beneath the perispore)	79
x	Spores smooth	91
91(90)	Cap at first at least at centre with minute white flocci of branched filamentous hyphae 2.5-4μm broad in addition to setules; (cap small; marginal cystidia vesiculose or setulose; spores 8-10/ 4.7-5.5μm, ellipsoid or slightly amygdaliform, germ-pore slightly excentric; on soil in woods)	

(heterothrix Kühner in Bull. Soc. Nat. Oyonnax 10-11
Suppl: 60, fig.29b (1957))

x	Cap without scales of filamentous hyphae, with setules only	92
92(91)	Basidia 2-spored	93
x	Basidia 4-spored	94
93(92)	On twigs or dead wood; cap with thick-walled setules when fresh (walls sienna or fulvous); spores (10.5-)11.5-15/ (5.5-)6-8μm, ellipsoid slightly amygdaliform in side view, ovoid or elongate-ovoid with slight kink on both sides near germ-pore, slightly to distinctly excentric	**82 bisporiger**
x	On soil; cap with hyaline setules, sometimes yellowish or brownish at base only; spores 11.2-15.6(-17)/6.2-8.3μm sec. M. Lange & Smith, 15-17.2/7-8.7μm sec. Kühner, germ-pore slightly to distinctly excentric	

(amphithallus M.Lange & A.H.Smith, Mycologia 45: 774, 1953)

94(92)	Spores relatively broad, lentiform, broadly wedge-shaped with rounded corners or subglobose in face view , ellipsoid amygdaliform in side-view, 9-10.3/ 6.1-7.8μm, germ-pore broad (about 2.5μm) ± central; cap small; gregarious on sticks; marginal cystidia vesiculose and lageniform) (*eurysporus* M. Lange & A.H. Smith in Mycologia 45: 773, 1953)

x Spores longer or narrower, not or only slightly
lentiform, ellipsoid, ovoid or slightly amygdaliform 95

95(94) Setules on cap markedly swollen or capitate at apex,
which is often rather broad 5-12μm; (spores
11-13/6-7μm, germ-pore ± excentric; marginal
cystidia vesiculose or pyriform) **79 plagioporus**

x Setules on cap not or hardly swollen at apex, which
is often narrower (2-9(-15)μm broad) 96

96(95) Cap (also stem at least in part) tinged purplish date or
brown-vinaceous when expanding; spores very dark
brown or almost black sub micr. rather large,
(11-)12-14(-15.5)/(5.5-6)6-7(-7.5)μm, germ-pore
excentric; solitary or gregarious in leaves or soil in
wet places

92 subpurpureus

x Cap paler when expanding, without purplish tinge;
greyish, fulvous or cinnamon, more rarely rusty
tawny or date-brown; spores often paler sub micr.
(umber or reddish brown), sizes and germ-pore various;
(all species become ± plicate-striate and often incised
with age) 97

97(96) Marginal cystidia all vesiculose, ellipsoid or pyriform;
setules on cap ± acute; spores with ± excentric germ-
pore; facial cystidia absent 98

x Marginal cystidia of two sorts, vesiculose or ellipsoid or ±
lageniform (setulose); setules on cap acute or obtuse; spores
with central or excentric germ-pore; facial cystidia present
or absent 100

98(97) Caespitose or gregarious on dungy straw, silage or compost
(rarely apparently on soil); facial cystidia present; spores
11-13/6-7μm, germ-pore distinctly excentric; setules
obtuse see § 88; **71 congregatus**

x Not so; facial cystidia absent; if caespitose, characters
otherwise 99
Note: if densely gregarious on or about dead or buried
wood but sometimes apparently on soil, see § 89; **63 disseminatus**

99(98) Setules on cap of two distinct sorts, *either* long and
± entirely thick-walled, 43-166/5-13μm, apex acute,
walls subhyaline to yellowish brown, *or* rather
shorter, hyaline and thin-walled, 42-100/7.5-15μm;
spores rather broad, (11.2-)12-13.5(-15)/(6.2-)6.5-7(-7.5)μm
(*sclerocystidiosus* M. Lange & A.H. Smith in Mycologia 45:
769, 1953).

x Long setules on cap all hyaline, 75-154/10-20μm, apex
3.5-10μm broad, sometimes a few short thick-walled
brownish ones may also be present; spores narrower,
9-11(-13)/5-6μm; (more especially in damp or wet places) **77 callinus**

100(97)   Facial cystidia present; spores with germ-pore slightly
          to distinctly excentric, 9.3-13.5/5.7-7.5μm; (setules on
          cap hyaline, rather short, 62-130/9-18.2μm, apex obtuse
          5.5-13μm broad, sometimes a few brownish thick-
          walled ones are also present; cap 15-23mm high before
          expanding   **81 subimpatiens**
x   Facial cystidia absent; spores often narrower, with ±
          central germ-pore; setules all hyaline   101
101(100) Cap very small, 3-8mm high before expanding; setules
          on cap subcylindric or with slightly swollen base,
          59-121/10-22μm, apex obtuse, 7.5-15μm broad;
          (spores 8.7-12.7/5-6.5μm)   **80 subdisseminatus**
x   Cap usually larger, 10-30mm high before expanding;
          setules on cap with ± acute apex   102
102(101) Often rather robust (stem 2-4mm broad), usually
          solitary or in small groups; in leaves (especially
          beech) or on soil in woods or shady places; spores
          obtuse at base with small apiculus, (9-)10-12/5-6μm;
          setules on cap rather short, 50-86/10-16μm   **76 impatiens**
x   Less robust (stem 1-2(-3)mm broad), often caespitose;
          on soil or in grass, often in the open; spores narrowed
          at base with large conspicuous apiculus, 9-11/4.5-5μm;
          setules on cap longer, 70-175/8-25μm, apex 4-9μm
          broad   **75 hiascens**
103(1)   On dung; spores distinctly lentiform   104
x   On soil or in grass; spores distinctly to only slightly
          lentiform   106
104(103) Basidia 2-spored see obs. to *90 miser*
x   Basidia 4-spored   105
105(104) Spores 7-8/5-6/6-7μm; fruit-bodies very small   **90 miser**
x   Spores 13-15.5/8.5-9.5/10-12μm; fruit-bodies
          more robust   **89 nudiceps**
106(103) Spores distinctly lentiform   107
x   Spores not or only slightly lentiform   109
107(106) Spores 8-11/5.5-6.6/7-8.5μm, ellipsoid or slightly
          amygdaliform in side view, broadly ovoid sometimes
          slightly angled in face view, germ-pore excentric in
          side view, appearing on the profile in face view (Fig. 219);
          on soil, generally in damp places   **88 leiocephalus**
x   Spores 10μm or more long, broader in face view
          (8.5-11μm), angled or not, germ-pore central or
          excentric in side view, variable in face view; on
          soil or in grass   108

108(107)   Spores with germ-pore appearing on the profile in face
view (Fig. 218) ellipsoid or slightly amygdaliform in
side view, broadly ovoid often distinctly 5- or 6-angled
in face view, (10-)11-13/6.5-7.5/8.5-10.5μm; in open
grassland or grassy places in woods   **86 plicatilis**
           Note: If spores larger see obs. to *86 plicatilis*

x   Spores with germ-pore inset in face view, not appearing
on the profile (Fig. 223), ellipsoid or ellipsoid-
amygdaliform in side view, subglobose-triangular not or
hardly angled in face view, 10-12.5/5-7/9-11μm; on
soil (? with preference for clay soils)   **87 galericuliformis**

109(106)   Spores 11.5-12.5/6.5-7/7-8μm   **84 hemerobius**

x   Spores 15-18/8.5-9.5/10-11μm   **85 megaspermus**

SECTION I : COPRINUS

Stirps 1: Comatus

1. C. comatus (Müller ex Fries) S.F. Gray, A Natural Arrangement of British Plants, I : 633, 1821. See Figs. 12 & 13, 37 & 45.

Syn.: *Agaricus comatus* Müller ex Fries, Systema Mycologicum, I:307, 1821.

Icon.: Cke (644) 658; L 156 E; M30; Ri 20[1]; Z 27. Figs.: Horak Beitrage Krypt. Schweiz sub Coprinus.

CAP at first (40-)50-150(-225)/(20-) 30-70mm ± cylindric or elongate-ovoid,then elongate campanulate or conical 50-80mm broad and soon becoming torn or revolute at margin, white becoming pinkish towards the margin then blackish, centre smooth and ochraceous cream, buff or pale fulvous at first with shaggy white to pale brownish scales often darkest at the tips. GILLS white then pinkish or vinaceous, finally black. STEM 100-370/11-26mm (20-35mm at base) attenuated upwards from the thickened or bulbous sometimes rooting base, white then pinkish, vinaceous or clay-buff sometimes saffron or pale sienna at base, smooth and shiny but becoming brownish fibrillose when handled, base white tomentose; ring white, movable, sometimes dropping to the base of the stem. SMELL none or slight, pleasant. SPORE-PRINT fuscous black.

SPORES blackish brown (9-)10-13(-14)/(6-)6.5-8 μm, ellipsoid-amygdaliform, germ-pore central and truncate, apiculus prominent (Fig. 37), thick walled. BASIDIA 4-spored, dimorphic. MARGINAL CYSTIDIA sphaeropedunculate, vesiculose or pyriform, 20-84/15-40μm. FACIAL CYSTIDIA absent. CAP CUTICLE of radially arranged ± cylindric cells, 5-20μm broad, with hyaline or brownish walls. VEIL on cap of ± cylindric cells 6-24 μm broad, hyaline or slightly encrusted brownish pigmented.

CLAMP-CONNECTIONS present. GENETICS heterothallic, bipolar, OIDIA absent, replaced by spherical conidia borne on dendroid branches which neither germinate in culture nor cause homing. Fruit-bodies are only obtained in soil culture with difficulty and after a long time.

HABITAT on soil or in grass by roadsides and paths, or on lawns or rubbish dumps, more especially on recently disturbed soil; gregarious. Widespread in Britain and Ireland, sometimes common but not found everywhere. Edible.

This well known and striking agaric, popularly known as 'Shaggy Ink Cap' (so called because of the way the cap deliquesces into a black inky liquid which drips away) or 'Lawyer's Wig' is considered good eating by some. A variant with cap subglobose at first is figured by J. Lange (L 156 D) as forma *sphaerocephalus*

J. Lange; its status awaits further investigation. The name *C. ovatus* (Schaeff. ex Fr.) Fr. has been used for specimens with cap ovoid at first, but the description of Fries in Epicrisis suggests something quite different. Experience in other agaric genera suggests caution in synonymising Fries' species. *C. ovatus* has also been used for *C. sterquilinus* in the past and there has also probably been confusion between *comatus* and *sterquilinus*, but the distinct spore size and habitat difference enables these two to be clearly distinguished.

2. **C. sterquilinus** (Fries)Fries, Epicrisis Systematis Mycologici, 242, 1838. See Figs. 38 & 44.

Syn: *Agaricus sterquilinus* Fries, Systema Mycologicum, I : 388, 1821.

Icon.: L 157 F; KM 21; Ri 20^2. Photo,: Buller, Researches on Fungi IV 78. figs: 49; 50.

CAP at first 40-60/20-30mm ellipsoid or ovoid, then up to 60mm broad expanded conical or plane or with upturned soon torn or incised margin, white or whitish with pale or deep cream centre then grey or vinaceous grey from margin in, at first entirely finely white fibrillose-floccose then sometimes more coarsely scaly, becoming striate at margin as cap expands. GILLS whitish then pinkish, finally purplish umber to blackish. STEM 80-150/4-8mm (8-12mm at base), attenuated upwards from thickened or ± bulbous base, white then buff or clay-pinkish at least in part, base sometimes with mycelial strands; ring white, movable, frequently basal, sometimes fugacious. SMELL not noted. SPORE-PRINT fuscous black.

SPORES blackish brown, (16-)17-22(-23)/10-13(-13.5)μm, ellipsoid or ovoid, germ-pore rounded and ± excentric, apiculus small. BASIDIA 4-spored, dimorphic. MARGINAL CYSTIDIA vesiculose. FACIAL CYSTIDIA absent. VEIL on cap of filamentous hyphae.

CLAMP-CONNECTIONS present. GENETICS apparently homothallic. OIDIA absent in culture (Buller).

HABITAT on dung (horse or rabbit), solitary or in small groups. Rarely recorded but widespread in Britain.

Easily recognised by the ring, very large spores and habitat on dung. It is rather smaller and less conspicuously scaly than *C. comatus*, which does not grow on dung. No doubt it has sometimes been recorded, as *C. ovatus*, the status of which name is, however, uncertain. *C. oblectus* [Bolt.] ex Fr. has been given as a synonym but Fries' description is based on Bolton's illustration (Pl. 142) which looks distinct, having a marked flaring volvate base, much as is indicated for *C. vosoustii* Pilát which could be the same. *C. oblectus* is therefore rejected for the moment pending rediscovery of fresh material.

The presence of a second closely related taxon is suggested by the fact that certain isolates produce thallic arthrospores in addition to spherical conidia borne on specialised dendroid branches.

Stirps 2 : Atramentarius

3. C. atramentarius (Bulliard ex Fries) Fries, Epicrisis Systematis Mycologici, 243, 1838. See Figs. 11, 15 & 16, 18, 40 & 46.

Syn: *Agaricus atramentarius* Bulliard ex Fries, Systema Mycologicum, I:308, 1821.

Icon.: Boud 138; Cke 648(662); Hennig I 38; Hvass 173; L 157 H; LH 137; M 31; NB 356; Ri 22[1]; Romag PA 89; RMT 151; W 56; WD 82. Figs.: Horak Beitrage Krypt. Schweiz sub *Pselliophora*

CAP at first 30-65/30-70mm ovoid, then convex or conical, finally expanded-convex or -conical 40-80mm broad, with margin often lobed or irregularly puckered at first then torn or split radially, smoke- or mouse-grey, minutely adpressed or slightly reflexed cinnamon to sepia scaly especially at centre, outer part soon becoming ± smooth and sulcate-plicate or radially ribbed. GILLS whitish then umber, purplish date or brown vinaceous, finally black. STEM 70-175/9-15mm, equal or attenuated at base and apex, white, smooth but apex minutely pruinose at first, with a ring-like mark from veil (often at the thickest part) above the base, topped by a raised ridge or simply a faint line and sometimes angularly grooved above this. SMELL none or faint, pleasant, SPORE-PRINT umber or purplish-date to blackish umber.

SPORES dark date-brown, 8-11/5-6μm, ellipsoid or ellipsoid-amygdaliform, germ-pore central and truncate. BASIDIA 4-spored, dimorphic. MARGINAL CYSTIDIA cylindric or slightly clavate to narrowly fusiform or elongate-ovoid, 24-80/10-30μm, apex obtuse. FACIAL CYSTIDIA elongate-cylindric, often flexuose, about 150-200/20-32μm. CAP CUTICLE of short radially arranged cylindric cells, 10-30μm broad. VEIL on cap and at stem-base of filamentous hyphae 2-12μm broad with slightly coloured walls.

CLAMP-CONNECTIONS absent. GENETICS unknown; spores very difficult to germinate in culture.

HABITAT on wood or apparently on soil but in reality attached to buried wood; solitary or caespitose. Common throughout lowland Britain. Edible.

Easily recognised by stature, veil-mark at base of stem and spore width. It is only likely to be confused with either *acuminatus*, which is usually smaller and has relatively narrow spores (4-5.2μm broad instead of 5-6μm for the same length), or *insignis*, which has rough spores and a more distinct veil on the cap. The cap and gills produce copious quantities of inky fluid as they deliquesce. *C. romagnesianus* is a more scaly taxon with coloured velar material *C. fuscescens* is another name which has been used for specimens with a ± smooth cap, but its status is doubtful.

4. C. acuminatus (Romagnesi) P.D. Orton in Notes from the Royal Garden, Edinburgh, 29 : 86, 1969. See Figs. 39 & 42.

Syn.: *C. atramentarius* var. *acuminatus* Romagnesi in Rev. Mycol. Paris, 16: 120, 1951.

Icon.: none. Figs.: NRBG 29 : 91; figs. 1c′, c″; 93; figs 3a, b, c; RM 16.: 120, fig. 4.

CAP at first 10-30(-35)/12-23(-30)mm from rounded-convex to elongate ellipsoid with mammiform umbo, then expanded 22-60(-80)mm broad, with revolute and split margin, greyish, often with darker clay-buff or sepia centre, smooth outer part often smoke-grey, usually fulvous to sepia minutely scaly at centre, smooth, silky atomate and often radially wrinkled or striate in outer part. GILLS whitish then pinkish, finally blackish umber. STEM 22-60(-90)/2-5(-9)mm, ± equal or attenuated upwards, often slightly swollen at base or more rarely slightly fusiform and attenuated at base, white then sometimes discoloured pale clay-buff at base, silky striate, base usually with volva-like zone of scales like those at cap-centre, topped by a ring-like mark, sometimes with white mycelial strands. SMELL none or faint, pleasant. SPORE-PRINT very dark umber.

SPORES umber, (7.5-)8-10/4-5.2μm, ellipsoid-amygdaliform in side view, ellipsoid in face view, germ-pore truncate and central. BASIDIA 4-spored. MARGINAL CYSTIDIA shortly cylindric or vesiculose, 10-18μm broad. FACIAL CYSTIDIA elongate cylindric, sometimes slightly curved, (64-)84-230/12-40μm. CAP CUTICLE of radially arranged cylindric cells, 4-15μm broad. VEIL on cap and at stem-base of filamentous hyphae with pale grey or brownish walls.

CLAMP-CONNECTIONS present. GENETICS tetrapolar. OIDIA not seen in culture.

HABITAT on buried wood, sawdusty soil, or apparently just on soil; singly or subcaespitose, often gregarious. Widespread in Britain, but not yet recorded from Ireland. Edible.

Readily distinguished from *atramentarius* by the narrower spores (4-5.2μm broad instead of 5-6μm for the same length), relatively smaller size of most fruit-bodies and perhaps not always growing on wood. Probably eaten by mistake for *atramentarius,* but said to be equally as good.

5. C. romagnesianus Singer in Lilloa, 22: 459, 1951. See Figs. 41 & 43.

Syn.: *C. atramentarius* var *squamosus* Bresadola, Iconographia Mycologia (1931): 878 sensu Bresadola (non *C. squamosus* Morgan, 1883)

Icon.: Bres. 878 var *squamosus*

CAP at first 30-40/30-45mm ellipsoid or conical, then expanded 40-60mm broad, with torn, split or revolute sometimes wavy margin, slate grey to sepia beneath veil, at first entirely covered by thick smooth sienna, apricot or rusty veil which may fade to cinnamon or fulvous and splits into adpressed scales, largest at centre and smallest at margin, finally smooth and sulcate striate from margin in. GILLS white then pinkish, finally slate-grey. STEM 60-95/5-15mm (10-15mm at base), equal or thickened in middle or lower part of stem, white, silky- and sometimes sulcate-striate above fibrillose median or apical ring-zone, below this with apricot or rusty fibrillose scales from veil as on cap. SMELL none. SPORE-PRINT violaceous black.

SPORES dark sepia, 8-9.5/4.5-5.5µm, ellipsoid very slightly amygdaliform in side view, ellipsoid or cylindric-ellipsoid in face view, germ-pore central and rather rounded. BASIDIA 4-spored. MARGINAL CYSTIDIA subglobose or ± clavate, 25-50/12-20µm, sometimes with cylindrical apical point 5-8µm broad and up to 10µm long. FACIAL CYSTIDIA cylindric or lageniform with tapered neck, 45-50/17.5-25µm, apex 9-12µm broad. CAP CUTICLE of radially arranged filamentous hyphae. VEIL on cap of dark brown filamentous hyphae.

CLAMP-CONNECTIONS present. GENETICS unknown.

HABITAT caespitose about roots of old trees. Distribution unknown but recently collected from Perth, probably widespread though presumably rare or uncommon.

It differs from other members of Stirps *Atramentarius* in its bright apricot or rust veil, especially noticeable on young specimens, and the fact that the veil covers the lower half or two-thirds of the stem instead of the base only.

This collection agrees quite well with Bresadola's description, especially as to colours and spore size and shape, but not with Romagnesi's interpretation (RM 10 : 77, fig. 2 (1945)) which is described as having longer and differently shaped spores (11-12.5/4.7-5.3µm, fusiform-amygdaliform or irregularly fusiform in side view, elongate ellipsoid in face view). There is no evidence of such a taxon in Britain as yet, and it would seem to require description as a new species.

6. C. insignis Peck in Twenty Sixth Report of the New York State Museum, 60, 1874.

Icon.: BSMF 44: Atlas pl. 23; TBMS 41: 430, text fig. 1, Pl. 24[5].

CAP at first 40-150/20-70mm ovoid sometimes slightly umbonate or conico-convex, then expanded, whitish or greyish with buff or clay-buff centre, at first white, silvery silky fibrillose from veil then ± smooth, margin becoming blackish, slightly wrinkled at first then sulcate-striate almost to centre. GILLS white then reddish brown, finally black. STEM 80-200/7-15mm, ± equal or slightly thickened towards base, white, then pale buff, base white tomentose. SMELL none. SPORE-PRINT fuscous black.

SPORES (10-)11-14.5/(6-)7-8μm, amygdaliform in side view, ellipsoid in face view, rough with low irregular warts thus appearing crenulate in optical section, germ-pore prominent, hyaline, and truncate but rather narrow. BASIDIA 4-spored. MARGINAL CYSTIDIA vesiculose. FACIAL CYSTIDIA vesiculose, 80-180/60μm (sec. Kühner). VEIL on cap of chains of cylindric cells, 52-143/8-26μm and also filamentous hyphae 6-12μm broad (sec. Kühner, Atlas pl. 23).

CLAMP-CONNECTIONS present. GENETICS unknown.

Description from Kühner and Reid.

HABITAT on stumps of broad-leaved trees; caespitose. Seemingly uncommon and as yet only recorded from southern England.

This species is easily recognised microscopically by its rough spores but may be confused with *C. atramentarius* in the field, from which it differs by the white silky-fibrillose veil, visible at least on the young cap. The other British species with rough spores are all smaller and with different habitat and veil characters.

Stirps 3 : Erythrocephalus

7. C. erythrocephalus (Leveillé) Fries, Hymenomycetes Europaei, 327, 1874. See Figs. 50 & 56.

Syn.: *Agaricus erythrocephalus* Leveillé in Ann. Sci. Nat., Series 2, 16 : 237, 1841. Misident. : *C. dilectus* Fries sensu J.E. Lange in Dansk bot. Arkiv. 2 : 40, 1915 and Fl. Ag. Dan.4 : 109, 1939.

Icon.: L 157 A, dilectus; BSMF 57 : 39, fig. 1, Pl. 3.

CAP at first 10-20/5-8mm, cylindric-ellipsoid or cylindric-campanulate, then expanded ± plane 10-25mm broad with torn or recurved margin, orange-red or coral from the veil then whitish, greyish or clay-buff from margin inwards, centre sometimes buff or ± fulvous, at first entirely minutely orange-red or coral fibrillose scaly, then ± smooth and wrinkled-sulcate from margin inwards. GILLS white or whitish then date-brown finally black. STEM 30-85/1-2mm (3-5mm at base), attenuated upwards at least in upper part, white at first with coral fibrillose scales as on cap, which become scattered and finally disappear as stem elongates, base ± persistently coral tomentose. SMELL none. SPORE-PRINT black.

SPORES dark brown, 8-10/4.5-5.5μm, ellipsoid or ovoid, germ-pore central, BASIDIA 4-spored. MARGINAL CYSTIDIA vesiculose, clavate or fusiform, 24-40/12-20μm. FACIAL CYSTIDIA cylindric vesiculose, 60-80/20-26μm. CAP CUTICLE of radially arranged filamentous hyphae 6-20μm broad. VEIL on cap of buff, yellowish or fulvous encrusted-pigmented or hyaline ± cylindric hyphae 6-10(-12)μm broad.

CLAMP-CONNECTIONS present. GENETICS unknown.

HABITAT on bare soil, old bonfire sites or on rubbish dumps, solitary or ± gregarious. Uncommon in England, not yet recorded from Scotland or Ireland.

It is easily recognised by the coloured veil of filamentous hyphae and spores of medium size. Another taxon with pink veil is *C. roseotinctus* Rea, which possibly belongs to Stirps *Niveus*; see obs. on 32 *C. niveus*.

Stirps 4 : Echinosporus

8. C. echinosporus Buller in Transactions of the British Mycological Society, 6 : 363, 1920. See Figs. 52a & b.

Syn.: *C. giganteoporus* Huijsman in Fungus 25: 19, 1955.

Icon.: none. Figs.: Fungus 25 : 21, Pl, 1. Fig. 1.

CAP at first 10-20/5-10mm ovoid, then conico-campanulate or ± expanded 13-30mm broad, and split or revolute at margin, white then grey often with vinaceous buff or clay-buff centre, at first with scattered adpressed white or whitish silky floccose scales from veil then ± smooth and sulcate-striate from margin inwards. GILLS black at maturity. STEM 40-90/1.4-3.5mm, equal or slightly thickened at base, white then hyaline whitish, at first white silky floccose scaly like cap, becoming ± smooth at least in upper part, base white tomentose. SMELL none. SPORE-PRINT black.

SPORES brownish-black, (8-)8.5-10.5/5.5-7μm, limoniform or amygdaliform in side view, ovoid in face view, closely and rather finely warted, germ-pore central and truncate, (2-)2.5-3(-3.5)μm broad. BASIDIA 4-spored. MARGINAL CYSTIDIA vesiculose or pyriform, 10-20μm broad. FACIAL CYSTIDIA cylindric ellipsoid often fugacious (70-105/23-57μm sec. Buller). CAP CUTICLE of radially arranged cells 10-20μm wide. VEIL on cap of ± cylindric hyaline branched hyphae 4-10(-12)μm broad.

HABITAT on sticks or twigs, usually solitary. Uncommon in England and Scotland, not yet recorded for Ireland.

It is easily recognised microscopically by the warted spores with broad flat truncate germ-pore, and macroscopically it looks like a small *C. lagopus*. *C. phlyctidosporus* also with warted spores has a different habitat, on burnt ground, and ellipsoid spores.

Buller recorded this originally 'on sticks dredged from a pool' which has led people to suppose that it occurred solely in wet places. Actually this is not so at all, for it is lignicolous and has been found in woods nowhere near any water; what had happened was that the sticks were dumped near the pond and the *Coprinus* came up on them. Hora (*Mycopath & Myc.Appl.*48 : 43, 1972) records this same fungus from pine-woods after treatment with washing soda. *C. giganteoporus* by virtue of the broad germ-pore (confirmed in type material, see Fig. 52b) is surely therefore a synonym. Romagnesi has described a different taxon under the name *C. echinosporus* (RM 6 : 109, 1941) which is in all probability *C. insignis* as suggested by Kühner & Romagnesi in Flore Analytique 391, footnote 12.

9. C. phlyctidosporus Romagnesi in Revue de Mycologie, 10: 73, 1945. See Fig. 51.

Icon.: none. Figs.: RM 10: 73, fig. 1.

CAP at first 13-20/8-15mm ovoid or conico-convex, then expanded slightly umbonate up to 40mm broad, pale to dark grey-brown (drab), whitish fibrillose veil forming small scales in outer part and a pale creamy-yellowish covering at centre, becoming ± smooth and grooved sulcate from margin inwards. GILLS white then blackening. STEM 40-50/3-4mm, attenuated upwards, white then dis-colouring slightly, minutely tomentose. SMELL none. SPORE-PRINT blackish.

SPORES dark red-brown, 8-10/6-7.5μm, ellipsoid or ovoid, with conspicuous rounded dark warts and also with hyaline pointed warts near the small central germ-pore and below the apiculus. BASIDIA 4-spored. MARGINAL CYSTIDIA ellipsoid or cylindric-vesiculose, 60-65/25-30μm. FACIAL CYSTIDIA irregularly vesiculose, not fully investigated. CAP CUTICLE of radially arranged hyphae 6.5-10μm broad. VEIL on cap of filamentous thin-walled branched hyphae 4-8μm broad.

CLAMP-CONNECTIONS not observed. GENETICS unknown.

HABITAT on burnt ground. Seemingly rare, as yet only recorded from Dodderhill Common, Worcs.

Description mainly from Romagnesi.

It is distinguished from other species of *Coprinus* that grow on burnt ground by its rough spores and veil characters. Further study on fresh material is required to complete the description.

Stirps 5 : Picaceus

10. C. picaceus (Bulliard ex Fries) S.F. Gray, A Natural Arrangement of British Plants, I: 634, 1821. See Figs. 47 & 55.

Syn.: *Agaricus picaceus* Bulliard ex Fries, Systema Mycologicum, |I:308, 1821.

Icon.: Cke 652(665), L 158 E, KM 36[1], Ri 21[1].

CAP at first 50-80/30-40 cylindric-ellipsoid or conical then expanded conical or campanulate 40-60mm broad, white then grey, finally sepia or fuscous black beneath veil scales, at first entirely covered with thick felty whitish, clay-pink or vinaceous buff veil which splits into adpressed often broad patches, margin becoming striate and radially split. GILLS white then clay-pinkish or fawn, finally black, often rather broad. STEM 90-300/6-15mm (20-25mm at base), attenuated upwards from bulbous base, white, at first flocculose but soon smooth, base white strigose-tomentose. SMELL faint to fairly strong, unpleasant. SPORE-PRINT fuscous black.

SPORES black, (12-)13-17(-18)/10-12μm, ellipsoid, slightly amygdaliform in side view, broadly ovoid in face view, germ-pore central. BASIDIA 4-spored. MARGINAL CYSTIDIA cylindric or vesiculose to narrowly lageniform, 60-80/20-30μm. FACIAL CYSTIDIA cylindric-vesiculose and fusiform, 100-200/30-50μm. CAP CUTICLE of radially arranged ± cylindric cells. VEIL of interwoven filamentous hyphae 4-20μm broad.

CLAMP-CONNECTIONS present. GENETICS heterothallic, tetrapolar (Brunswick and Chow). OIDIA not seen.

HABITAT on soil or in leaves, more especially in beech woods on basic soil; solitary or in small groups. Widespread in Britain but rather local, not occurring in Northern Scotland.

One of the most easily recognised species in the genus on account of its tall stem, large size and conspicuous white patches on the otherwise dark cap, from which it gets its common name of Magpie Toadstool. It is said to be poisonous. *C. episcopalis* and *C. scobicola* are smaller and different microscopically but may look rather like miniature specimens of *C. picaceus*.

11. C. episcopalis P.D. Orton in Transactions of the British Mycological Society, 40: 270, 1957. See Figs. 53, 57, 58 & 59.

Icon.: none. Figs.: TBMS 40: 270, figs. 5, 6.

CAP at first 20-30/10-18mm cylindrical or ± conical, then expanded convex sometimes broadly umbonate to ± plane and 30-55mm broad with white margin soon torn and reflexed, finally split or revolute, then pale to dark grey with paler or greyish cream centre, at first entirely covered by white veil which splits up into adpressed separable whitish patches, those at centre clay pinkish or cream-buff, those near margin smaller and floccose-fibrillose, becoming striate or sulcate in outer part. GILLS whitish then grey, finally blackish. STEM 60-95/3-5mm (8-15mm at base), attenuated upwards from marginate, or less frequently rounded, bulbous base, white then whitish, lower part finely white silky floccose when fresh, bulb whitish or pale grey-cream, white tomentose beneath. SMELL none at first, then as cap expands dung-like and disagreeable but not strong. SPORE-PRINT blackish.

SPORES dark-brown, 7.5-10/5.5-6.5/6.5-8μm, lentiform, ellipsoid-amygdaliform in side view, markedly mitriform in face view (Fig. 53), germ-pore truncate and central. BASIDIA 4-spored. MARGINAL CYSTIDIA vesiculose, clavate or slightly fusiform, more rarely cylindric, 30-40(-60)/16-30μm. FACIAL CYSTIDIA elongate ellipsoid or fusiform-cylindric often narrowed and occasionally bifurcate at apex, 90-180/20-60μm. CAP CUTICLE of ± cylindric cells up to 30μm broad. VEIL on cap of hyaline hyphae 3-9μm broad, those at centre often with thick brownish walls.

CLAMP-CONNECTIONS present. GENETICS unknown; not yet obtained in culture.

HABITAT in leaves in beech woods on basic soil, usually solitary. So far only recorded from Surrey (Boxhill area, several collections) and Berkshire (one collection). It may well occur in beech woods on basic soil elsewhere in England, possibly as far north as Yorkshire. A footnote in Kühner & Romagnesi, Flora Analytique (1953): 391, no. 11 suggests that this species may also occur in France.

Easily recognised sub micr. by mitriform spores similar to that of *C. angulatus* but recognisable in the field by habitat, marginate bulbous stem, small adpressed patches of veil on cap (making it look like a miniature *C. picaceus*) and rather weak disagreeable smell.

12. C. scobicola P.D. Orton in Notes from the Royal Botanic Garden, Edinburgh, 32 : 147, 1972. See Figs. 49 & 54.

Icon.: none. Figs.: NRBG 32: 147, fig. 2, h-j.

CAP at first 16-22/9-11mm. ovoid or cylindric-ovoid, then expanded-convex up to 30mm broad with torn or split margin, grey then tinged clay-buff at centre, at first covered with white ± recurved fibrillose scales, those at centre often clay-buff or drab and thick and shaggy, then becoming scattered adpressed scaly with outer part finally smooth and plicate-striate. GILLS soon grey then black. STEM 35-50/2.5-4mm, white, attenuated upwards, at first minutely flocculose then becoming smooth as cap expands, base white tomentose. SMELL none. SPORE-PRINT blackish.

SPORES fuscous black, 11.5-14/7-8.5μm, ellipsoid or ellipsoid amygdaliform, germ-pore central. BASIDIA 2(3)-spored. MARGINAL CYSTIDIA pyriform or shortly vesiculose, 30-54/24-44μm. FACIAL CYSTIDIA cylindric-vesiculose, 80-110/30-40μm. VEIL on cap of filamentous hyphae with cells ± cylindric or narrowed at the septa, 50-100/8-20μm.

HABITAT on sawdust, gregarious. Only recorded from S. Devon.

It most closely resembles *C. episcopalis* from which it differs not only in habitat and 2-spored basidia but also in spore shape and lack of markedly bulbous stem base. From members of Stirps *Lagopus* it differs in having narrower hyphae in the veil forming more distinct scales on the cap.

13. C. extinctorius (Bulliard ex St Amans) Fries, Epicrisis Systematis Mycologici, 245, 1838. See Fig. 48.

Syn.: *Agaricus extinctorius* Bulliard ex St Amans, Flore Agenaise, 567, 1821.

Icon.: none. Figs.: RM 6 : 112, fig, 2; KR 387, fig. 544.

CAP at first 15-24/11-24mm elongate-conical or cylindrical to ovoid, then expanded with strongly incurved revolute margin, 20-35mm broad, white then greyish with drab or clay-buff centre, at first with small rather pointed white fibrillose scales from veil, those at or around centre often tinged buff or grey-cream at ± reflexed tips, margin soon smooth and striate. GILLS white then greyish or pale purplish date, finally black. STEM 35-55/2-4mm (up to 6mm at base), equal or attenuated upwards from slightly thickened or bulbous base, white or whitish, apex minutely white pruinose, white scaly like cap at first, then ± smooth, base white tomentose. SMELL none. SPORE-PRINT black.

SPORES blackish brown, 8-10/5.5-6.5/6.5-7.5µm slightly lentiform, limoniform or amygdaliform in side view, ovoid-fusiform in face view, germ-pore broad and truncate. BASIDIA 4-spored. MARGINAL CYSTIDIA vesiculose, ellipsoid, ovoid or fusiform, 24-100/14-40µm. FACIAL CYSTIDIA ellipsoid or cylindric-ellipsoid, 60-120/28-50µm. CAP CUTICLE of radially arranged shortly cylindric cells 10-25µm broad. VEIL on cap a mixture of narrow often brownish thick-walled filamentous hyphae 1-6µm broad, and hyaline thin-walled hyphae of cylindric-ellipsoid cells often constricted at septa 10-36µm broad.

CLAMP-CONNECTIONS present. GENETICS heterothallic, tetrapolar (sec. Quintanilha et al.). OIDIA absent.

HABITAT on stumps or in wounds of broad-leaved trees, solitary or in small groups. Infrequently recorded but widespread in Britain.

It is recognised amongst other macroscopically similar species growing on wood by the veil with two kinds of hyphae and ± limoniform spores with broad truncate germ-pore. It seems very doubtful if this is the agaric described by St Amans as *Agaricus extinctorius*, which is said to have the cap 'fauve au sommet et parsemé de vésicules brillantes'. It may therefore have to be described as a new species.

Stirps 6 : Lagopus

14. C. lagopus (Fries) Fries, Epicrisis Systematis Mycologici, 250, 1838. See Figs. 61 & 70.

Syn.: *Agaricus lagopus* Fries, Systema Mycologicum, I : 312, 1821.

Icon.: L 158 F: KM 34: Ri 21[2]. Figs.: TBMS 40 : 270, fig. 1.

CAP at first 10-35/7-20mm, conical or cylindric-ellipsoid, then expanded ± plane or slightly depressed 25-50mm broad, white then grey, sometimes clay-buff at centre, often dirty whitish when spores have been shed, veil at first covering the whole cap then forming erect or recurved white or pale grey floccose-fibrillose often pointed easily separable ± fugacious scales, those at centre sometimes brownish, when mature ± smooth and striate or plicate, when quite old often entire and thin and papery but sometimes split or more rarely revolute at margin. GILLS white then grey, finally black. STEM 65-130/2-3mm, 3-6mm broad at base, equal or attenuated upwards, more rarely with slightly swollen base, white, at first entirely white floccose-fibrillose like the cap then ± smooth. SMELL none. SPORE-PRINT violaceous black.

SPORES dark brown, (10-)11-13.5/6-7μm, ellipsoid or ellipsoid-amygdaliform, germ-pore central. BASIDIA 4-spored, tetramorphic. MARGINAL CYSTIDIA vesiculose, pyriform, or fusiform-lageniform, 30-80/12-38μm. FACIAL CYSTIDIA fusiform-vesiculose or elongate ellipsoid to broadly lageniform, 80-130/25-50μm. CAP CUTICLE of radially arranged ± cylindric cells. VEIL of hyaline thin-walled hyphae with cells ± cylindric, 40-200/12-40μm often constricted at septa, end-cells sometimes narrowed at apex.

CLAMP-CONNECTIONS present. GENETICS heterothallic, probably tetrapolar. OIDIA formed in moist heads in culture.

HABITAT on soil or in leaves on paths in shady places or in woods, more rarely in fields or gardens; often solitary but sometimes in small groups (especially on saw-dusty soil). Widespread and common in Britain and recorded from Ireland, but past records must be treated with suspicion because this name has been used for dung-inhabiting taxa.

Recognisable in the field by habitat, coarse white fibrils of veil on cap, and the tendency of the cap to persist after the gills have deliquesced. The broad hyphae of the veil and spore-size are confirmatory microscopic characters.

A very similar fungus has been collected in Warwickshire and Knapdale, Scotland, and in Kortenhoef, Netherlands. It differs only in minor details of spore shape and size; the spores are slightly narrower, shorter and usually shouldered about the germ-pore. It is not interfertile with typical *C. lagopus*. This species has been called *C. pseudolagopus* Kemp nom. prov. (TBMS 65 : 380, 1975).

It is unfortunate that Buller (1922, 1924) and others after him have used this epithet wrongly for dung-inhabiting taxa (see obs. on 16 *C. cinereus*) in spite of

Fries clearly indicating a habitat on soil. The only other British member of Stirps *Lagopus* so far described not growing on dung is *C. lagopides,* which can look macroscopically similar but grows on burnt soil, has much smaller ± subglobose spores and is usually more robust and less fragile; it also deliquesces more quickly.

15. C. lagopides Karsten in Meddelanden of Societas pro Fauna et Flora Fennica, 9 : 48, 1852. See Figs. 60 & 69.

Syn.: *C. jonesii* Peck, in Bull. Torrey Bot. Club, 22: 206 1895; *C. funariarum* Métrod, in Bull. Soc. mycol. Fr., 53: 287, 1937; *C. lagopus* var. *sphaerosporus* Kühner & Josserand, in Bull. Soc. mycol. Fr., 60: 31,1944.

Icon.: none. Figs.: TBMS 40: 264, figs. 2, 3; BSMF 60: 31, fig. 5, var.*sphaerosporus.*

CAP at first 17-57/10-35mm ellipsoid, conical or cylindrical, then expanded with margin 15-50mm broad, often split or torn or revolute, white or whitish then grey and often vinaceous buff, clay-buff or fawn at centre, at first entirely covered with erect or recurved white then greyish easily separable floccose-fibrillose scales, then ± smooth, and striate or sulcate from margin inwards. GILLS becoming fuscous black to black. STEM 30-110/3-12mm equal or attenuated upwards, sometimes slightly ventricose at first rarely slightly thickened at base, white, entirely white floccose-fibrillose scaly at first becoming smooth in places, base white tomentose. SMELL none. SPORE-PRINT violaceous black.

SPORES dark brown, 6-9/4.5-6/5-7μm, lentiform, ellipsoid slightly amygdaliform in side view, subglobose or ovoid in face view, germ-pore central and truncate. BASIDIA 4-spored, trimorphic. MARGINAL CYSTIDIA vesiculose-clavate or cylindric-vesiculose, 40-100/20-30μm. FACIAL CYSTIDIA cylindric-vesiculose or elongate broadly lageniform, 80-160/25-50μm. CAP CUTICLE of radially arranged ± cylindric cells 10-20μm broad. VEIL on cap of thin-walled hyaline hyphae constricted at septa of ± cylindric or elongate-ellipsoid cells, (40-)50-200/(12-)20-40μm, those on stem similar but sometimes narrower 8-20μm broad.

CLAMP-CONNECTIONS present. GENETICS heterothallic, probably tetrapolar. OIDIA formed in moist heads in culture.

HABITAT on burnt soil, charred wood or plaster; gregarious or subcaespitose, less commonly solitary. Widespread and rather common in Britain.

It can be recognised in the field by habitat and conspicuous fibrillose scales on the cap, but is best distinguished by the relatively small lentiform spores. It is more substantial than *C. lagopus* and the cap deliquesces more completely in age so that it is never found papery and entire as in *C. lagopus.*

16. C. cinereus (Schaeffer ex Fries) S.F. Gray, A Natural Arrangement of British Plants, I:634, 1821. See Figs. 17, 63 & 68, 71-73.

Syn.: *Agaricus cinereus* Schaeffer ex Fries, Systema Mycologicum, I : 310, 1821; *Agaricus macrorhizus* Persoon ex Fries, Systema Mycologicum, I : 311, 1821; *Coprinus macrorhizus* (Persoon ex Fries) Rea, British Basidiomycetae, 503, 1922; *C. delicatulus* Apinis, in Trans. Brit. myc. Soc., 48 : 653, 1965; *C. fimetarius* [L.] ex Fries, Epicrisis Systematis Mycologici, 245, 1838 pro parte. Misident. : *C. lagopus* (Fr.) Fr. sensu Day in Heredity, 13 : 81; *idem*. sensu Lewis in Genet. Res., 2 : 141, 1961; *idem* sensu Fincham & Day, Fungal genetics, 19, 1959; idem sensu Anderson, The Life history and genetics of *Coprinus lagopus,* (1971).

Icon.: Bres 879, *fimetarius*; Cke 658(671); Cke 657(670), var. *macrorhizus;* KM 35; L 158 G, *fimetarius.*

CAP at first 10-50/6-30mm ellipsoid, conical or elongate-cylindric, then expanded 20-50mm broad, at first whitish with centre tinged smoke-grey or vinaceous buff, then smoke-grey or leaden-grey especially in outer part, at first entirely densely flocculose-fibrillose white or sometimes greyish or buff-tipped scaly then ± smooth with plicate-striate margin. GILLS white soon whitish or greyish then fawn to fuscous black finally black. STEM 40-120/3-6mm, equal or slightly attenuated upwards from the often thickened and sometimes rooting base, white then sometimes tinged pale vinaceous buff in lower part, apex smooth or slightly pruinose, lower part with white soon collapsing flocculose-fibrillose scales. SMELL none to fairly strong, pleasant. SPORE-PRINT fuscous black.

SPORES date-brown, 9-12/6-7µm, ellipsoid or ellipsoid-ovoid, germ-pore central. BASIDIA 4-spored, dimorphic. MARGINAL CYSTIDIA globose, ovoid or pyriform, 20-70/16-38µm. FACIAL CYSTIDIA elongate cylindric or ellipsoid, (or broadly lageniform), 60-98/18-45µm. CAP CUTICLE of radially arranged ± cylindric cells. VEIL on cap of hyaline thin-walled filamentous hyphae 10-40(-60)µm broad, constricted at septa.

CLAMP-CONNECTIONS present. GENETICS heterothallic, tetrapolar. OIDIA in moist heads in culture.

HABITAT on dung-heaps or manured straw, especially if these are heating up through bacterial activity; solitary or caespitose. Common and widespread in the British Isles.

It differs from other members of Stirps *Lagopus,* except *C. macrocephalus,* in the habitat and relatively large size of fruit-bodies, and from *C. macrocephalus* in narrower spores and sometimes rooting stem. *C. radiatus* and *C. pseudoradiatus* both usually produce very small fruit-bodies; the latter has much smaller spores.

C. cinereus readily grows and fruits in culture and has been used extensively in genetical studies, unfortunately frequently misnamed *C. lagopus,* a name which should not be used for dung-inhabiting taxa. The variant with rooting stem has been named *C. macrorhizus,* but interfertility experiments indicate that this is not a separate taxon (Kemp, TBMS 65: 380, 1975). *C. delicatulus* has also been shown by interfertility experiments to be conspecific (Kemp, TBMS 65: 380, 1975).

17. C. macrocephalus (Berkeley) Berkeley, Outlines of British Fungology, 180, 1860. See Figs 64 & 74.

Syn.: *Agaricus macrocephalus* Berkeley, Hooker's British Flora, 5; 122, 1836.
Icon.: Cke 670(682): L 158 B.

CAP at first 10-30/4-15mm, cylindrical or elongate ellipsoid, then expanded ± plane often with revolute or split margin, 11-40mm broad, white then grey, centre sometimes buff or pale fulvous, at first entirely white or whitish and often rather coarsely floccose-fibrillose, fibrils often in rather long bundles, these then breaking up into separable sometimes buff-tinged scales, finally almost smooth and striate to centre. GILLS white then grey, soon black, STEM 40-190/2-7mm, attenuated upwards, not or only slightly thickened at base, but sometimes slightly pointed and rooting, white then hyaline whitish, at first with scattered often spreading white fibrils especially in lower part, then almost smooth except at base. SMELL none. SPORE-PRINT violaceous black.

SPORES black or very dark brown, 11-14(-15)/7.5-8.5µm, ellipsoid or ellipsoid ovoid, germ-pore central and rather truncate. BASIDIA 4-spored. MARGINAL CYSTIDIA globose or vesiculose, 25-40µm broad. FACIAL CYSTIDIA absent. CAP CUTICLE of radially arranged cells. VEIL on cap of filamentous hyphae with ± cylindric cells constricted at the septa, 12-44µm broad, end-cells sometimes narrowed at apex.

CLAMP-CONNECTIONS present. GENETICS heterothallic, tetrapolar.

HABITAT on manured straw or dung heaps, less frequently on fresh dung; solitary or gregarious. Uncommon, although it may be widespread in Great Britain.

It can be recognised in the field by the rather coarse veil fibrils and lack of marked swollen or rooting stem base. Small specimens may appear like large specimens of *C. radiatus* but can be recognised by the clearly broader spores. *C. cinereus,* although it may have spores as long as *C. macrocephalus* has them narrower (6-7)µm broad and rather less coarsely scaly cap.

18. C. radiatus (Bolton ex Fries) S.F. Gray, A Natural Arrangement of British Plants, I:635, 1821. See Figs. 65, 67 & 75.

Syn.: *Agaricus radiatus* Bolton ex Fries, Systema Mycologicum I: 313, 1821.
C. fimetarius [Linn.] ex Fries, Epicrisis Systematis Mycologici, 245, 1838, pro parte. Misident. : *C. lagopus* (Fries) Fries sensu Buller, Researches on Fungi 2 : 86, 1922 et seq.

Icon.: L 158 C. Figs. : BSMF 60 : 23, fig. 1; KR 388, figs. 549, 550.

CAP at first 2-6/1-3mm ellipsoid or ovoid, then expanded or conico-expanded with split or revolute margin 2-10mm broad, whitish soon pale or deep grey, at first with white then whitish recurved fibrils from veil then ± smooth and striate or plicate to centre. GILLS whitish then black. STEM 20-50/0.5-1mm, equal or slightly attenuated upwards, sometimes rooting at base, white then hyaline, with scattered white fibrils from veil at first then smooth except at base. SMELL none. SPORE-PRINT violaceous black.

SPORES brownish black, 11-14/6-7μm, ellipsoid or cylindric-ellipsoid, sometimes slightly phaseoliform in side view, germ-pore central or slightly excentric. BASIDIA 4-spored. MARGINAL CYSTIDIA ellipsoid or ovoid, up to 50/30μm. FACIAL CYSTIDIA cylindric or cylindric ovoid, up to 100/32μm. CAP CUTICLE of radially arranged ± cylindric cells. VEIL on cap of ± cylindric cells constricted at septa 10-20μm broad.

CLAMP-CONNECTIONS present. GENETICS heterothallic, tetrapolar. OIDIA in moist heads in culture.

Description partly from J.E. Lange and also Kühner & Josserand.

HABITAT on dung, especially horse; often gregarious. Common and widespread in Great Britain.

It is classically recognised by the small size together with relatively broad hyphae of the veil and fairly large spores. *C. pseudoradiatus* is very similar but has very much smaller spores.

Larger fruit bodies have been called by some *C. fimetarius*, but culture work has shown these collections are interfertile with typical *C. radiatus*. Small specimens of *C. macrocephalus* are easily separable by broader spores and broader hyphae on the cap. *C. cinereus* has larger fruit bodies and the spores are never phaseoliform in any view.

19. C. pseudoradiatus Kühner & Josserand ex Watling in Notes from the Royal Botanic Garden, Edinburgh, 35 : 154, 1976.

Syn.: (not validly published, no latin description) *C. pseudoradiatus* Kühn. & Joss. in Bull. Soc. mycol. France, 60: 26, 1944. Misident: *C. radiatus* (Bolt. ex Fr.) S.F. Gray sensu Rea, British Basidiomycetae, 512, 1922.

Icon.: none. Figs.: BSMF 60: 26, figs. 2, 3: KR 388, fig. 551.

CAP at first 3-5/2-3mm ellipsoid or ovoid, then expanded and often revolute 6-10mm broad, pale grey, sometimes tinged buff at centre then dark grey, at first entirely fibrillose-scaly becoming ± smooth and striate or plicate to centre. GILLS white then black. STEM 15-55/0.5-2.3mm, equal or attenuated upwards from not or only slightly swollen base, white then hyaline or greyish, finely fibrillose-scaly from veil at first then ± smooth except at base. SMELL none. SPORE-PRINT violaceous black.

SPORES brownish black, 7.5-8.5/4.5-5.5μm, ellipsoid or elongate ellipsoid, germ-pore small and central. BASIDIA 4-spored, polymorphic. MARGINAL CYSTIDIA subglobose or slightly ellipsoid, 30-40/22-28μm. FACIAL CYSTIDIA vesiculose or ellipsoid ovoid, 25-60/16-25μm. CAP CUTICLE of radially arranged ± cylindric cells, 25-100/8-25μm. VEIL on cap of filamentous hyphae with cylindric or elongate ellipsoid cells constricted at septa 10-30μm or more broad, end-cells sometimes thinner at apex.

CLAMP-CONNECTIONS present. GENETICS probably heterothallic and tetrapolar.

HABITAT on dung. Uncommon in Britain, probably overlooked as no recent collections have been made.

Macroscopically, it is much the same as *C. radiatus,* the only other member of Stirps *Lagopus* with very small fruit-bodies, but is immediately distinguished microscopically by the much smaller spores. Kemp TBMS 65; 377, (1975) suggests that there may be even more than one taxon involved.

Stirps 7 : Friesii

20. C. friesii Quélet, Les Champignons du Jura et des Vosges I : 129,1872. See Fig. 83.

Icon.: L 158 D; Quélet, Champ. Jura Vosges 1: 129, Pl 23[5].

CAP at first 4-6/3-4mm ellipsoid or ellipsoid ovoid, then expanded ± plane 10-15mm, with split or revolute margin white then greyish or grey-violaceous from margin inwards, centre sometimes pale cream, at first minutely white floccose-fibrillose scaly especially at centre, then ± wrinkled striate from margin inwards. GILLS white then purplish date or brown-vinaceous. STEM 12-30/0.5-1mm, equal or attenuated upwards from swollen disc-like white tomentose base (2-3mm broad), entirely white minutely floccose at first. SMELL none. SPORE-PRINT dark umber or date brown.

SPORES rather dark brown, 7-9(-11)/6-7/7-8(-9)μm, slightly lentiform, broadly ellipsoid ovoid in side view, subglobose or slightly angular in face view, germ-pore rounded and central. BASIDIA 4-spored. MARGINAL and FACIAL CYSTIDIA and CAP CUTICLE not investigated. VEIL on cap of hyaline filamentous branched diverticulate hyphae 1-5μm broad.

CLAMP-CONNECTIONS present. GENETICS heterothallic, bipolar according to Brunswick.

HABITAT on dead grass or rush leaves or stems in damp places, often early in summer. Probably not uncommon in suitable localities in Southern England but less frequently recorded further north.

It is distinguished among other members of Stirps *Friesii* by relatively large slightly lentiform subglobose spores, whereas the others all have shorter or narrower spores. This stirps needs further investigation in the field and fruit-bodies should be looked for more especially in June, July or early August.

This stirps has been studied in Central Europe by Pilát and Svrček who have found it necessary to describe several new species both in this stirps and in Stirps *Tigrinellus* but British species do not appear to agree in details with their novelties, so it has been necessary to describe new ones for Britain also (see Key ξ 66).

21. C. argenteus P. D. Orton, in Notes from the Royal Botanic Garden, Edinburgh 32 : 139, 1972. See Figs. 76 & 77.

Icon.: none. Figs.: NRBG 31 : 139, fig. 1, a-c.

CAP at first up to 10/4mm elongate conico-cylindric, then expanded up to 15mm broad, with split or torn margin, sometimes ± acutely umbonate, white then greyish or tinged leaden-grey or vinaceous grey, centre sometimes clay-buff, finally almost entirely silvery-grey and wrinkled striate, at first with adpressed patches of white veil. GILLS white then blackish. STEM up to 20/2mm, attenuated upwards with pronounced swollen disc-like base, white then hyaline, minutely white pruinose striate when fresh. SMELL none. SPORE-PRINT blackish.

SPORES rather pale brownish, 5-7/4-5/5-5.5μm, lentiform, ellipsoid in side view, globose-triangular often flattened at base in face view, germ-pore broad truncate, and central. BASIDIA believed to be 4-spored. MARGINAL and FACIAL CYSTIDIA and CAP CUTICLE not investigated. VEIL on cap of hyaline filamentous hyphae 5-14(-20)μm broad.

GENETICS unknown.

HABITAT in chalk grassland probably attached to grass stems. Known only from near Boxhill, Surrey, but is probably more widespread.

It resembles *C. saichiae* most closely but has characteristically shaped smaller, more conspicuously flattened spores and is seemingly more robust. The description is somewhat incomplete and further collections are needed to expand it. It should be looked for more especially in June, July or August like other members of Stirps *Friesii*.

22. C. gonophyllus Quélet in Annales des Sciences Naturelles, Bordeaux 14, Suppl. 5 : Pl. 1, 1884. See Figs. 93 & 94.

Icon.: none. Figs.: BSMF 71 : 120, fig. 15; RM 10: 79, fig. 3; TBMS 40 : 273, fig. 7.

CAP at first 4-15/3-12mm subglobose, ovoid or ellipsoid, then expanded or expanded-convex 10-30mm broad with torn or revolute margin, white sometimes tinged buff at centre, then grey or mouse-grey, at first entirely covered with white silky-floccose veil which breaks up into separable adpressed scales which often become brownish in places, soon striate or sulcate from margin inwards. GILLS white then pale mouse-grey, soon purplish date or brown-vinaceous, finally blackish. STEM 20-65/0.5-2mm (1-2.5mm at base), attenuated upwards or at apex with thickened or ± marginately bulbous base, white, minutely pruinose then ± smooth. SMELL none. SPORE-PRINT dark brown-vinaceous.

SPORES dark brown, 6.5-9/5-6/6-7.5μm, lentiform, broadly ellipsoid in side view, subglobose or broadly ovoid, sometimes slightly flattened at base in face view, germ-pore broad, truncate and central. BASIDIA 4-spored. MARGINAL CYSTIDIA fusiform-clavate, 45-50/11-16.5μm. FACIAL CYSTIDIA cylindric-fusiform or broadly obtusely lageniform, 50-100/12-25(-35)μm. CAP CUTICLE of filamentous radially arranged hyphae 5-10(-12)μm broad. VEIL on cap of hyaline thin- to rather thick-walled sometimes diverticulate branched hyphae 1.5-5μm broad.

CLAMP-CONNECTIONS present. GENETICS heterothallic, bipolar. OIDIA not seen (conidia formed according to Yen).

HABITAT on burnt ground or old plaster. Widespread and not uncommon in Britain.

It resembles other members of Stirps *Friesii* microscopically but is readily recognised by habitat, rather small lentiform spores and veil characters. Undue emphasis has been placed on gill shape in the past but since the gills can be found narrow or broad, this character is not of taxonomic significance.

A similar taxon with larger spores growing on wool stuffing was shown to be infertile with *C. kimurae* (see pg. 148). *C. spilosporus* Romagnesi (RM 16 : 112, 1951), growing on soil, not yet recorded in Britain, likewise has subglobose spores, which are, however, slightly larger than those of *C. gonophyllus* and have the germ-pore reduced to a less pigmented spot.

23. C. urticaecola (Berkeley & Broome) Buller in Transactions of the British Mycological Society, 5 : 485, 1917. See Fig. 78.

Syn.: *Agaricus urticaecola* Berkeley & Broome, in Annals & Magazine of Natural History, series 3, 7 : 376, 1961; *Psathyra urticaecola* (Berk. & Br.) Saccardo, Sylloge Fungorum 5: 1073, 1887; *C. brassicae* Peck, in 43rd Report of the New York State Museum 18, 1890.

Icon.: Cke 622(595)B. Figs. : RM 16: 117, fig. 2, brassicae; TBMS 43: 411, fig. 251.

CAP at first 3-8/2-4mm subglobose or ovoid, then expanded-conical or expanded-campanulate up to 10mm broad with torn or split margin, white then greyish, entirely minutely white floccose silky scaly at first then ± smooth. GILLS white then purplish date or brown-vinaceous. STEM 20-40/0.5-1mm, equal or attenuated upwards from swollen disc-like base, white then hyaline, minutely pruinose when fresh. SMELL none. SPORE-PRINT umber or brown-vinaceous.

SPORES pale brown, (6-)6.5-8.5/4.5-5.5(-6)μm, ellipsoid or ellipsoid ovoid, germ-pore central and rather truncate. BASIDIA 4-spored, dimorphic. MARGINAL CYSTIDIA ellipsoid or pyriform (sec. Romagnesi). FACIAL CYSTIDIA cylindric ellipsoid, 80-150/10-20μm. CAP CUTICLE not investigated. VEIL on cap of hyaline or slightly coloured filamentous, branched but not diverticulate, thin-walled hyphae 2-5(-6)μm broad.

CLAMP-CONNECTIONS apparently absent. GENETICS of British material un-known (but heterothallic, bipolar in N. American material, sec. Hanna).

HABITAT on *Juncus, Carex,* grass, nettle (*Urtica*) or other rotting plant debris, more particularly in damp places. Probably widespread in southern England, more especially in summer.

It is distinguished from *C. friesii* by smaller ellipsoid or ovoid spores and non-diverticulate cells in the veil and from *C. argenteus* and *C. saichiae* by the spores not being subglobose and not or only slightly lentiform.

Stirps 8 : Tigrinellus

24. C. tigrinellus Boudier in Bulletin de la Societé Botanique de France, 32 : 283, 1885.

Icon.: Boud 139. Figs.: Bull. Soc. Bot. Fr. 32 : 283, Pl. IX, fig. 3,

CAP at first 4-7/3-7mm ovoid or ellipsoid, then expanded 10-18mm broad with split or torn margin white then whitish grey, at first with dark sepia or blackish adpressed ± pointed fibrillose scales, which are denser at centre and more scattered towards margin, becoming ± smooth, except at often more persistently scaly centre, and sulcate striate in outer part. GILLS white then fuscous black. STEM 15-25/1-1.5mm, ± equal or attenuated upwards, white, sometimes minutely white silky-striate, apex white pruinose, base white tomentose. SMELL none. SPORE-PRINT dark purplish-date.

SPORES rather pale brown, 7.5-9/6-7μm, subglobose or broadly ellipsoid, germ-pore central and minute, apiculus small. BASIDIA 4-spored. MARGINAL CYSTIDIA clavate or slightly lageniform, 20-30/10-14μm. FACIAL CYSTIDIA cylindric-vesiculose, 100-150/18-24μm. VEIL on cap of ± cylindric hyphae 3-10μm broad, pigment irregularly distributed in masses and not so well defined sub micr. as the colour of the scales would suggest.

CLAMP-CONNECTIONS not investigated. GENETICS unknown.

HABITAT on *Typha* and *Carex* debris, often in early summer. Probably not uncommon in suitable localities at least in England, but infrequently recorded.

It differs from other members of Stirps *Friesii* and *Tigrinellus* in dark scales on cap and spore shape and size. The description based on material from Frensham, Surrey, may need modification when more fresh material is forthcoming. Boudier says the cap may be 20-30mm high, gives the spores as $11/7\mu m$ and records it on *Carex riparia* and also *Iris pseudoacorus.*

25. C. rhombisporus P.D. Orton in Notes from the Royal Botanic Garden, Edinburgh, 32 : 145, 1972. See Figs. 79 & 80.

Icon.: none. Figs.: NRBG 32 : 145, fig. 2, a-c.

CAP at first 3-10/4-7mm ± ovoid or conical, then expanded ± plane or slightly umbonate often with revolute margin, 7-12mm broad, white then greyish, at first with rather thick white to grey, ochraceous or buff fibrillose scales especially at centre, becoming striate or ± smooth, except at the persistently paler and scaly centre. GILLS white then pale umber or purplish date, finally blackish. STEM 25-50/0.5-1.5mm equal or slightly attenuated upwards often with slightly swollen base, white or hyaline-white, ± smooth above but white pruinose or with scales as on cap towards white tomentose or strigose base. SMELL none. SPORE-PRINT umber or dark bay.

SPORES red-brown, $7-9/5-5.5/5.5-6.5\mu m$, lentiform, ellipsoid-amygdaliform in side view, ± rhomboid or obscurely angled - amygdaliform in face view, germ-pore central. BASIDIA 4-spored. MARGINAL CYSTIDIA sphaeropedunculate, vesiculose or clavate, $10-22\mu m$ broad, more rarely broadly lageniform, $30-60/16-26\mu m$. FACIAL CYSTIDIA cylindric-vesiculose, $60-90/14-24\mu m$. VEIL on cap of narrow filamentous branched often diverticulate hyphae $3-8\mu m$ broad, with walls $0.5-1\mu m$ broad and diverticulae $1-2\mu m$ broad.

CLAMP-CONNECTIONS not noted. GENETICS unknown.

HABITAT on grass or sedge debris. Distribution unknown but recorded from Norfolk (type locality where it is not uncommon in summer) and Devon. It probably occurs elsewhere at least in southern England.

It is best recognised by the combination of coloured scales on the cap and relatively large rhomboid spores. A similar fungus has been found in Warwickshire but with broader pip-shaped spores; the veil is typically diverticulate (Fig. 92).

26. C. xantholepis P.D. Orton in Notes from the Royal Botanic Garden, Edinburgh, 32: 150, 1972. See Figs. 81 & 82.

Icon.: none. Figs.: NRBG 32: 150, fig. 2, d-e.

CAP at first 9-10/4.5mm elongate cylindric-ellipsoid, then expanded 10-20mm broad, sometimes umbonate or radially split, white then grey sometimes vinaceous grey before expanding or with cream centre when expanded, at first with numerous ochraceous or buff adpressed fibrillose scales, those at apex sometimes rather thick and slightly recurved. GILLS white then violaceous clay, finally umber. STEM 42-58/1-1.5mm, equal or slightly attenuated upwards, white silky-striate, base often slightly swollen and with veil remnants at first as on cap. SMELL none. SPORE-PRINT not noted.

SPORES red-brown, 5.5-7/4.5-5/5-5.5μm, lentiform, ovoid-amygdaliform in side view, submitriform or ellipsoid-rhomboid in face view, germ-pore central and truncate. BASIDIA 4-spored. MARGINAL CYSTIDIA ± vesiculose, 15-30μm broad. FACIAL CYSTIDIA ± cylindric or elongate ellipsoid, 80-138/18-32μm. VEIL on cap of irregularly diverticulate hyphae 2-8μm broad with rather thick buff-tinted refringent walls, together with some colourless hyaline hyphae 6-10μm broad.

CLAMP-CONNECTIONS not investigated. GENETICS unknown.

HABITAT on dead grass stems; so far only recorded from Loch Skene, Aberdeen-shire, but no doubt awaits discovery elsewhere.

It differs from the other members of Stirps *Tigrinellus* by the small submitriform spores with conspicuous truncate germ-pore. This description will probably need modification when further material is forthcoming.

27. C. saichiae Reid in Transactions of the British Mycological Society, 41 : 430, 1958. See Fig. 66.

Icon.: none. Figs.: TBMS 41 : 430, fig. 6.

CAP at first about 3/2mm ovoid, then expanded with revolute margin, white often tinged cream at centre, becoming greyish or blackish from margin inwards from veil, becoming sulcate striate from margin inwards. GILLS becoming black. STEM up to 22/1mm, equal or slightly swollen at base, white. SMELL and SPORE-PRINT not noted.

SPORES, grey-brown 6.5-8/4.5-5/5-7.5μm, ellipsoid in side view, subglobose-triangular in face view, germ-pore rather small and central. BASIDIA 4-spored. MARGINAL and FACIAL CYSTIDIA and CAP CUTICLE not noted. VEIL on cap of hyaline or yellow-brown, thick-walled diverticulate hyphae 2-2.5μm broad.

GENETICS unknown.
(Description from Reid)

HABITAT on dead grass stems. So far only known from Hertfordshire and Edinburgh but may be more widespread especially in southern England.

It is distinguished from others in Stirps *Tigrinellus* by its spores and very small fruit-bodies. More work on fresh material is needed to complete the above description. A somewhat similar taxon has been collected also in Herts. with more rounded slightly smaller spores, germ-pore barely truncate and often with fragments (? of perispore) attached to the spore-wall in places. A good description of fresh material is needed before this can be named, although a parallel taxon with slightly roughened spore has been described as *C. herinkii* Pilát & Svrček from Czechoslovakia.

Stirps 9 : Filamentifer

28. C. filamentifer Kühner in Bulletin de la Société des Naturalistes d'Oyonnax, 10-11, Suppl., : 64, 1957. See Figs. 95-98.

Icon.: none. Figs.: Bull. Soc. nat. Oyonnax 10-11, Suppl.: 64, figs. 29c, 31; NRBG 28: 40, fig. 1, D-d.

CAP at first 7-10/4-5.5mm ellipsoid or conical, then expanded ± plane with deeply split margin, at first entirely covered with whitish or pale greyish flocculose veil which splits up without forming definite scales as cap expands. GILLS grey then brownish, finally violaceous black. STEM 40-100/0.7-1.5mm, attenuated upwards, white, at first with whitish or grey veil as on cap. SMELL none. SPORE-PRINT violaceous black.

SPORES dark brown, 7-8/4-5μm, ovoid or ellipsoid in side view, ovoid-submitriform in face view (appearing shouldered), germ-pore central and fairly small. BASIDIA 4-spored. MARGINAL CYSTIDIA elongate-vesiculose up to 58μm long. FACIAL CYSTIDIA elongate-vesiculose, 60-70/25-30μm. CAP CUTICLE of radially arranged filamentous hyphae 8-14μm broad. VEIL on cap of cylindric thin-walled hyphae 3-7μm broad.

CLAMP-CONNECTIONS present in some collections. GENETICS homothallic. OIDIA absent.

HABITAT on dung of herbivores and rabbit pellets. Recently recorded from England, Ireland and Scotland.

This is distinguished from other coprophilous species producing small fruit-bodies by veil without sphaerocysts and consisting entirely of narrow, cylindric smooth, thin-walled hyphae, and small submitriform spores.

29. C. vermiculifer [Josserand ex] Dennis in Kew Bulletin 19 : 112,1964. See Figs. 88-91.

Syn.: (not validly published no Latin description): *C. vermiculifer* Josserand in Bull. de la Soc. mycol. Fr. 60 ; 7, 1944.

Icon.: none. Figs. BSMF 60 : 7, fig. 1; Kew Bull. 19 : 112, fig. 1; NRBG 28: 50, figs. 3D, d, d'.

CAP at first about 6/3-4mm ovoid or ellipsoid, then expanded 8-16mm broad, often slightly depressed with upturned margin, whitish or greyish often tinged sepia at centre, at first covered with adpressed fibrillose-floccose veil. GILLS whitish then dark umber or fuscous black. STEM 30-80/1-1.2mm, white, at first minutely white villose-pruinose (short ± cylindric hairs) then ± smooth. SMELL none. SPORE-PRINT dark umber.

SPORES dark brown, 9.5-10/5.5-6μm, ellipsoid, germ-pore central and rather small. BASIDIA 4-spored, polymorphic. MARGINAL CYSTIDIA pyriform of clavate, 25-50/15-25μm. FACIAL CYSTIDIA ellipsoid or cylindric-ellipsoid, 45-80/25-32μm. CAP CUTICLE of radially arranged ± cylindric cells. VEIL on cap of interwoven hyaline thin- or thick- walled, smooth filamentous hyphae 4-8μm broad.

CLAMP-CONNECTIONS present. GENETICS unknown.

HABITAT on dung, especially of sheep. Not uncommon in northern England and Scotland although infrequently recorded. It may well occur throughout Britain where there are sheep.

It differs from other coprophilous species with filamentous veil in producing small fruit-bodies having non-diverticulate but often thick-walled hyaline hyphae in the veil and moderate sized ellipsoid spores.

30. C. xenobius P.D. Orton in Notes from the Royal Botanic Garden, Edinburgh 35 : 148, 1976. See Fig. 87.
Icon.: none. Fig.: none.

CAP at first 2-7/1-4mm ellipsoid or cylindric-ellipsoid, then expanded-convex to depressed, 2-8mm broad, sometimes splitting radially at margin, at first white then whitish often clay-buff at centre, turning pale then deep grey as spores mature, but dirty whitish or pale grey-cream after spores have been shed, at first white pilose-tomentose from veil, then ± adpressedly finely flocculose-fibrillose, either as fairly long loosely entwined fibrils or as scattered easily separable loosely interwoven patches, ± smooth at maturity, becoming striate-sulcate from margin inwards. GILLS whitish then clay-buff, soon fuscous to violaceous-black. STEM 20-40/ 0.3-1mm, equal or slightly swollen at base, white then hyaline or grey, entirely white or whitish flocculose-fibrillose when fresh, becoming ± smooth except at extreme base. SMELL none. SPORE-PRINT date-brown or cigar-brown to fuscous black.

SPORES dark red-brown, ellipsoid or cylindric-ellipsoid, (9-)10-13.5/(5-)5.5-6.5μm rather thick-walled, germ-pore central. BASIDIA 4-spored. MARGINAL CYSTIDIA sphaeropedunculate or vesiculose to cylindric-pyriform 14-54μm broad. FACIAL CYSTIDIA ± cylindric often with slightly narrower apex, 58-100/20-30μm, apex 15-25μm broad. CAP CUTICLE of radially arranged ± cylindric cells 6-18μm broad. VEIL on cap of branched hyphae of cylindric or slightly fusiform some-times diverticulate thin-walled hyaline cells 3-12 (-14)μm broad.

CLAMP-CONNECTIONS none seen. GENETICS unknown.

HABITAT on old cow dung; gregarious. So far only recorded from Perthshire and Inverness-shire in May and June. Doubtless widespread, but easily overlooked since it often appears on the undersides of the old dung-masses, and may be summer fruiting.

It differs from the other very small dung-inhabiting species with filamentous cap cuticle in having the veil hyphae sometimes diverticulate. *C. filamentifer* also differs in smaller spores, and *C. vermiculifer* in having the veil at least in part of thick-walled non-diverticulate hyphae, although the spores are of similar size.

Stirps 10 : Utrifer

31. C. utrifer [Josserand ex] Watling in Notes from the Royal Botanic Garden, Edinburgh, 31: 362, 1972.. See Figs. 84-86.

Syn.: (not validly published no Latin description): *C. utrifer* Josserand Bull. Soc. mycol. Fr. 64 : 20, 1948.

Icon.: none. Figs.: BSMF 64 : 26, fig. 7; NRBG 28 : 50, figs. 3C, c, c'; ibid. 31 : 362, figs. 1 F-M.

CAP at first 7-15/4-7mm ellipsoid or ovoid, then expanded or depressed with revolute margin, ash-grey, then clay or sepia at centre, at first covered with pale grey or ochraceous filamentous scurfy veil which may persist as ± concentric scales, margin becoming sulcate-striate. GILLS whitish or clay then tinged vinaceous grey, finally blackish brown. STEM 10-50/1-2mm (up to 3mm at base), white then hyaline at first with whitish or greyish veil fragments, becoming smooth except at scurfy-fibrillose to tomentose base which may be seated in a socket of mycelium sometimes joining 2 or 3 fruit-bodies. SMELL none. SPORE-PRINT violaceous black.

SPORES purplish date, 7.5-9/4.5-5.5μm, ellipsoid or cylindric-ellipsoid in side view, cylindric-ovoid or slightly strangulated in face view, germ-pore central and fairly small. BASIDIA 4-spored, polymorphic. MARGINAL CYSTIDIA subglobose, ovoid-ellipsoid or irregularly vesiculose, 25-40/25-35μm. FACIAL CYSTIDIA vesiculose, elongate-ellipsoid or cylindric-fusiform, 40-100/17-23μm. CAP CUTICLE of radially arranged elongate fusiform cells. VEIL on cap a mixture of pyriform, vesiculose or fusiform cells 12-70μm broad, and thin- or thick-walled filamentous, sometimes diverticulate, hyphae 3-8μm broad.

CLAMP-CONNECTIONS present. GENETICS heterothallic. OIDIA formed in culture in moist heads.

HABITAT on dung, especially sheep; not uncommon in northern England and Scotland.

It is distinguished from other coprophilous species producing small fruit-bodies by the mixture of broad and narrow cells in the veil and rather small spores. As yet this is the only member of Stirps *Utrifer* (characterized by the varied shapes of the cells of the veil) but a similar taxon differing in spore size and shape and some cultural characters awaits further investigation; this may be *C. heterocomus* Malencon recorded from Morocco (Champ. Sup. du Maroc - I: 237, 1970).

SECTION II : MICACEUS

Stirps 11 : Micaceus

32. C. micaceus (Bulliard ex Fries) Fries, Epicrisis Systematis Mycologici, 247, 1838. See Figs. 14, 100, 106 & 112.

Syn.: *Agaricus micaceus* Bull. ex Fr., Systema Mycologicum, I : 309, 1821.

Icon.: L 160 I; Ri 22[4]; M 32; Bres 880.Figs.: KR 382, fig. 526.

CAP at first 10-35/8-25mm ovoid or cylindric, then campanulate or expanded-campanulate, sometimes umbonate or with irregular wavy-lobed margin, finally expanded 8-30mm broad with revolute or split margin, ochraceous or fulvous often with darker cinnamon or umber centre, then pale ochraceous or buff from margin inwards, soon deeply sulcate-striate to centre, white or whitish atomate granular-mealy then ± smooth from margin inwards except in the grooves and at centre, which may be buff or fulvous mealy especially when fresh. GILLS white then date brown or purplish date, finally fuscous black. STEM 40-100/2-5mm, equal or slightly attenuated upwards, white then sometimes discolouring pale dirty cream from base up, at first white velvety-pruinose or pubescent then ± smooth especially in lower part, at first also with atomate white to buff or fulvous veil as on cap, this often persisting at white-tomentose base. SMELL none. SPORE-PRINT umber or date brown.

SPORES red-brown, (6.5-)7-10/4-5/4.5-6µm, lentiform, markedly amygdaliform or fusiform in side view, ovoid or submitriform in face view, germ-pore central and truncate. BASIDIA 4-spored. MARGINAL CYSTIDIA globose, vesiculose or ovoid, 30-120/20-74µm. FACIAL CYSTIDIA vesiculose-clavate or elongate-ellipsoid, up to 130-155µm. CAP CUTICLE cellular. VEIL on cap of ± globose, hyaline thin-walled or brownish encrusted thick-walled cells 20-72µm broad (walls up to 1µm thick).

CLAMP-CONNECTIONS present. GENETICS heterothallic, probably tetrapolar. OIDIA in moist heads.

HABITAT on and around stumps or logs of broad-leaved trees or attached to buried wood, singly or caespitose, sometimes densely so. Common throughout the British Isles and fruiting at any time of year in suitable weather conditions.

This species and *C. truncorum,* the other species in stirps Micaceus, are easily recognisable by the atomate mealy veil and the habitat on wood. *C. truncorum* is immediately distinguishable microscopically for it has ellipsoid or ovoid spores with less conspicuous more rounded germ-pore (Fig. 101). It is said to have a smooth stem and paler cap, but these characters do not give a clear distinction, for *C. micaceus* may also seem to have a smooth stem (especially when old) and the cap may be much the same colour. Recently a taxon has been found in Warwickshire and Lancashire which possesses similar mitriform spores but they are minutely, although distinctly, ornamented at the plage; the fruit-bodies are also invariably associated with a red-brown *Ozonium* much as in *C. domesticus. sticus.*

33. C. truncorum [Schaeffer] ex Fries, Epicrisis Systematis Mycologici, 248,1838. See Fig. 101.

Icon.: none. Figs.: KR 382, fig. 525.

CAP at first about 10-20/10-20mm convex or conico-convex, then expanded-convex 18-40mm broad, cream-buff or buff tinged cinnamon at centre then greyish buff, at first entirely white or whitish atomate granular mealy then becoming smooth from margin inwards and deeply sulcate or wrinkled striate except at centre. GILLS white or pale cream then clay-violaceous finally brown-vinaceous to fuscous black. STEM 55-85/3-5mm, ± equal, white then discolouring pale dirty cream, very minutely pubescent when young and fresh then soon appearing smooth and often rather shiny at least in upper half, base white tomentose. SMELL none. SPORE-PRINT fuscous-black.

SPORES red-brown, (6-)6.5-8.5/4.5-5.5/5-6.5μm, lentiform, ellipsoid or slightly amygdaliform in side view, ovoid or ellipsoid in face view, germ-pore central and rather rounded. BASIDIA 4-spored. MARGINAL CYSTIDIA globose, ellipsoid or vesiculose, 30-90/20-46μm. FACIAL CYSTIDIA vesiculose, or cylindric-ellipsoid, 50-120/25-50μm. CAP CUTICLE cellular. VEIL on cap of globose or ovoid thin-walled not or only slightly encrusted cells 18-48(-62)μm broad.

CLAMP-CONNECTIONS present. GENETICS unknown.

HABITAT on or about stumps or logs, often densely caespitose. Uncommon, though probably overlooked because of confusion with *C. micaceus.* It is definitely known from South and Central England but may well be more widespread.

It is macroscopically indistinguishable from *C. micaceus* but can readily be distinguished by spore shape when these are inspected. The stem is reported to be smoother than that of *C. micaceus,* but this character does not seem to be a reliable means of separating the two. No doubt past records of *C. micaceus* may refer to this species sometimes if spores have not been examined. It may be a nuisance having to examine the spores of what is suspected to be *C. micaceus* every time, but this seems to be the only way to make a really positive determination. There seems to be no real evidence for regarding L 160 I or Maublanc 32, *micaceus* as being this species and these quotations should be removed in the New Check List (1960).

Stirps 12 : Domesticus

34. C. domesticus (Bolton ex Fries) S.F. Gray, A Natural Arrangement of British Plants, I : 635, 1821. See Figs. 103 & 109.

Syn.: *Agaricus domesticus* Bolton ex Fries, Systema Mycologium, I : 311, 1821.

Icon.: L 159 G. Figs.: RM 5: 79; fig. 1.

CAP at first 10-30/6-20mm ellipsoid, ovoid or cylindric-ovoid, then convex or campanulate, finally expanded 26-67mm broad, with revolute or split margin, pale ochraceous or buff with darker fulvous, cinnamon or rusty-tawny centre, at first covered with whitish, buff, fulvous or rust fibrillose-floccose mealy scales which are often pointed at tips, then ± smooth and sulcate-striate from margin inwards. GILLS white then pale purplish date or umber finally violaceous black. STEM 40-155/1.5-7mm (2-11mm at base), attenuated upwards or thickened towards usually swollen or bulbous base, whitish or tinged cream-colour or buff towards the base, smooth or minutely silky striate, sometimes minutely white floccose above base which may be white flocculose scaly and ridged, sometimes growing from a sienna or rust mycelial mat (*Ozonium*). SMELL none. SPORE-PRINT dark date brown.

SPORES red-brown (sometimes rather pale) (7-)7.5-10/4-5µm, cylindric ellipsoid or cylindric phaseoliform in side view, ellipsoid in face view, germ-pore central, BASIDIA 4-spored. MARGINAL CYSTIDIA subglobose or clavate, 20-80/ 12-50µm. FACIAL CYSTIDIA ellipsoid or vesiculose to cylindric-ovoid, 65-150/ 30-60µm. CAP CUTICLE cellular. VEIL on cap a mixture of globose or ellipsoid hyaline cells 14-46µm broad and chains of cylindric or ellipsoid hyaline or thick-walled and yellowish brown 5-12µm broad sometimes encrusted cells, end-cells often broadly clavate or fusiform and up to 22µm broad.

CLAMP-CONNECTIONS absent. GENETICS bipolar, heterothallic. OIDIA in moist heads.

HABITAT on broad-leaved stumps, logs or branches, singly or in small groups. Not uncommon in England and Scotland often early in the season; recorded from Ireland but this may refer to other species of Stirps *Domesticus*.

Members of Stirps *Domesticus* can be recognised in the field by cap colour, habitat on wood and the appearance of the veil which is made up of two kinds of cells, often forming coloured scales on the cap centre, but can only be separated with certainty by examination of spores. The species *C. domesticus* is distinguished from *C. ellisii* by longer rather broader spores, and from *C. radians* by smaller spores. *C. xanthothrix* has spores not or hardly phaseoliform in any view and broader in outline.

In the New Check List *C. domesticus* sensu J.E. Lange was stated to be *C. xanthothrix* following French authors. Re-appraisal of Lange's description does not confirm this, however, and Lange's plant is now quoted for *C. domesticus* (see observations on 36. *C. xanthothrix*.)

35. C. ellisii P.D. Orton in Transactions of the British Mycological Society, 43: 199, 1960. See Figs. 99 & 107.

Icon.: none. Figs.: TBMS 43: figs. 11, 248, 405-406.

CAP at first 6-35/6-23mm ovoid, cylindric-ovoid or ellipsoid, then expanded 10-40mm broad with revolute or split or torn margin, pale cream or buff often with darker fulvous centre, then grey in outer part, at first entirely covered with whitish or pale cream floccose-scurfy separable scales, those at centre often pointed and buff, cinnamon or umber, becoming smooth and sulcate-striate from the margin in. GILLS white or whitish then fawn, finally purplish date or violaceous black. STEM 45-90/1-6mm (3-15mm at base), attenuated upwards from thickened or bulbous base, white or whitish or tinged cream buff especially in lower part, minutely pruinose-pubescent when fresh then ± smooth, base with volva-like veil zone often with flocculose sometimes reflexed fringe when fresh, cream above, cream buff beneath with buff, cinnamon or umber scales as on cap, tomentose or velvety strigose at extreme base, sometimes growing from a rusty mycelial mat (*Ozonium*). SMELL none. SPORE-PRINT umber or sepia-date brown.

SPORES pale reddish brown, 6.5-8.5(-9)/3-4.5(-5)μm, cylindric-phaseoliform or cylindric-ellipsoid, germ-pore central and not very noticeable. BASIDIA 4-spored. MARGINAL CYSTIDIA vesiculose, ellipsoid or shortly cylindric-ellipsoid, 16-60/10-35μm. FACIAL CYSTIDIA cylindric-ellipsoid or slightly ovoid, 60-90/22-45μm. CAP CUTICLE cellular. VEIL on cap a mixture of ± globose hyaline smooth cells 24-60μm broad, and chains of cylindric-ellipsoid or fusiform sometimes encrusted cells 5-13μm broad, which are hyaline or with yellowish-brown (buff) or fulvous-brick walls, end-cells often markedly fusiform or almost lageniform and up to 28μm broad.

CLAMP-CONNECTIONS present. GENETICS heterothallic. OIDIA in moist heads.

HABITAT on twigs or logs, solitary or in small groups. Not uncommon in England but not recorded elsewhere.

It is easily recognised as a member of Stirps *Domesticus* (see observations on *C. domesticus*) and is readily distinguished by small narrow spores. The volva-like veil remnants on the stem base are usually conspicuous. This feature seems constant and has not been noted consistently for other members of this stirps, but it must be treated with caution as a distinguishing character until more field work has been done.

36. C. xanthothrix Romagnesi in Revue de Mycologie, 6: 127, 1941. See Fig. 104. Icon.: none. Figs.: RM 10: 86, fig. 8.

CAP at first 14-20/8-13mm, ellipsoid or conico-ellipsoid then expanded to ± plane 20-37mm broad with torn, split or slightly revolute margin, sometimes obtusely umbonate, ochraceous cream or cream buff with slightly darker centre, then ochraceous clay or greyish from margin in, at first with whitish rather thick scattered floccose-scurfy scales which are often darker fulvous or cinnamon at their tips, becoming smooth and striate-sulcate from margin in. GILLS grey-cream or vinaceous buff then clay-umber finally date-brown-umber. STEM 60-90/2-3mm, ± equal, but often with slightly swollen or bulbous base, white or whitish, minutely striate, and finely white pruinose *sub lente* when fresh, base often with slight ridge and a few veil scales as on cap. SMELL none. SPORE-PRINT date brown-umber.

SPORES rather pale red-brown (cinnamon), 7-9/4.5-5.5(-6)μm, ellipsoid slightly amygdaliform in side view, ovoid or ellipsoid in face view, germ-pore central and often rather truncate, apiculus barely visible. BASIDIA 4-spored. MARGINAL CYSTIDIA sphaeropedunculate or vesiculose with long apical point to lageniform with long narrow neck, 30-50/9-18μm, apex 3-4μm. CAP CUTICLE cellular. VEIL on cap a mixture of smooth hyaline ± globose cells 12-44μm broad, and chains of cylindric or fusiform, hyaline or coloured, thin - or thick-walled sometimes slightly encrusted cells 8-15μm broad, with end-cells sometimes swollen and up to 20μm broad.

CLAMP-CONNECTIONS absent. GENETICS not investigated. OIDIA in dry heads.

HABITAT on twigs or stumps of broad-leaved trees, singly or in small groups; has been found in beech litter but probably attached to buried wood. Uncommon and recorded so far only from England.

It differs from other members of Stirps *Domesticus* (see observations on *C. domesticus*) in relatively short broad spores which are not phaseoliform in any view, possibly also in paler cap colour and less strongly encrusted cells in the veil.

In the New Check List this was stated to be *C. domesticus* sensu J. Lange following French authors. Re-appraisal of Lange's description does not confirm this, however, for the spores are given as subphaseoliform and 4.5-5μm broad, which is not so for *C. xanthothrix* but is true for *C. domesticus*. Lange's plate is therefore cited for *C. domesticus*.

37. C. radians (Desmazières) Fries, Epicrisis Systematis Mycologici : 248, 1838. See Fig. 105.

Syn.: *Agaricus radians* Desmazières in Ann. Sci. Nat. 13 : 214, 1828; *C. similis* Berkeley & Broome in Ann. Mag. nat. Hist. ser. 3, 15 : 317, 1865; *C. hortorum* Métrod in Rev. Mycol. 5 : 80, 1940.

Icon.: Ri 21[4]. Figs.: RM 5 (1940) 80, fig. 2; BSMF 53 (1937) 126, fig. 2, *similis.*

CAP at first 20-40/10-25mm, cylindric-ellipsoid or conical, then expanded 27-67mm broad with ± revolute or split margin, pale cream or buff, often deeper buff or fulvous at centre then greyish from margin inwards, at first entirely covered with thick white or pale cream floccose-scurfy separable scales, those at centre often cinnamon or umber, becoming smooth and sulcate-striate from margin in. GILLS whitish or pale cream then umber or purplish date, finally violaceous black. STEM 30-80/3-4mm (5-10mm at base), white, pruinose-striate when fresh, base white tomentose and sometimes with volva-like veil zone of scales as on cap, sometimes growing from a sienna or rust coloured mycelioid mat (*Ozonium*) (Fig. 114). SMELL none. SPORE-PRINT purplish date to violaceous black.

SPORES reddish brown, 8.5-11/5-6.5μm, ellipsoid-phaseoliform in side view, ovoid or ellipsoid in face view, germ-pore central and rather rounded, apiculus barely visible. BASIDIA 4-spored. MARGINAL CYSTIDIA lageniform with obtuse apex, 30-60/15-20μm. FACIAL CYSTIDIA ellipsoid or irregularly vesiculose, 100-200/60-80μm. CAP CUTICLE cellular. VEIL on cap a mixture of ellipsoid or globose smooth hyaline cells up to 60μm broad, and chains of narrower cylindric or fusiform, hyaline or coloured, thin-or thick-walled smooth to strongly encrusted cells 5-12μm broad, end-cells often vesiculose or fusiform-clavate to ± lageniform 20-30μm broad.

CLAMP-CONNECTIONS seemingly absent. GENETICS heterothallic, bipolar. OIDIA in moist heads.

HABITAT on stumps, logs or branches of broad-leaved trees, singly or in small groups usually arising from a rust mycelium (*Ozonium auricomum*). Rather uncommon in England but may be overlooked if spores are not examined.

It is distinguished from other members of Stirps *Domesticus* (see observations on *C. domesticus*) by the relatively large spores which are ellipsoid-phaseoliform in side view.

Elsewhere in Europe different results have been obtained for the pattern of sexuality of different collections of *C. radians* (cf. Vandendries and Quintanilha). This may reflect either misidentifications or a complex of closely related taxa.

Stirps 13 : Flocculosus

38. C. flocculosus De Candolle ex Fries, Epicrisis Systematis Mycologici, 245, 1838. See Figs. 102, 108, 113.

Misident.: *C. rostrupianus* E.C. Hansen sensu J. Lange, Flora Agaricina Danica 4: 109, 1939.

Icon.: L 157 E *rostrupianus;* Figs.: RM 10: 83; fig. 6; TBMS 41: 429; fig. 12.

CAP at first 10-37/7-25mm ovoid or cylindric ovoid, then campanulate, finally expanded-conical or -convex and sometimes slightly umbonate 24-40mm broad with margin torn, split or revolute, whitish then grey or blackish from margin inwards, at first with thick whitish adpressed floccose-fibrillose scales, those at centre sometimes tinged buff or fulvous, becoming smooth in outer part but not or only slightly striate. GILLS white then grey, finally blackish. STEM 40-70/ 2-4mm, equal or attenuated upwards and then up to 10mm broad at base, white then whitish, smooth, extreme base white tomentose. SMELL none. SPORE-PRINT black.

SPORES sepia, 11-15(-16)/6.5-7.5/7-9.5μm, lentiform, ellipsoid or slightly amygdaliform in side view, ellipsoid or ovoid in face view, germ-pore markedly excentric. BASIDIA 4-spored. MARGINAL CYSTIDIA subglobose, 20-65/35-65μm (sec Romagnesi). FACIAL CYSTIDIA cylindric ovoid 30-50μm broad, (65-111/ 28-65 sec Romagnesi). CAP CUTICLE cellular. VEIL on cap of chains of ellipsoid ovoid or subglobose to fusiform or cylindric cells, end-cells often vesiculose-clavate or sphaeropedunculate, 20-80/12-54μm, walls thin and hyaline or more rarely slightly thickened and sometimes yellowish, rarely slightly encrusted. (This description is based on British material but is supplemented by information from Romagnesi's description of 1945.)

CLAMP-CONNECTIONS seemingly absent. GENETICS heterothallic, bipolar (Newton, Buller).

HABITAT on soil, sawdust or amongst manured straw. Uncommon. It has been authentically but infrequently recorded from England and Scotland.

It is easily recognised by large dark spores with markedly excentric germ-pore and veil of cells of various shapes. The species is taken in the sense of Romagnesi, so older British records of *C. flocculosus* may not necessarily be of the same taxon.

39. C. poliomallus Romagnesi in Revue de Mycologie, 10: 81, 1954. See Figs. 110 & 111.

Icon.: none. Figs.: RM 10: 82; fig. 5; BSMF 63: 80, fig. 4.

CAP at first 3-7mm broad ovoid to cylindric ovoid or conico-cylindric, then expanded 4-5mm broad with revolute margin, white beneath veil then greyish, at first entirely covered with floccose pubescence or mealy grey veil which may be ±

clay-buff at centre, becoming ± smooth and sulcate-striate from margin inwards. GILLS white then grey, finally blackish. STEM 20-40/0.2-0.5mm, equal or attenuated upwards, hyaline greyish or whitish, at first grey floccose pubescent from veil then silky striate in upper part, veil persisting only at base. SMELL none. SPORE-PRINT sepia tinged violaceous.

SPORES sepia, 7-9/3.7-4.5μm, ellipsoid slightly amygdaliform in side view, ellipsoid or cylindric ellipsoid in face view, germ-pore central and truncate, BASIDIA 4-spored. MARGINAL CYSTIDIA ellipsoid or fusiform vesiculose, 30-35/11.5-18μm. FACIAL CYSTIDIA not observed. CAP CUTICLE cellular. VEIL on cap a mixture of rather thick-walled often yellowish encrusted ± globose cells 20-42μm broad, and chains of ± cylindric or fusiform cells, often also thick-walled and encrusted 4-15μm broad, end-cells sometimes pyriform or ellipsoid, 25-45/13-16μm.

CLAMP-CONNECTIONS absent. GENETICS unknown.

Description from Romagnesi and Locquin.

HABITAT on cow dung. Probably widely distributed although so far recorded only from Midlothian and Perthshire.

It may be recognised by the small fruit bodies, rather small spores and the veil being a mixture of globose and fusiform or cylindric cells some of which are heavily encrusted and strongly coloured. It appears to have been seen most frequently by those who incubate dung in the laboratory, possibly because it may only fruit in the early morning in the field.

Stirps 14 : Cortinatus

40. C. cortinatus J. Lange in Dansk Botanisk Arkiv, 2: 45, 1915. See Figs. 115, 119 & 123.

Icon.: L 159 B.

CAP at first 4-11/3-8mm, ovoid or ellipsoid then expanded ± plane, 4-15mm broad, sometimes slightly umbonate, white with slight clay-buff or pale cream-buff tinge at centre, then grey with paler centre, at first entirely minutely scurfy floccose, margin fringed with white veil at first then striate sulcate. GILLS pale then dark purplish date finally fuscous black. STEM 8-50/0.3-1mm, equal, white or hyaline white, minutely floccose when fresh but becoming smooth, veil leaving fugacious ring zone near apex, base sometimes slightly white strigose. SMELL none. SPORE-PRINT fuscous black.

SPORES sepia, 9.5-11/5-6μm, amygdaliform in side view, ovoid-ellipsoid in face view, germ-pore central and truncate. BASIDIA 4-spored. MARGINAL CYSTIDIA cylindric-clavate or slightly vesiculose or lageniform, 22-40/10-14(-18)μm. FACIAL CYSTIDIA absent. CAP CUTICLE cellular. VEIL on cap a mixture of globose or subglobose cells covered with crystals, which disappear in HCl, 16-52μm broad, and narrower filamentous hyphae with end-cells 6-18μm broad and ± clavate especially noticeable on the outer part of the cap; veil on the stem similar.

GENETICS unknown. OIDIA in moist heads.

HABITAT on soil, often under *Mercurialis perennis* and probably with preference for basic soils. Uncommon but easily overlooked and as yet only recorded from England.

It is best recognised by habitat, veil of two kinds of cells on cap, cortina on stem, and amygdaliform medium spores. It differs from *C. filiformis* in cortinate veil and from *C. luteocephalus* in not being yellowish and in habitat not on dung.

41. C. filiformis Berkeley & Broome in Annals and Magazine of Natural History, series 3, 7: 379, 1861. See Figs. 116, 118, 122.

Icon.: Cke 674(686) B. Figs.: TBMS 40: 274; fig. 9.

CAP at first 4-7/2-6mm ± cylindrical or conical sometimes slightly umbonate then expanded with upturned margin, pale whitish grey then deeper grey with centre tinged drab or mouse-grey, at first with whitish mealy veil, which may be cream or buff at centre, becoming smooth with wrinkled sulcate margin. GILLS whitish then greyish, finally blackish. STEM 15-40/0.2-1mm, equal or slightly thickened downwards, base often thickened or disc-like, whitish, minutely hairy or pubescent especially in lower part. SMELL none. SPORE-PRINT not recorded.

SPORES red-brown, 8-10/4.7-5.5μm, ellipsoid or very slightly amygdaliform, germ-pore central and rather truncate. BASIDIA 4-spored. MARGINAL and FACIAL CYSTIDIA and CAP CUTICLE not investigated. VEIL on cap a mixture of ± ellipsoid or globose, hyaline thin-walled cells 20-40μm broad, and cylindric often diverticulate thick-walled cells 4-6μm broad with walls sometimes brownish or encrusted.

CLAMP-CONNECTIONS present. GENETICS not known.

HABITAT on bare soil in shady places, solitary or scattered. Uncommon in England, not recorded for Ireland or Scotland, but easily overlooked.

It is best recognised by small size, veil of two kinds of cells and habitat. It may prefer basic soil.

42. C. luteocephalus Watling in Notes from the Royal Botanic Garden, Edinburgh, 31: 359, 1972. See Figs. 8-10, 117, 120 & 121, 124 & 125.

Icon.: none. Figs.: NRBG 31: 359, figs. A-E.

CAP at first 8-18mm high elongate conico-cylindric, then expanded-conical or expanded-convex to ± plane, 8-22mm broad, often distinctly umbonate, greenish yellow or lemon-yellow, darker yellow at centre then pale cream at margin, entirely fibrillose-scurfy then becoming smooth and striate or sulcate in outer part. GILLS greyish becoming violaceous black. STEM 40-60/1-1.5mm (2-3mm at base), equal often with ± bulbous base, hyaline or slightly brownish, base greenish yellow or citrine tomentose. SMELL none. SPORE-PRINT violaceous black.

SPORES purplish date, 10.5-12.5/5-7.5μm, ellipsoid-amygdaliform in side view, ± ellipsoid in face view, germ-pore central and up to 2μm broad. BASIDIA 4-spored. MARGINAL CYSTIDIA ellipsoid or vesiculose, 13-18μm broad. FACIAL CYSTIDIA sparse, fusiform-lageniform with long neck or obovoid, 85-100/35-45μm, apex obtuse. CAP CUTICLE cellular of rather ellipsoid cells. VEIL on cap a mixture of thin-walled filamentous, irregularly branched hyphae 2-5μm broad, with granular or vacuolar yellow contents and sometimes yellowish encrusted pigmented, and fusiform-elongate ellipsoid or vesiculose cells 10-12μm broad.

CLAMP-CONNECTIONS present. GENETICS heterothallic, tetrapolar. OIDIA formed in culture in moist heads.

HABITAT on horse dung. Seemingly uncommon, so far only recorded from Midlothian and Cumberland.

Readily recognised by yellow veil. Although otherwise macroscopically resembling *C. vermiculifer* it differs fundamentally in having a cellular cuticle of broadly ellipsoid cells. *C. poliomallus,* which is also small and on dung, has the veil consisting of broader elements.

Stirps 15 : Niveus

43. C. niveus (Persoon ex Fries) Fries, Epicrisis Systematis Mycologici, 246, 1838. See Figs. 128 & 130.

Syn.: *Agaricus niveus* Persoon ex Fries, Systema Mycologicum, I: 311, 1821.

Icon.: L 159 I; KM 33; Ri 20[4].

CAP at first 15-30/9-17mm cylindric-ellipsoid to ovoid, then ± campanulate, finally expanded 20-40mm broad with radially split or revolute margin, white, at first rather thickly snow-white mealy flocculose, then smoother and striate and sometimes tinged grey from margin inwards. GILLS white soon greyish then black. STEM 30-90/3-6mm, equal or slightly attenuated upwards, or with slightly thickened base, white, mealy flocculose like the cap when fresh, apex often white silky-floccose and base white tomentose. SMELL none. SPORE-PRINT black or violaceous black.

SPORES fuscous black or black, 15-19/8.5-10.5/11-13μm, ellipsoid, slightly amygdaliform in side view, broadly ellipsoid ovoid and indistinctly limoniform-angular in face view, germ-pore central. BASIDIA 4-spored. MARGINAL CYSTIDIA globose or vesiculose 16.5-25/(10-)12.5-20μm. FACIAL CYSTIDIA vesiculose 30-55/27-42.5μm. VEIL on cap of globose or ellipsoid, smooth or slightly crystalline granular cells 20-40μm broad.

CLAMP-CONNECTIONS present. GENETICS heterothallic, probably tetrapolar. OIDIA in moist heads in culture.

HABITAT on dung (especially cow and horse). Common and widespread in the British Isles.

It is characterised by smooth or crystalline granular veil cells and is easily recognised by the rather copious persistent snow-white veil, medium to large fruit-bodies and large indistinctly angular spores. *C. latisporus* is also white, but has shorter subglobose-angular spores with slightly excentric germ-pore and smaller fruit-bodies. Microscopical details in the above description may need modification when further material has been critically examined from this point of view. The granulations on the cells of the veil are removed by acid in all members of Stirps *Niveus.*

C. roseotinctus Rea (TBMS 1 23: 1897) may belong in Stirps *Niveus.* It has a fuscous cap at first cylindrical 7-11mm high and densely powdered with rose-coloured meal, the stem white and also densely powdered with deep-rose meal, spores pip-shaped 9-11/5-6μm and was found in an ash plantation and also under trees (details from Rea). In the absence of type material and of information on the veil it cannot be included, but it seems likely to be a good species awaiting re-discovery in Britain. Pearson and Dennis (1948) suggest that *C. frustulosus* Sacc. is the same as Rea's species. An agaric agreeing with Rea's description has been found recently in Czechoslovakia.

44. C. latisporus P.D. Orton in Notes from the Royal Botanic Garden, Edinburgh, 32: 140, 1972. See Fig. 133.

Icon.: none. Figs.: NRBG 32: 140, fig. 1, m-n.

CAP at first 5-6/4-5mm ovoid, then expanded, snow-white then greyish from margin inwards, at first minutely white atomate granular mealy and with margin slightly fringed-crenate. GILLS white then blackish. STEM 20-24/1-1.5mm ± equal, white, white granular mealy like the cap. SMELL none. SPORE-PRINT fuscous black.

SPORES dark date-brown to fuscous black, 14-16/8-9/10-12.5μm, markedly lentiform, ellipsoid or ovoid in side view, subglobose indistinctly angular in face view, germ-pore slightly excentric. MARGINAL CYSTIDIA present but shape not noted. FACIAL CYSTIDIA not seen. CAP CUTICLE cellular. VEIL on cap of globose to broadly ellipsoid smooth cells, 26-90μm broad, with some narrow hyaline hyphae.

CLAMP CONNECTIONS not noted. GENETICS unknown.

HABITAT on cow dung. Recorded from Somerset, Norfolk and Perthshire, so it is probably widespread but uncommon or confused with *C. niveus*.

It closely resembles *C. niveus* but has a smaller fruit-body and shorter relatively broader spores with slightly excentric germ-pore.

The above description is incomplete and will need modification when further material has been examined, especially as to range of size of fruit-body and cystidial details.

45. C. pachyspermus P.D. Orton in Notes from the Royal Botanic Garden, Edinburgh, 32: 144, 1972. See Figs. 131 & 132.

Icon.: none. Figs.: NRBG 32: 144, figs. 1 j-l.

CAP at first 6-30/4-18mm, ovoid or ellipsoid sometimes rather pointed at apex, then conical to expanded umbonate with revolute sometimes radially split margin, grey or cream-grey, at first entirely minutely granular mealy to coarsely often ± pointed warty mealy-floccose scaly especially at centre, scales sometimes (especially in larger specimens) darker sepia-brownish at tips, margin fringed at first with dirty white. GILLS grey then blackish. STEM 30-110/1-4mm, ± equal or slightly thickened in lower part, white or hyaline, more rarely hyaline grey, finely white silky-flocculose in lower part, apex very minutely flocculose-punctate, base sometimes with remains of mealy veil as on cap. SMELL none. SPORE-PRINT fuscous black.

SPORES fuscous black, (14-)15-17/8.5-10/12.5-14μm, markedly lentiform, ellipsoid or slightly ovoid in side view, broadly ovoid or subglobose often indistinctly angled in face view, germ-pore central and in some views showing as a truncate papilla. BASIDIA 2-spored. MARGINAL CYSTIDIA ± globose to pyriform, a few ± clavate, 30-50/28-37μm. FACIAL CYSTIDIA clavate to elongate vesiculose, 80-200/32-74μm. CAP CUTICLE cellular. VEIL on cap of globose or more rarely slightly ellipsoid hyaline sometimes encrusted crystalline cells 18-90μm broad, together with narrow hyaline hyphae 2-4μm broad.

CLAMP CONNECTIONS not investigated. GENETICS unknown.

HABITAT on old cow dung. Uncommon and as yet only known from the Nethy Bridge area, Inverness-shire.

It is immediately recognisable microscopically by the 2-spored basidia and large lentiform spores. It is sometimes more robust than other members of Stirps *Niveus* and is then distinguishable in the field by its grey colour. Possibly it will only grow on old cow dung and may therefore be restricted in occurrence.

46. C. cothurnatus Godey apud Gillet, Hyménomycetes de France, 605, 1874. See Figs. 127 & 136.

Icon.: none. Figs.: NRBG 29: 87, figs. 1e, 3d-f.

CAP at first 7-20/5-12mm ellipsoid, conical or elongate-cylindric,then expanded ± umbonate 14-40mm broad with split and grooved-striate or revolute margin, white or tinged ivory then greyish from margin inwards, at first entirely white or greyish granular flocculose scaly, sometimes with darker clay-buff or drab scales at centre. GILLS whitish then blackish umber to black. STEM 50-100/2-4.5(-6)mm, equal or slightly thickened at the base, sometimes fusiform at first, white then whitish and dissolving clay-buff or pale buff in lower part, at first entirely white flocculose scaly, becoming smoother with age, apex minutely floccose-pruinose when fresh, lower part often with mealy granular scales as on cap, which may turn pinkish, clay-buff, or pale drab when bruised, extreme base sometimes with pinkish or pale drab tomentum as well. SMELL none. SPORE-PRINT fuscous black.

SPORES umber, 11.5-14.5/6-8/7.5-9μm, slightly lentiform, ellipsoid or slightly amygdaliform in side view, broadly ellipsoid or ovoid often obscurely hexagonal in face view, germ-pore central. BASIDIA 4-spored, dimorphic. MARGINAL CYSTIDIA sphaeropedunculate or vesiculose, sometimes a few with papillate apex, 10-44μm broad. FACIAL CYSTIDIA rather fugacious, clavate to broadly lageniform, 30-44/8-14μm, apex 7-10μm broad. CAP CUTICLE cellular. VEIL on cap of globose or broadly ellipsoid fairly thick-walled smooth cells 20-144μm broad, sometimes with brownish pigment masses among them.

CLAMP-CONNECTIONS not observed but are said to develop in culture. GENETICS heterothallic, bipolar (sec M Lange).

HABITAT on dungy straw, solitary or gregarious. Uncommon, so far only recorded from Norfolk, but probably widespread in suitable habitats.

It is distinguished from other members of Stirps *Niveus* by greyish, sometimes discolouring veil and more particularly by the rather large obscurely hexagonal spores. *C. roseotinctus* Rea is more distinctly pinkish mealy and has different spores; see obs. on *C. niveus.*

This description seems to agree with *C. cothurnatus* as redescribed by M. Lange and A. H. Smith in Mycologia 40 (1948): 739, but the exact identity of Godey's taxon is not really certain.

47. C. cordisporus Gibbs in The Naturalist, London: 100, 1898 See Figs. 126, 134 & 137.

Syn.: *C. volvaceominimus* Crossland in The Naturalist, London 372, 1892.

Misident.: *C. patouillardii* Quélet sensu Josserand (et al.) in Ann. Soc. Linn. Lyon 77: 104, 1933; sensu Dennis, Orton & Hora, 1960.

Icon.: L 159 E. Figs.: Ann. Soc. Linn. Lyon 77: 104, fig. 9, *patouillardii*

CAP at first 1-4/1-3mm ovoid or cylindric-ellipsoid, then convex or expanded sometimes depressed at the centre 5-10mm broad, at first with whitish to buff or ochraceous mealy or granular scales, outer part becoming grey and plicate-striate to centre. GILLS whitish or greyish then blackish. STEM 10-35(-60)/0.5-1mm, ± equal, filiform, white then hyaline, smooth except for slightly pruinose base. SMELL none. SPORE-PRINT fuscous-black.

SPORES dark date-brown, (6-)6.5-8.5(-9)/4-5/5.5-7μm, lentiform, ellipsoid ± amygdaliform in side view, subglobose-triangular or ± pentagonal in face view, germ-pore truncate and central. BASIDIA 4-spored. MARGINAL CYSTIDIA cylindric-ovoid or broadly lageniform. FACIAL CYSTIDIA elongate ellipsoid or ± lageniform, 40-55/13-32μm. CAP CUTICLE cellular. VEIL on cap of smooth or punctate crystalline, hyaline or pale ochraceous globose cells 15-40μm broad.

CLAMP-CONNECTIONS absent. GENETICS undertermined.

HABITAT on relatively fresh dung. Common throughout the British Isles.

It differs from the other small-spored members of Stirps *Niveus* by its relatively small fruit-bodies. *C. patouillardii* differs in producing relatively large fruit-bodies and in growing on kitchen refuse or old dung or burnt soil. *C. ephemeroides* has a clearly marked apical or basal veil zone on the stem and is white ± flushed yellow when fresh. This is listed as *C. patouillardii* in the New Check List (1960).

A 2-spored microscopically similar taxon exists with larger more angular spores about 9-11/6-6.5/8-9μm. Its exact status remains to be investigated but it seems likely that it will be a distinct species.

48. C. ephemeroides (Bulliard ex Fries) Fries, Epicrisis Systematis Mycologici,: 250, 1838. See Figs. 129 & 138.

Syn.: *Agaricus ephemeroides* Bulliard ex Fries, Systema Mycologicum, I 313; 1821; *Agaricus hendersonii* Berkeley apud Hooker, English Flora, 122, 1836; *C. hendersonii* (Berkeley) Fries, Epicrisis Systematis Mycologici, 250, 1838; *C. bulbillosus* Patouillard, Tabulae Analyticae Fungorum, fasc. VII: 60, Pl. 658, 1889.

Icon.: L 159 H; TBMS 3: 126, Pl. 7. Figs.: RM 10: 80, fig. 4.

CAP at first 2-6/1-2.5mm ellipsoid or cylindric, then expanded ± plane 2-7mm broad often with upturned margin or depressed at centre, white or greyish in outer part with cream, pale straw or yellowish centre, entirely white or cream granular mealy-scaly when fresh, outer part becoming plicate-striate and sometimes ± smooth, sometimes with fragments of ring at first. GILLS whitish then blackish. STEM 10-30/0.3-0.8mm, equal or attenuated upwards from swollen or bulbous base, white then hyaline, smooth except for finely tomentose or adpressed silky base; ring from basal to half-way up the stem, sheathing at first, white or pale cream, floccose-membranous, sometimes torn and split and partly adhering to edge of cap. SMELL none. SPORE-PRINT fuscous black.

SPORES dark date-brown, 6-9/5-6/6.5-8µm, lentiform, ellipsoid in side view, subglobose-pentagonal in face view, germ-pore central and truncate. BASIDIA 4-spored. MARGINAL CYSTIDIA globose or ovoid, 30-50/25-40µm. FACIAL CYSTIDIA absent. CAP CUTICLE cellular. VEIL on cap of globose or ellipsoid hyaline, smooth cells 14-60µm broad.

CLAMP-CONNECTIONS absent. GENETICS homothallic. OIDIA absent in culture.

HABITAT on dung of various kinds. Widespread and not uncommon in the British Isles.

It can be distinguished from the other small-spored members of Stirps *Niveus* by the ring on the stem and cream or yellowish fresh cap centre. If the ring has been washed off or left at the cap edge, the whitish cap with coloured centre will distinguish it from the greyer *C. cordisporus*.

A 2-spored taxon somewhat similar in appearance has been recorded and may warrant separation as a distinct species. It has larger spores 9-10/6-7/8-9µm and seems to produce larger, greyer fruit-bodies, but a well-described collection is needed for further investigation. This may in part be what Berkeley referred to as *C. hendersonii*, although the spores of the type material agree in all respects with *C. cordisporus*.

49. C. patouillardii Quélet apud Patouillard, Tabulae Analyticae Fungorum, 107, 1884. See Figs. 135 & 139.

Syn.: *C. nycthemerus var. patouillardii* Quél. in C.R. Ass. franc. Av. Sci. (Blois 1884) 13: 280, 1885; *C. patouillardii var. lipophilus* Heim & Romagnesi in Bull. Soc. Mycol. Fr. 50: 187, 1934. Misident.: *C. angulatus* Peck sensu J. Lange in Dansk. Bot. Arkiv. 2: 45, 1915.

Icon.: Pat 240; L 157 D angulatus. Figs.: BSMF 50: 187, fig. 15, var. lipophilus.

CAP at first 8-12mm high ovoid, then expanded-convex 10-20mm broad sometimes slightly depressed at centre, whitish or pale cream then greyish in outer part, at first with mealy or granular scales, those at centre ochraceous buff or cinnamon often coarser and sometimes pointed, those in outer part whitish or pale cream, becoming smoother and plicate-striate to centre. GILLS whitish then greyish, finally black. STEM 25-35/1-2mm, ± equal with swollen or slightly bulbous base, white or hyaline, smooth but at first at the base with scales like those on cap which may persist and form a volvate zone. SMELL none. SPORE-PRINT black.

SPORES dark date-brown, 7-9/5-6/7-8µm, lentiform, ellipsoid in side view, indistinctly 5-angled in face view, germ-pore central and 2-2.5µm broad. BASIDIA 4-spored. MARGINAL CYSTIDIA globose or ovoid, hyaline or tinged ochraceous,

25-45/22-35μm. FACIAL CYSTIDIA absent. CAP CUTICLE cellular. VEIL on cap of hyaline to strongly ochraceous ± globose or ellipsoid slightly roughened or smooth cells 18-35μm broad.

CLAMP-CONNECTIONS absent. GENETICS unknown.

HABITAT on kitchen refuse, silage, straw, soil mixed with old dung, in small groups or subcaespitose. Distribution unknown but recorded from Yorkshire, Edinburgh and Mull.

The original collection of Patouillard was recorded from 'le marc de raisin pourrissant' and the cap was said to be 10-20mm broad. Confusion has arisen because Josserand and other authors have used this name for a taxon growing on fresh dung producing very small fruit-bodies which is included in this work as *C. cordisporus* Gibbs. Josserand's interpretation was followed in the New Check List (1960).

Rea (Trans. Brit. Myc. Soc., 3: 126, 1909) correctly described *C. patouillardii* from spent tea leaves. It can be distinguished from the other small-spored species in Stirps *Niveus* by its habitat, small to medium sized cap and lack of ring. It would seem that it also occurs on burnt soil and on old dung, but further field work is necessary before we can be sure that this is really the same taxon, for there is undoubtedly a complex of species in this group which await further investigation.

Stirps 16 : Narcoticus

50. C. narcoticus (Batsch ex Fries) Fries, Epicrisis Systematis Mycologici, 250, 1838. See Fig. 167.

Syn.: *Agaricus narcoticus* Batsch ex Fries, Systema Mycologicum, I: 311, 1821.

Icon.: none. Fig.: Persoonia 5: 142; fig. 1, 9, 15-17, 28, 35, 42.

CAP at first 8-15/5-10mm broadly ellipsoid or ovoid, or conical-ovoid then conico-convex and up to 30mm high, finally ± plane 20-25mm broad with revolute or split margin, pale to dark grey, entirely whitish mealy granular scaly, then more coarsely often pale clay-buff warty scaly in centre part, outer part becoming grooved striate to centre. GILLS white then grey finally black. STEM 15-60(-75)/ 1.5-3mm, equal or attenuated at apex, base sometimes swollen or more rarely slightly rooting, white then whitish, densely white woolly-hairy when fresh especially at base. SMELL strong of gas (like *Tricholoma sulphureum*). SPORE-PRINT fuscous black or black.

SPORES umber, 10.8-13.5/5.4-6.8μm (without perispore), ellipsoid or ellipsoid-amygdaliform, narrowed to conspicuous apiculus, perispore (0.5-)1-1.5(-2)μm broad, marked with blackish dots or short thick lines beneath this, germ-pore central. BASIDIA 4-spored. MARGINAL CYSTIDIA sphaeropedunculate, globose, vesiculose or slightly elongate, 30-80/20-50μm. FACIAL CYSTIDIA broadly

69

ellipsoid or ovoid with very short stalk, 50-105/35-50(-65)μm. CAP CUTICLE cellular. VEIL on cap of slightly brownish globose to vesiculose, minutely diverticulate cells 40-112μm broad, together with some cylindric or slightly swollen or diverticulate hyphae 1.6-6.4μm broad. VEIL on stem a dense network of branching narrow hyphae together with a few globose cells as on the cap, some of which may be almost smooth.

Description from van Waveren.

CLAMP-CONNECTIONS present. GENETICS probably homothallic with freely self-anastomosing hyphae. OIDIA not seen.

HABITAT on dung or manured soil. Distribution unknown.

It is distinguished from other coprophilous members of Stirps *Narcoticus* by the smell of gas, spores with conspicuous elongate apiculus, marked with black lines or dots beneath the ± conspicuous perispore.

Much confusion exists over the use of the epithet *narcoticus*. In the past any evil-smelling taxon has been named thus. This, however, will not do and there are included in this work four clearly recognisable taxa of this nature: *C. narcoticus* sensu van Waveren, *C. trisporus*, *C. triplex* (= *C. narcoticus* sensu Buller) and *C. radicans*. *C. narcoticus* sensu Lange grows on soil (possibly originating from decaying vegetable matter) and not on dung, and is known to occur in Britain, but needs describing as a new species after gathering adequate material. It differs from *C. narcoticus* sensu van Waveren in having a different (stercoraceous) smell as well as a different habitat. A taxon with a stercoraceous smell growing on old tea leaves with stem-base often rooted and branching as in *C. radicans*, with spores of the other type in the stirps with inconspicuous perispore and apiculus is also known and likewise waits a proper description. It is hoped that interfertility tests may eventually confirm or disprove the need to separate these taxa.

Older descriptions under the name *C. narcoticus* must therefore be treated with suspicion and are not quoted above. The original description of Fries indicates a coprophilous habitat ('in fimo locis nemorosis') and this is why van Waveren's taxon is described here. Too much importance should not be attached to the presence or absence of a root on the stem, which is a variable feature, but the presence of a sclerotium, in the group in general, is a different matter.

51. C. radicans Romagnesi in Revue de Mycologie 16: 122, 1951.
Icon.: none. Figs.: RM 16: 122, fig. 5

CAP at first 10-30/7-25mm ellipsoid or ovoid, then convex or conico-convex, finally expanded ± plane or slightly umbonate 17-44mm broad with revolute margin at first entirely greyish floccose mealy scaly on a grey or mouse-grey back-ground, scales at centre often thick, ± pointed and darker, becoming ± smooth from margin inwards. GILLS whitish then greyish, finally black. STEM 50-80/ 1.5-3mm at apex, 3-6mm at base which is often prolonged into a tough greyish 'root', which may be branched and connected to other fruit-bodies, white or whitish then pale grey especially in lower part, entirely white floccose-fibrillose at first, base often white or whitish silky floccose or tomentose. SMELL powerful, disagreeable, pungent-stercoraceous, developing as soon as spores start to ripen.

SPORES blackish, 11.5-14.5/5.5-7/6.5-8.5µm (with perispore), slightly amygdaliform in side view, narrowed rather gradually to ± conspicuous apiculus, germ-pore central and truncate, perispore conspicuous at least over most of the spore surface but sometimes rather thin and often folded, 0.5-2µm broad. BASIDIA 4-spored. MARGINAL CYSTIDIA vesiculose or ellipsoid, 24-62µm broad. FACIAL CYSTIDIA ellipsoid-vesiculose or cylindric-ellipsoid 80-100/30-36µm. CAP CUTICLE cellular. VEIL on cap of globose or slightly ellipsoid minutely warty punctate cells 46-104µm broad, together with some ± cylindric hyphae 4-12µm broad.

CLAMP-CONNECTIONS not recorded. GENETICS unknown.

HABITAT on very rotten plant refuse (old potatoes and straw). Distribution unknown, probably uncommon. Recorded from Glenesk, Kincardine.

The above description of British material is included under this name with the reservation that it differs from Romagnesi's description in that the perispore was visible on the mature spore and the habitat is not on dung; all other features agree well. A similar taxon from Stratford-on-Avon, on old tea leaves, with spores slightly narrower 10.5-13.5/5-6.5/6.6µm seems likely to be the same.

It is distinguished from *C. narcoticus* by habitat, a different smell and rather larger spores seemingly without dark marks on the surface, and from *C. trisporus* in 4-spored basidia and darker cap and from *C. triplex* in 4-spored basidia and more robust habit. Most specimens were rooting, some extensively so, but a few were apparently without roots - so this character is not reliable enough to be clearly diagnostic. A macroscopically similar taxon with rooting stem but with spores lacking conspicuous apiculus and perispore was collected on old tea leaves and awaits further investigation; this collection closely approaches Romagnesi's fungus.

52. C. laanii van Waveren in Persoonia 5: 146, 1968. See Figs. 161-164.

Icon.: none. Figs.: Persoonia 5: 146, figs. 10, 18-21, 29-31, 36-37, 43-44, Pl. 6; NRBG 28: 45, figs. 2 D-d", aff. martini

CAP at first 5-22/3-12mm ellipsoid, ovoid or elongate conical, then convex conico-campanulate, finally expanded 10-30mm broad with upturned margin, pale grey to mouse-grey, at first entirely greyish mealy with margin granular floccose scaly, more finely and sparsely so in outer part, often more coarsely and darkly (drab) so at centre, outer part becoming grooved-striate and radially cracked or split. GILLS white then grey, or slightly clay-pinkish then purplish date or date-brown, finally fuscous black to violaceous black. STEM 20-55/1-4mm, equal or ± attenuated upwards, silvery-whitish then pale grey or hyaline-grey, at first entirely grey

71

floccose-mealy (then minutely silky fibrillose), base sometimes with darker mealy flocci as on cap, more rarely with a few mycelial threads. SMELL none. SPORE-PRINT fuscous black to violaceous black.

SPORES dark date-brown, 10-11.5/4.8-6µm (without perispore), ± ellipsoid in all views, narrowed gradually to the ± conspicuous apiculus, germ-pore central, perispore conspicuous and often thick with wavy or folded outline 0.5-3µm broad marked with blackish dots or lines beneath this. BASIDIA 4-spored dimorphic. MARGINAL CYSTIDIA globose, sphaeropedunculate, pyriform or vesiculose (30-75/20-45µm), to elongate fusiform or broadly lageniform (50-100(-120)/ 20-45µm). FACIAL CYSTIDIA vesiculose to lageniform or slightly utriform, 80-130/25-38µm. CAP CUTICLE cellular. VEIL on cap of hyaline or slightly brownish globose, ellipsoid or ovoid, minutely diverticulate cells 32-100µm broad, together with some ± cylindric branching often diverticulate hyphae (1.6-6.4 (-11.2)µm broad); veil on stem of dense network of ± cylindric branched hyaline often diverticulate hyphae 3-10µm broad, together with a few ± globose cells as on cap and sometimes some ± fusiform cells at stem base.

CLAMP-CONNECTIONS present. GENETICS heterothallic, bipolar. OIDIA absent in culture.

HABITAT on algal scum or moss on cut surfaces of stumps or logs, or in wood chips or sawdust. Probably not uncommon; recorded from Somerset, Surrey, Yorkshire, Perthshire, Midlothian & Wales.

It is rather easily distinguished from other members of Stirps *Narcoticus* firstly by habitat, by absence of smell and spores narrowed to conspicuous apiculus with prominent perispore. The spore is marked with dark lines or dots beneath the perispore as in *C. narcoticus* only more so. The above description of British material agrees well with van Waveren's original description from which some extra details are included in brackets. No doubt this species has been overlooked in the past; it has certainly been recorded as *C. cineratus* and was included under that name in the New Check List (1960).

53. C. semitalis P.D. Orton in Notes from the Royal Botanic Garden, Edinburgh, 32: 147, 1972. See Fig. 154.

Syn.: *C. cinereofloccosus var. angustisporus* Reid in Ill. Rare & Interesting Fungi, 5: 22, 1972. Misident.: *C. cineratus* Quélet in Trans. Brit. Mycol. Soc., 43 Suppl: 37.

Icon.: none. Figs.: NRBG 32: 147, fig. 2f.

CAP at first 13-22/6-10mm ovoid or conico-ellipsoid, then expanded ± plane 10-22mm broad with torn or revolute margin, whitish to grey, at first entirely greyish granular mealy, sometimes more coarsely clay-buff or pale sepia mealy-scaly at centre or more finely mealy in outer part, margin becoming smoother and slightly striate. GILLS white soon grey then blackish. STEM 65-96/1.5-3mm, equal or slightly attenuated upwards or thickened at base, hyaline or silvery grey, ± entirely white or whitish scattered silky flocculose when fresh, base with clay buff or greyish granular mealy flocci as on cap when fresh. SMELL none, or rarely slightly earthy (when old). SPORE-PRINT fuscous black.

SPORES dark date-brown, 10.5-13.5/4.5-5.5/6.5-8μm (with perispore), ellipsoid slightly amygdaliform in side view, elongate ellipsoid in face view, gradually narrowed to the conspicuous apiculus, germ-pore central and truncate, perispore conspicuous, often folded 1-3.5μm broad, BASIDIA 4-spored. MARGINAL CYSTIDIA sphaeropedunculate, pyriform or vesiculose to slightly lageniform, 40-110/20-52μm. FACIAL CYSTIDIA cylindric-ellipsoid, fusiform or slightly utriform, 120-170/28-36μm. CAP CUTICLE cellular. VEIL on cap of globose or broadly ellipsoid minutely verrucose cells 36-80μm broad; veil on stem base similar but some cylindric or fusiform branched often diverticulate cells also present, 4-14μm, or when fusiform 16-48μm, broad; flocci on stem of narrow, hyaline filamentous hyphae 2-8(-10)μm broad.

CLAMP-CONNECTIONS present. GENETICS homothallic. OIDIA absent in culture.

HABITAT on soil (often on paths) or amongst grass in fields or in woods, singly, in groups or subcaespitose. Not uncommon and widespread in England and Scotland (probably also in Wales and Ireland).

It differs from other members of Stirps *Narcoticus* in lack of smell, terrestrial habitat, rather long narrow spores, with conspicuous perispore, and 4-spored basidia. *C. laanii* and *C. cinereofloccosus* are macroscopically similar, but the former grows on stumps or logs or sawdust and has rather shorter spores marked with dots or lines and the latter is 2-spored. It was included in the New Check List in part as *C. cineratus* Quélet, but the identity of this name is not certain.

54. C. cinereofloccosus P.D. Orton in Transactions of the British Mycological Society, 43: 198, 1960. See Figs. 153, 156 & 160.

Icon.: none. Figs.: TBMS 43: 198, figs. 247, 403-4.

CAP at first 11-22/8-20mm ellipsoid, ovoid or conical-ovoid, then expanded-convex or conico-expanded 10-38mm broad, finally expanded ± plane with revolute margin, pale grey sometimes darker grey at centre, at first entirely grey floccose mealy-scaly, more finely and palely so in outer part, often coarsely or lumpy pale vinaceous buff or dark grey granular scaly in centre part, outer part becoming smoother and ± plicate-sulcate. GILLS white then greyish, finally black. STEM 60-100(-150)/1-5mm (2-6mm at base), ± equal or attenuated upwards or at apex, white soon whitish or pale grey, entirely finely pale grey or pale vinaceous buff floccose-mealy when fresh, becoming smoother and finely or interruptedly white silky striate when old, base often with darker mealy scales as on cap. SMELL none. SPORE-PRINT black.

SPORES dark date-brown, 11-15/5.5-7/7-9μm (with perispore), ellipsoid, slightly amygdaliform in side-view, longer ones sometimes irregularly phaseoliform in face-view, rather gradually narrowed to fairly conspicuous apiculus, germ-pore central and truncate, perispore conspicuous, often folded, 1-3(4)μm broad. BASIDIA 2-spored. MARGINAL CYSTIDIA sphaeropedunculate, clavate, pyriform or vesiculose, sometimes irregularly constricted, 40-100/20-45μm. FACIAL CYSTIDIA cylindric-vesiculose or elongate fusiform, 86-175/24-40μm. CAP CUTICLE cellular. VEIL on cap of globose or broadly ellipsoid minutely warty punctate (diverticulate) cells, 24-100μm broad, together with some cylindric or slightly fusiform cells 8-14μm broad. VEIL on stem similar, at base often also with some more strongly fusiform sometimes diverticulate cells 20-30μm broad.

CLAMP-CONNECTIONS not recorded. GENETICS unknown.

HABITAT on grass or on soil, singly or in groups. Distribution unknown but seemingly uncommon; recorded from England and Scotland.

It is recognised amongst other odourless members of Stirps *Narcoticus* by 2-spored basidia, terrestrial habitat and rather long spores.

The name *C. cinereofloccosus* should be restricted to 2-spored collections. In the original description of this species the basidia were said to be 4-spored, but in fact the type material has 2-spored basidia. The error arose because of confusion with *C. semitalis,* under which the 4-spored taxon is included in this work.

These two species and *C. laanii* are macroscopically very similar and have spores of the same type, but *C. laanii* grows on wood or sawdust and has spores marked with conspicuous lines and dots beneath the perispore, and *C. semitalis* has spores of much the same length but narrower.

C. saccharomyces is also similar macroscopically to *C. cinereofloccosus* but smells of yeast or beer, and, although 2-spored, has much larger spores (14-20/9-10μm) with inconspicuous apiculus and perispore.

Interfertility tests have not yet been possible between this and *C. semitalis* because of the difficulty in inducing spores of members of this stirps to germinate. Although these two taxa may be found in the same area (e.g. at Rannoch), this does not necessarily mean they *must* be the same species, and it seems best to keep them separate pending evidence to the contrary. For *C. cinereofloccosus* var. *angustisporus* Reid see notes on *C. semitalis.*

55. C. triplex P.D. Orton in Notes from the Royal Botanic Garden, Edinburgh, 35: 147, 1976.

Misident: *C. narcoticus* (Batsch ex Fr.) Fr, sensu Buller non al.

Icon.: none. Figs. L Buller, Researches on Fungi III: 294, fig. 125.

CAP at first 6-12/5-9mm subglobose or ovoid, then expanded 7-15mm broad with ± revolute or split margin, grey, at first often with very coarse grey or buff-tipped lumps of meal at centre, elsewhere minutely finely floccose--mealy, becoming grooved striate from margin in. GILLS whitish then umber or purplish date finally blackish. STEM 30-35/1-2mm, equal or slightly attenuated upwards from the ± marginately bulbous base, entirely minutely white mealy floccose when fresh, bulb with radially arranged grey mealy flocci, base sometimes continued into a thin mycelial cord. SMELL fairly strong, especially when opening out, nauseous, of human faeces or like acetylene. SPORE-PRINT fuscous black.

SPORES dark date-brown, 8.5-11/5-6.2μm, (without perispore), ellipsoid or slightly ovoid in both views, germ-pore central, perisporial sac not or barely visible in places only (in water). BASIDIA 3- or very rarely 4-spored. MARGINAL CYSTIDIA vesiculose or pyriform often pedunculate, 30-70/16-34μm. FACIAL CYSTIDIA not seen. VEIL on cap of ± globose verruculose cells 34-84μm broad.

GENETICS unknown.

HABITAT on cow dung. Recorded only from Mull as yet, but probably widespread though uncommon.

Recognised by the small, 3-spored basidia and marginately bulbous stem base. The other 3-spored member of this stirps *C. trisporus* lacks the latter and is whiter and has broader spores. This is one of the *C. narcoticus* complex and is *C. narcoticus* sensu Buller judging by the photographs he gives which show an exactly similar stem shape and habit.

56. C. trisporus Kemp & Watling in Notes from the Royal Botanic Garden, Edinburgh, 32: 128, 1972. See Figs. 141, 148 & 152.

Icon.: none. Figs.: NRBG 32: 128, fig. 1. G-K.

CAP at first 5-17.5/7-8mm ovoid, elongate-ellipsoid or cylindric-ovoid, then expanded-convex 12-18mm broad, sometimes umbonate, white or whitish often greyish or pale clay-buff at centre, at first entirely white mealy floccose and often very coarsely floccose mealy-scaly at centre, becoming smoother and plicate-striate from margin in. GILLS whitish then black. STEM 10-25/2-3.5mm (3.5-4.5mm at base), ± equal or attenuated upwards, white or greyish, finely pruinose becoming smooth. SMELL strong, nauseous, resembling that of gas works. SPORE-PRINT fuscous black.

SPORES dark date-brown, 9-10(-10.5)/(5.5-)6-6.5/6-7μm (with perispore), slightly amygdaliform in side view, broadly ellipsoid or ovoid in face view, germ-pore central, perispore thin and hyaline barely visible in water but more prominent after treatment with sulphuric acid. BASIDIA 3-spored. MARGINAL CYSTIDIA sphaeropedunculate, pyriform or vesiculose, 30-60/15-40μm. FACIAL CYSTIDIA similar or more cylindric-vesiculose, 70-100/28-48μm. CAP CUTICLE cellular. VEIL on cap of hyaline, verruculose minutely diverticulate cells mostly globose 20-75μm broad, but with some ± ellipsoid, 20-75/10-40μm together with a few ± cylindric hyphae 4-8μm broad.

GENETICS heterothallic. OIDIA formed in dry heads on monokaryons in culture. CLAMP-CONNECTIONS present in culture but irregular.

HABITAT on dung especially of horse, in small groups. Widely distributed in Britain and probably not uncommon.

It is easily recognised by the habitat, pale cap, strong smell and 3-spored basidia, but has no doubt been recorded in the past as *C. narcoticus* or *C. stercorarius* or possibly *C. niveus* if the smell was missed. It differs from *C. narcoticus* not only in number of spores on the basidia but also in whiter cap and a more nauseous smell, and should therefore be distinguishable in the field. *C. triplex,* which is also 3-spored, has narrower spores and a greyer cap and the stem base often marginately bulbous and mealy-floccose striate.

57. C. foetidellus P.D. Orton in Notes from the Royal Botanic Garden, Edinburgh, 31: 139, 1971. See Figs. 157 & 159.

Icon.: none. Figs.: NRBG 31: 139; figs. 1 d, e.

CAP at first 1-4/0.5-2mm elongate cylindric-ellipsoid,then expanded up to 10mm broad, sometimes depressed when old, or radially split at margin, at first pale grey with slightly darker grey thick mealy scales, those at centre coarser and sometimes tinged buff or saffron and pointed, then becoming floccose to ± smooth. GILLS becoming black. STEM 28-60/0.5mm, equal, pale greyish, entirely tomentose-pruinose when fresh. SMELL quite strong, stercoraceous. SPORE-PRINT fuscous black.

SPORES dark date-brown, 9-11(5-)5.5-6μm, ellipsoid or slightly oblong ellipsoid, germ-pore central, apiculus small and indistinct, perispore showing as a complete or incomplete thin transparent outline in water and in ammonia. BASIDIA 4-spored. MARGINAL CYSTIDIA clavate, cylindric-clavate, or irregular, 20-40/10-16(-20)μm. FACIAL CYSTIDIA cylindric, about 64/20μm. CAP CUTICLE cellular. VEIL cells on cap globose or ellipsoid, verruculose or minutely diverticulate 16-46μm broad together with some filamentous hyphae 2-6μm broad here and there. VEIL cells on stem a similar mixture but filamentous hyphae more numerous and some up to 18μm broad.

CLAMP-CONNECTIONS not observed. GENETICS unknown.

HABITAT on dung. So far known only from Somerset and probably uncommon, but distribution unknown.

This species is recognised by smell, small fruit-bodies and spores with inconspicuous perispore and apiculus. *C. stercoreus* is somewhat similar macroscopically but has smaller much narrower spores and a stronger smell. The absence of a sclerotium, its smell and very small size separate it from *C. tuberosus*. The above description may need modification, especially as regards size of fruit-body when further material has been found.

58. C. tuberosus Quélet in Bulletin de la Société Botanique de France, 25: 289, 1879. See Figs. 142 & 147.

Misident.: *C. stercorarius* (Bull.ex St Amans) J. Lange sensu J. Lange in Dansk Bot. Arkiv 2: 44, 1915.

Icon.: L 159 A *stercorarius;* Figs.: NRBG 32: 127, fig. 1F.

CAP at first 5-15/2-7mm ellipsoid or elongate-cylindric, then expanded 10-20mm broad and soon with revolute margin, pale grey sometimes darker at centre, at first entirely minutely pale grey mealy then sometimes rather smooth. GILLS grey then black. STEM 25-60/0.8-2mm, equal or attenuated upwards, white or whitish, fibrillose-downy when fresh especially in lower part, base often elongated-rooting and attached to an often deep-seated roundish black sclerotium up to 5mm broad. SMELL none. SPORE-PRINT fuscous black.

SPORES date-brown, 9-11/5.5-7μm, ellipsoid or slightly ovoid, germ-pore central, apiculus inconspicuous, perispore apparently lacking. BASIDIA 4-spored. MARGINAL CYSTIDIA vesiculose. CAP CUTICLE cellular. VEIL on cap of globose or ellipsoid verruculose minutely diverticulate cells 30-70μm broad, together with narrow filamentous hyphae especially towards the cap margin.

CLAMP-CONNECTIONS not observed. GENETICS heterothallic.

HABITAT in richly manured gardens or hothouses or on horse dung. Recorded from England, Scotland and Ireland, but Irish material has not been examined. The distribution of this and other related and recently described species is as yet unknown.

This species is recognised among other members of Stirps *Narcoticus* by habitat, lack of smell, spores without conspicuous perispore and rather small fruit-bodies. It is one of the constituents of *C. tuberosus* sensu van Waveren in Persoonia 5: 164 (1968). Care must be taken in searching for the sclerotium at the base of the stem or rooting base as it is small and insignificant and frequently decomposes leaving only the darkened cortex as a hull. This is in contrast to *C. sclerotiger* where the sclerotium originates at or on the surface of the substrate and persists for some time after the fruit-body has fructified.

A similar taxon has been found at Rannoch appearing amongst leaf litter and moss under birch and possibly growing on vole dung with narrower spores 8.5-10/ 4.5-5μm and long rooting stem base which was blackish at the tip. In one specimen some remains were present at the tip of the rooting stem base which looked sclerotioid, but no complete sclerotium could be found. This awaits further investigation but may well be a different species.

59. C. sclerotiger Watling in Notes from the Royal Botanic Garden, Edinburgh, 32: 130, 1972. See Figs. 140, 143, 149-151.

Icon.: none. Figs.: NRBG 32: 130, fig. 1 A-D.

CAP at first 8-22/9-11mm subglobose or ovoid,then elongate-ellipsoid or cylindric-ovoid, finally expanded 11-30mm broad with revolute margin, sometimes umbonate, pale grey or mouse-grey, darker or tinged ochraceous at centre, finally dark grey-brown, at first entirely floccose-mealy with thicker clay or ochraceous sometimes warty scales at centre, becoming smooth and striate-sulcate from margin inwards. GILLS white soon greyish then dark date-brown. STEM 55-90/ 2-3mm, (3-4mm at base), ± equal or attenuated upwards or thickened at base, pale-grey, densely floccose-pruinose especially in lower part, base white fibrillose and often with thick radiating fibrils, arising directly from a ± globose white-centred dark-brown sometimes convoluted sclerotium up to 18mm broad. SMELL strong, pleasant of fried mushrooms. SPORE-PRINT violaceous black.

SPORES dark date-brown to purplish date (9.5-)10-11/5-6.5μm (without perispore), ellipsoid-amygdaliform in side-view, ellipsoid or ellipsoid-ovoid in face-view, germ-pore central, perispore 0.5-2.5μm broad,prominent, hyaline irregular. BASIDIA 4-spored. MARGINAL CYSTIDIA globose or vesiculose, 40-80/25-45μm. FACIAL CYSTIDIA ovoid, ellipsoid or cylindric-ellipsoid, 55-140/20-40μm. CAP CUTICLE cellular. VEIL on cap of globose cells 21-70μm broad, and some ellipsoid or vesiculose cells, 11-80/8-38μm, yellowish or yellow-brown in ammonia with small diverticulae 1-1.5μm long, together with branching ± filamentous hyphae 2.5-6.5μm broad.

CLAMP-CONNECTIONS present. GENETICS unknown. OIDIA absent.

HABITAT on dung heaps or manured straw, solitary or gregarious but not caespitose. Described from Mull but probably widely distributed.

It is distinguished from all other coprophilous members of Stirps *Narcoticus* except *C. tuberosus* by growing from a sclerotium and from the latter by its more robust habit, coarse veil, larger sclerotia and spores with more voluminous perispore. It is one of several taxa probably formerly recorded as *C. stercorarius*.

60. C. stercoreus Fries, Epicrisis Systematis Mycologici, 251, 1838. See Figs. 144-146.

Syn.: *Agaricus stercorarius* Bull ex St. Amans, Flore Agenaise, 569, 1821 non *A. stercorarius* Schum. ex. Fr., Systema Mycologicum I: 291, 1821; *C. stercorarius*

(Bull. ex St. Amans) J.E. Lange sensu Kühner & Romagnesi non J.E. Lange et al. Misident.: *C. velox* Godey apud Gillet sensu van Waveren in Persoonia 5: 154, 1968.

Icon.: none. Figs.: NRBG 28: 48, figs. 2F, f, f[1]; Persoonia 7: 154, figs. 5-7, 11, 22, 23, 32, 38, 39, *velox*.

CAP at first 3-12/1-4mm ovoid or ellipsoid, then expanded 2-10mm broad, with revolute or split margin, white or whitish then pale or smoke-grey darkening to mouse- or slate-grey when mature, at first entirely white then whitish or pale grey minutely floccose mealy or scurfy-scaly, scales at centre sometimes slightly coarser and darker grey or tinged clay-buff, margin finely tomentose-fringed at first, becoming ± smooth and plicate-striate. GILLS whitish then date brown or umber, finally blackish. STEM 10-40/0.5-1mm, filiform, equal or slightly attenuated upwards, white or pale grey then hyaline, at first entirely white or very pale grey silky fibrillose-floccose or mealy-scurfy becoming smoother with age, sometimes with a denser zone of scales where cap joins stem when young, base sometimes white tomentose-strigose or more rarely slightly thickened. SMELL none to very faintly stercoraceous, strongest as cap is just opening out. SPORE-PRINT fuscous black.

SPORES umber, (6.5-)7-8(-9)/3.5-4μm, elongate-ellipsoid, cylindric-ovoid or slightly phaseoliform in side view, elongate-ellipsoid or slightly ovoid in face view, germ-pore central, apiculus small, perisporial sac none or not visible in water, though sometimes traces may be seen after treatment with acids. BASIDIA 4-spored. MARGINAL CYSTIDIA mostly globose or vesiculose, but often a few are ellipsoid or elongate-fusiform, 20-60/12-24μm. FACIAL CYSTIDIA ovoid or ellipsoid to slightly fusiform, (30-50/15-25μm) sec van Waveren. CAP CUTICLE cellular. VEIL on cap of ± globose warty-punctate minutely diverticulate cells 14-78μm broad together with some cylindric or slightly or irregularly swollen sometimes branched cells with short blunt diverticulae in places 2-5μm broad, and more especially near the cap margin some ± vesiculose cells 50-100/15-20μm. VEIL on stem of cylindric or slightly swollen minutely diverticulate sometimes branched cells 2-10μm broad and a few globose cells as on cap, and often also some vesiculose ones at stem base.

CLAMP-CONNECTIONS present. GENETICS heterothallic. OIDIA formed in dry heads in culture.

HABITAT on dung (rabbit, deer, sheep, cow or horse), especially if old and water-logged, solitary or more often gregarious. Common and authentically recorded from England, Wales and Scotland, and probably also common in Ireland.

It most closely resembles *C. cordisporus* macroscopically but differs clearly from that species in narrow elongate spores, cells of the veil with short diverticulae rather than crystalline granules, and in the smell, which however, is easily missed and not always noticeable. From the other coprophilous species of Stirps *Narcoticus* it is immediately distinguished by the small narrow spores and very small fruit-bodies. The other two species in this stirps producing small fruit-bodies *C. foetidellus* and *C. tuberosus,* both have larger spores showing at least traces of perispore, and the former has a stronger smell and the latter grows from a sclerotium and may have a stouter stem with a rooting base.

C. stercoreus is so named in this work in the belief that Fries renamed *Agaricus stercorarius* Bull. ex St. Amans in order to avoid confusion with *Agaricus stercorarius* Schum ex Fr. It is not regarded as a misprint as some would have it, but the exact identity of *A. stercorarius* Bull. ex St. Amans is still a matter of dispute.

C. velox sensu J.E. Lange (L159C) seems likely to be a different taxon with slightly larger broader spores (about 8-9/4-4.5μm) which requires further study. The identity of *C. velox* Godey apud Gillet in the original sense is not certain, so it seems best to drop this name since it cannot be established from type material.

61. C. martinii Favre ex P.D. Orton in Transactions of the British Mycological Society, 43: 201, 1960. See Figs. 158 & 166.

Icon.: none. Figs.: BSMF 53: 286; figs. 6, 7; TBMS 38: 395; fig. 14; NRBG 28: 45, fig. 2e.

CAP at first 5-22/3-8mm ovoid or cylindric, often elongate, then expanded 8-12mm broad with revolute margin, sometimes umbonate, grey, at first mealy-pulverulent, then smooth and sulcate especially in outer part. GILLS grey, then black. STEM 32-60/1.5-2mm (up to 5mm at base), equal with thickened base or attenuated upwards, pale grey, darker grey in lower part when old, hyaline, minutely silky fibrillose when fresh, base white tomentose. SMELL none. SPORE-PRINT fuscous black.

SPORES dark brick or umber, 12-16/6.5-8.5μm, (without perispore) ellipsoid slightly amygdaliform in side view, ellipsoid or ovoid in face view, germ-pore central, apiculus small but distinct, perispore sometimes fairly conspicuous and complete but usually incomplete or absent. BASIDIA 4-spored, dimorphic. MARGINAL CYSTIDIA ± cylindric fusiform (sec Favre). FACIAL CYSTIDIA cylindric-fusiform or elongate-ovoid, about 115μm long (sec Favre). CAP CUTICLE cellular. VEIL on cap of globose or vesiculose diverticulate cells 14-52μm broad, together with some narrower, branching often diverticulate hyphae.

CLAMP-CONNECTIONS present. GENETICS unknown.

HABITAT on *Carex, Scirpus* or *Juncus* debris. Probably not uncommon where suitable habitats exist. Not recorded for Ireland.

It is distinguished from the other odourless members of Stirps *Narcoticus* by the habitat and the rather large broad spores with ± inconspicuous or incomplete perispore.

The above description may need modification when further material is examined especially as regards cystidial details, which are taken from Favre's description. He collected it from dead erect stems of *Carex* near the edge of ditches in peat. British material has been collected also on both *Scirpus* and *Juncus*.

62. C. saccharomyces P.D. Orton in Transactions of the British Mycological Society, 43: 202, 1960. See Figs. 155 & 165.

Icon.: none. Figs.: TBMS 43 (1960): 202, figs, 12, 250.

CAP at first 7-15/5-7mm ovoid, then expanded-conical or obtusely umbonate with radially split and recurved margin, ± uniformly pale grey, at first minutely mealy-flocculose, sometimes with coarser or slightly darker grey or clay-buff flocci at centre, becoming grooved-striate in outer part. GILLS white soon grey then blackish. STEM 24-72/1-2mm, equal or slightly attenuated at apex, hyaline-grey or whitish, sometimes slightly darker in lower part, at first pale grey or whitish mealy flocculose like the cap, then silky flocculose to ± smooth especially in upper part, mealy floccules often persisting at the base. SMELL strong of wet yeast or beer, especially after being enclosed in a tin. SPORE-PRINT fuscous black.

SPORES umber, (14-)15-18(-20)/8-10μm, ellipsoid slightly amygdaliform in side view, ellipsoid or ovoid in face view, germ-pore central, apiculus small and often indistinct, perispore none or incomplete, very thin. BASIDIA 2-spored. MARGINAL CYSTIDIA ± sphaeropedunculate, pyriform or clavate often with long stalk, sometimes ± cylindric, 42-90/14-44μm. FACIAL CYSTIDIA elongate-fusiform or cylindric-ellipsoid, 64-90/20-44μm. CAP CUTICLE cellular. VEIL on cap of globose, ellipsoid, pyriform or vesiculose warty-punctate minutely diverticulate sometimes slightly brownish encrusted cells 23-67μm broad, together with some narrower fusiform or ± cylindric cells.

CLAMP-CONNECTIONS not observed. GENETICS unknown.

HABITAT on bare soil or in grass. So far recorded from Lanarkshire, Aberdeen-shire and New Forest, Hants, so it is probably widespread but uncommon.

This species is easily distinguished from its allies by the marked smell of yeast or beer, 2-spored basidia, terricolous habitat and very large spores with inconspicuous perispore.

SECTION III : PSEUDOCOPRINUS

Stirps 17 : Disseminatus

63. C. disseminatus (Pers. ex Fries) S.F. Gray, A Natural Arrangement of British Plants, I: 634, 1821. See Figs. 169, 178, 179 & 182.

Syn.: *Agaricus disseminatus* Pers. ex Fr., Systema Mycologicum I: 305, 1821; *Psathyrella disseminata* (Pers. ex Fr.) Quélet, Champ. Jura Vosges, 123, 1928.

Icon.: L 156 A; Bres 889[2]; Cke 641(657)B; Ri 23[4]. Figs.: Dansk Bot. Arkiv 14: 128, figs. 1, 8.

CAP 6-15mm ovoid or convex,then expanded convex or campanulate, pale buff or cream-buff then pale to slightly violaceous grey from margin inwards with buff or pale fulvous centre, entirely minutely pubescent and mealy scurfy when young, becoming smooth except for centre of cap and along the sides of the grooves, becoming plicate-striate from margin in, fragile. GILLS whitish soon grey then pale violaceous umber, finally fuscous black. STEM 15-40/0.5-2.5mm, equal or slightly thickened downwards, white or pale grey, often hyaline, sometimes tinged vinaceous-buff at base, entirely minutely pubescent when fresh, soon fragile, base white tomentose. SMELL none. SPORE-PRINT date-brown or umber. FRUIT-BODY not deliquescent.

SPORES pale brown, 7-9.5/4-5μm, ellipsoid,amygdaliform in side view, ellipsoid or slightly ovoid in face view, germ-pore central, large and truncate. BASIDIA 4-spored, tetramorphic. MARGINAL CYSTIDIA lageniform, similar to setules on cap, 60-150/15-20μm, apex obtuse 8-10μm broad. FACIAL CYSTIDIA absent. CAP CUTICLE cellular. SETULES on cap lageniform, 75-200/20-30μm, apex obtuse 8-14μm broad, hyaline or slightly encrusted at base. VEIL on cap of encrusted or ovoid cells, 10-60μm broad.

CLAMP-CONNECTIONS present. GENETICS heterothallic, probably bipolar. OIDIA absent.

HABITAT on old stumps or dead wood or on soil near buried wood. Densely gregarious, but not truly caespitose. Common throughout the British Isles.

Easily recognised by the habitat, gregarious habit and setulose scurfy fragile cap. Care must be taken to distinguish this from *Psathyrella pygmaea* (Bull. ex Fr.) Sing. which often grows with it, but which is easily separated by presence of encrusted cystidia, much smaller spores and absence of setules on cap.

64. C. silvaticus Peck in Twenty-fourth Report of the New York State Museum 71, 1871. See Figs. 172 & 181.

Syn.: *Coprinellus tardus* Karsten in Bidrag till Kännedom af Finlands Natur och Folk 32: 266, 1879; *Coprinus tardus* (Karsten) Karsten in Meddelanden of societas pro Fauna et Flora Fennica 5: 34, 1880. Misident.: *C. tergiversans* (Fries)

Fries sensu Ricken, Die Blätterpilze 63, 1915; *idem* sensu Josserand in Ann. Soc. Linn. Lyon 66: 154, 1930.

Icon.: L 160 F, tardus; Ri 22[6], tergiversans. Figs.: Ann. Soc. Linn. Lyon 76: 154, figs. A, B, *idem*; Dansk Bot. Arkiv 14: 127, figs. 1, 8; TBMS 41: 431, text-fig. 14.

CAP at first 13-30(-38)/8-18mm, ovoid or subglobose, then conico-convex or expanded-convex 25-45mm broad, cream-buff or buff usually with darker fulvous, sienna or cinnamon centre, then often greyish at margin and sometimes ± rusty-tawny at centre, apparently smooth but minutely pubescent sub lente, becoming deeply plicate-striate or grooved to centre, often with incised margin. GILLS whitish then greyish umber finally blackish. STEM 40-85/2-6mm, ± equal, white then discolouring pale buff or clay-buff especially in lower part, silky striate, apex pruinose-pubescent, lower part often becoming smooth, becoming rather fragile. SMELL none. SPORE-PRINT fuscous black. FRUIT-BODY deliquescing slowly or not at all.

SPORES dark brown to black, 11-15/7-9/8-10μm, amygdaliform or limoniform in side view, ellipsoid or ovoid in face view, germ-pore central and truncate and often prominent, ornamented with low warts or ridges to almost smooth but minutely rugulose. BASIDIA 4-spored, tetramorphic. MARGINAL CYSTIDIA vesiculose-fusiform to lageniform, 42-84/13-24μm, apex obtuse 4-8μm broad. FACIAL CYSTIDIA absent. CAP CUTICLE cellular. SETULES on cap lageniform with walls hyaline or slightly brownish, thickened and usually with neck slightly narrowed upwards, 90-180/16-25μm, apex 4-7μm. SETULES on stem similar (100-150/12-28μm sec Joss.). VEIL of scattered sphaerocysts 20-48μm broad with encrusted brownish walls.

CLAMP-CONNECTIONS present. GENETICS heterothallic, probably tetrapolar. OIDIA apparently absent (see M. Lange).

HABITAT on wood or if on soil or in leaves probably attached to buried wood. Not uncommon in England and lowland Scotland.

It is best recognised by the ± limoniform ornamented spores, together with habitat and large setules. It can easily be confused in the field with *C. micaceus,* but can readily be distinguished by inspection of spores and cap surface. The spores, as mentioned by Josserand (loc. cit.: 157, 'structure de la spore'), may appear smooth unless very carefully examined under oil immersion, when they can be seen to be very minutely rugulose.

65. C. hexagonosporus Josserand in Revue de Mycologie, Paris 13: 82, 1948. See Figs. 170, 173 & 180.

Syn.: *C. hexagonosporus f. stephanosporus* Josserand in Rev. Mycol, Paris, 13: 82, 1948.

Icon.: none. Figs.: RM 13: 82; Dansk Bot. Arkiv 14: 108, figs. 1, 9; NRBG 29: figs. lf, 2b, 3g.

CAP at first 5-15/4-8mm ± cylindric, then conical or conico-convex to expanded conical, 9-33mm broad, finally often plane or depressed with margin soon crenate and sometimes splitting or becoming slightly revolute, fawn or umber with paler greyish margin, becoming purplish date or brown-vinaceous in and around centre, when old with margin persistently greyer, apparently smooth but very minutely pubescent *sub lente,* soon furrowed radially fragile and thin and papery when old. GILLS whitish or grey then black. STEM 38-74/0.5-2mm, equal, white or hyaline while, sometimes discolouring vinaceous buff or clay-buff in lower part, very minutely pubescent like the cap, base white tomentose, very fragile. SMELL none. SPORE-PRINT dark chocolate or umber. FRUIT-BODY soon deliquescing.

SPORES blackish brown, 10.5-13.5/6-7/7-8µm lentiform, ± ellipsoid in side view, ± hexagonal in face view, sometimes with peg-like projections near the apiculus, germ-pore slightly to distinctly excentric. BASIDIA 4-spored, trimorphic. MARGINAL CYSTIDIA vesiculose to cylindric-clavate, 40-75/32-48µm. FACIAL CYSTIDIA absent or rare, 60-90/20-35µm. CAP CUTICLE cellular. SETULES on cap hyaline lageniform, 40-84/12-16µm, apex often slightly swollen 7-12µm broad. VEIL of globose or broadly ellipsoid encrusted cells 20-42µm broad (best seen on young cap).

CLAMP-CONNECTIONS present. GENETICS heterothallic, tetrapolar. OIDIA formed in moist heads in culture.

HABITAT on dung or manured straw. Distribution unknown but has occurred in Norfolk and Edinburgh; uncommon.

Macroscopically distinguishable by the purplish date mature cap which is rather like that of *C. sassii* M. Lange & A.H. Smith, which is, however, 2-spored and lacks sphaerocysts; easily recognised microscopically by the ± hexagonal spores with ± excentric germ-pore and sometimes with peg-like projections near the apiculus. Josserand named specimens producing spores with these peg-like projections forma *stephanosporus* but this appears to be a variable feature within the species. Malençon (Champ. sup. du Maroc I : 239, 1970) has recently described var. *homosetulosus* in which vesiculose cells are absent from the gill-margin and are replaced by cells similar to those on the cap.

66. C. dilectus Fries, Epicrisis Systematis Mycologici, 250, 1838. See Fig. 168.

Icon.: none. Figs.: BSMF 57: 46, fig. 2.

CAP at first 3-5/4-7mm ellipsoid or conical, then conico-expanded 10-14mm broad, rusty-tawny or brick sometimes tinged apricot, paler at margin, fading to greyish rust with more persistently rusty-tawny centre, entirely minutely adpressed scurfy-scaly when fresh, becoming ± smooth and wrinkled-sulcate to centre, but scurfiness sometimes remaining in the grooves. GILLS pale buff or slightly tinged with the colour of the cap, then grey or greyish sepia finally violaceous umber. STEM 17-32/0.5-1mm, equal or slightly thickened at the base, hyaline greyish or tinged ochraceous buff, more rarely pale rusty-tawny at base, entirely minutely whitish floccose-pruinose at first, becoming ± smooth except near base. SMELL none. SPORE-PRINT violaceous umber. FRUIT-BODY not deliquescent or only slowly.

SPORES umber, 11-13(-14)/6-7μm, ellipsoid, germ-pore central sometimes indistinct. BASIDIA 4-spored. MARGINAL CYSTIDIA vesiculose or sphaero-pedunculate to broadly lageniform, 30-80/16-28μm, neck often slightly attenuated upwards, apex obtuse 6-12μm broad. FACIAL CYSTIDIA absent. CAP CUTICLE cellular. SETULES on cap like those on stem, sometimes only visible at margin. SETULES on stem thin-walled ± lageniform with rounded or irregularly swollen base 65-124/(16-)18-24(-30)μm, neck cylindric to slightly attenuated upwards, apex obtuse 5-8μm broad. A few pyriform or vesiculose cells may also be present on stem. VEIL on cap of hyaline or encrusted sphaerocysts 16-40μm broad.

CLAMP-CONNECTIONS present. GENETICS unknown, probably heterothallic (Vandendries).

HABITAT on muddy soil. Uncommon; so far only collected from Innerhadden, Perthshire on wet peaty soil under heather.

Easily recognised by cap colour, habitat, rather large spores and presence of setules and sphaerocysts on cap. The collection from which the above description was made agrees quite well with the description given by Josserand (1941), which was also recorded from muddy soil (terre limoneuse). It is perhaps debatable whether this is really *C. dilectus* sensu Fries, and a new name may be necessary if *C. dilectus* Fries should be otherwise typified. *C. dilectus* sensu J. Lange is included in this work as *C. erythrocephalus*.

67. C. curtus Kalchbrenner in Grevillea, 9: 138, 1881. See Fig. 175.

Syn.: *C. plicatiloides* Buller in Trans. Brit. mycol. Soc., 6: 364, 1920.

Icon.: L 160 G. Figs.: Ann. Soc. Linn. Lyon 77: 109; fig. 11.

CAP at first 2-9/1-5mm ovoid, then expanded-convex or ± plane, 3-9mm broad, sometimes slightly depressed at centre, at first entirely covered by the rust, brick or rusty-tawny veil, then whitish or pale clay-buff becoming grey from margin in, at first minutely pubescent sub lente then scattered granular mealy at centre, outer part becoming grooved-sulcate to centre. GILLS very pale greyish finally black. STEM 10-40/0.35-0.8mm, equal or slightly attenuated upwards, whitish or hyaline, at first minutely pubescent then ± smooth. SMELL not known. SPORE-PRINT blackish brown. FRUIT-BODY slowly deliquescent.

SPORES brownish black, 10-11/5.5-6.2μm (sec Josserand), ellipsoid in both views, germ-pore small and not truncate. BASIDIA 4-spored. MARGINAL CYSTIDIA ± lageniform rapidly collapsing. FACIAL CYSTIDIA none. CAP CUTICLE cellular. SETULES on cap ± capitate with globose brownish base, 60-80(-100)/4-5μm, apex 6-9μm broad, base 10-20μm broad. VEIL of clusters of subglobose sometimes encrusted yellowish brown cells 13-20μm broad. (Description from Josserand and J.E. Lange)

CLAMP-CONNECTIONS absent. GENETICS heterothallic bipolar (sec Brunswick).

HABITAT on horse-dung. Seemingly rare and recorded only recently from Britain. Distribution unknown.

Readily recognised amongst species growing on dung producing very small fruit-bodies by the cap with setules and reddish-brown granular veil and regularly ellipsoid spores. The more common *C. heptemerus* has longer spores with large excentric germ-pore and dull brownish cap.

68. C. heptemerus M. Lange & A.H. Smith in Mycologia, 45: 751, 1953. See Figs. 171, 174, 176 & 177.

Syn.: *C. curtus f. macrosporus* Romagnesi in Rev. Mycol., 6: 114, 1941.

Icon.: none. Figs.: Dansk bot. Arkiv 14: 108, figs. 2, 9; NRBG 28: 44, fig. 1 G/g".

CAP at first 1-10/0.5-5mm ovoid or subcylindric, then convex or convex-expanded with margin torn or revolute, whitish or greyish with pale buff or cinnamon-buff centre, minutely granular scaly at first especially at centre, becoming wrinkled striate to centre, margin crenate. GILLS whitish or greyish then blackish. STEM 5-50/0.1-1mm (up to 2mm at base), equal or slightly sub lente when fresh. SMELL none. SPORE-PRINT violaceous black. FRUIT-BODY deliquescent.

SPORES pale brown, (11-)11.5-14.5/(5-)6-7.5μm, ellipsoid or cylindric-ellipsoid, germ-pore large (2.5-3μm or more broad) and distinctly excentric, often fully visible and not touching the profile of the spore in face-view. BASIDIA 4-spored, dimorphic. MARGINAL CYSTIDIA subglobose, ellipsoid or vesiculose, 25-50μm broad. FACIAL CYSTIDIA absent. CAP CUTICLE cellular. SETULES on cap lageniform, 50-122/9-23μm neck attenuated upwards, apex rather pointed 2.5-4μm broad, sometimes forked hyaline or encrusted at base intergrading into sphaerocysts. SETULES on stem similar 40-80/8-12μm. VEIL on cap of ± globose encrusted brownish sphaerocysts 20-45μm broad.

CLAMP-CONNECTIONS absent. GENETICS homothallic. OIDIA absent.

HABITAT on rabbit, deer, sheep or cow dung, solitary or in small groups. Not uncommon and widely distributed but easily overlooked. It has been recorded from north-west Inverness-shire southwards to Yorkshire and from Holkham dunes, Norfolk.

It is best recognised amongst other coprophilous taxa producing very small fruit-bodies by the rather large spores with markedly excentric germ-pore, together with the presence of both sphaerocysts and setules on the cap. When the veil is lost it looks much like other coprophilous species in Section *Pseudocoprinus* (eg *C. pellucidus*) and it is necessary to make careful microscopic investigation of these very small taxa before making a determination.

It was first described briefly by Romagnesi (1941) as a form of *C. curtus*, from which it differs in larger paler spores, setules with non-capitate heads and lack of reddish veil.

Stirps 18 : Ephemerus

69. C. ephemerus (Bull. ex Fries) Fries, Epicrisis Systematis Mycologici, 252, 1838. See Figs. 1-7, 188, 199, 202, 216, 217, 219 & 220.

Syn.: *Agaricus ephemerus* Bulliard ex Fries, Systema Mycologicum, I: 313, 1821.

Icon.: L 160 H; Ri 22[3]. Figs.: Dansk Bot. Arkiv 14: 111, figs. 2, 10; Ann. Soc. Linn. Lyon 77: 101, fig. 8.

CAP at first (1.5-)5-15mm high cylindric-ellipsoid or ovoid then conico-convex, finally expanded ± plane 5-10(-20)mm broad with margin torn or revolute, whitish or grey with cream, buff, fulvous or cinnamon centre, then grey or drab sometimes with pale centre, pellucid-striate then plicate-sulcate in outer part. GILLS greyish then black, STEM 40-70/0.5-2mm, equal or slightly thickened at base (up to 3mm broad), white, minutely pubescent when young then ± smooth, base white tomentose or strigose. SMELL none. SPORE-PRINT fuscous black. FRUIT-BODY strongly deliquescent.

SPORES dark brown, (10.5-)11.5-15.5/(5.5-)6-7.5(-8.5)μm, ellipsoid slightly amygdaliform in side view, ellipsoid or slightly ovoid in face view, germ-pore excentric, BASIDIA 4-spored, dimorphic. MARGINAL CYSTIDIA vesiculose or subglobose, subcylindric or lageniform, 20-60/(15-)20-30μm. FACIAL CYSTIDIA vesiculose 60-120/25-45μm. CAP CUTICLE cellular. SETULES on cap hyaline, lageniform with tapering neck, 40-100/9-18μm, apex fairly acute 2.5-5μm broad.

CLAMP-CONNECTIONS present. GENETICS heterothallic, bipolar. OIDIA in moist heads in culture.

HABITAT on old cow or horse dung, or straw and dung mixtures. Widespread and not uncommon in Great Britain. Owing to confusion with related taxa, past records should be treated with caution.

It differs from other members of Stirps *Ephemerus* (except *C. congregatus*) in possessing abundant facial cystidia, rather large spores with excentric germ-pore, rather long hyaline setules, and not growing on fresh dung. *C. congregatus* is most often caespitose, has a paler cap, and grows on compost, silage or kitchen refuse as well as mixtures of dung and straw.

70. C. bisporus J. Lange in Dansk Botanisk Arkiv 2 (1915): 50. See Figs. 205 & 210.

Syn.: *C. ephemerus* var. *bisporus* (J. Lange) Konrad & Maublanc, Icones Selectae Fungorum, 6: 71, 1928.

Icon.: L 160 E. Figs.: Dansk Bot. Arkiv 14: 115; figs. 2, 11; NRBG 28: 39; figs. 1a, a'.

CAP at first 5-16mm high ellipsoid or convex, then expanded up to 20mm, pale fulvous at centre, white or whitish in outer part, darkening very little with age, appearing smooth at first but very minutely pubescent sub lente, then hoary, outer part becoming sulcate striate. GILLS white or pale buff at first then violaceous black. STEM 30-80/1-1.5mm (2-6mm at base), attenuated upwards from slightly to distinctly swollen base, frequently rooting and then often joined either above or below the surface of the substrate to stems of other fruit-bodies, white or whitish, minutely pubescent when fresh. SMELL none or faint, pleasant. SPORE-PRINT fuscous black. FRUIT-BODY deliquescent.

SPORES dark brown, 9.5-14.5/5.5-7.5μm, ellipsoid-amygdaliform in side view, elongate-ellipsoid in face view, germ-pore distinctly excentric in side view. MARGINAL CYSTIDIA vesiculose, 30-50/20-25μm. FACIAL CYSTIDIA absent. CAP CUTICLE cellular. SETULES on cap hyaline, subcylindrical with slightly to distinctly swollen base, thin-walled, 60-120/10-20μm, apex obtuse 5-7.5μm broad. SETULES on stem similar. VEIL absent.

CLAMP-CONNECTIONS absent. GENETICS homothallic. OIDIA present in moist heads.

HABITAT subfasciculate on dung, or mixture of dung and straw or soil. Probably widespread and not uncommon. Recorded from England and Scotland.

This species is very similar macroscopically to *C. congregatus,* especially in colour, but that species is 4-spored, has rather shorter, narrower setules on the cap and facial cystidia are present though not numerous and it also differs in habitat, not being found on pure dung and sometimes occurring on rotting vegetable refuse of other kinds. *C. sassii* (not yet recorded in Britain) is also 2-spored but has the cap soon brown-vinaceous and much larger spores 13-20/8-11μm. *C. ephemerus* besides being 4-spored differs in reddish brown (cinnamon) or sepia cap and in possessing numerous facial cystidia.

Other two-spored taxa exist in Section *Pseudocoprinus* (eg.*C. bisporiger*) and it should not be assumed that all 2-spored collections must necessarily be placed in *C. bisporus* or *C. sassii.*

71. C. congregatus (Bulliard ex St Amans) Fries, Epicrisis Systematis Mycologici, 249, 1838. See Figs. 186, 213 & 214.

Syn.: *Agaricus congregatus* Bulliard ex St Amans, Flore Agenaise,: 568, 1821.

Icon.: none. Figs.: Dansk Bot. Arkiv 14: 111, figs. 2, 11; NRBG 28: 40 figs, 1c, c'.

CAP at first (2-)5-20mm high, cylindric or elongate-ellipsoid, then expanded convex, cream-ochraceous or buff with paler margin becoming slate grey from margin inwards, appearing polished smooth when young but minutely pubescent sub lente, becoming matt and sulcate-striate almost to centre. GILLS pale buff then purplish date or brown-vinaceous, finally blackish. STEM 20-80/0.5-5mm, attenuated upwards from slightly swollen base, frequently somewhat rooting and joined to stems of other fruit-bodies to form a clump, pubescent becoming smooth. SMELL pleasant. SPORE-PRINT fuscous black. FRUIT-BODY deliquescent.

SPORES dark brown tinged olivaceous or sepia, 12-14/6-7μm, elongate ellipsoid, germ-pore slightly excentric. BASIDIA 4-spored, di- or tri-morphic. MARGINAL CYSTIDIA subglobose, ellipsoid, ovoid or vesiculose, 30-70/20-30μm. FACIAL CYSTIDIA vesiculose, 70-120/22-50μm. CAP CUTICLE cellular. SETULES on cap hyaline, subcylindric with swollen base to ± lageniform, 48-106/7.5-17μm with obtuse apex 4.5-12μn broad. SETULES at stem apex similar. VEIL absent.

CLAMP-CONNECTIONS absent. GENETICS heterothallic, bipolar. OIDIA formed in moist heads in culture.

HABITAT on rotten straw, compost, silage, kitchen refuse or mixtures of dung and soil or straw. Usually caespitose. Probably widespread but distribution unknown.

It is distinguished from other species of Stirps *Ephemerus* by the caespitose habit, 4-spored basidia, presence of facial cystidia, spore size and excentric germ-pore. It does not occur on pure dung, but a taxon similar both macro- and microscopically has been found on rabbit pellets, though it is not caespitose. Further observations are required on this taxon to ascertain its status, particularly by interfertility tests.

C. ephemerus also has facial cystidia and spores with excentric germ-pore but is less robust and not caespitose and grows on old dung or mixtures of dung and straw.

72. C. pellucidus Karsten in Meddelanden af Societas pro Fauna et Flora Fennica 9: 61, 1882. See Figs. 187 & 198.

Icon.: none. Figs.: Dansk bot. Arkiv 14: 116, figs. 3, 12; TBMS 40: 273, fig. 8.

CAP at first 0.5-8/1-4mm conico-convex, then expanded 2-9mm broad, whitish with cinnamon or date-brown centre and striae, to completely cinnamon, brick or tawny date-brown, becoming grey from margin inwards, minutely pubescent sub lente, outer part becoming striate-sulcate and splitting radially. GILLS whitish then fuscous black. STEM 8-50/0.2-1.5mm, filiform, equal or slightly thickened at base, whitish to pale buff or vinaceous-buff, hyaline, minutely white pruinose sub lente when fresh. SMELL none. SPORE-PRINT dark umber or date-brown. FRUIT-BODY deliquescing rather slowly.

SPORES reddish brown (7-)8-10(-11)/(3.5-)4-5μm, cylindric-ellipsoid, more rarely slightly phaseoliform, germ-pore central and truncate sometimes not very well marked, apiculus often indistinct, BASIDIA 4-spored, di- or trimorphic. MARGINAL CYSTIDIA vesiculose 12-40μm broad or lageniform, 20-30/10-12μm with ± acute apex. FACIAL CYSTIDIA absent. CAP CUTICLE cellular. SETULES on cap hyaline, lageniform, 35-70/8-14μm, with neck attenuated upwards to a ± acute apex 3-5μm broad. SETULES on stem similar, 38-80/9-14(-16)μm. VEIL absent.

CLAMP-CONNECTIONS absent. GENETICS homothallic. OIDIA in dry heads in culture.

HABITAT on dung (especially cow), solitary or gregarious. Common throughout the British Isles.

Readily distinguished amongst the coprophilous species of Section *Pseudocoprinus* by the narrow spores, rather acute setules and absence of facial cystidia and veil. *C. stellatus* sensu M. Lange differs in broader spores and presence of facial cystidia. In both taxa the cap may split radially with age, so this is hardly a character of any taxonomic significance. Further investigations are necessary to show whether *C. stellatus* sensu Buller is distinct from *C. pellucidus* or not.

M. Lange (1952) suggested further study of this species is required to see whether differences in length of spores and setules on the cap can be correlated with cap colour or abundance of setules on the cap and so indicate different taxonomic units. A taxon with rather larger fruit-bodies and brighter 'orange tawny' cap centre possesses clamp connections and produces wet oidia in culture. Its status remains to be investigated.

73. C. stellatus Buller apud Bisby, Buller and Dearness, Fungi of Manitoba, 119, 1929. See Fig. 189.

Icon.: none. Figs. none.

CAP at first 5-10/4-5mm conico-cylindric, then expanded conical with margin slightly recurved and splitting stellately into 12-16 rays, yellowish white with bay-brown centre becoming grey in outer part, minutely setulose sub lente. GILLS white then greyish. STEM 40-70/1-2mm attenuated upwards, bay-brown below, whitish upwards, minutely white pruinose (tufts of setules). FLESH thin except at cap centre where it is brown. FRUIT-BODY strongly deliquescent.

SPORES 8-10/4-5μm, ellipsoid. BASIDIA dimorphic. MARGINAL and FACIAL CYSTIDIA cylindrical, 130-170/20-26μm. SETULES on cap pointed, 40-50μm long, the projecting part 5-10μm broad.

HABITAT on horse-dung balls in laboratory cultures.

This description is from Buller (1929). *C. stellatus* sensu M. Lange (Dansk) Bot. Arkiv. 14 (1952): 115, figs. 3, 12) appears to differ as follows: spores broader (8-)9-12(13)/(4.5-)5-6(-6.5)μm, cap paler, 'pale clay colour' to 'tawny olive', centre 'brownish alutaceous', facial cystidia vesiculose, 70-130/17-40µm. What is believed to be M. Lange's taxon has been grown in the laboratory from dung samples collected in this country but adequate fresh material must be collected in the field and described before it can be validly named.

Material agreeing in all respects with M. Lange's description (Fig. 189), has been collected at Kindrogan in Perthshire on cow dung. The pileocystidia were hyaline except for faint hint of brown at base, acuminate and 50-55 (-66.5)   x 8.5-10(-13.3)µm; spores were 8.3 - 10 x 4.5-5.5µm, moderately broad in face view and very faintly amygdaliform in side view.

Authentic *C. stellatus* with spores 8-10/4-5µm may well exist in this country but it too must be collected in the field before it can be compared with *C. pellucidus.* Lange's fungus is homothallic and this may well explain the difference between N. American & European collections.

74. C. heterosetulosus [Locquin ex] Watling in Notes of the Royal Botanic Garden, Edinburgh 35; 153, 1976. See Figs. 187, 215-218.

Syn.: (not validly published, no latin description): *C. heterosetulosus* Locquin in Bull. Soc. Mycol. Fr. 63: 78, 1947.

Icon.: none. Figs.: BSMF 63: 78 figs. 2, 3; Dansk bot. Arkiv 14: 113, figs. 3, 10.

CAP at first 2-7mm high, globose or ellipsoid then conico-convex or conico-expanded, cigar-brown, date-brown, umber or bay with paler ± rust then dark grey margin, apparently smooth but minutely and densely pubescent sub lente, then hoary and plicate or sulcate-striate in outer part. GILLS pale ochraceous buff or vinaceous buff then fuscous black. STEM 15-45/0.2-1mm, equal or thickened downwards, white or whitish hyaline, sometimes tinged with colour of cap at base, minutely whitish pubescent when fresh. SMELL none. SPORE-PRINT black. FRUIT-BODY deliquescent.

SPORES dark red brown, 9.5-11(-12)/5.5-6.5(-7)µm, ellipsoid, slightly amygdali-form in side view, ellipsoid or slightly ovoid in face view, germ-pore slightly excentric. BASIDIA 4-spored, trimorphic. MARGINAL CYSTIDIA ± globose, more rarely lageniform, 15-30µm broad. FACIAL CYSTIDIA absent. CAP CUTICLE cellular. SETULES on cap ranging from thin-walled narrowly lageniform hyaline rarely slightly thick-walled at base, 60-105(-125)/10.5-13.5(-21)µm, apex obtuse 3-6(-9)µm broad thick-walled brownish, subcylindric with slightly swollen base 23-50/6-8µm. VEIL absent.

CLAMP-CONNECTIONS present. GENETICS homothallic and   tetrapolar (M. Lange). OIDIA present in culture.

HABITAT on cow, horse or goat dung, especially when old and washed out, or mixtures of straw and dung. Probably uncommon. Distribution unknown but recorded from various localities in Scotland.

91

This species has probably been overlooked in the past, but is readily recognisable by the spores of moderate size and presence of thin and thick-walled setules although the latter may be few in numbers. It was described by Locquin (1947) without a latin description; validation could not be carried out with the original material therefore suitable British material was chosen. It has been suggested that this is *C. ephemerus* sensu Josserand (Ann. Soc. Linn. Lyon 77: 101 1933), but this cannot be so as Josserand clearly described facial cystidia and rather larger spores; he makes no mention of thick-walled setules.

Stirps 19 : Hiascens

75. C. hiascens (Fries) Quélet, Flore Mycologique de la France, 42, 1888. See Figs. 185, 197, 207 & 208.

Syn.: *Agaricus hiascens* Fries, Systema mycologicum, I: 303, 1821 *Psathyrella hiascens* (Fries) Quélet, Les Champignons du Jura et des Vosges (1872): 123. Misident.: *P. crenata* (Lasch) Gillet sensu Rea, British Basidiomycetae (1922): 422.

Icon.: L 157 C. Figs.: Dansk Bot. Arkiv 14: 126, figs. 6, 16.

CAP at first 5-25/5-15mm convex to cylindric-ovoid, then expanded-convex 6-25mm broad, at first clay-buff often with fulvous, cinnamon or pale date-brown centre, then grey, apparently smooth but minutely pubescent sub lente at first, becoming wrinkled striate to centre, often thin and papery when old. GILLS whitish or greyish then pale purplish date, finally blackish. STEM 20-60/0.5-3mm, equal, often with slightly bulbous base, white then hyaline, entirely minutely pruinose when fresh, base white tomentose. SMELL none. SPORE-PRINT dark umber or date-brown. FRUIT-BODY slowly deliquescent.

SPORES umber, (8-)9-11(-12)/(4.2-)4.5-5.5μm, ellipsoid-amygdaliform in side view, rather narrowly ellipsoid or ovoid in face view, germ-pore central, truncate and rather broad. BASIDIA 4-spored, tetramorphic. MARGINAL CYSTIDIA ± lageniform, 25-75/12-18μm, apex acute, 4-7μm broad. FACIAL CYSTIDIA absent. CAP CUTICLE cellular. SETULES on cap hyaline or slightly brownish at base, elongate-lageniform with long neck attenuated upwards, to subcylindric with slightly swollen base and often slightly attenuated apex, (60)80-150/15-20μm apex obtuse or slightly acute 5-8μm broad. SETULES on stem similar, 80-130/14-26μm, apex 6-10μm broad. VEIL absent.

CLAMP-CONNECTIONS present. GENETICS heterothallic, tetrapolar. OIDIA in moist heads in culture.

HABITAT on soil or in grass, often along rides or near paths, solitary or more often caespitose in small groups. Not uncommon and recorded from England, Scotland and Ireland.

It is best recognised by the often caespitose habit, habitat, rather narrow ellipsoid-amygdaliform spores with broad truncate germ-pore and long setules on the cap.

It is one of the less deliquescent species of Section *Pseudocoprinus* and therefore looks rather like a *Psathyrella* at times. *C. impatiens* and *C. silvaticus* are both usually larger and the former is often solitary and has broader spores, whilst the latter has larger spores with low warts or ridges.

76. C. impatiens (Fries) Quélet, Flore Mycologique de la France 42, 1888. See Figs. 192 & 202.

Syn.: *Agaricus impatiens* Fries, Systema Mycologicum, I: 302, 1821; *Psathyrella impatiens* (Fries) Kühner in Bull. Soc. Myc. Fr. 52: 33, 1936.

Icon.: L 156 B: KM 38'. Figs.: Dansk Bot. Arkiv 14: 126, figs. 6, 15.

CAP 18-4mm broad, convex or ovoid then expanded ± plane, sometimes slightly umbonate, fawn or cinnamon, soon paler from margin in, drying whitish or grey in outer part, striate when moist, soon strongly sulcate to centre, often thin and papery when old. GILLS pale clay-buff or pale drab then drab or pale sepia. STEM 70-100/2-4mm, equal or slightly thickened at base, white, apex white flocculose, remainder minutely white pruinose when fresh, soon ± silky striate. SMELL none. SPORE-PRINT dark umber or date-brown. FRUIT-BODY not or hardly deliquescent but becoming fragile.

SPORES umber, 9-12/5-6µm, ellipsoid or slightly ellipsoid-amygdaliform in side-view, ellipsoid or ovoid in face-view, germ-pore central and often rounded. BASIDIA 4-spored, tetramorphic. MARGINAL CYSTIDIA subglobose, 20-35µm broad, or lageniform, 36-64/10-15µm, apex often rather acute 3-5µm broad. FACIAL CYSTIDIA absent. CAP CUTICLE cellular. SETULES on cap hyaline or slightly brownish below, ± lageniform, gradually or abruptly thickened towards base (50-)70-120/8-14µm, apex rather acute 2-4.5µm broad. SETULES on stem similar. VEIL absent.

CLAMP-CONNECTIONS present. GENETICS heterothallic, tetrapolar. OIDIA in moist heads in culture.

HABITAT on soil or in leaves (especially beech) in woods or shady places, often solitary. Not uncommon, at least in southern England.

This is one of the less deliquescent members of this genus, but is only likely to be confused with *C. silvaticus,* which is often caespitose and has larger spores with low warts or ridges. It is recognised by the relatively large size of the fruit-bodies, habitat and the ± acute setules. *C. hiascens* is usually ± caespitose and has narrower spores, as well as producing smaller fruit-bodies.

77. C. callinus M. Lange & A.H. Smith in Mycologia, 45: 770, 1953. See Fig. 196.

Misident.: *C. hiascens* (Fries) Quélet sensu Romagnesi in Rev. Mycol. Paris, 4: 119, 1941.

Icon.: none. Figs.: RM 6: 119, fig. 5, hiascens; Dansk Bot. Arkiv 14: 122, figs. 5, 14.

CAP at first 6-16/4-9mm narrowly ellipsoid or ovoid, then expanded-convex or sometimes conical 10-20mm broad, pale ochraceous buff or cream-buff with rusty-tawny, umber, bay or date-brown centre, becoming greyish from margin inwards, appearing smooth, but minutely pubescent sub lente, becoming wrinkled or sulcate then grooved-striate from the often ± crenate margin inwards. GILLS whitish or greyish then dark umber or date-brown, becoming ± remote. STEM 25-65/0.5-2mm, equal or attenuated upwards, white then hyaline whitish or grey, minutely pubescent when fresh, base white tomentose or strigose. SMELL none. SPORE-PRINT dark umber or date-brown. FRUIT-BODY deliquesces slowly or not at all.

SPORES umber, 9-11/5-6μm, ellipsoid or slightly amygdaliform in side view, ellipsoid or ovoid in face view, germ-pore slightly to distinctly excentric. BASIDIA 4-spored, tetramorphic. MARGINAL CYSTIDIA globose, vesiculose or ellipsoid to broadly pyriform, 26-80/20-44μm. FACIAL CYSTIDIA absent. CAP CUTICLE cellular. SETULES on cap hyaline or slightly brownish or thick-walled at base, lageniform or ± swollen at base with long tapered neck, 77-140(-180)/10-22μm, with ± acute apex 3-8μm broad. SETULES on stem similar but rather shorter, 50-110/12-20μm, apex from rather obtuse to ± acute 5-10μm broad. VEIL absent.

CLAMP-CONNECTIONS present. GENETICS heterothallic, tetrapolar.

HABITAT on soil or humus in damp places, occasionally attached to sticks, solitary or gregarious or in small clumps. Not uncommon and widespread in suitable localities, such as edges of ponds or lakes or damp hollows or in fenland.

Recognised among other members of Stirps *Hiascens* by habitat in damp places, long ± acute setules on the cap, moderate sized spores and globose or vesiculose marginal cystidia. M. Lange describes two intersterile groups within this species. He claims that the grouping correlates size of fruit body with presence or absence of thick-walled setules on the cap, and may indicate two closely related taxa. No such thick-walled setules have been reported in British material as yet, though some have been seen to be slightly thick-walled at the base. This problem requires further study.

78. C. angulatus Peck in Twenty-sixth Annual Report of the New York State Museum, 60, 1874. See Fig. 195.

Syn.: *C. boudieri* Quélet in Bull. Soc. Bot. Fr., 24: 321, 1877.

Icon.: KM 37[2], boudieri; Ri 22[2], idem; BSMF 54: 122 with Fig. 127 and Pl. 2. Figs.: Dansk. Bot. Arkiv 14: 117, figs. 1, 7.

CAP at first 4-25/5-20mm conico-cylindric, cylindric-ellipsoid, convex or broadly ovoid, then campanulate or expanded-convex 10-30mm broad, rusty tawny, umber or bay, sometimes deep chestnut at centre, then brick or cinnamon with fulvous or grey outer part, sometimes appearing shiny and smooth but minutely pubescent sub lente, margin pellucid-striate becoming split and sulcate. GILLS pale cream or grey then black. STEM 10-60/1-3mm, equal or attenuated upwards, white or whitish, minutely pruinose-striate, when fresh, base sometimes slightly thickened or white tomentose. SMELL none. SPORE-PRINT black. FRUIT-BODY strongly deliquescent.

SPORES fuscous black, 8.5-11/5-6.5/6.5-8.5μm, lentiform, ellipsoid slightly amygdaliform in side view, ± mitriform in face view, germ-pore central, truncate and 2.5-4μm broad, apiculus sometimes indistinct. BASIDIA 4-spored, trimorphic. MARGINAL CYSTIDIA either subglobose, vesiculose, or pyriform 15-38μm broad, or ± lageniform 25-55/100-16μm with apex 3.5μm broad. FACIAL CYSTIDIA vesiculose to elongate ellipsoid, 55-180/30-70μm. CAP CUTICLE cellular. SETULES on cap thin or thick-walled, hyaline or brownish, ± lageniform, 30-100(-117)/(7-)12-16(-23)μm, apex acute or obtuse 3-9μm broad. SETULES on stem similar, 25-85/10-20μm. VEIL absent.

CLAMP-CONNECTIONS present but few in number. GENETICS heterothallic, tetrapolar. OIDIA present in culture, although variable in quantity.

HABITAT on burnt ground or charred wood, solitary or gregarious. Not uncommon; widely distributed in Great Britain and probably also in Ireland.

Very distinct by habitat and spore shape. As yet amongst British species only *C. episcopalis* (Section *Coprinus*: Stirps *Picaceus*) has similar spores and this differs in habitat, cap cuticle and in possessing a filamentous veil and may well be the taxon mentioned by Josserand (BSMF 60: 16 (1944)) as being another species of *Coprinus* with similar spore but possessing a veil and a different habitat.

79. C. plagioporus Romagnesi in Revue de Mycologie, Paris, 6: 121, 1941. See Fig. 206.

Icon.: none. Figs.: RM 6: 121, fig. 6; Dansk Bot. Arkiv 14: 118, figs. 4, 13.

CAP at first 4-12/3-5mm ovoid or ellipsoid, then convex or conico-convex 10-15mm broad, before expanding whitish with ± cinnamon centre, then greyish or vinaceous buff to greyish milky-coffee, often with persistent brownish tinge at centre, outer part soon plicate-striate. GILLS white soon grey then chocolate or umber, finally blackish. STEM 20-60/0.5-1mm, equal or slightly thickened at base, white or whitish, sometimes hyaline when old, minutely pruinose when fresh, base white silky floccose. SMELL none. SPORE-PRINT fuscous black. FRUIT-BODY deliquescing slowly in humid conditions.

SPORES umber, 10.5-13.5/5.5-7μm, ellipsoid or ellipsoid-amygdaliform in side-view, ellipsoid or slightly ovoid in face view, germ-pore rounded and excentric, sometimes not touching the profile in face view. BASIDIA 4-spored, tetramorphic. MARGINAL CYSTIDIA vesiculose to elongate pyriform,14-38μm broad. FACIAL CYSTIDIA not noted (vesiculose 25-50μm broad, sec Romagnesi). CAP CUTICLE cellular. SETULES on cap hyaline, lageniform, mostly subcapitate, 60-100/

14-22μm, apex 7-12μm broad, obtuse. SETULES on stem similar, 50-90/10-16μm, apex 7-10μm broad. VEIL absent.

CLAMP-CONNECTIONS not seen. GENETICS amphithallic, tetrapolar (sec M. Lange).

HABITAT on soil or mud in damp places (sometimes attached to sticks, sec M. Lange), solitary or in small groups. Seemingly uncommon; so far only recorded from Norfolk.

Recognised from other non-coprophilous species of Section *Pseudocoprinus* by habitat, subcapitate setules and fairly large spore with excentric germ-pore. No doubt the above description may need some modifications when more material has been collected and carefully studied.

80. C. subdisseminatus M. Lange in Mycologia, 45: 777, 1953. See Figs. 183, 201, 203 & 204.

Syn.: *Pseudocoprinus subdisseminatus* (M. Lange) McKnight & Allison in Morris Arb. Bull., 20: 75, 1969.

Icon.: none. Figs.: Dansk Bot. Arkiv 14: 125, figs. 6, 16; NRBG 28: 51, figs. 3A.

CAP at first 3-8mm high convex or ovoid, then expanded-convex but not becoming revolute, pale buff to cinnamon, becoming grey in outer part, sulcate-striate to centre, minutely pubescent sub lente. GILLS pale vinaceous-buff then date-brown, STEM 35-45/0.4-1.5mm, white then hyaline, at first slightly fibrillose. SMELL none. SPORE-PRINT dark date-brown, FRUIT-BODY not or hardly deliquescing.

SPORES date-brown tinged slightly sepia, 9-12(-12.5)/5-6(-6.5)μm, ellipsoid or slightly ovoid, germ-pore central or more often subcentral, BASIDIA 4-spored, trimorphic. MARGINAL CYSTIDIA subcylindric or broadly lageniform, 30-75/11-20μm, apex obtuse 7-12μm broad. FACIAL CYSTIDIA absent. CAP CUTICLE cellular. SETULES on cap subcylindric or slightly swollen at base, 60-120/10-22μm, apex obtuse 7.5-15μm broad. VEIL absent. SMELL of ink.

CLAMP-CONNECTIONS present. GENETICS heterothallic, tetrapolar. OIDIA present although rare in culture.

HABITAT on leaves, sticks and other plant debris in damp places, solitary or in small troops, not usually fasciculate. Uncommon, distribution unknown, but recorded from Edinburgh, Hertfordshire and Staffordshire, and may well be wide-spread.

It is best recognised amongst other species of Stirps *Hiascens* by the habitat, small fruit-bodies, absence of facial cystidia and cap setules with broad obtuse apex. Macroscopically it resembles single specimens of *C. disseminatus* but that species differs in growing densely crowded on or about wood and has smaller ellipsoid-amygdaliform spores and sphaerocysts on the cap.

81. C. subimpatiens M. Lange & A.H. Smith in Mycologia, 45: 772, 1953. See Fig. 194.

Icon.: none. Figs.: Dansk Bot. Arkiv 14: 123, figs. 5, 14, 15.

CAP at first 15-23mm high cylindric or ellipsoid, then expanded conico-campanulate, whitish, ochraceous or buff with cinnamon or rusty tawny centre, becoming grey from margin inwards and plicate-striate to the centre, margin some-times splitting. GILLS white becoming black. STEM 25-100/1.5-3mm, equal. white, minutely setulose-pubescent when fresh, base loosely fibrillose. SMELL none. SPORE-PRINT black. FRUIT-BODY not or hardly deliquescing.

SPORES dark date-brown to fuscous black, 9.3-13.5/5.7-7.1μm ((10-)11-13/6.5-7.5μm in British collection), ellipsoid slightly amygdaliform in side view, ellipsoid or ovoid in face view, germ-pore subcentral to distinctly excentric. BASIDIA 4-spored, tetramorphic. MARGINAL CYSTIDIA vesiculose up to 50μm broad, or $\pm$ lageniform, 25-85/10-18μm, apex 5-7μm broad. FACIAL CYSTIDIA vesiculose to cylindric ellipsoid 26-38μm broad. CAP CUTICLE cellular. SETULES on cap hyaline or slightly brownish at base, lageniform, 62-110/9-17μm, apex obtuse 5.5-8.5μm broad. Shorter subcylindric thick-walled brownish setules some-times also present.

CLAMP-CONNECTIONS present. GENETICS heterothallic, tetrapolar.

Description from M. Lange and A.H. Smith

HABITAT on soil or humus, solitary, gregarious or subcaespitose. Distribution unknown, but recorded from Kew Green, Surrey.

It resembles *C. impatiens* most closely, but is not quite so large and has broader spores with $\pm$ excentric germ-pore. From other terrestrial members of section *Pseudocoprinus* it can be distinguished by possessing facial cystidia as well as two sorts of marginal cystidia (vesiculose and lageniform), broad spores, and rather obtuse cap-setules.

82. C. bisporiger Buller ex P.D. Orton. Notes from the Royal Botanic Garden, Edinburgh. See Fig. 200.

Syn.: *C. bisporiger* Buller in Trans. Br. mycol. Soc. 3: 350, 1911; nomen nudum (as *C. bisporigera*) Misident.: *C. bisporus* J.E. Lange sensu Buller in Trans. Br. mycol. Soc., 6: 363, 1920.

Icon.: none. Figs.: Buller, Researches on Fungi II (1922): 315, fig. 106.

CAP 5-12mm high and broad, pallid or ochraceous then greyish hyaline ovate-conical, then revolute and radially sulcate up to the disc which remains prominent, covered with erect, minute hairs, 45-120/12-24μm. STEM 3-8cm/1-3mm, white, equal, strigose at the base. GILLS white, then blackish, adnexed; narrow, 2mm wide. FLESH white, ochraceous under the pellicle of the pileus, thin except at the disc.

SPORES purplish brown in the mass, dark brown under the microscope, oval or oblong elliptical, 12-14/6-7μm; BASIDIA broadly ovate, 8-10μm in diameter, with 2 sterigmata. CYSTIDIA inflated, ovate, 80-90/45-55μm.

HABITAT on sticks Kew, Surrey.

Buller's description of 1920 is quoted verbatim for lack of any other description. The type material is in quite good condition, 2-spored basidia can be found and spores drawn from it are 12.5-15/6.5-8μm, ellipsoid-amygdaliform in side view, ellipsoid or slightly ovoid in face-view with ± central germ-pore. Another collection from the same place dated 2 Sep 1911 is stated on the packet to have yellow hairs on the cap and stem. These collections were gathered from sticks taken from a pond then dumped on the ground beside it, after which the fruit bodies appeared.

Buller confused this with *C. bisporus* J.E. Lange no doubt because it had 2-spored basidia, but did not realise the significance of the difference in habitat. It seemingly differs also in the presence of thick-walled setules. A good modern description awaits the collection of adequate fresh material.

A collection from Madehurst, W. Sussex, on the ground between beech trunk and buttresses and labelled '*C. sclerocystidiosus* 2-spored form' seems likely to be the same, for it has similarly shaped although slightly smaller spores (10.5-)11.5-14/ (5.5-)6-7.5μm and thick-walled setules about 120/6μm. Even so one must beware of thinking that any *Coprinus* of this type which is 2-spored and growing on or near wood must necessarily be *C. bisporiger*.

Stirps 20 : Auricomus

83. C. auricomus Patouillard, Tabulae Analyticae Fungorum, 5: 200, 1886. See Figs. 230 & 231.

Icon.: none. Figs.: BSMF 50: 53; figs. 1, 2; *idem:* 60, fig. 5.

CAP at first 12-16/12-13mm ovoid or broadly ellipsoid, then expanded ± plane 15-30mm broad, sometimes slightly papillate, centre not becoming depressed, rusty tawny, chestnut or bay then ± cinnamon or sienna with often persistently darker centre, then greyish in outer part, smooth and shiny at first, outer part becoming grooved-striate, margin sometimes crenate. GILLS whitish then clay-buff, soon umber or dark date-brown, finally fuscous black, becoming remote but not separated from stem by a collar. STEM 45-75/1.5-2.5mm, attenuated upwards or ± equal, base sometimes slightly swollen or interruptedly silky striate, base slightly white tomentose. SMELL none. SPORE-PRINT fuscous black. FRUIT-BODY deliquescent when old.

SPORES fuscous black, 10-13(-14)/6-7(-8)/7-7.5μm (sec Kühner & Josserand), ellipsoid or slightly amygdaliform in side view, ellipsoid or slightly ovoid in face view, germ-pore central. BASIDIA 4-spored, polymorphic. MARGINAL CYSTIDIA pyriform, vesiculose or broadly obtusely lageniform, 24-64/8-20μm, apex 4-8μm when lageniform. FACIAL CYSTIDIA lageniform or fusiform-lageniform, 70-130/ 20-38μm apex ca. 18-20μm. CAP CUTICLE cellular. SETAE on cap long, narrow, flexuose, acute, with ± fulvous or sienna walls progressively thicker towards base, 100-350/3-6(-10)μm apex 2-3μm broad, most numerous in centre of cap. VEIL absent.

CLAMP-CONNECTIONS present. GENETICS heterothallic, tetrapolar (Quintanilha).

HABITAT on soil, singly or in small groups, often appearing early (May to July), Infrequently recorded in England perhaps because of its early appearance.

It is easily recognised by the long thick-walled setae on the cap. It differs from many other members of section *Pseudocoprinus* in its terrestrial habitat, rather robust habit and dark cap colours.

Some authors quote *C. hansenii* J.E. Lange (Dansk Botanisk Arkiv 2: 48, (1915)) as a synonym. This seems doubtful for Lange clearly states 'surface of cap without setulae' for *C. hansenii*, which is best regarded as a different species awaiting re-discovery and clarification (Icon: L 160 B). Lange was surely too good an observer to miss setae as distinct as those of *C. auricomus*.

Stirps 21 : Hemerobius

84. C. hemerobius Fries, Epicrisis Systematis Mycologici,: 253, 1838 (sensu J. Lange non Ricken). See Fig. 221.

Icon.: L 160 C.

CAP at first about 10mm high ovoid, then ± convex but not expanding fully, ochraceous or buff with centre tinged fulvous, smooth but atomate when dry, becoming radially split at margin and grooved almost to centre. GILLS greyish then blackish. STEM 15-50/1-2mm, equal or slightly thickened towards apex, whitish, smooth. SMELL none. SPORE-PRINT dark umber. FRUIT-BODY hardly deliquescent.

SPORES date-brown, 11.5-12.5/6.5-7/7-8μm, not or only slightly lentiform, ellipsoid-amygdaliform in side view, ellipsoid in face view, germ-pore central. BASIDIA 4-spored. MARGINAL CYSTIDIA inflated flask-shaped with broad neck (sec J. Lange). FACIAL CYSTIDIA not seen. CAP CUTICLE cellular, of globose or vesiculose cells 20-40μm broad. VEIL absent.

CLAMP-CONNECTIONS present or not. GENETICS not tested. OIDIA in moist heads in culture.

HABITAT in grass by footpaths, in copses and shady places, solitary. Not common but authentically recorded from England and Scotland. Owing to confusion with related taxa, past records should be treated with caution. This description may need modification when further fresh material has been examined.

When young it looks much like *C. plicatilis* but differs from this in that the cap does not expand fully and in having spores that are only slightly lentiform and not angled or so broad. The not or only slightly lentiform spores distinguish it from all other terrestrial members of this stirps except *C. megaspermus* which has much larger spores and also a darker cap.

J. Lange describes and illustrates a related taxon, *C. hansenii* J. Lange, 1940 (L 160 B) differing in more robust caespitose habit and darker rusty tawny or bay young cap, but with spores of similar size and shape. It grows on soil, sometimes attached to sticks and may well occur in Britain too.

85. C. megaspermus P.D. Orton in Notes from the Royal Botanic Garden, Edinburgh, 32: 141, 1972. See Fig. 220.

Icon.: none. Figs.: NRBG l.c., fig. 1f (bottom left spore excluded).

CAP at first 11-12mm broad, ovoid, then expanded with depressed centre, 25-30mm broad, ± rusty tawny at first then fulvous, sienna or cinnamon at centre, often also cinnamon around centre when mature, with outer part clay-buff and strongly plicate-striate, hardly deliquescing. GILLS blackening. STEM 52-60/2mm, equal or with slightly swollen base, white then discolouring pale clay-buff, smooth, base white tomentose. SMELL none. SPORE-PRINT blackish umber. FRUIT-BODY hardly deliquescing.

SPORES fuscous black, 15-18/8.5-9.5/10-11μm, ellipsoid or ellipsoid-ovoid, sometimes slightly lentiform, germ-pore central. BASIDIA 4-spored. MARGINAL CYSTIDIA ± lageniform, ca. 50-60/18-20μm, apex from conical to cylindric-obtuse and 8-10μm broad. FACIAL CYSTIDIA not seen. CAP CUTICLE cellular, cells 12-28μm broad. VEIL absent.

CLAMP-CONNECTIONS not studied. GENETICS not studied.

HABITAT on soil. So far only recorded from Norfolk.

Readily distinguished microscopically from the other terrestrial members of the Stirps *Hemerobius* by the large, not or barely lentiform spores, although also from 4-spored basidia, possibly also by fairly robust habit and dark coloured cap. The above description may need modification especially as regards size of fruit-body when further collections have been made.

86. C. plicatilis (Fries) Fries, Epicrisis Systematis Mycologici, 252, 1838. See Figs. 218, 228 & 229.

Basionym: *Agaricus plicatilis* Fries, Systema Mycologicum (1821): 312; Misident.: *Coprinus hemerobius* Fries sensu Ricken, Die Blatterpilze (1915): 65.

Icon.: L 160 A; KM 37'; Ri 23', *hemerobius*. Figs.: KR 376, fig. 516.

CAP at first 5-13/4-10mm ovoid or cylindric-ovoid, then expanded or expanded-convex with depressed centre, 10-25mm broad, ochraceous, buff or cinnamon, sometimes rusty tawny or umber at centre, soon grey or greyish buff but often retaining original colour at centre for some time, smooth but soon deeply sulcate-striate to centre, not deliquescing but becoming thin and papery. GILLS clay-buff or grey then blackish, remote because attached to a collar of flesh at stem apex. STEM 32-70/1-2mm, ± equal but often slightly thickened at base, white or hyaline-whitish then often discoloured pale clay-buff or greyish, smooth. SMELL none. SPORE-PRINT fuscous black. FRUIT-BODY hardly deliquescent.

SPORES dark date-brown, (9.5-)10-13/(6-)6.5-7.5(-8)/8.5-10.5μm, strongly lentiform, ellipsoid or ellipsoid-amygdaliform and with excentric germ-pore in side view, subglobose-triangular or obscurely to rather distinctly 5- or 6-angled with central germ-pore visible on the profile in face view. BASIDIA 4-spored. MARGINAL CYSTIDIA vesiculose, clavate, or broadly lageniform, 30-60/12-44μm. FACIAL CYSTIDIA numerous at first, cylindric-clavate or broadly lageniform, 60-80/20-35μm. CAP CUTICLE cellular with cells globose or ellipsoid in surface view but hymeniform of elongate clavate cells when seen in longitudinal section. VEIL absent.

CLAMP-CONNECTIONS present. GENETICS heterothallic (tetrapolar for North American material sec Routien).

HABITAT in grass in fields and lawns or on path sides, singly or in scattered groups. Common throughout the British Isles.

Recognised by absence of veil, habitat, non-deliquescent umbrella-like soon papery cap and strongly lentiform often slightly angular relatively large spores. More field work is necessary before stating that the collar to which the gills are attached is characteristic of this species. Other related terrestrial taxa are macroscopically similar but can be separated on habitat or spore differences. *C. leiocephalus* has smaller spores and grows in shady places on bare soil or in leaves, more rarely in grass. *C. galericuliformis* also appears to favour shady places but has less angular spores with germ-pore excentric in face view as well as in side view and therefore not showing on the profile in face view.

A related but as yet unnamed taxon with rather larger spores (about 13-15/10-12μm in face-view) found in grass but growing in small clusters awaits description. It seems also to be rather more robust then *plicatilis*. It is best to examine spores before naming taxa in this group and past records of *C. plicatilis* should therefore

101

be treated with caution. In our experience although *C. plicatilis* may produce fruit-bodies in a small group they are never joined at the base and are most frequently seen as isolated specimens.

87. C. galericuliformis [Losa ex] Watling in Notes from the Royal Botanic Garden, Edinburgh. 28: 42, 1966. See Figs. 223 & 225.

Syn.: (Not validly published; no latin descriptions): *C. galericuliformis* Losa in Ann. Jard. bot. Madrid 3: 154 1943; *Pseudocoprinus galericuliformis* ([Losa ex] Watling) McKnight & Allison Morris Arb. Bull. 20: 74, 1969.

Icon.: none. Figs.: NRBG l.c.: 41, 1F & f.

CAP at first 5-15/3-10mm ovoid or cylindric-ovoid, then convex or expanded convex often with depressed centre 5-23mm broad, ochraceous buff with darker date-brown centre to entirely rust or rusty tawny, then grey or greyish buff at least in the outer part, smooth but atomate sub lente, soon sulcate-striate in outer part. GILLS greyish or tinged sepia blackish. STEM 25-67/0.5-3mm, equal or ± thickened at base, white then whitish or hyaline clay-buff, smooth or slightly white fibrillose at base. SMELL none. SPORE-PRINT fuscous-black. FRUIT-BODY not or hardly deliquescent.

SPORES, 10-12(-12.5)/6-7/8.5-10.5(-11)μm, strongly lentiform, ellipsoid in side-view, subglobose-triangular not or occasionally very indistinctly angled in face view, germ-pore distinctly excentric in side view, ± central but not appearing on the profile in face-view. BASIDIA 4-spored. MARGINAL CYSTIDIA globose to ellipsoid. FACIAL CYSTIDIA not seen, probably absent. CAP CUTICLE cellular, cells globose to ellipsoid in surface view. VEIL absent.

CLAMP-CONNECTIONS present. GENETICS unknown. OIDIA not observed.

HABITAT on bare soil in woods or along paths in shady places, especially on recently disturbed ground. Recorded from Surrey and Hampshire and in Edinburgh in cool glasshouse; probably not uncommon and widespread.

It is best distinguished by the absence of veil, together with the particular shape of the spore with the germ-pore not showing on the profile in face view. The habitat seems distinctive and a preference for recently disturbed soil is likely. Macroscopically it may look much like *C. plicatilis*. The collections from southern England might be a different taxon in view of the paler and seemingly more expanded mature cap, but the spores and habitat seem identical and further field work is necessary to clarify this. It is probably unwise to base specific differences on cap shape in this genus.

88. C. leiocephalus P.D. Orton in Notes from the Royal Botanic Garden, Edinburgh 29: 88, 1969. See Fig. 219.

Syn.: *C. plicatilis* var. *microsporus* Kühner in Bull. Soc. mycol Fr., 50: 57 1934.

Icon.: none. Figs.: BSMF 50: 57, fig. 4 var. *microsporus*; NRBG 29, figs. lg', g", 3h.

CAP at first ovoid, ellipsoid or cylindric-ellipsoid, 5-15/4-13mm, then conico-convex, finally expanded-convex to ± plane, less commonly with ± depressed centre when mature, from rusty tawny or umber to fulvous or cinnamon with brick or dark brick-colour centre, drying pale buff or greyish cream usually with darker central spot, smooth, outer part becoming grey and radially grooved-striate. GILLS whitish then greyish or tinged colour of cap, finally ± black, remote. STEM (30-)62-90/1-2mm, equal or slightly attenuated upwards, white or whitish then buff, greyish or tinged colour of cap in lower part, smooth, base often white tomentose or strigose. SMELL none. SPORE-PRINT fuscous black. FRUIT-BODY not or hardly deliquescing.

SPORES dark umber, 8.5-11/5.5-6.5/7-8.5μm, lentiform, ellipsoid in side view, broadly ovoid or ovoid-triangular sometimes slightly rounded-angular in face view, germ-pore excentric in side view, central and on the profile in face view. BASIDIA 4-spored. MARGINAL CYSTIDIA vesiculose-clavate, 30-42/16-32μm, or lageniform with broad apex, 40-84(-92)/12-32μm with apex 10-18(-24)μm broad. FACIAL CYSTIDIA vesiculose-clavate, pyriform or lageniform with broad apex to slightly utriform 50-90/16-42μm. CAP CUTICLE cellular with cells globose or ellipsoid in surface view, but hymeniform with elongate clavate cells when seen in longitudinal section. VEIL absent.

CLAMP-CONNECTIONS absent. GENETICS untested. OIDIA formed in moist heads in culture.

HABITAT on soil or occasionally attached to sticks, more especially in damp shady places, solitary, or in small troops or sub-caespitose. Rather common and widely distributed in England and Scotland and probably also elsewhere.

It is rather distinct in its smooth cap without veil and relatively small lentiform spores, which besides being narrower and mostly shorter are less angular than those of *C. plicatilis*. Any '*plicatilis*' found on soil in damp woods or under bushes is most likely this species. *C. galericuliformis* also grows in such situations but has clearly larger spores with the germ-pore not on the profile in face view. It is yet to be ascertained whether the gills are always attached to a collar at the apex of the stipe as they are in *C. plicatilis*.

89. C. nudiceps P.D. Orton in Notes from the Royal Botanic Garden, Edinburgh, 32: 142, 1972. See Figs. 222 & 227.

Icon.: none. Figs.: NRBG, l.c.: 143, fig. 1, g-h.

CAP at first 5-15/3-8mm ellipsoid or ovoid, then expanded plane 8-24mm broad, ochraceous (G in colour chart) or saffron then becoming grey from margin inwards and fulvous, sienna or cinnamon at centre, smooth and rather shiny at first, soon plicate or grooved-striate from margin inwards and conspicuously split or lacerate

103

radially at margin. GILLS, pale ochraceous or pale saffron then buff, umber or date-brown and finally blackish. STEM 30-60/0.5-1.5mm (1.5-3mm at base), attenuated upwards from slightly bulbous base, white or whitish then greyish cream or pale creamy buff, smooth but at first minutely adpressed silky fibrillose and ± interruptedly striate, base with conspicuous adpressed white silky fibrils when fresh. SMELL none. SPORE-PRINT blackish umber. FRUIT-BODY not or hardly deliquescent.

SPORES dark umber, 12-15.5/8-9.5/10-12µm, lentiform, ellipsoid-ovoid in side view, subglobose-triangular or slightly 5-6-angled in face view, germ-pore central. BASIDIA 4-spored. MARGINAL CYSTIDIA vesiculose or pyriform to utriform, irregularly or broadly fusiform, or ± cylindric, 30-60/14-28µm. FACIAL CYSTIDIA ± cylindric. CAP CUTICLE cellular, cells ± globose 10-26µm broad. VEIL absent.

CLAMP-CONNECTIONS and GENETICS not investigated.

HABITAT on old cow or horse dung. As yet recorded only from Scotland (Midlothian, Perthshire, Inverness-shire) but probably widespread.

Recognised by habitat, absence of veil and large spores. The conspicuously split cap margin seems to be constant and is also characteristic. It is related to *C. miser* but has clearly larger spores and produces larger fruit-bodies. It may be Ricken's interpretation of *C. subtillis* (Fr.) Quél. (Die Blätterpilze: 68 (1915), but the identity of Fries' *C. subtilis* cannot be firmly established.

90. C. miser Karsten in Bidrag till Kannedom af Finlands Natur och Folk, 37: 236, 1882. See Figs. 224 & 226.

Misident.: *C. subtilis* (Fries) Quélet sensu Josserand in Ann. Soc. Linn. Lyon 77: 107, 1953

Icon.: L 157 B. Figs.: Ann. Soc. Linn. Lyon: 108, fig. 10, *subtilis*.

CAP at first 2-5/1-3mm ellipsoid or ovoid, then convex or conico-convex, finally expanded ± plane 2-8mm broad, cinnamon, brick, rusty tawny or umber at first soon discolouring ochraceous or buff then greyish from margin inwards, smooth, wrinkled-striate almost to centre when mature. GILLS pale grey or grey-violaceous then fuscous black. STEM 5-40/0.1-0.5mm, filiform, equal, whitish or hyaline grey, sometimes tinged cream at base, smooth but base sometimes minutely tomentose. SMELL none. SPORE-PRINT fuscous black. FRUIT-BODY not or hardly deliquescent.

SPORES umber, 7-9(-9.5)/5-6/6-8µm, lentiform, ellipsoid slightly amygdaliform in side view, subglobose-triangular in face view, germ-pore central. BASIDIA 4-spored. MARGINAL CYSTIDIA vesiculose or pyriform 12-24µm broad, or ± lageniform, 22-30/8-12µm with apex 3-6µm broad. FACIAL CYSTIDIA absent. CAP CUTICLE cellular, cells globose or ellipsoid 12-32µm broad. VEIL absent.

CLAMP-CONNECTIONS present. GENETICS not completely analysed. OIDIA present.

HABITAT on cow or horse dung. Fairly common and widespread throughout Great Britain.

Recognised by very small cap, lack of setules on cap or stem, habitat and relatively small subglobose-triangular spores. A similar taxon with 2-spored basidia is known but cannot be dealt with here because of insufficient fresh material and lack of description. It may well be a distinct species. *C. nudiceps* is more robust and has much larger spores. *C. cordisporus* is similar in size and has a conspicuous veil of globose cells when fresh but could be confused with *C. miser* when old. However, some veil cells are usually visible somewhere in *C. cordisporus*, especially at base of stem even when quite old.

ECOLOGICAL LIST OF SPECIES

On dung or dungy straw

bisporus	*niveus*
cinereus	*nudiceps*
congregatus	*pachyspermus*
cordisporus	*pellucidus*
cothurnatus	*poliomallus*
curtus	*pseudoradiatus*
ephemeroides	*radiatus*
ephemerus	*sclerotiger*
filamentifer	*stellatus*
foetidellus	*stercoreus*
heptemerus	*sterquilinus*
heterosetulosus	*triplex*
hexagonosporus	*trisporus*
latisporus	*tuberosus*
luteocephalus	*utrifer*
macrocephalus	*vermiculifer*
miser	*xenobius*
narcoticus	

On kitchen refuse or rotting plant material

congregatus	*radicans*
erythrocephalus	*urticaecola*
patouillardii	

On wood

acuminatus	*laanii*
atramentarius	*micaceus*
bisporiger	*radians*
disseminatus	*romagnesianus*
domesticus	*silvaticus*
echinosporus	*subdisseminatus*
ellisii	*truncorum*
extinctorius	*xanthothrix*
insignis	

On sawdust

acuminatus	*lagopus*
flocculosus	*scobicola*

On *Typha, Juncus* or *Carex*

martinii	*tigrinellus*
rhombisporus	*urticaecola*

On grass stems or in grassland
  argenteus
  auricomus
  comatus
  friesii
  hemerobius
  hiascens
  plicatilis

  rhombisporus
  saccharomyces
  saichiae
  semitalis
  urticaecola
  xantholepis

On soil
  acuminatus
  auricomus
  callinus
  cinereofloccosus
  comatus
  cortinatus
  dilectus
  episcopalis
  erythrocephalus
  filiformis
  flocculosus
  galericuliformis

  hiascens
  impatiens
  lagopus
  leiocephalus
  megaspermus
  picaceus
  plagioporus
  saccharomyces
  semitalis
  silvaticus
  subdisseminatus
  subimpatiens
  subpurpureus

In beech leaves
  episcopalis
  impatiens
  lagopus

  picaceus
  silvaticus

On burnt ground
  angulatus
  erythrocephalus
  gonophyllus

  lagopides
  phlyctidosporus

On refuse
  kimurae

CULTURAL CHARACTERISTICS

Members of the genus *Coprinus* have been long used as genetic and physiological tools, indeed there is probably more known about this genus than any other group of agarics. Some of this work has been listed in the references in the introduction. However, there has been much confusion as to the true identity of many of the species used in laboratory tests. Experimenters are referred to the diagnostic characters of the fruit-bodies pg 1-105 but identification in culture can be eased by the examination of the following characters (Figs. 29 - 36):-

1   presence or absence of oidia (and/or conidia).

2   if oidia or conidia present whether borne in dry or in moist heads.

3   presence or not of chlamydospores.

4   formation or not of sclerotia or sclerotial plates.

5   formation or not of rhizoidal (coloured or not) growth.

6   presence or absence of clamp-connections.

7   consistency and frequency of branching and angle of development of lateral hyphae.

8   thickness of vegetative hyphae.

9   density of aerial hyphae, if any.

10   homing characters of vegetative hyphae towards oidia.

INDEXES OF SYNONYMS & MISIDENTIFICATIONS

Synonyms

acuminatus, atramentarius var.	= *acuminatus*	4
angustisporus, cinereofloccosus var.	= *semitalis*	53
bisporus, ephemerus var.	= *bisporus*	70
boudieri	= *angulatus*	78
brassicae	= *urticaecola*	23
bulbillosus	= *ephemeroides*	48
delicatulus	= *cinereus*	16
fimetarius	= *radiatus/cinereus*	18/16
funariarum	= *lagopides*	15
giganteoporus	= *echinosporus*	8
hendersonii	= *ephemeroides*	48
hortorum	= *radians*	37

jonesii	= *lagopides*	15
lipophilus, patouillardii var.	= *patouillardii*	49
macrorhizus	= *cinereus*	16
macrosporus, curtus f.	= *heptemerus*	68
microsporus, plicatilis var.	= *leiocephalus*	88
patouillardii, nycthemerus var.	= *patouillardii*	49
plicatiloides	= *curtus*	67
similis	= *radians*	37
sphaerosporus, lagopus var.	= *lagopides*	15
squamosus, atramentarius var.	= *romagnesianus*	5
stephanosporus, hexagonosporus f.	= *hexagonosporus*	65
stercorarius	= *stercoreus*	60
tardus	= *silvaticus*	64
volvaceominimus	= *cordisporus*	47
Psathyra urticicola	= *Coprinus urticaecola*	23
Psathyrella disseminatus	= *C. disseminatus*	63
P. hiascens	= *C. hiascens*	75
P. impatiens	= *C. impatiens*	76
Pseudocoprinus disseminatus	= *C. disseminatus*	63
P. galericuliformis	= *C. galericuliformis*	87
P. impatiens	= *C. impatiens*	76
P. subdisseminatus	= *C. subdisseminatus*	80

Misidentifications

angulatus sensu J. Lange	= *patouillardii*	49
bisporus sensu Buller	= *bisporiger*	82
cineratus sensu Dennis, Orton & Hora	= laanii 52 and semitalis	53
dilectus sensu J. Lange	= *erythrocephalus*	7
domesticus sensu J. Lange	= *xanthothrix*	36
hemerobius sensu Ricken	= *plicatilis*	86
hiascens sensu Romagnesi	= *callinus*	77
lagopus sensu Buller p.p. et al.	= *cinereus* 16 and/or *radiatus*	18
micaceus sensu Lange	= *truncorum*	33
narcoticus sensu Buller	= *triplex*	55
narcoticus sensu J. Lange	not yet clarified, see obs. to 50	
	narcoticus	

109

patouillardii sensu Josserand et al.	= *cordisporus*	47
radiatus sensu Rea	= *pseudoradiatus*	19
rostrupianus sensu J. Lange	= *flocculosus*	38
stercorarius sensu J. Lange	= *tuberosus*	58
subtilis sensu Josserand	= *miser*	90
tergiversans sensu Ricken	= *silvaticus*	64
velox sensu J. Lange	= *stercoreus*	60
Psathyrella crenata sensu Rea et al.	= *Coprinus hiascens*	75

Note: *P. crenata* s. Lange 1915   = *C. hansenii* which is not yet
authentically British

REJECTED NAMES

Lists of species occurring in British literature although of doubtful nature; probable aliens are indicated by an asterisk*.

C. alternatus (Schum.) Fries, 1838: unknown in original sense. Cooke's Illust. 664 (677) could possibly represent *C. silvaticus.*

C. aphthosus Fries, 1838: Cooke's Illust. 653 (666) possibly represents *Psathyrella cotonea:* var. *boltonii* Mass. is said to differ in repand, olivaceous cap; it might be an alien: sensu Lange (L 157 G) is not authentically British.

C. aquatilis Peck, 1875: Crossland's illustration in Halifax Fungus Flora possibly represents a member of Section *Pseudocoprinus.*

C. aratus Berk. & Br. 1861: Described from King's Cliffe. Cooke's Illust. 661 (674) shows a distinctive fungus probably of Stirps *Micaceus,* whereas 662 (675) depicts a fungus more in keeping with Stirps *Domesticus.*

C. bresadolae Schulz., 1885: doubtful record of poorly known fungus.

C. deliquescens (Bull.) Fries, 1838: unknown in original sense; Cooke's Illust. 665 (678) could represent a member of Stirps *Atramentarius.*

C. digitalis (Batsch) Fries, 1838: listed by Massee, 1896 & Rea, 1922 but needs clarification; appears to belong to Section *Pseudocoprinus.* Romagnesi (RM 6, 1941) interprets this as a species close to *C. hiascens.*

C. eburneus Quélet, 1883: listed by Massee, 1896 & Rea, 1922; doubtful whether even a *Coprinus.*

C. frustulosus sacc. see under 43 *C. niveus*

C. fuscescens (Schaeff.) Fries, 1838: unknown in original sense although said to be allied to *C. atramentarius.* Cooke's Illust. 650 (663) depicts a fungus probably belonging to Section *Micacei:* Stirps *Micaceus/Domesticus:* var *rimososquamosus* Cke. said to differ from the type only in the cap becoming cracked into angular patches.

C. hydrophorus (Bull.) Quél., 1888: often placed in *Psathyrella* but even then of doubtful status.

C. nycthemerus Fries, 1838: unknown in original sense; Cooke's Illust. 670 (682) depicts *C. heptemerus* or *C. curtus.*

C. papillatus (Batsch) Fries, 1838 (incl var. *óxygenus*): Cooke's Illust. 663 (676) could represent a member of Stirps *Niveus* close to *C. cordisporus.*

C. platypus Berk. 1885 in Cooke's Illust. 675 (687) depicts a fungus on Palm stems from a conservatory probably referable to Stirps *Tigrinellus* or Stirps *Friesii,* possibly of foreign origin. Also recorded on *Phalaris arundinacea.* (Rea, 1922).

C. schroeteri, Karst., 1879 said to be allied to *C. angulatus:* var. *proximellus* (Karst.) Mass. (= *C. proximellus* Karst. 1879) is also referable to Section *Pseudocoprinus.*

C. sociatus Fries, 1838: listed by Massee, 1896 & Rea, 1922. Said to be the same as *Psathyrella crenata* (Lasch) Fries.

C. spegazzinii Karsten, 1879: on soil in plant-pot; originally described from Finland.

C. spraguei Berk. & Curt., 1859: originally described from New England; possibly introduced and no recent collections known.

C. stellaris Quélet, 1878: listed by Rea, although very doubtful.

C. tomentosus (Bull.) Fries, 1838: not known in original sense: Cooke's Illust. 659 (672) probably refers to a species in Stirps *Filamentifer*.

C. umbrinus Cooke & Massee, 1896: on soil at Kew; doubtful whether this is really synonymous with *C. sterquilinus,* as has been suggested. Probably an alien.

INDEX OF EPITHETS MENTIONED IN OBSERVATIONS

acuminatus in obs. to 3
angulatus 11
angustisporus
   cinereofloccosus var. 53
argenteus 23
atramentarius 4
 6
bisporiger 70
bisporus 82
cineratus 52
 53
cinereofloccosus 53
cinereus 17
 18
comatus 2
congregatus 69
 78
cordisporus 48
 49
 60
 90
curtus 68
delicatulus 16
disseminatus 80
domesticus 32
 35
 37
 36
ellisii 34
ephemeroides 47
 49
ephemerus 70
 71
 74
episcopalis 10
 12
 78

atramentarius
episcopalis

semitalis
urticaecola
acuminatus
insignis
bisporus
bisporiger
laanii
semitalis
semitalis
macrocephalus
radiatus
sterquilinus
ephemerus
bisporus
ephemeroides
patouillardii
stercoreus
miser
heptemerus
cinereus
subdisseminatus
micaceus
ellisii
radians
xanthothrix
domesticus
cordisporus
patouillardii
bisporus
congregatus
heterosetulosus
picaceus
scobicola
angulatus

erythrocephalus in obs. to	66	*dilectus*	
filamentifer	30	*xenobius*	
filiformis	40	*cortinatus*	
foetidellus	60	*stercoreus*	
friesii	23	*urticaecola*	
fuscescens	3	*atramentarius*	
galericuliformis	86	*plicatilis*	
	88	*leiocephalus*	
giganteoporus	8	*echinosporus*	
hansenii	83	*auricomus*	
	84	*hemerobius*	
heptemerus	67	*curtus*	
herinkii	27	*saichiae*	
heterocomus	31	*utrifer*	
hiascens	76	*impatiens*	
homosetulosus			
hexagonosporus var.	65	*hexagonosporus*	
impatiens	75	*hiascens*	
	81	*subimpatiens*	
insignis	3	*atramentarius*	
	8	*echinosporus*	
kimurae	22	*gonophyllus*	
laanii	53	*semitalis*	
	54	*cinereofloccossus*	
lagopides	14	*lagopus*	
lagopus	8	*echinosporus*	
	15	*lagopides*	
	16	*xinwewua*	
latisporus	43	*niveus*	
leiocephalus	86	*plicatilis*	
luteocephalus	40	*cortinatus*	
macrocephalus	16	*cinereus*	
	18	*radiatus*	
macrorhizus	16	*cinereus*	
magespermus	84	*hemerobius*	
micaceus	33	*truncorum*	
	64	*silvaticus*	
miser	89	*nudiceps*	
narcoticus	51	*radicans*	
	52	*laanii*	
	55	*triplex*	
	56	*trisporus*	
niveus	44	*latisporus*	
	56	*trisporus*	
nudiceps	90	*miser*	
oblectus	2	*sterquilinus*	
ovatus	1	*comatus*	
	2	*sterquilinus*	

113

patouillardii in obs. to	47	*cordisporus*	
pellucidus	68	*heptemerus*	
	73	*stellatus*	
phlyctidosporus	8	*echinosporus*	
picaceus	11	*episcopalis*	
plicatilis	84	*hemerobius*	
	87	*galericuliformis*	
	88	*leiocephalus*	
poliomallus	42	*luteocephalus*	
pseudolagopus	14	*lagopus*	
pseudoradiatus	16	*cinereus*	
	18	*radiatus*	
pygmaea, Psathyrella	63	*disseminatus*	
radians	34	*domesticus*	
radicans	50	*narcoticus*	
radiatus	16	*cinereus*	
	17	*macrocephalus*	
	19	*pseudoradiatus*	
romagnesianus	3	*atramentarius*	
roseotinctus	7	*erythrocephalus*	
	43	*niveus*	
	46	*cothurnatus*	
saccharomyces	54	*cinereofloccosus*	
saicheae	21	*argenteus*	
	23	*urticaecola*	
sassii	65	*hexagonosporus*	
	70	*bisporus*	
sclerocystidiosus	82	*bisporiger*	
sclerotiger	58	*tuberosus*	
scobicola	10	*picaceus*	
semitalis	54	*cinereofloccosus*	
silvaticus	75	*hiascens*	
	76	*impatiens*	
sphaerocephalus			
comatus f.	1	*comatus*	
spilosporus	22	*gonophyllus*	
stellatus	72	*pellucidus*	
stephanosporus			
hexagonosporus f.	65	*hexagonosporus*	
stercorarius	56	*trisporus*	
	59	*sclerotiger*	
	60	*stercoreus*	
stercoreus	57	*foetidellus*	
sterquilinus	1	*comatus*	
subtilis	89	*nudiceps*	
triplex	50	*narcoticus*	
	51	*radicans*	
	56	*trisporus*	

trisporus in obs to	50	*narcoticus*
	51	*radicans*
	55	*triplex*
truncorum	32	*micaceus*
tuberosus	57	*foetidellus*
	59	*sclerotiger*
	60	*stercoreus*
velox	60	*stercoreus*
vermiculifer	42	*luteocephalus*
	30	*xenobius*
vosoustii	2	*sterquilinus*
xanthorthrix	34	*domesticus*

INDEX OF SPECIES DESCRIBED

species	serial no.	species	serial no
acuminatus	4	*friesii*	20
angulatus	78	*galericuliformis*	87
argenteus	21	*gonophyllus*	22
atramentarius	3	*hemerobius*	84
auricomus	83	*heptemerus*	68
bisporiger	82	*heterosetulosus*	74
bisporus	70	*hexagonosporus*	65
callinus	77	*hiascens*	75
cinereofloccosus	54	*impatiens*	76
cinereus	16	*insignis*	6
comatus	1	*laanii*	52
congregatus	71	*lagopides*	15
cordisporus	47	*lagopus*	14
cortinatus	40	*latisporus*	44
cothurnatus	46	*leiocephalus*	88
curtus	67	*luteocephalus*	42
delictus	66	*macrocephalus*	17
disseminatus	63	*martinii*	61
domesticus	34	*megaspermus*	85
echinosporus	8	*micaceus*	32
ellisii	35	*miser*	90
ephemeroides	48	*narcoticus*	50
ephemerus	69	*niveus*	43
episcopalis	11	*nudiceps*	89
erythrocephalus	7	*pachyspermus*	45
extinctorius	13	*patouillardii*	49
filamentifer	28	*pellucidus*	72
filiformis	41	*phlyctidosporus*	9
flocculosus	38	*picaceus*	10
foetidellus	57	*plagioporus*	79

British Fungus Flora

species	serial no.	species	serial no.
plicatilis	86	*stercoreus*	60
poliomallus	39	*sterquilinus*	2
pseudoradiatus	19	*subdisseminatus*	80
radians	37	*subimpatiens*	81
radicans	51	*tigrinellus*	24
radiatus	18	*triplex*	55
rhombisporus	25	*trisporus*	56
romagnesianus	5	*truncorum*	33
saccharomyces	62	*tuberosus*	58
saichiac	27	*urticaecola*	23
sclerotiger	59	*utrifer*	31
scobicola	12	*vermiculifer*	29
semitalis	53	*xantholepis*	26
silvaticus	64	*xanthothrix*	36
stellatus	73	*xenobius*	30

additional species

kimurae	91	*subpurpureus*	92

COPRINUS : GENERAL

Fig. 1-7   Development of typical setulose *Coprinus: C. ephemereus* (Stirps *Ephemerus*).

Fig. 8-10   Development of veiled *Coprinus: C. luteocephalus* (Stirps *Cortinatus*).

Fig. 11   Habitat sketch of *C. atramentarius* (Stirps *Atramentarius*) showing volvate base to stem.

Fig. 12   Section of *C. comatus* (Stirps *Comatus*) showing ring and hollow stem.

Fig. 12A   Section of non-coprinoid agaric for comparison: *Agrocybe semiorbicularis.*

Fig. 13   Plan of gills in *Coprinus comatus* showing facial and marginal cystidia, and parallel-sided gills.

Fig. 13A   Section of *Agrocybe semiorbicularis* showing wedge-shaped gills common to most agarics.

Fig. 14   "Scalp" showing round outline of cells in 'cellular' cuticle (*C. micaceus:* Stirps *Micaceus*).

Fig. 15   Face-view of gill-surface showing developing basidia separated by sterile cells (= basidioles) (*C. atramentarius:* Stirps *Atramentarius*).

Fig. 16   Section of gill showing parallel gill-trama and onset of deliquescence (*C. atramentarius:* Stirps *Atramentarius*).

Fig. 17   "Scalp" showing elongate inflated cells in radially arranged 'filamentous' cuticle (*C. cinereus:* Stirps *Lagopus*).

Fig. 18   Adjacent gill-faces separated by voluminous facial cystidia (*C. atramentarius:* Stirps *Atramentarius*).

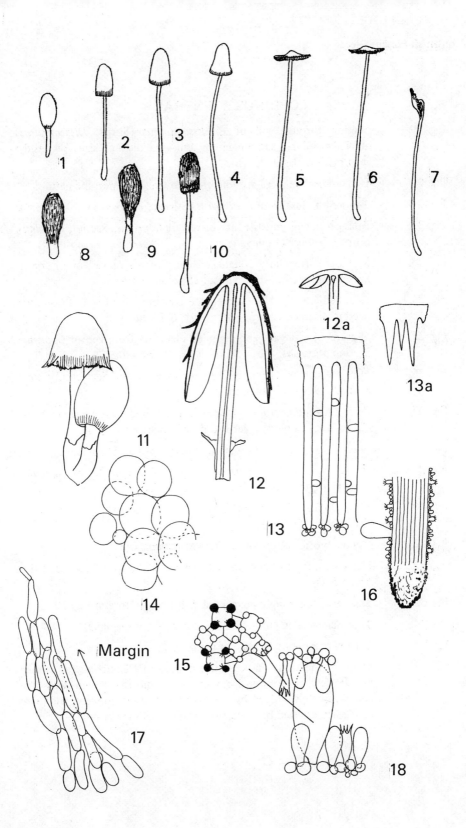

COPRINUS : GENERAL

Fig. 19.   Section through gill of *C. disseminatus* (Stirps: *Disseminatus*) showing cellular subhymenium and two distinct sizes of basidia separated by basidioles (b).

Fig. 20.   Isolated basidia of *C. disseminatus* showing polymorphic nature.

Fig. 21.   2-spored basidia from *C. bisporus* (Stirps: *Ephemerus*).

Fig. 22.   Sausage-shaped constituents of veil of *Coprinus*, Section *Coprinus*, Stirps *Lagopus: C. cinereus.*

Fig. 23.   Rounded, irregularly roughened constituents of veil of *Coprinus*, Section *Micaceus*, Stirps *Niveus: C. patouillardii.*

Fig. 24.   Rounded, structurally ornamented constituents of veil of *Coprinus*, Section *Micaceus*, Stirps *Narcoticus: C. laanii.*

Fig. 25.   Mixture of elongate and rounded elements from veil of *Coprinus*, Section *Micaceus*, Stirps *Domesticus: C. domesticus.*

Fig. 26.   Elongate narrow elements from veil of *Coprinus*, Section *Coprinus*, Stirps *Picaceus: C. episcopalis.*

Fig. 27.   Fruit-body of *Coprinus pellucidus* (Section *Pseudocoprinus;* Stirps *Ephemerus*) as seen under low-power microscope or lens.

Fig. 28.   as Fig. 27 but *C. miser* (Section *Pseudocoprinus;* Stirps *Hemerobius*).

Fig. 29 a & b.   Oidial apparatus in *C. cinereus* (Section *Coprinus*; Stirps *Lagopus*), showing development of oidia held in sticky heads.

Fig. 30.   as Fig. 29 from *C. congregatus* (Section *Coprinus;* Stirps *Ephemerus*) - oidia held in dry chains.

Fig. 31.   Monocaryotic culture of *C. cinereus* showing oidia.

Fig. 32.   Pigmented areas in culture of *C. trisporus* (Section *Micaceus*, Stirps *Narcoticus*).

Fig. 33.   Thick-walled strongly pigmented cells from culture in Fig. 32.

Fig. 34.   'Microsclerotia' in culture of *C. cinerus* (Stirps *Lagopus*).

Fig. 35.   Chlamydospore on hyphae of *C. cinereus.*

Fig. 36.   Clamp-connections on vegetative hyphae of *C. cinereus* (a) as seen in side view, (b) as seen from above, (c) and (d) as seen when half and completely hidden by overlaying hypha respectively, and (e) as seen when crushed between two enlarged cells (as in veil).

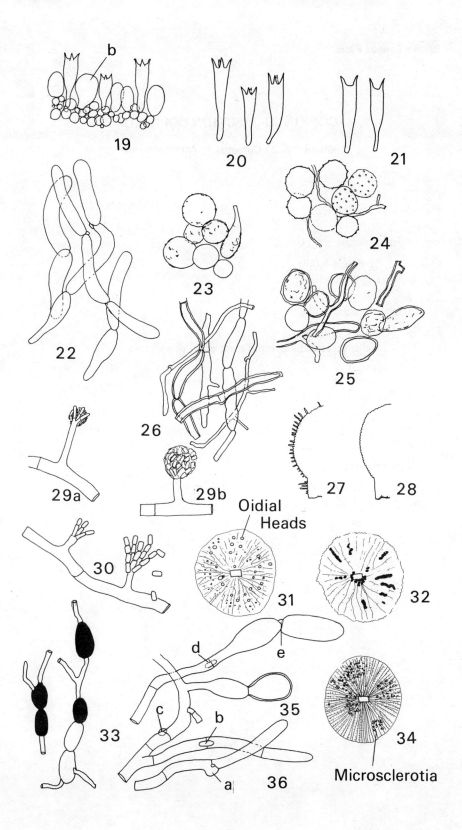

Oidial
Heads

Microsclerotia

121

COPRINUS : SECTION COPRINUS

Stirps 1 & 2 - Comatus & Atramentarius

C. comatus　　(1)

Fig. 37.　　Spores. x 1,000
Fig. 45.　　Habit sketch.

C. sterquilinus　　(2)

Fig. 38.　　Spores. x 1,000
Fig. 44.　　Habit sketch.

C. acuminatus　　(4)

Fig. 39.　　Spores. x 1,000
Fig. 42　　Habit sketches: a & b different collections

C. atramentarius　(3)

Fig. 40.　　Spores. x 1,000
Fig. 46.　　Habit sketch.

C. romagnesianus　　(5)

Fig. 41.　　Spores. x 1,000
Fig. 43.　　Habit sketch.

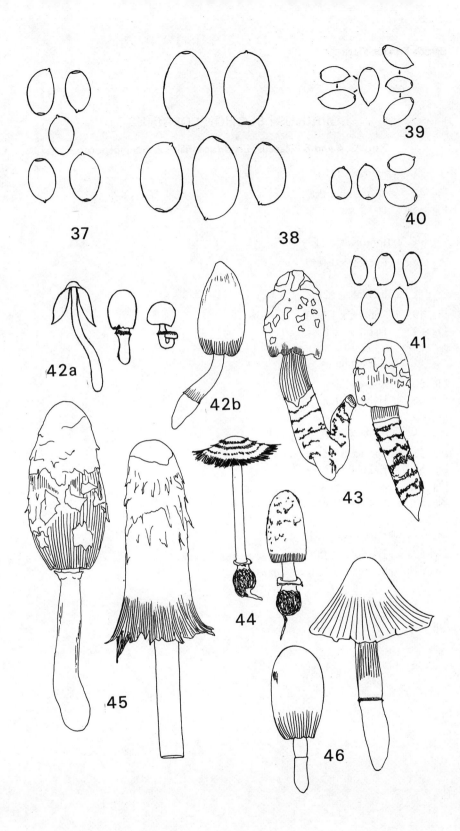

37

38

39

40

41

42a

42b

43

44

45

46

COPRINUS : SECTION COPRINUS

Stirps 3, 4 and 6 Picaceus; Erythrocephalus & Echinosporus

C. picaceus   (10)

Fig. 47.   Spores. x 1,000
Fig. 55.   Habit sketch

C. extinctorius   (13)

Fig. 48.   Spores, x 1,000

C. scobicola   (12)

Fig. 49.   Spores. x 1,000
Fig. 54.   Habit sketch

C. erythrocephalus   (7)

Fig. 50.   Spores.
Fig. 56.   Habit sketch

C. episcopalis (11)

Fig. 53.   Spores. x 1,000
Fig. 57.   Habit sketch.
Fig. 58.   Velar fragments. x250
Fig. 59.   Facial cystidia. x250

C. echinosporus (8)

Fig. 52a.   Spores. x 1,000
Fig. 52b.   Spores of *C. giganteoporus*

C. phlyctidosporus (9)

Fig. 51.   Spores. x 1,250

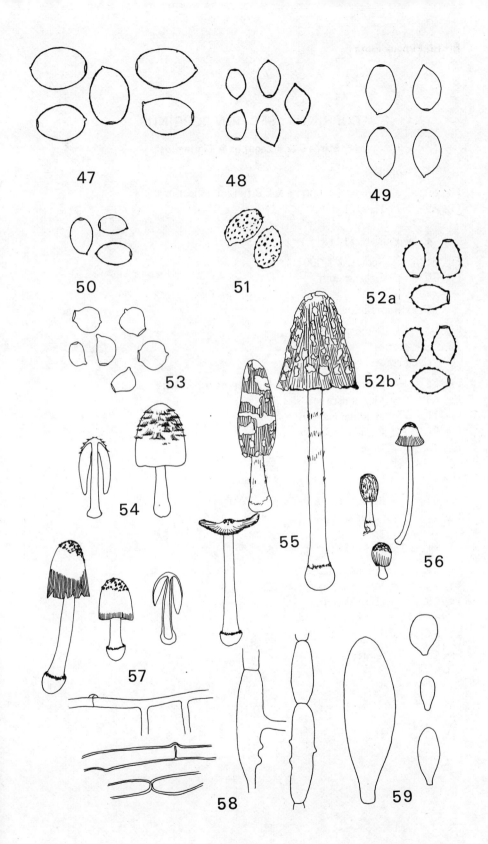

47

48

49

50

51

52a

52b

53

54

55

56

57

58

59

COPRINUS : SECTION COPRINUS

Stirps 5 & 8 Lagopus & Tigrinellus

C. lagopides

Fig. 60.   Spores. x 1,000 : a & b different collections
Fig. 69.   Habit sketch.

C. lagopus   (14)

Fig. 61.   Spores. x 1,000
Fig. 70.   Habit sketch.

C. pseudoradiatus   (19)

Fig. 62.   Spores. x 1,000

C. cinereus   (16)

Fig. 63.   Spores. x 1,000 : a & b different collections
Fig. 68.   Veil constituents. x 500
Fig. 71.   Marginal cystidia. x 500
Fig. 72.   Facial cystidia. x 500
Fig. 73.   Habit sketch.

C. macrocephalus   (17)

Fig. 64.   Spores. x 1,000
Fig. 74.   Habit sketch.

C. radiatus   (18)

Fig. 65.   Spores. x 1,250
Fig. 67.   Veil constituent. x 500
Fig. 75.   Habit sketch.

C. saichiae   (27)

Fig. 66.   Spores

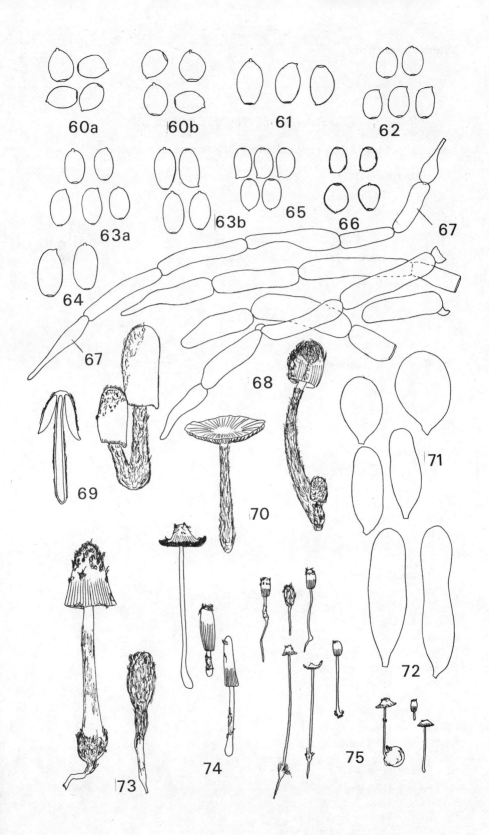

COPRINUS : SECTION COPRINUS

Stirps 7-10 - Friesii, Tigrinellus. Filamentifer & Utrifer

C. argenteus   (21)

Fig. 76.   Habit sketch.
Fig. 77.   Spores. x 1,000

C. urticaecola (23)

Fig. 78.   Spores. x 1,000 : a & b different collections

C. rhombisporus (25)

Fig. 79.   Habit sketch.
Fig. 80.   Spores. x 1,000 : a & b different collections

C. aff. rhombisporus   (25)

Fig. 92.   Veil constituents. x 500

C. xantholepis   (26)

Fig. 81.   Habit sketch.
Fig. 82.   Spores. x 1,000

C. friesii   (20)

Fig. 83.   Spores. x 1,000

C. utrifer   (31)

Fig. 84.   Habit sketch.
Fig. 85.   Spores.
Fig. 86.   Veil constituents. x 500

C. xenobius   (30)

Fig. 87.   Spores. x 1,000: a & b different collections

C. vermiculifer   (29)

Fig. 88.   Veil constituents. x 500
Fig. 89.   Facial cystidia. x 500
Fig. 90.   Spores. x 1,000
Fig. 91.   Habit sketch

C. gonophyllus   (22)

Fig. 93.   Spores. x 1,000
Fig. 94.   Habit sketch.

C. filamentifer   (28)

Fig. 95.   Habit sketch.
Fig. 96.   Spores. x 1,250
Fig. 97.   Facial cystidia. x 500
Fig. 98.   Veil constituents. x 500

128

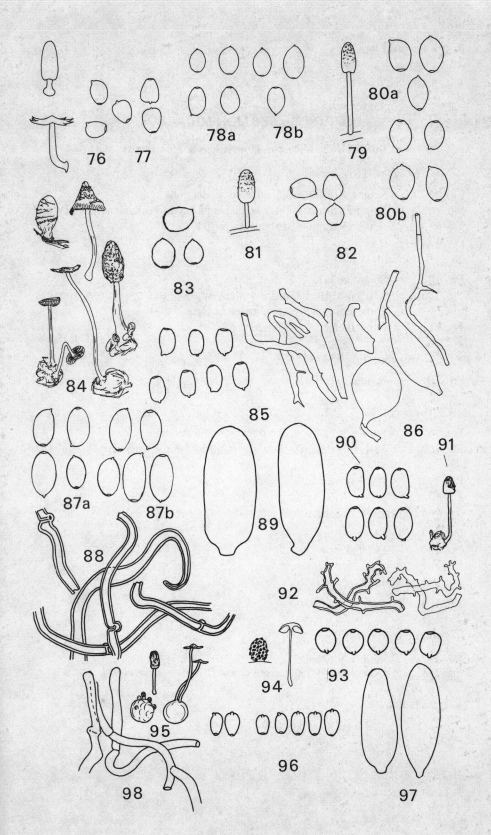

76   77   78a   78b   79   80a

80b   81   82   83   84   85   86

87a   87b   88   89   90   91

92   93   94   95   96   97   98

129

COPRINUS : SECTION MICACEUS

Stirps 11-13 - Micaceus, Domesticus & Flocculosus

C. ellisii   (35)

Fig. 99.   Spores x 1,000: a & b different collections
Fig. 107.   Veil constituents; thick-walled, smooth and ornamented units, and thin-walled rounded elements. x 500

C. micaceus   (32)

Fig. 100.   Spores. x 1,000
Fig. 106.   Veil constituents; thick-walled, smooth and ornamented-rounded units, and irregular, pigmented hyphae. x 500
Fig. 112.   Habit sketch.

C. truncorum   (33)

Fig. 101.   Spores. x 1,000

C. flocculosus   (38)

Fig. 102.   Spores. x 1,000: a & b different collections
Fig. 108.   Veil constituents showing swollen faintly ornamented end-cells. x 500
Fig. 113.   Habit sketch.

C. domesticus   (34)

Fig. 103.   Spores. x 1,000
Fig. 109.   Habit sketch.

C. xanthothrix   (36)

Fig. 104.   Spores. x 1,000

C. radians   (37)

Fig. 105.   Spores. x 1,000
Fig. 114.   Orange-tawny vegetative state (= *Ozonium auriconium*).

C. poliomallus   (39)

Fig. 110.   Veil constituents. x 500
Fig. 111.   Spores. x 2,000

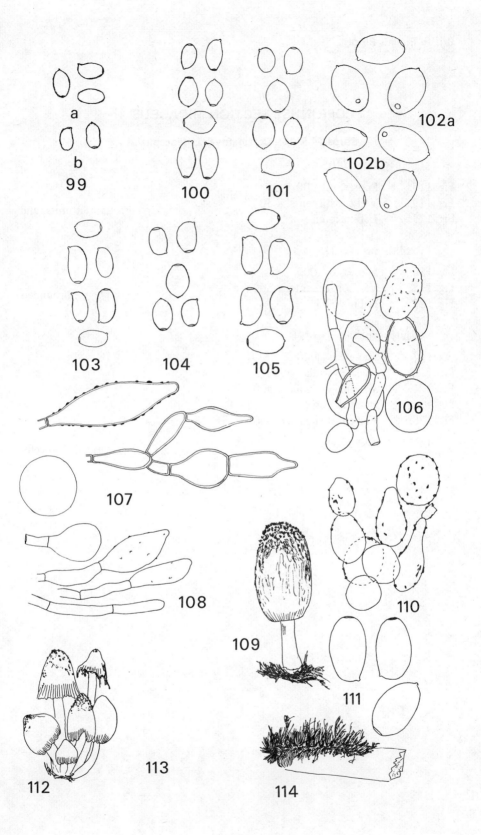

COPRINUS : SECTION MICACEUS

Stirps 14 & 15 - Cortinatus & Luteocephalus

C. cortinatus   (40)

Fig. 115.   Spores. x 1,000
Fig. 119.   Veil constituents. x 500
Fig. 123.   Habit sketch

C. filiformis   (41)

Fig. 116.   Spores. x 1,000
Fig. 118.   Veil constituents. x 500
Fig. 122.   Habit sketch.

C. luteocephalus   (42)

Fig. 117.   Spores. x 1,000
Fig. 120.   Facial cystidia. x 500
Fig. 121.   Marginal cystidia. x 500
Fig. 124.   Habit sketch.
Fig. 125.   Veil constituents. x 500

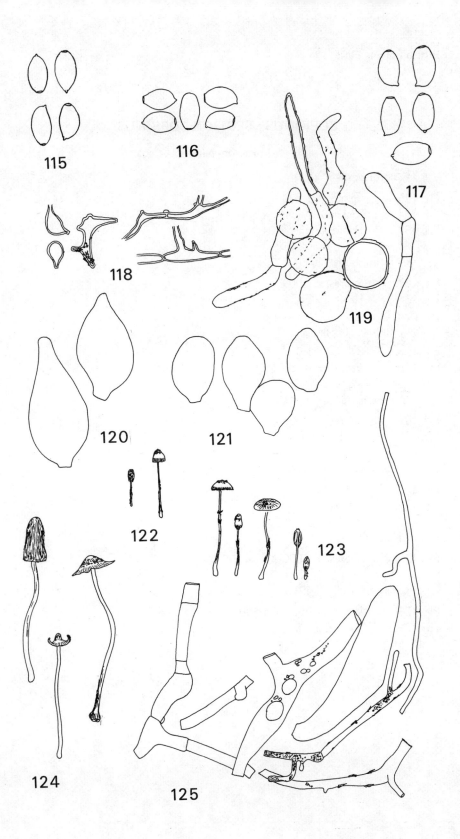

COPRINUS : SECTION COPRINUS

Stirps 15 - Niveus

C. cordisporus   (47)

Fig. 126.   Spores. x 1,000
Fig. 134.   Veil constituents. x 500
Fig. 137.   Habit sketch.

C. cothurnatus   (46)

Fig. 127.   Spores. x 1,000
Fig. 136.   Habit sketch.

C. niveus   (43)

Fig. 128.   Spores. x 1,000
Fig. 130.   Veil constituents. x 500

C. ephemeroides   (48)

Fig. 129.   Spores. x 1,000
Fig. 138.   Habit sketch.

C. pachyspermus   (45)

Fig. 131.   Habit sketch.
Fig. 132.   Spores. x 1,000

C. latisporus   (44)

Fig. 133.   Spores. x 1,000

C. patouillardii   (49)

Fig. 135.   Veil constituents. x 500
Fig. 139.   Habit sketch.

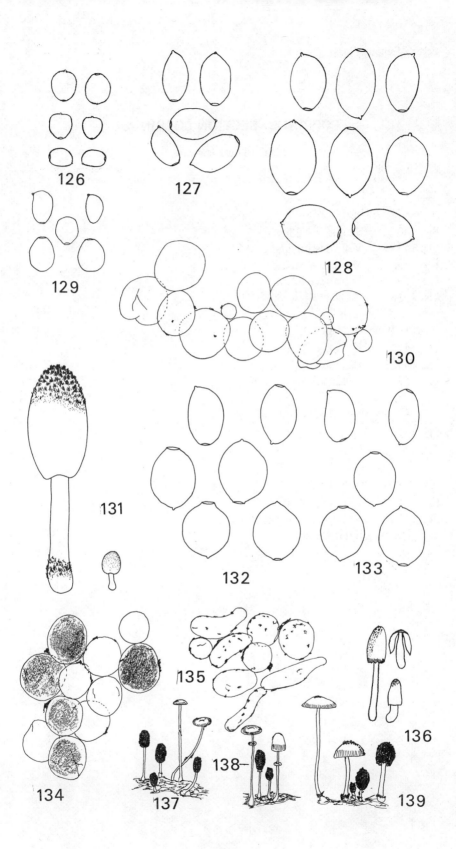

126

127

128

129

130

131

132

133

134

135

136

137

138

139

COPRINUS : SECTION COPRINUS

Stirps 16 - Narcoticus

1 - C. tuberosus group & C. stercoreus

C. sclerotiger   (59)

Fig. 140.	Spores. x 1,250
Fig. 143.	Veil constituents. x 500
Fig. 149.	Marginal cystidia. x 750
Fig. 150.	Habit sketch.
Fig. 151.	Facial cystidia. x 750

C. trisporus   (56)

Fig. 141.	Spores. x 1,250
Fig. 148.	Habit sketch.
Fig. 152.	Veil constituents. x 500

C. tuberosus   (58)

Fig. 142.	Spores. x 1,250
Fig. 147.	Habit sketch.

C. stercoreus   (60)

Fig. 144.	Spores. x 1,000
Fig. 145.	Veil constituents. x 500
Fig. 146.	Habit sketch.

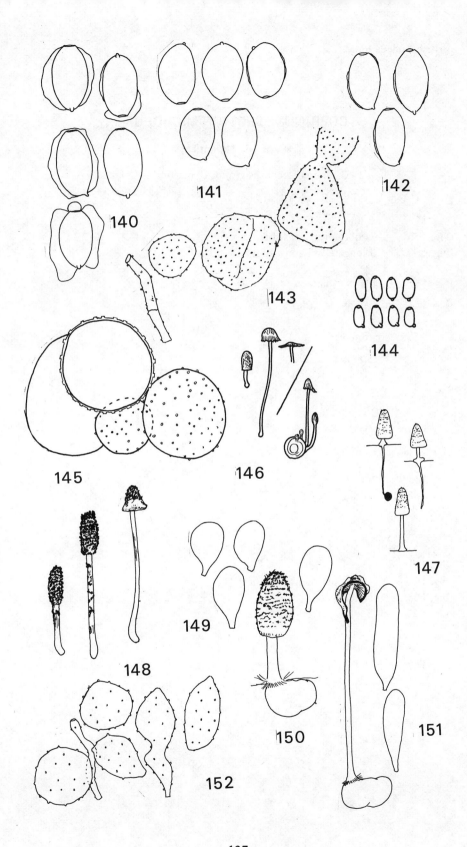

COPRINUS : SECTION MICACEUS

Stirps 16 - Narcoticus

2 - C. cinereofloccosus group, C. martinii & C. laanii

C. cinereofloccosus (54)

Fig. 153.   Spores. x 1,000
Fig. 156.   Globose veil constituents. x 500
Fig. 160.   Elongate veil constituents. x 500

C. semitalis   (53)

Fig. 154.   Spores. x 1,000

C. saccharomyces   (62)

Fig. 155.   Spores. x 1,000
Fig. 165.   Habit sketch.

C. foetidellus (57)

Fig. 157.   Habit sketch.
Fig. 159.   Spores. x 1,000

C. martinii   (61)

Fig. 158.   Spores. x 1,000
Fig. 166.   Habit sketch.

C. laanii   (52)

Fig. 161.   Facial cystidia.
Fig. 162.   Veil constituents. x 1,000
Fig. 163.   Habit sketch.
Fig. 164.   Spores. x 1,000

C. narcoticus (50)

Fig. 167.   Habit sketch; modified from Cooke

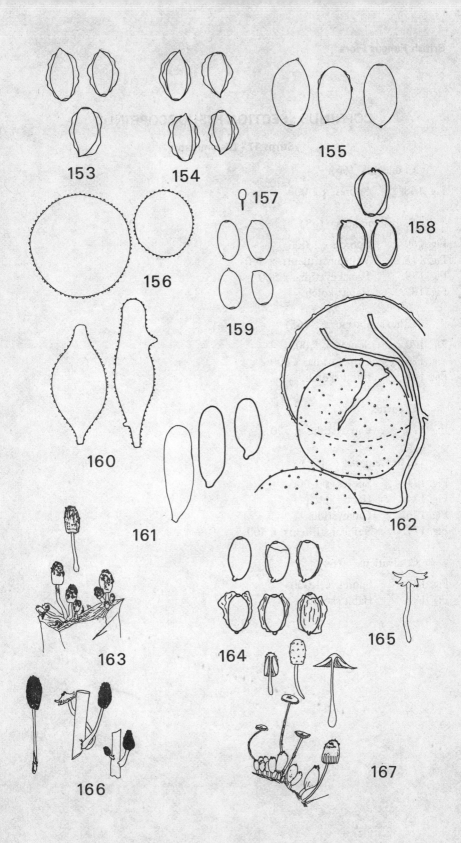

153

154

155

156

157

158

159

160

161

162

163

164

165

166

167

COPRINUS : SECTION PSEUDOCOPRINUS

Stirps 17 - Disseminatus

C. dilectus (66)

Fig. 168.   Spores. x 1,000

C. disseminatus   (63)

Fig. 169.   Spores. x 1,000
Fig. 178.   Veil constituents. x 500
Fig. 179.   Facial cystidia. x 500
Fig. 182.   Habit sketch.

C. hexagonosporus   (65)

Fig. 170.   Spores. x 1,000
Fig. 173.   Cap cystidia. x 500
Fig. 180.   Habit sketch.

C. curtus   (67)

Fig. 175.   Cap cystidia. x 500

C. heptemerus   (68)

Fig. 171.   Spores. x 1,000
Fig. 174.   Habit sketch.
Fig. 176.   Cap cystidia.
Fig. 177.   Veil constituents. x 500

C. silvaticus (64)

Fig. 172.   Spores. x 1,000
Fig. 181.   Habit sketch.

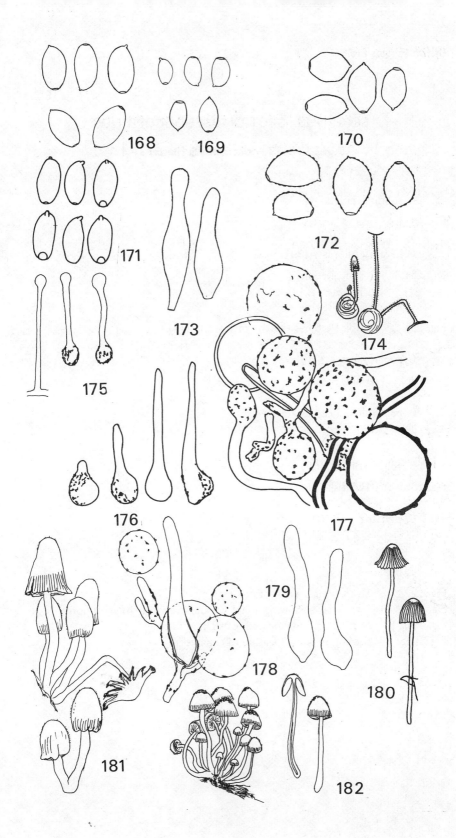

168   169   170

171   172

173   174

175

176   177

179

178   180

181   182

141

COPRINUS : SECTION PSEUDOCOPRINUS

Stirps 18 & 19 - Ephemerus & Hiascens — I

C. subdisseminatus   (80)

Fig. 183.   Habit sketch.

C. heterosetulosus   (74)

Fig. 184.   Habit sketch.

C. hiascens   (75)

Fig. 185.   Habit sketches (a & b) with section (c)

C. congregatus   (71)

Fig. 186.   Habit sketch.

C. pellucidus   (72)

Fig. 187.   Habit sketch.

C. ephemerus   (69)

Fig. 188.   Habit sketch.

C. stellatus   (73)

Fig. 189.   Habit sketch.

C. impatiens   (76)

Fig. 192.   Habit sketch and section.
Fig. 190.   Spore-views showing apical (a) and excentric (b) germ-pores
Fig. 191.   Section to show location of stem cystidia
Fig. 193.   Section to show location of cap cystidia

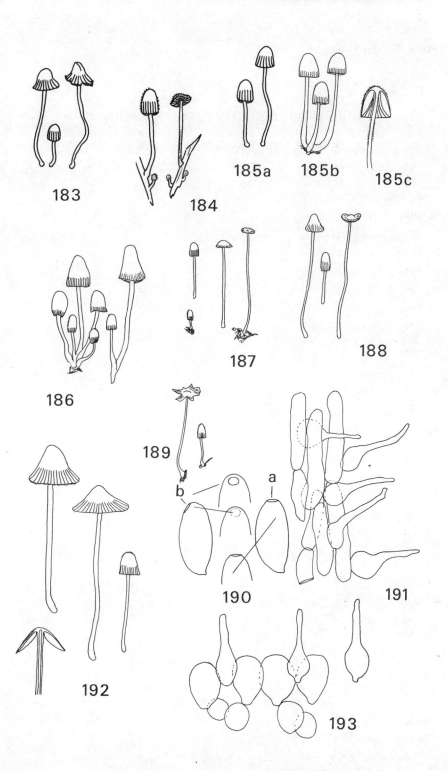

183

184

185a   185b   185c

186

187

188

189

b   a

190   191

192   193

COPRINUS : SECTION PSEUDOCOPRINUS

Stirps 18 & 19 - Ephemerus & Hiascens — 2

C. subimpatiens (81)
Fig. 194.   Spores. x 1,000

C. angulatus (78)
Fig. 195.   Spores. x 1,000

C. callinus (77)
Fig. 196.   Spores. x 1,000

C. hiascens (75)
Fig. 197.   Spores. x 1,000
Fig. 207.   Marginal cystidia. x 500
Fig. 208.   Cap cystidia. x 500

C. pellucidus (72)
Fig. 198.   Spores. x 1,000

C. ephemerus (69)
Fig. 199.   Spores. x 1,000
Fig. 216.   Cap cystidia. x 500
Fig. 217.   Facial cystidia. x 500

C. bisporiger (82)
Fig. 200 a & b. Spores. x 1,000

C. subdisseminatus (80)
Fig. 201.   Spores. x 1,000
Fig. 203.   Marginal cystidia. x 500
Fig. 204.   Cap cystidia. x 500

C. impatiens (76)
Fig. 202.   Spores. x 1,000

C. plagioporus (79)
Fig. 206.   Spores. x 1,000

C. bisporus (70)
Fig. 205.   Spores. x 1,000
Fig. 210.   Cap cystidia. x 500

C. congregatus (71)
Fig. 209.   Spores.
Fig. 211.   Cap cystidia. x 500

C. heterosetulosus (74)
Fig. 212.   Thin-walled cap cystidia. x 500
Fig. 216.   Thick-walled cap cystidia. x 500
Fig. 214.   Marginal cystidia. x 500
Fig. 215.   Spores. x 1,000

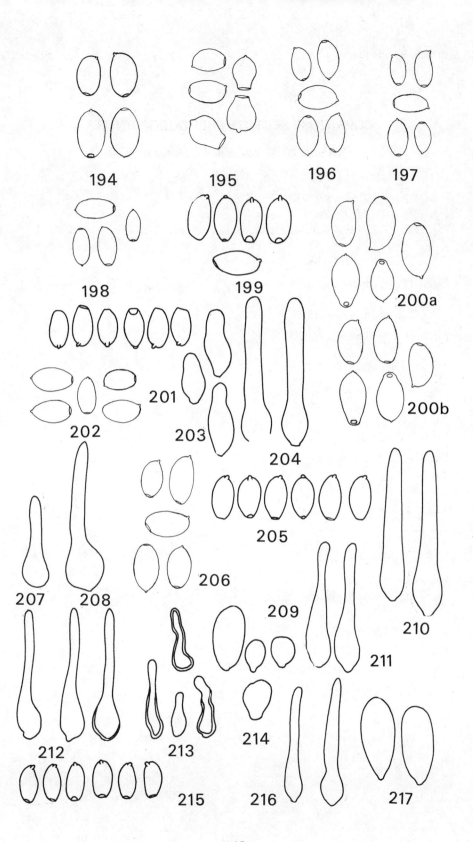

194   195   196   197

198   199   200a

201   202   203   204   200b

205   206   207   208   209   210   211

212   213   214   215   216   217

145

COPRINUS : SECTION PSEUDOCOPRINUS

Stirps 20 & 21 - Auricomus & Hemerobius

C. plicatilis   (86)

Fig. 218.   Spores. x 1,000
Fig. 228.   Habit sketch.
Fig. 229.   Section showing attachment of gills to apical collar.

C. leiocephalus   (88)

Fig. 219.   Spores. x 1,000

C. megaspermus   (85)

Fig. 220.   Spores. x 1,000

C. nudiceps   (89)

Fig. 222.   Spores. x 1,000
Fig. 227.   Habit sketch.

C. hemerobius   (84)

Fig. 221.   Spores. x 1,250

C. galericuliformis   (87)

Fig. 223 a & b. Spores. x 1,000
Fig. 225.   Habit sketch.

C. miser   (90)

Fig. 224.   Spores.
Fig. 226.   Habit sketch.

C. auricomus   (83)

Fig. 230.   Cap setae. x 500
Fig. 231.   Section of cap surface. x 500

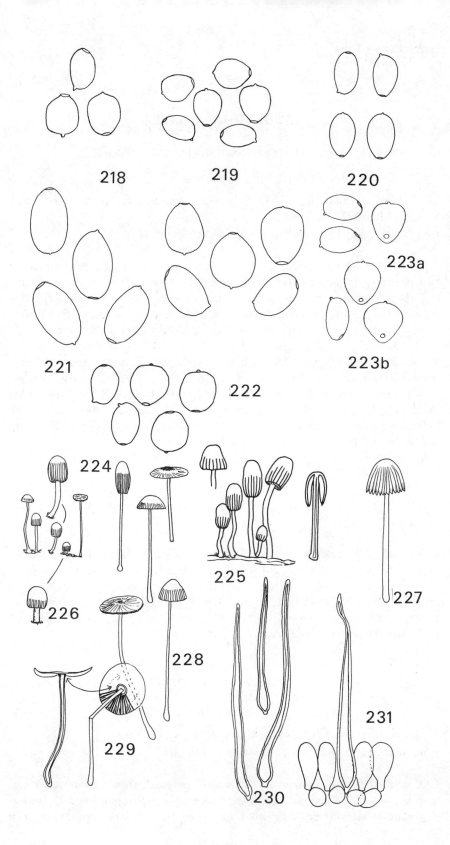

218

219

220

221

222

223a

223b

224

225

226

227

228

229

230

231

ADDITIONAL SPECIES

Section Coprinus

Stirps Picaceus

91. C. kimurae Hongo & Aoki in Aoki and Hongo in Transactions Mycological Society of Japan 7: 16, 1966.

Icon.: none. Figs.: Trans. mycol. Soc. Japan 7: 17, figs. 1, III-VI.

CAP at first 10-20mm ovoid, then expanded-convex or campanulate, whitish or buff becoming tinted fulvous and finally grey, with whitish or buff veil splitting to form patches on a grey background, margin striate, soon reflexed and splitting radially. GILLS whitish soon black. STEM 40-60/0.75-1.5mm, equal or with slightly swollen base pale grey, silky fibrillose. SPORE-PRINT dark umber.

SPORES very umber, 10-13.5/8.5-10μm, subglobose to broadly ovoid with large central germ-pore. BASIDIA 4-spored. MARGINAL CYSTIDIA pyriform to broadly clavate, up to 45μm broad, smooth, hyaline. FACIAL CYSTIDIA sparse, soon collapsing, fusoid-ventricose, smooth, hyaline, up to 100μm long. CAP CUTICLE of filamentous radially arranged hyphae with swollen cells. VEIL on cap of filamentous thin-walled hyphae, 3-30μm broad.

CLAMP-CONNECTIONS present. GENETICS heterothallic.

HABITAT on damp stuffing of couch in a hospital. Recorded once in Britain; as yet only from Yorkshire.

It was originally described from rotting rice-straw in Japan, but the British material has been successfully crossed with N. American and Japanese isolates. It looks like a small *C. picaceus,* but differs from that species and other members of Stirps Picaceus in subglobose spores with broad germ-pore. It differs from *C. spilosporus* Romagn. (RM 16: 112, 1951) and *C. gonophyllus* more especially in the broader germ-pore of the spores, which are also larger.

Section Pseudocoprinus

Stirps Hiascens

92. C. subpurpureus A.H. Smith in Mycologia 40: 684, 1948.

Icon.: none. Figs.: Dansk Bot. Ark. 14, figs. 4 & 13.

CAP at first 8-10/7-11mm ovoid or broadly ellipsoid, then conico-convex and soon expanded 24-40mm often with reflexed margin, at first purplish date, brown-vinaceous or date brown, grey when expanded, at first striate to centre then plicate-striate with crenate margin sometimes radially split, appearing smooth but setulose sub lente. GILLS milky-coffee or fawn then black. STEM 45-70/1-3mm, equal or slightly narrowed upwards, whitish soon tinged vinaceous grey and more conspicuously so as cap expands, entirely white pruinose when fresh and sometimes appearing striate, base white tomentose. SMELL none. SPORE-PRINT cigar-brown.

SPORES ± umber, 10-13(-14)/6-7μm, ellipsoid with excentric germ-pore. BASIDIA 4-spored. MARGINAL CYSTIDIA subglobose or vesiculose to broadly clavate, 14-32μm broad. FACIAL CYSTIDIA not investigated. CAP CUTICLE cellular. SETULES on cap hyaline, lageniform with ± cylindric or slightly narrowed neck and obtuse sometimes slightly thicker apex, 70-90/12-20μm with apex 7-10μm broad. VEIL none.

HABITAT on soil (from Devon in grassy patch where logs had been burnt a few years before). Distribution unknown but recorded from Devon and Yorkshire.

The above description is of British material from Membury, Devon. Readily recognised by purplish-date or brown-vinaceous cap and vinaceous grey stem, together with rather large spores, with excentric germ-pore, and setules on cap with obtuse not or only slightly capitate apex.

Produced in Scotland by Her Majesty's Stationery Office Reprographic Division, Edinburgh
Dd 589869/3800 K8/4179

Mark Twain

THE ADVENTURES OF HUCKLEBERRY FINN
by Mark Twain (1835–1910)
Originally published in 1884
This edition © 2009 Sam Torode
Printed in the USA

www.AmericanRenaissanceBooks.com

The Adventures of

HUCKLEBERRY
FINN

Mark Twain

American Renaissance
NASHVILLE, TENNESSEE

NOTICE

Persons attempting to find a motive in this narrative will be prosecuted;
persons attempting to find a moral in it will be banished;
persons attempting to find a plot in it will be shot.

BY ORDER OF THE AUTHOR
Per G.G., Chief of Ordnance

EXPLANATORY

In this book a number of dialects are used, to wit: the Missouri negro dialect; the extremest form of the backwoods Southwestern dialect; the ordinary "Pike County" dialect; and four modified varieties of this last. The shadings have not been done in a haphazard fashion, or by guesswork; but painstakingly, and with the trustworthy guidance and support of personal familiarity with these several forms of speech.

I make this explanation for the reason that without it many readers would suppose that all these characters were trying to talk alike and not succeeding.

THE AUTHOR

HUCKLEBERRY FINN

SCENE: The Mississippi Valley
TIME: Forty to fifty years ago

Chapter I

You don't know about me without you have read a book by the name of THE ADVENTURES OF TOM SAWYER; but that ain't no matter. That book was made by Mr. Mark Twain, and he told the truth, mainly. There was things which he stretched, but mainly he told the truth. That is nothing. I never seen anybody but lied one time or another, without it was Aunt Polly, or the widow, or maybe Mary. Aunt Polly—Tom's Aunt Polly, she is—and Mary, and the Widow Douglas is all told about in that book, which is mostly a true book, with some stretchers, as I said before.

Now the way that the book winds up is this: Tom and me found the money that the robbers hid in the cave, and it made us rich. We got six thousand dollars apiece— all gold. It was an awful sight of money when it was piled up. Well, Judge Thatcher he took it and put it out at interest, and it fetched us a dollar a day apiece all the year round —more than a body could tell what to do with. The Widow Douglas she took me for her son, and allowed she would sivilize me; but it was rough living in the house all the time, considering how dismal regular and decent the widow was in all her ways; and so when I couldn't stand it no longer I lit out. I got into my old rags and my sugar-hogshead again, and was free and satisfied. But Tom Sawyer he hunted me up and said he was going to start a band of robbers, and I might join if I would go back to the widow and be respectable. So I went back.

The widow she cried over me, and called me a poor lost lamb, and she called me a lot of other names, too, but she never meant no harm by it. She put me in them new clothes again, and I couldn't do nothing but sweat and sweat, and feel all cramped up. Well, then, the old thing commenced again. The widow rung a bell for supper, and you had to come to time. When you got to the table you couldn't go right to eating, but you had to wait for the widow to tuck down her head and grumble a little over the victuals, though there warn't really anything the matter with them,—that is, nothing only everything was cooked by itself. In a barrel of odds and ends it is different; things get mixed up, and the juice kind of swaps around, and the things go better.

After supper she got out her book and learned me about Moses and the Bulrushers, and I was in a sweat to find out all about him; but by and by she let it out that Moses had been dead a considerable long time; so then I didn't care no more about him, because I don't take no stock in dead people.

Pretty soon I wanted to smoke, and asked the widow to let me. But she wouldn't. She said it was a mean practice and wasn't clean, and I must try to not do it any more. That is just the way with some people. They get down on a thing when they don't know nothing about it. Here she was a-bothering about Moses, which was no kin to her, and no use to anybody, being gone, you see, yet finding a power of fault with me for doing a thing that had some good in it. And she took snuff, too; of course that was all right, because she done it herself.

Her sister, Miss Watson, a tolerable slim old maid, with goggles on, had just come to live with her, and took a set at me now with a spelling-book. She worked me middling hard for about an hour, and then the widow made her ease up. I couldn't stood it much longer. Then for an hour it was deadly dull, and I was fidgety. Miss Watson would say, "Don't put your feet up there, Huckleberry;" and "Don't scrunch up like that, Huckleberry—set up straight;" and pretty soon she would say, "Don't gap and stretch like that, Huckleberry—why don't you try to behave?" Then she told me all about the bad place, and I said I wished I was there. She got mad then, but I didn't mean no harm. All I wanted was to go somewheres; all I wanted was a change, I warn't particular. She said it was wicked to say what I said; said she wouldn't say it for the whole world; she was going to live so as to go to the good place. Well, I couldn't see no advantage in going where she was going, so I made up my mind I wouldn't try for it. But I never said so, because it would only make trouble, and wouldn't do no good.

Now she had got a start, and she went on and told me all about the good place. She said all a body would have to do there was to go around all day long with a harp and sing, forever and ever. So I didn't think much of it. But I never said so. I asked her if she reckoned Tom Sawyer would go there, and she said not by a considerable sight. I was glad about that, because I wanted him and me to be together.

Miss Watson she kept pecking at me, and it got tiresome and lonesome. By and by they fetched the niggers in and had prayers, and then everybody was off to bed. I went up to my room with a piece of candle, and put it on the table. Then I set down in a chair by the window and tried to think of something cheerful, but it warn't no use. I felt so lonesome I most wished I was dead. The stars were shining, and the leaves rustled in the woods ever so mournful; and I heard an owl, away off, who-whooing about somebody that was dead, and a whippowill and a dog crying about somebody that was going to die; and the wind was trying to whisper something to me, and I couldn't make out what it was, and so it made the cold shivers run over me. Then away out in the woods I heard that kind of a sound that a ghost makes when it wants to tell about something that's on its mind and can't make itself understood, and so can't rest easy in its grave, and has to go about that way every night grieving. I got so down-hearted and scared I did wish I had some company. Pretty soon a spider went crawling up my shoulder, and I flipped it off and it lit in the candle; and before I could budge it was all shriveled up. I didn't need anybody to tell me that that was an awful bad sign and would fetch me some bad luck, so I was scared and most shook the clothes off of me. I got up and turned around in my tracks three times and crossed my breast every time; and then I tied up a little lock of my hair with a thread to keep witches away. But I hadn't no confidence. You do that when you've lost a horseshoe that you've found, instead of nailing it up over the door, but I hadn't ever heard anybody say it was any way to keep off bad luck when you'd killed a spider.

I set down again, a-shaking all over, and got out my pipe for a smoke; for the house was all as still as death now, and so the widow wouldn't know. Well, after a long time I heard the clock away off in the town go BOOM—BOOM—BOOM—twelve licks; and all still again—stiller than ever. Pretty soon I heard a twig snap down in the dark amongst the trees —something was a stirring. I set still and listened. Directly I could just barely hear a "me-yow! me-yow!" down there. That was good! Says I, "me-yow! me-yow!" as soft as I could, and then I put out the light and scrambled out of the window on to the shed. Then I slipped down to the ground and crawled in among the trees, and, sure enough, there was Tom Sawyer waiting for me.

Chapter II

We went tiptoeing along a path amongst the trees back towards the end of the widow's garden, stooping down so as the branches wouldn't scrape our heads. When we was passing by the kitchen I fell over a root and made a noise. We scrouched down and laid still. Miss Watson's big nigger, named Jim, was setting in the kitchen door; we could see him pretty clear, because there was a light behind him. He got up and stretched his neck out about a minute, listening. Then he says:

"Who dah?"

He listened some more; then he come tiptoeing down and stood right between us; we could a touched him, nearly. Well, likely it was minutes and minutes that there warn't a sound, and we all there so close together. There was a place on my ankle that got to itching, but I dasn't scratch it; and then my ear begun to itch; and next my back, right between my shoulders. Seemed like I'd die if I couldn't scratch. Well, I've noticed that thing plenty times since. If you are with the quality, or at a funeral, or trying to go to sleep when you ain't sleepy—if you are anywheres where it won't do for you to scratch, why you will itch all over in upwards of a thousand places. Pretty soon Jim says:

"Well, I know what I's gwyne to do: I's gwyne to set down here and listen tell I hears it agin."

So he set down on the ground betwixt me and Tom. He leaned his back up against a tree, and stretched his legs out till one of them most touched one of mine. My nose begun to itch. It itched till the tears come into my eyes. But I dasn't scratch. Then it begun to itch on the inside. Next I got to itching underneath. I didn't know how I was going to set still. This miserableness went on as much as six or seven minutes; but it seemed a sight longer than that. I was itching in eleven different places now. I reckoned I couldn't stand it more 'n a minute longer, but I set my teeth hard and got ready to try. Just then Jim begun to breathe heavy; next he begun to snore—and then I was pretty soon comfortable again.

Tom he made a sign to me—kind of a little noise with his mouth—and we went creeping away on our hands and knees. When we was ten foot off Tom whispered to me, and wanted to tie Jim to the tree for fun. But I said no; he might wake and make a disturbance, and then they'd find out I warn't in. Then Tom said he hadn't got candles enough, and he would slip in the kitchen and get some more. I didn't want him to try. I said Jim might wake up and come. But Tom wanted to resk it; so we slid in there and got three candles, and Tom laid five cents on the table for pay. Then we got out, and I was in a sweat to get away; but nothing would do Tom but he must crawl to where Jim was, on his hands and knees, and play something on him. I waited, and it seemed a good while, everything was so still and lonesome.

As soon as Tom was back we cut along the path, around the garden fence, and by and by fetched up on the steep top of the hill the other side of the house. Tom said he slipped Jim's hat off of his head and hung it on a limb right over him, and Jim stirred a little, but he didn't wake. Afterwards Jim said the witches bewitched him and put him in a trance, and rode him all over the State, and then set him under the trees again, and hung his hat on a limb to show who done it. And next time Jim told it he said they rode him down to New Orleans; and, after that, every time he told it he spread it more and more, till by and by he said they rode him all over the world, and tired him most to death, and his back was all over saddle-boils. Jim was monstrous proud about it, and he got so he wouldn't hardly notice the other niggers. Niggers would come miles to hear Jim tell about it, and he was more looked up to than any nigger in that country. Strange niggers would stand with their mouths open and look him all over, same as if he was a wonder. Niggers is always talking about witches in the dark by the kitchen fire; but whenever one was talking and letting on to know all about such things, Jim would happen in and say, "Hm! What you know 'bout witches?" and that nigger was corked up and had to take a back seat. Jim always kept that five-center piece round his neck with a string, and said it was a charm the devil give to him with his own hands, and told him he could cure anybody with it and fetch witches whenever he wanted to just by saying something to it; but he never told what it was he said to it. Niggers would come from all around there and give Jim anything they had, just for a sight of that five-center piece; but they wouldn't touch it, because the devil had had his hands on it. Jim was most ruined for a servant, because he got stuck up on account of having seen the devil and been rode by witches.

Well, when Tom and me got to the edge of the hilltop we looked away down into the village and could see three or four lights twinkling, where there was sick folks, maybe; and the stars over us was sparkling ever so fine; and down by the village was the river, a whole mile broad, and awful still and grand. We went down the hill and found Jo Harper and Ben Rogers, and two or three more of the boys, hid in the old tanyard. So we unhitched a skiff and pulled down the river two mile and a half, to the big scar on the hillside, and went ashore.

We went to a clump of bushes, and Tom made everybody swear to keep the secret, and then showed them a hole in the hill, right in the thickest part of the bushes. Then we lit the candles, and crawled in on our hands and knees. We went about two hundred yards, and then the cave opened up.

Tom poked about amongst the passages, and pretty soon ducked under a wall where you wouldn't a noticed that there was a hole. We went along a narrow place and got into a kind of room, all damp and sweaty and cold, and there we stopped. Tom says:

"Now, we'll start this band of robbers and call it Tom Sawyer's Gang. Everybody that wants to join has got to take an oath, and write his name in blood."

Everybody was willing. So Tom got out a sheet of paper that he had wrote the oath on, and read it. It swore every boy to stick to the band, and never tell any of the secrets; and if anybody done anything to any boy in the band, whichever boy was ordered to kill that person and his family must do it, and he mustn't eat and he mustn't sleep till he had killed them and hacked a cross in their breasts, which was the sign of the band. And nobody that didn't belong to the band could use that mark, and if he did he must be sued; and if he done it again he must be killed. And if anybody that belonged to the band told the secrets, he must have his throat cut, and then have his carcass burnt up and the ashes scattered all around, and his name blotted off of the list with blood and never mentioned again by the gang, but have a curse put on it and be forgot forever.

Everybody said it was a real beautiful oath, and asked Tom if he got it out of his own head. He said, some of it, but the rest was out of pirate-books and robber-books, and every gang that was high-toned had it.

Some thought it would be good to kill the FAMILIES of boys that told the secrets. Tom said it was a good idea, so he took a pencil and wrote it in. Then Ben Rogers says:

"Here's Huck Finn, he hain't got no family; what you going to do 'bout him?"

"Well, hain't he got a father?" says Tom Sawyer.

"Yes, he's got a father, but you can't never find him these days. He used to lay drunk with the hogs in the tanyard, but he hain't been seen in these parts for a year or more."

They talked it over, and they was going to rule me out, because they said every boy must have a family or somebody to kill, or else it wouldn't be fair and square for the others. Well, nobody could think of anything to do—everybody was stumped, and set still. I was most ready to cry; but all at once I thought of a way, and so I offered them Miss Watson—they could kill her. Everybody said: "Oh, she'll do. That's all right. Huck can come in."

Then they all stuck a pin in their fingers to get blood to sign with, and I made my mark on the paper.

"Now," says Ben Rogers, "what's the line of business of this Gang?"

"Nothing only robbery and murder," Tom said.

"But who are we going to rob?—houses, or cattle, or—"

"Stuff! stealing cattle and such things ain't robbery; it's burglary," says Tom Sawyer. "We ain't burglars. That ain't no sort of style. We are highwaymen. We stop stages and carriages on the road, with masks on, and kill the people and take their watches and money."

"Must we always kill the people?"

"Oh, certainly. It's best. Some authorities think different, but mostly it's considered best to kill them—except some that you bring to the cave here, and keep them till they're ransomed."

"Ransomed? What's that?"

"I don't know. But that's what they do. I've seen it in books; and so of course that's what we've got to do."

"But how can we do it if we don't know what it is?"

"Why, blame it all, we've GOT to do it. Don't I tell you it's in the books? Do you want to go to doing different from what's in the books, and get things all muddled up?"

"Oh, that's all very fine to SAY, Tom Sawyer, but how in the nation are these fellows going to be ransomed if we don't know how to do it to them?—that's the thing I want to get at. Now, what do you reckon it is?"

"Well, I don't know. But per'aps if we keep them till they're ransomed, it means that we keep them till they're dead."

"Now, that's something like. That'll answer. Why couldn't you said that before? We'll keep them till they're ransomed to death; and a bothersome lot they'll be, too— eating up everything, and always trying to get loose."

"How you talk, Ben Rogers. How can they get loose when there's a guard over them, ready to shoot them down if they move a peg?"

"A guard! Well, that IS good. So somebody's got to set up all night and never get any sleep, just so as to watch them. I think that's foolishness. Why can't a body take a club and ransom them as soon as they get here?"

"Because it ain't in the books so—that's why. Now, Ben Rogers, do you want to do things regular, or don't you?—that's the idea. Don't you reckon that the people that made the books knows what's the correct thing to do? Do you reckon YOU can learn 'em anything? Not by a good deal. No, sir, we'll just go on and ransom them in the regular way."

"All right. I don't mind; but I say it's a fool way, anyhow. Say, do we kill the women, too?"

"Well, Ben Rogers, if I was as ignorant as you I wouldn't let on. Kill the women? No; nobody ever saw anything in the books like that. You fetch them to the cave, and you're always as polite as pie to them; and by and by they fall in love with you, and never want to go home any more."

"Well, if that's the way I'm agreed, but I don't take no stock in it. Mighty soon we'll have the cave so cluttered up with women, and fellows waiting to be ransomed, that there won't be no place for the robbers. But go ahead, I ain't got nothing to say."

Little Tommy Barnes was asleep now, and when they waked him up he was scared, and cried, and said he wanted to go home to his ma, and didn't want to be a robber any more.

So they all made fun of him, and called him cry-baby, and that made him mad, and he said he would go straight and tell all the secrets. But Tom give him five cents to keep quiet, and said we would all go home and meet next week, and rob somebody and kill some people.

Ben Rogers said he couldn't get out much, only Sundays, and so he wanted to begin next Sunday; but all the boys said it would be wicked to do it on Sunday, and that settled the thing. They agreed to get together and fix a day as soon as they could, and then we elected Tom Sawyer first captain and Jo Harper second captain of the Gang, and so started home.

I clumb up the shed and crept into my window just before day was breaking. My new clothes was all greased up and clayey, and I was dog-tired.

Chapter III

Well, I got a good going-over in the morning from old Miss Watson on account of my clothes; but the widow she didn't scold, but only cleaned off the grease and clay, and looked so sorry that I thought I would behave awhile if I could. Then Miss Watson she took me in the closet and prayed, but nothing come of it. She told me to pray every day, and whatever I asked for I would get it. But it warn't so. I tried it.

Once I got a fish-line, but no hooks. It warn't any good to me without hooks. I tried for the hooks three or four times, but somehow I couldn't make it work. By and by, one day, I asked Miss Watson to try for me, but she said I was a fool. She never told me why, and I couldn't make it out no way.

I set down one time back in the woods, and had a long think about it. I says to myself, if a body can get anything they pray for, why don't Deacon Winn get back the money he lost on pork? Why can't the widow get back her silver snuffbox that was stole? Why can't Miss Watson fat up? No, says I to my self, there ain't nothing in it. I went and told the widow about it, and she said the thing a body could get by praying for it was "spiritual gifts." This was too many for me, but she told me what she meant—I must help other people, and do everything I could for other people, and look out for them all the time, and never think about myself. This was including Miss Watson, as I took it. I went out in the woods and turned it over in my mind a long time, but I couldn't see no advantage about it—except for the other people; so at last I reckoned I wouldn't worry about it any more, but just let it go. Sometimes the widow would take me one side and talk about Providence in a way to make a body's mouth water; but maybe next day Miss Watson would take hold and knock it all down again. I judged I could see that there was two Providences, and a poor chap would stand considerable show with the widow's Providence, but if Miss Watson's got him there warn't no help for him any more. I thought it all out, and reckoned I would belong to the widow's if he wanted me, though I couldn't make out how he was a-going to be any better off then than what he was before, seeing I was so ignorant, and so kind of low-down and ornery.

Pap he hadn't been seen for more than a year, and that was comfortable for me; I didn't want to see him no more. He used to always whale me when he was sober and could get his hands on me; though I used to take to the woods most of the time when he was around. Well, about this time he was found in the river drownded, about twelve mile above town, so people said. They judged it was him, anyway; said this drownded man was just his size, and was ragged, and had uncommon long hair, which was all like pap; but they couldn't make nothing out of the face, because it had been in the water so long it warn't much like a face at all. They said he was floating on his back in the water. They took him and buried him on the bank. But I warn't comfortable long, because I happened to think of something. I knowed mighty well that a drownded man don't float on his back, but on his face. So I knowed, then, that this warn't pap, but a woman dressed up in a man's clothes. So I was uncomfortable again. I judged the old man would turn up again by and by, though I wished he wouldn't.

We played robber now and then about a month, and then I resigned. All the boys did. We hadn't robbed nobody, hadn't killed any people, but only just pretended. We used to hop out of the woods and go charging down on hog-drivers and women in carts taking garden stuff to market, but we never hived any of them. Tom Sawyer called the hogs "ingots," and he called the turnips and stuff "julery," and we would go to the cave and powwow over what we had done, and how many people we had killed and marked. But I couldn't see no profit in it. One time Tom sent a boy to run about town with a blazing stick, which he called a slogan (which was the sign for the Gang to get together), and then he said he had got secret news by his spies that next day a whole parcel of Spanish merchants and rich A-rabs was going to camp in Cave Hollow with two hundred elephants, and six hundred camels, and over a thousand "sumter" mules, all loaded down with di'monds, and they didn't have only a guard of four hundred soldiers, and so we would lay in ambuscade, as he called it, and kill the lot and scoop the things. He said we must slick up our swords and guns, and get ready. He never could go after even a turnip-cart but he must have the swords and guns all scoured up for it, though they was only lath and broomsticks, and you might scour at them till you rotted, and then they warn't worth a mouthful of ashes more than what they was before. I didn't believe we could lick such a crowd of Spaniards and A-rabs, but I wanted to see the camels and elephants, so I was on hand next day, Saturday, in the ambuscade; and when we got the word we rushed out of the woods and down the hill. But there warn't no Spaniards and A-rabs, and there warn't no camels nor no elephants. It warn't anything but a Sunday-school picnic, and only a primer-class at that. We busted it up, and chased the children up the hollow; but we never got anything but some doughnuts and jam, though Ben Rogers got a rag doll, and Jo Harper got a hymn-book and a tract; and then the teacher charged in, and made us drop everything and cut. I didn't see no di'monds, and I told Tom Sawyer so. He said there was loads of them there, anyway; and he said there was A-rabs there, too, and elephants and things. I said, why couldn't we see them, then? He said if I warn't so ignorant, but had read a book called Don Quixote, I would know without asking. He said it was all done by enchantment. He said there was hundreds of soldiers there, and elephants and treasure, and so on, but we had enemies which he called magicians; and they had turned the whole thing into an infant Sunday-school, just out of spite. I said, all right; then the thing for us to do was to go for the magicians. Tom Sawyer said I was a numskull.

"Why," said he, "a magician could call up a lot of genies, and they would hash you up like nothing before you could say Jack Robinson. They are as tall as a tree and as big around as a church."

"Well," I says, "s'pose we got some genies to help US—can't we lick the other crowd then?"

"How you going to get them?"

"I don't know. How do THEY get them?"

"Why, they rub an old tin lamp or an iron ring, and then the genies come tearing in, with the thunder and lightning a-ripping around and the smoke a-rolling, and everything they're told to do they up and do it. They don't think nothing of pulling a shot-tower up by the roots, and belting a Sunday-school superintendent over the head with it—or any other man."

"Who makes them tear around so?"

"Why, whoever rubs the lamp or the ring. They belong to whoever rubs the lamp or the ring, and they've got to do whatever he says. If he tells them to build a palace forty miles long out of di'monds, and fill it full of chewing-gum, or whatever you want, and fetch an emperor's daughter from China for you to marry, they've got to do it—and they've got to do it before sun-up next morning, too. And more: they've got to waltz that palace around over the country wherever you want it, you understand."

"Well," says I, "I think they are a pack of flat-heads for not keeping the palace themselves 'stead of fooling them away like that. And what's more—if I was one of them I would see a man in Jericho before I would drop my business and come to him for the rubbing of an old tin lamp."

"How you talk, Huck Finn. Why, you'd HAVE to come when he rubbed it, whether you wanted to or not."

"What! and I as high as a tree and as big as a church? All right, then; I WOULD come; but I lay I'd make that man climb the highest tree there was in the country."

"Shucks, it ain't no use to talk to you, Huck Finn. You don't seem to know anything, somehow—perfect saphead."

I thought all this over for two or three days, and then I reckoned I would see if there was anything in it. I got an old tin lamp and an iron ring, and went out in the woods and rubbed and rubbed till I sweat like an Injun, calculating to build a palace and sell it; but it warn't no use, none of the genies come. So then I judged that all that stuff was only just one of Tom Sawyer's lies. I reckoned he believed in the A-rabs and the elephants, but as for me I think different. It had all the marks of a Sunday-school.

Chapter IV

Well, three or four months run along, and it was well into the winter now. I had been to school most all the time and could spell and read and write just a little, and could say the multiplication table up to six times seven is thirty-five, and I don't reckon I could ever get any further than that if I was to live forever. I don't take no stock in mathematics, anyway.

At first I hated the school, but by and by I got so I could stand it. Whenever I got uncommon tired I played hookey, and the hiding I got next day done me good and cheered me up. So the longer I went to school the easier it got to be. I was getting sort of used to the widow's ways, too, and they warn't so raspy on me. Living in a house and sleeping in a bed pulled on me pretty tight mostly, but before the cold weather I used to slide out and sleep in the woods sometimes, and so that was a rest to me. I liked the old ways best, but I was getting so I liked the new ones, too, a little bit. The widow said I was coming along slow but sure, and doing very satisfactory. She said she warn't ashamed of me.

One morning I happened to turn over the salt-cellar at breakfast. I reached for some of it as quick as I could to throw over my left shoulder and keep off the bad luck, but Miss Watson was in ahead of me, and crossed me off. She says, "Take your hands away, Huckleberry; what a mess you are always making!" The widow put in a good word for me, but that warn't going to keep off the bad luck, I knowed that well enough. I started out, after breakfast, feeling worried and shaky, and wondering where it was going to fall on me, and what it was going to be. There is ways to keep off some kinds of bad luck, but this wasn't one of them kind; so I never tried to do anything, but just poked along low-spirited and on the watch-out.

I went down to the front garden and clumb over the stile where you go through the high board fence. There was an inch of new snow on the ground, and I seen somebody's tracks. They had come up from the quarry and stood around the stile a while, and then went on around the garden fence. It was funny they hadn't come in, after standing around so. I couldn't make it out. It was very curious, somehow. I was going to follow around, but I stooped down to look at the tracks first. I didn't notice anything at first, but next I did. There was a cross in the left boot-heel made with big nails, to keep off the devil.

I was up in a second and shinning down the hill. I looked over my shoulder every now and then, but I didn't see nobody. I was at Judge Thatcher's as quick as I could get there. He said:

"Why, my boy, you are all out of breath. Did you come for your interest?"

"No, sir," I says; "is there some for me?"

"Oh, yes, a half-yearly is in last night—over a hundred and fifty dollars. Quite a fortune for you. You had better let me invest it along with your six thousand, because if you take it you'll spend it."

"No, sir," I says, "I don't want to spend it. I don't want it at all—nor the six thousand, nuther. I want you to take it; I want to give it to you—the six thousand and all."

He looked surprised. He couldn't seem to make it out. He says:

"Why, what can you mean, my boy?"

I says, "Don't you ask me no questions about it, please. You'll take it—won't you?"

He says:

"Well, I'm puzzled. Is something the matter?"

"Please take it," says I, "and don't ask me nothing—then I won't have to tell no lies."

He studied a while, and then he says:

"Oho-o! I think I see. You want to SELL all your property to me—not give it. That's the correct idea."

Then he wrote something on a paper and read it over, and says:

"There; you see it says 'for a consideration.' That means I have bought it of you and paid you for it. Here's a dollar for you. Now you sign it."

So I signed it, and left.

Miss Watson's nigger, Jim, had a hair-ball as big as your fist, which had been took out of the fourth stomach of an ox, and he used to do magic with it. He said there was a spirit inside of it, and it knowed everything. So I went to him that night and told him pap was here again, for I found his tracks in the snow. What I wanted to know was, what he was going to do, and was he going to stay? Jim got out his hair-ball and said something over it, and then he held it up and dropped it on the floor. It fell pretty solid, and only rolled about an inch. Jim tried it again, and then another time, and it acted just the same. Jim got down on his knees, and put his ear against it and listened. But it warn't no use; he said it wouldn't talk. He said sometimes it wouldn't talk without money. I told him I had an old slick counterfeit quarter that warn't no good because the brass showed through the silver a little, and it wouldn't pass nohow, even if the brass didn't show, because it was so slick it felt greasy, and so that would tell on it every time. (I reckoned I wouldn't say nothing about the dollar I got from the judge.) I said it was pretty bad money, but maybe the hair-ball would take it, because maybe it wouldn't know the difference. Jim smelt it and bit it and rubbed it, and said he would manage so the hair-ball would think it was good. He said he would split open a raw Irish potato and stick the quarter in between and keep it there all night, and next morning you couldn't see no brass, and it wouldn't feel greasy no more, and so anybody in town would take it in a minute, let alone a hair-ball. Well, I knowed a potato would do that before, but I had forgot it.

Jim put the quarter under the hair-ball, and got down and listened again. This time he said the hair-ball was all right. He said it would tell my whole fortune if I wanted it to. I says, go on. So the hair-ball talked to Jim, and Jim told it to me. He says:

"Yo' ole father doan' know yit what he's a-gwyne to do. Sometimes he spec he'll go 'way, en den agin he spec he'll stay. De bes' way is to res' easy en let de ole man take his own way. Dey's two angels hoverin' roun' 'bout him. One uv 'em is white en shiny, en t'other one is black. De white one gits him to go right a little while, den de black one sail in en bust it all up. A body can't tell yit which one gwyne to fetch him at de las'. But you is all right. You gwyne to have considable trouble in yo' life, en considable joy. Sometimes you gwyne to git hurt, en sometimes you gwyne to git sick; but every time you's gwyne to git well agin. Dey's two gals flyin' 'bout you in yo' life. One uv 'em's light en t'other one is dark. One is rich en t'other is po'. You's gwyne to marry de po' one fust en de rich one by en by. You wants to keep 'way fum de water as much as you kin, en don't run no resk, 'kase it's down in de bills dat you's gwyne to git hung."

When I lit my candle and went up to my room that night there sat pap—his own self!

Chapter V

I had shut the door. Then I turned around and there he was. I used to be scared of him all the time, he tanned me so much. I reckoned I was scared now, too; but in a minute I see I was mistaken—that is, after the first jolt, as you may say, when my breath sort of hitched, he being so unexpected; but right away after I see I warn't scared of him worth bothring about.

He was most fifty, and he looked it. His hair was long and tangled and greasy, and hung down, and you could see his eyes shining through like he was behind vines. It was all black, no gray; so was his long, mixed-up whiskers. There warn't no color in his face, where his face showed; it was white; not like another man's white, but a white to make a body sick, a white to make a body's flesh crawl—a tree-toad white, a fish-belly white. As for his clothes—just rags, that was all. He had one ankle resting on t'other knee; the boot on that foot was busted, and two of his toes stuck through, and he worked them now and then. His hat was laying on the floor—an old black slouch with the top caved in, like a lid.

I stood a-looking at him; he set there a-looking at me, with his chair tilted back a little. I set the candle down. I noticed the window was up; so he had clumb in by the shed. He kept a-looking me all over. By and by he says:

"Starchy clothes—very. You think you're a good deal of a big-bug, DON'T you?"

"Maybe I am, maybe I ain't," I says.

"Don't you give me none o' your lip," says he. "You've put on considerable many frills since I been away. I'll take you down a peg before I get done with you. You're educated, too, they say—can read and write. You think you're better'n your father, now, don't you, because he can't? I'LL take it out of you. Who told you you might meddle with such hifalut'n foolishness, hey?—who told you you could?"

"The widow. She told me."

"The widow, hey?—and who told the widow she could put in her shovel about a thing that ain't none of her business?"

"Nobody never told her."

"Well, I'll learn her how to meddle. And looky here—you drop that school, you hear? I'll learn people to bring up a boy to put on airs over his own father and let on to be better'n what HE is. You lemme catch you fooling around that school again, you hear? Your mother couldn't read, and she couldn't write, nuther, before she died. None of the family couldn't before THEY died. I can't; and here you're a-swelling yourself up like this. I ain't the man to stand it—you hear? Say, lemme hear you read."

I took up a book and begun something about General Washington and the wars. When I'd read about a half a minute, he fetched the book a whack with his hand and knocked it across the house. He says:

"It's so. You can do it. I had my doubts when you told me. Now looky here; you stop that putting on frills. I won't have it. I'll lay for you, my smarty; and if I catch you about that school I'll tan you good. First you know you'll get religion, too. I never see such a son."

He took up a little blue and yaller picture of some cows and a boy, and says:

"What's this?"

"It's something they give me for learning my lessons good."

He tore it up, and says:

"I'll give you something better—I'll give you a cowhide."

He set there a-mumbling and a-growling a minute, and then he says:

"Ain't you a sweet-scented dandy, though? A bed; and bedclothes; and a look'n'-glass; and a piece of carpet on the floor—and your own father got to sleep with the hogs in the tanyard. I never see such a son. I bet I'll take some o' these frills out o' you before I'm done with you. Why, there ain't no end to your airs—they say you're rich. Hey?—how's that?"

"They lie—that's how."

"Looky here—mind how you talk to me; I'm a-standing about all I can stand now—so don't gimme no sass. I've been in town two days, and I hain't heard nothing but about you bein' rich. I heard about it away down the river, too. That's why I come. You git me that money to-morrow—I want it."

"I hain't got no money."

"It's a lie. Judge Thatcher's got it. You git it. I want it."

"I hain't got no money, I tell you. You ask Judge Thatcher; he'll tell you the same."

"All right. I'll ask him; and I'll make him pungle, too, or I'll know the reason why. Say, how much you got in your pocket? I want it."

"I hain't got only a dollar, and I want that to—"

"It don't make no difference what you want it for—you just shell it out."

He took it and bit it to see if it was good, and then he said he was going down town to get some whisky; said he hadn't had a drink all day. When he had got out on the shed he put his head in again, and cussed me for putting on frills and trying to be better than him; and when I reckoned he was gone he come back and put his head in again, and told me to mind about that school, because he was going to lay for me and lick me if I didn't drop that.

Next day he was drunk, and he went to Judge Thatcher's and bullyragged him, and tried to make him give up the money; but he couldn't, and then he swore he'd make the law force him.

The judge and the widow went to law to get the court to take me away from him and let one of them be my guardian; but it was a new judge that had just come, and he didn't know the old man; so he said courts mustn't interfere and separate families if they could help it; said he'd druther not take a child away from its father. So Judge Thatcher and the widow had to quit on the business.

That pleased the old man till he couldn't rest. He said he'd cowhide me till I was black and blue if I didn't raise some money for him. I borrowed three dollars from Judge Thatcher, and pap took it and got drunk, and went a-blowing around and cussing and whooping and carrying on; and he kept it up all over town, with a tin pan, till most midnight; then they jailed him, and next day they had him before court, and jailed him again for a week. But he said HE was satisfied; said he was boss of his son, and he'd make it warm for HIM.

When he got out the new judge said he was a-going to make a man of him. So he took him to his own house, and dressed him up clean and nice, and had him to breakfast and dinner and supper with the family, and was just old pie to him, so to speak. And after supper he talked to him about temperance and such things till the old man cried, and said he'd been a fool, and fooled away his life; but now he was a-going to turn over a new leaf and be a man nobody wouldn't be ashamed of, and he hoped the judge would help him and not look down on him. The judge said he could hug him for them words; so he cried, and his wife she cried again; pap said he'd been a man that had always been misunderstood before, and the judge said he believed it. The old man said that what a man wanted that was down was sympathy, and the judge said it was so; so they cried again. And when it was bedtime the old man rose up and held out his hand, and says:

"Look at it, gentlemen and ladies all; take a-hold of it; shake it. There's a hand that was the hand of a hog; but it ain't so no more; it's the hand of a man that's started in on a new life, and'll die before he'll go back. You mark them words—don't forget I said them. It's a clean hand now; shake it—don't be afeard."

So they shook it, one after the other, all around, and cried. The judge's wife she kissed it. Then the old man he signed a pledge—made his mark. The judge said it was the holiest time on record, or something like that. Then they tucked the old man into a beautiful room, which was the spare room, and in the night some time he got powerful thirsty and clumb out on to the porch-roof and slid down a stanchion and traded his new coat for a jug of forty-rod, and clumb back again and had a good old time; and towards daylight he crawled out again, drunk as a fiddler, and rolled off the porch and broke his left arm in two places, and was most froze to death when somebody found him after sun-up. And when they come to look at that spare room they had to take soundings before they could navigate it.

The judge he felt kind of sore. He said he reckoned a body could reform the old man with a shotgun, maybe, but he didn't know no other way.

Chapter VI

Well, pretty soon the old man was up and around again, and then he went for Judge Thatcher in the courts to make him give up that money, and he went for me, too, for not stopping school. He catched me a couple of times and thrashed me, but I went to school just the same, and dodged him or outrun him most of the time. I didn't want to go to school much before, but I reckoned I'd go now to spite pap. That law trial was a slow business—appeared like they warn't ever going to get started on it; so every now and then I'd borrow two or three dollars off of the judge for him, to keep from getting a cowhiding. Every time he got money he got drunk; and every time he got drunk he raised Cain around town; and every time he raised Cain he got jailed. He was just suited—this kind of thing was right in his line.

He got to hanging around the widow's too much and so she told him at last that if he didn't quit using around there she would make trouble for him. Well, WASN'T he mad? He said he would show who was Huck Finn's boss. So he watched out for me one day in the spring, and catched me, and took me up the river about three mile in a skiff, and crossed over to the Illinois shore where it was woody and there warn't no houses but an old log hut in a place where the timber was so thick you couldn't find it if you didn't know where it was.

He kept me with him all the time, and I never got a chance to run off. We lived in that old cabin, and he always locked the door and put the key under his head nights. He had a gun which he had stole, I reckon, and we fished and hunted, and that was what we lived on. Every little while he locked me in and went down to the store, three miles, to the ferry, and traded fish and game for whisky, and fetched it home and got drunk and had a good time, and licked me. The widow she found out where I was by and by, and she sent a man over to try to get hold of me; but pap drove him off with the gun, and it warn't long after that till I was used to being where I was, and liked it—all but the cowhide part.

It was kind of lazy and jolly, laying off comfortable all day, smoking and fishing, and no books nor study. Two months or more run along, and my clothes got to be all rags and dirt, and I didn't see how I'd ever got to like it so well at the widow's, where you had to wash, and eat on a plate, and comb up, and go to bed and get up regular, and be forever bothering over a book, and have old Miss Watson pecking at you all the time. I didn't want to go back no more. I had stopped cussing, because the widow didn't like it; but now I took to it again because pap hadn't no objections. It was pretty good times up in the woods there, take it all around.

But by and by pap got too handy with his hick'ry, and I couldn't stand it. I was all over welts. He got to going away so much, too, and locking me in. Once he locked me in and was gone three days. It was dreadful lonesome. I judged he had got drowned, and I wasn't ever going to get out any more. I was scared. I made up my mind I would fix up some way to leave there. I had tried to get out of that cabin many a time, but I couldn't find no way. There warn't a window to it big enough for a dog to get through. I couldn't get up the chimbly; it was too narrow. The door was thick, solid oak slabs. Pap was pretty careful not to leave a knife or anything in the cabin when he was away; I reckon I had hunted the place over as much as a hundred times; well, I was most all the time at it, because it was about the only way to put in the time. But this time I found something at last; I found an old rusty wood-saw without any handle; it was laid in between a rafter and the clapboards of the roof. I greased it up and went to work. There was an old horse-blanket nailed against the logs at the far end of the cabin behind the table, to keep the wind from blowing through the chinks and putting the candle out. I got under the table and raised the blanket, and went to work to saw a section of the big bottom log out—big enough to let me through. Well, it was a good long job, but I was getting towards the end of it when I heard pap's gun in the woods. I got rid of the signs of my work, and dropped the blanket and hid my saw, and pretty soon pap come in.

Pap warn't in a good humor—so he was his natural self. He said he was down town, and everything was going wrong. His lawyer said he reckoned he would win his lawsuit and get the money if they ever got started on the trial; but then there was ways to put it off a long time, and Judge Thatcher knowed how to do it. And he said people allowed there'd be another trial to get me away from him and give me to the widow for my guardian, and they guessed it would win this time. This shook me up considerable, because I didn't want to go back to the widow's any more and be so cramped up and sivilized, as they called it. Then the old man got to cussing, and cussed everything and everybody he could think of, and then cussed them all over again to make sure he hadn't skipped any, and after that he polished off with a kind of a general cuss all round, including a considerable parcel of people which he didn't know the names of, and so called them what's-his-name when he got to them, and went right along with his cussing.

He said he would like to see the widow get me. He said he would watch out, and if they tried to come any such game on him he knowed of a place six or seven mile off to stow me in, where they might hunt till they dropped and they couldn't find me. That made me pretty uneasy again, but only for a minute; I reckoned I wouldn't stay on hand till he got that chance.

The old man made me go to the skiff and fetch the things he had got.

There was a fifty-pound sack of corn meal, and a side of bacon, ammunition, and a four-gallon jug of whisky, and an old book and two newspapers for wadding, besides some tow. I toted up a load, and went back and set down on the bow of the skiff to rest. I thought it all over, and I reckoned I would walk off with the gun and some lines, and take to the woods when I run away. I guessed I wouldn't stay in one place, but just tramp right across the country, mostly night times, and hunt and fish to keep alive, and so get so far away that the old man nor the widow couldn't ever find me any more. I judged I would saw out and leave that night if pap got drunk enough, and I reckoned he would. I got so full of it I didn't notice how long I was staying till the old man hollered and asked me whether I was asleep or drownded.

I got the things all up to the cabin, and then it was about dark. While I was cooking supper the old man took a swig or two and got sort of warmed up, and went to ripping again. He had been drunk over in town, and laid in the gutter all night, and he was a sight to look at. A body would a thought he was Adam—he was just all mud. Whenever his liquor begun to work he most always went for the govment, this time he says:

"Call this a govment! why, just look at it and see what it's like. Here's the law a-standing ready to take a man's son away from him—a man's own son, which he has had all the trouble and all the anxiety and all the expense of raising. Yes, just as that man has got that son raised at last, and ready to go to work and begin to do suthin' for HIM and give him a rest, the law up and goes for him. And they call THAT govment! That ain't all, nuther. The law backs that old Judge Thatcher up and helps him to keep me out o' my property. Here's what the law does: The law takes a man worth six thousand dollars and up'ards, and jams him into an old trap of a cabin like this, and lets him go round in clothes that ain't fitten for a hog. They call that govment! A man can't get his rights in a govment like this. Sometimes I've a mighty notion to just leave the country for good and all. Yes, and I TOLD 'em so; I told old Thatcher so to his face. Lots of 'em heard me, and can tell what I said. Says I, for two cents I'd leave the blamed country and never come a-near it agin. Them's the very words. I says look at my hat—if you call it a hat—but the lid raises up and the rest of it goes down till it's below my chin, and then it ain't rightly a hat at all, but more like my head was shoved up through a jint o' stove-pipe. Look at it, says I —such a hat for me to wear—one of the wealthiest men in this town if I could git my rights.

"Oh, yes, this is a wonderful govment, wonderful. Why, looky here. There was a free nigger there from Ohio—a mulatter, most as white as a white man. He had the whitest shirt on you ever see, too, and the shiniest hat; and there ain't a man in that town that's got as fine clothes as what he had; and he had a gold watch and chain, and a silver-headed cane—the awfulest old gray-headed nabob in the State. And what do you think? They said he was a p'fessor in a college, and could talk all kinds of languages, and knowed everything. And that ain't the wust. They said he could VOTE when he was at home. Well, that let me out. Thinks I, what is the country a-coming to? It was 'lection day, and I was just about to go and vote myself if I warn't too drunk to get there; but when they told me there was a State in this country where they'd let that nigger vote, I drawed out. I says I'll never vote agin. Them's the very words I said; they all heard me; and the country may rot for all me—I'll never vote agin as long as I live. And to see the cool way of that nigger—why, he wouldn't a give me the road if I hadn't shoved him out o' the way. I says to the people, why ain't this nigger put up at auction and sold?—that's what I want to know. And what do you reckon they said? Why, they said he couldn't be sold till he'd been in the State six months, and he hadn't been there that long yet. There, now—that's a specimen. They call that a govment that can't sell a free nigger till he's been in the State six months. Here's a govment that calls itself a govment, and lets on to be a govment, and thinks it is a govment, and yet's got to set stock-still for six whole months before it can take a hold of a prowling, thieving, infernal, white-shirted free nigger, and—"

Pap was agoing on so he never noticed where his old limber legs was taking him to, so he went head over heels over the tub of salt pork and barked both shins, and the rest of his speech was all the hottest kind of language—mostly hove at the nigger and the govment, though he give the tub some, too, all along, here and there. He hopped around the cabin considerable, first on one leg and then on the other, holding first one shin and then the other one, and at last he let out with his left foot all of a sudden and fetched the tub a rattling kick. But it warn't good judgment, because that was the boot that had a couple of his toes leaking out of the front end of it; so now he raised a howl that fairly made a body's hair raise, and down he went in the dirt, and rolled there, and held his toes; and the cussing he done then laid over anything he had ever done previous. He said so his own self afterwards. He had heard old Sowberry Hagan in his best days, and he said it laid over him, too; but I reckon that was sort of piling it on, maybe.

After supper pap took the jug, and said he had enough whisky there for two drunks and one delirium tremens. That was always his word. I judged he would be blind drunk in about an hour, and then I would steal the key, or saw myself out, one or t'other. He drank and drank, and tumbled down on his blankets by and by; but luck didn't run my way. He didn't go sound asleep, but was uneasy. He groaned and moaned and thrashed around this way and that for a long time. At last I got so sleepy I couldn't keep my eyes open all I could do, and so before I knowed what I was about I was sound asleep, and the candle burning.

I don't know how long I was asleep, but all of a sudden there was an awful scream and I was up. There was pap looking wild, and skipping around every which way and yelling about snakes. He said they was crawling up his legs; and then he would give a jump and scream, and say one had bit him on the cheek—but I couldn't see no snakes. He started and run round and round the cabin, hollering "Take him off! take him off! he's biting me on the neck!" I never see a man look so wild in the eyes. Pretty soon he was all fagged out, and fell down panting; then he rolled over and over wonderful fast, kicking things every which way, and striking and grabbing at the air with his hands, and screaming and saying there was devils a-hold of him. He wore out by and by, and laid still a while, moaning. Then he laid stiller, and didn't make a sound. I could hear the owls and the wolves away off in the woods, and it seemed terrible still. He was laying over by the corner. By and by he raised up part way and listened, with his head to one side. He says, very low:

"Tramp—tramp—tramp; that's the dead; tramp—tramp—tramp; they're coming after me; but I won't go. Oh, they're here! don't touch me —don't! hands off— they're cold; let go. Oh, let a poor devil alone!"

Then he went down on all fours and crawled off, begging them to let him alone, and he rolled himself up in his blanket and wallowed in under the old pine table, still a-begging; and then he went to crying. I could hear him through the blanket.

By and by he rolled out and jumped up on his feet looking wild, and he see me and went for me. He chased me round and round the place with a clasp-knife, calling me the Angel of Death, and saying he would kill me, and then I couldn't come for him no more. I begged, and told him I was only Huck; but he laughed SUCH a screechy laugh, and roared and cussed, and kept on chasing me up. Once when I turned short and dodged under his arm he made a grab and got me by the jacket between my shoulders, and I thought I was gone; but I slid out of the jacket quick as lightning, and saved myself. Pretty soon he was all tired out, and dropped down with his back against the door, and said he would rest a minute and then kill me. He put his knife under him, and said he would sleep and get strong, and then he would see who was who.

So he dozed off pretty soon. By and by I got the old split-bottom chair and clumb up as easy as I could, not to make any noise, and got down the gun. I slipped the ramrod down it to make sure it was loaded, then I laid it across the turnip barrel, pointing towards pap, and set down behind it to wait for him to stir. And how slow and still the time did drag along.

Chapter *VII*

"**G**it up! What you 'bout?"

I opened my eyes and looked around, trying to make out where I was. It was after sun-up, and I had been sound asleep. Pap was standing over me looking sour and sick, too. He says:

"What you doin' with this gun?"

I judged he didn't know nothing about what he had been doing, so I says:

"Somebody tried to get in, so I was laying for him."

"Why didn't you roust me out?"

"Well, I tried to, but I couldn't; I couldn't budge you."

"Well, all right. Don't stand there palavering all day, but out with you and see if there's a fish on the lines for breakfast. I'll be along in a minute."

He unlocked the door, and I cleared out up the river-bank. I noticed some pieces of limbs and such things floating down, and a sprinkling of bark; so I knowed the river had begun to rise. I reckoned I would have great times now if I was over at the town. The June rise used to be always luck for me; because as soon as that rise begins here comes cordwood floating down, and pieces of log rafts—sometimes a dozen logs together; so all you have to do is to catch them and sell them to the wood-yards and the sawmill.

I went along up the bank with one eye out for pap and t'other one out for what the rise might fetch along. Well, all at once here comes a canoe; just a beauty, too, about thirteen or fourteen foot long, riding high like a duck. I shot head-first off of the bank like a frog, clothes and all on, and struck out for the canoe. I just expected there'd be somebody laying down in it, because people often done that to fool folks, and when a chap had pulled a skiff out most to it they'd raise up and laugh at him. But it warn't so this time. It was a drift-canoe sure enough, and I clumb in and paddled her ashore. Thinks I, the old man will be glad when he sees this—she's worth ten dollars. But when I got to shore pap wasn't in sight yet, and as I was running her into a little creek like a gully, all hung over with vines and willows, I struck another idea: I judged I'd hide her good, and then, 'stead of taking to the woods when I run off, I'd go down the river about fifty mile and camp in one place for good, and not have such a rough time tramping on foot.

It was pretty close to the shanty, and I thought I heard the old man coming all the time; but I got her hid; and then I out and looked around a bunch of willows, and there was the old man down the path a piece just drawing a bead on a bird with his gun. So he hadn't seen anything.

When he got along I was hard at it taking up a "trot" line. He abused me a little for being so slow; but I told him I fell in the river, and that was what made me so long. I knowed he would see I was wet, and then he would be asking questions. We got five catfish off the lines and went home.

While we laid off after breakfast to sleep up, both of us being about wore out, I got to thinking that if I could fix up some way to keep pap and the widow from trying to follow me, it would be a certainer thing than trusting to luck to get far enough off before they missed me; you see, all kinds of things might happen. Well, I didn't see no way for a while, but by and by pap raised up a minute to drink another barrel of water, and he says:

"Another time a man comes a-prowling round here you roust me out, you hear? That man warn't here for no good. I'd a shot him. Next time you roust me out, you hear?"

Then he dropped down and went to sleep again; but what he had been saying give me the very idea I wanted. I says to myself, I can fix it now so nobody won't think of following me.

About twelve o'clock we turned out and went along up the bank. The river was coming up pretty fast, and lots of driftwood going by on the rise. By and by along comes part of a log raft—nine logs fast together. We went out with the skiff and towed it ashore. Then we had dinner. Anybody but pap would a waited and seen the day through, so as to catch more stuff; but that warn't pap's style. Nine logs was enough for one time; he must shove right over to town and sell. So he locked me in and took the skiff, and started off towing the raft about half-past three. I judged he wouldn't come back that night. I waited till I reckoned he had got a good start; then I out with my saw, and went to work on that log again. Before he was t'other side of the river I was out of the hole; him and his raft was just a speck on the water away off yonder.

I took the sack of corn meal and took it to where the canoe was hid, and shoved the vines and branches apart and put it in; then I done the same with the side of bacon; then the whisky-jug. I took all the coffee and sugar there was, and all the ammunition; I took the wadding; I took the bucket and gourd; I took a dipper and a tin cup, and my old saw and two blankets, and the skillet and the coffee-pot. I took fish-lines and matches and other things—everything that was worth a cent. I cleaned out the place. I wanted an axe, but there wasn't any, only the one out at the woodpile, and I knowed why I was going to leave that. I fetched out the gun, and now I was done.

I had wore the ground a good deal crawling out of the hole and dragging out so many things. So I fixed that as good as I could from the outside by scattering dust on the place, which covered up the smoothness and the sawdust. Then I fixed the piece of log back into its place, and put two rocks under it and one against it to hold it there, for it was bent up at that place and didn't quite touch ground. If you stood four or five foot away and didn't know it was sawed, you wouldn't never notice it; and besides, this was the back of the cabin, and it warn't likely anybody would go fooling around there.

It was all grass clear to the canoe, so I hadn't left a track. I followed around to see. I stood on the bank and looked out over the river. All safe. So I took the gun and went up a piece into the woods, and was hunting around for some birds when I see a wild pig; hogs soon went wild in them bottoms after they had got away from the prairie farms. I shot this fellow and took him into camp.

I took the axe and smashed in the door. I beat it and hacked it considerable a-doing it. I fetched the pig in, and took him back nearly to the table and hacked into his throat with the axe, and laid him down on the ground to bleed; I say ground because it was ground—hard packed, and no boards. Well, next I took an old sack and put a lot of big rocks in it—all I could drag—and I started it from the pig, and dragged it to the door and through the woods down to the river and dumped it in, and down it sunk, out of sight. You could easy see that something had been dragged over the ground. I did wish Tom Sawyer was there; I knowed he would take an interest in this kind of business, and throw in the fancy touches. Nobody could spread himself like Tom Sawyer in such a thing as that.

Well, last I pulled out some of my hair, and blooded the axe good, and stuck it on the back side, and slung the axe in the corner. Then I took up the pig and held him to my breast with my jacket (so he couldn't drip) till I got a good piece below the house and then dumped him into the river. Now I thought of something else. So I went and got the bag of meal and my old saw out of the canoe, and fetched them to the house. I took the bag to where it used to stand, and ripped a hole in the bottom of it with the saw, for there warn't no knives and forks on the place —pap done everything with his clasp-knife about the cooking. Then I carried the sack about a hundred yards across the grass and through the willows east of the house, to a shallow lake that was five mile wide and full of rushes—and ducks too, you might say, in the season. There was a slough or a creek leading out of it on the other side that went miles away, I don't know where, but it didn't go to the river. The meal sifted out and made a little track all the way to the lake. I dropped pap's whetstone there too, so as to look like it had been done by accident. Then I tied up the rip in the meal sack with a string, so it wouldn't leak no more, and took it and my saw to the canoe again.

It was about dark now; so I dropped the canoe down the river under some willows that hung over the bank, and waited for the moon to rise. I made fast to a willow; then I took a bite to eat, and by and by laid down in the canoe to smoke a pipe and lay out a plan. I says to myself, they'll follow the track of that sackful of rocks to the shore and then drag the river for me. And they'll follow that meal track to the lake and go browsing down the creek that leads out of it to find the robbers that killed me and took the things. They won't ever hunt the river for anything but my dead carcass. They'll soon get tired of that, and won't bother no more about me. All right; I can stop anywhere I want to. Jackson's Island is good enough for me; I know that island pretty well, and nobody ever comes there. And then I can paddle over to town nights, and slink around and pick up things I want. Jackson's Island's the place.

I was pretty tired, and the first thing I knowed I was asleep. When I woke up I didn't know where I was for a minute. I set up and looked around, a little scared. Then I remembered. The river looked miles and miles across. The moon was so bright I could a counted the drift logs that went a-slipping along, black and still, hundreds of yards out from shore. Everything was dead quiet, and it looked late, and SMELT late. You know what I mean—I don't know the words to put it in.

I took a good gap and a stretch, and was just going to unhitch and start when I heard a sound away over the water. I listened. Pretty soon I made it out. It was that dull kind of a regular sound that comes from oars working in rowlocks when it's a still night. I peeped out through the willow branches, and there it was—a skiff, away across the water. I couldn't tell how many was in it. It kept a-coming, and when it was abreast of me I see there warn't but one man in it. Think's I, maybe it's pap, though I warn't expecting him. He dropped below me with the current, and by and by he came a-swinging up shore in the easy water, and he went by so close I could a reached out the gun and touched him. Well, it WAS pap, sure enough—and sober, too, by the way he laid his oars.

I didn't lose no time. The next minute I was a-spinning down stream soft but quick in the shade of the bank. I made two mile and a half, and then struck out a quarter of a mile or more towards the middle of the river, because pretty soon I would be passing the ferry landing, and people might see me and hail me. I got out amongst the driftwood, and then laid down in the bottom of the canoe and let her float. I laid there, and had a good rest and a smoke out of my pipe, looking away into the sky; not a cloud in it. The sky looks ever so deep when you lay down on your back in the moonshine; I never knowed it before. And how far a body can hear on the water such nights! I heard people talking at the ferry landing. I heard what they said, too—every word of it. One man said it was getting towards the long days and the short nights now. T'other one said THIS warn't one of the short ones, he reckoned—and then they laughed, and he said it over again, and they laughed again; then they waked up another fellow and told him, and laughed, but he didn't laugh; he ripped out something brisk, and said let him alone. The first fellow said he 'lowed to tell it to his old woman—she would think it was pretty good; but he said that warn't nothing to some things he had said in his time. I heard one man say it was nearly three o'clock, and he hoped

ı't wait more than about a week longer. After that the talk got further
y, and I couldn't make out the words any more; but I could hear the
ıw and then a laugh, too, but it seemed a long ways off.

below the ferry now. I rose up, and there was Jackson's Island, about
two mile and a half down stream, heavy timbered and standing up out of the middle
of the river, big and dark and solid, like a steamboat without any lights. There warn't
any signs of the bar at the head—it was all under water now.

It didn't take me long to get there. I shot past the head at a ripping rate, the current
was so swift, and then I got into the dead water and landed on the side towards the
Illinois shore. I run the canoe into a deep dent in the bank that I knowed about; I had
to part the willow branches to get in; and when I made fast nobody could a seen the
canoe from the outside.

I went up and set down on a log at the head of the island, and looked out on the
big river and the black driftwood and away over to the town, three mile away, where
there was three or four lights twinkling. A monstrous big lumber-raft was about a mile
up stream, coming along down, with a lantern in the middle of it. I watched it come
creeping down, and when it was most abreast of where I stood I heard a man say,
"Stern oars, there! heave her head to stabboard!" I heard that just as plain as if the man
was by my side.

There was a little gray in the sky now; so I stepped into the woods, and laid down
for a nap before breakfast.

Chapter *VIII*

The sun was up so high when I waked that I judged it was after eight o'clock. I laid
there in the grass and the cool shade thinking about things, and feeling rested and
ruther comfortable and satisfied. I could see the sun out at one or two holes, but mostly
it was big trees all about, and gloomy in there amongst them. There was freckled places
on the ground where the light sifted down through the leaves, and the freckled places
swapped about a little, showing there was a little breeze up there. A couple of squirrels
set on a limb and jabbered at me very friendly.

I was powerful lazy and comfortable—didn't want to get up and cook breakfast.
Well, I was dozing off again when I thinks I hears a deep sound of "boom!" away up
the river. I rouses up, and rests on my elbow and listens; pretty soon I hears it again. I
hopped up, and went and looked out at a hole in the leaves, and I see a bunch of smoke
laying on the water a long ways up—about abreast the ferry. And there was the ferryboat full of people floating along down. I knowed what was the matter now. "Boom!"
I see the white smoke squirt out of the ferryboat's side. You see, they was firing can-

non over the water, trying to make my carcass come to the top.

I was pretty hungry, but it warn't going to do for me to start a fire, because they might see the smoke. So I set there and watched the cannon-smoke and listened to the boom. The river was a mile wide there, and it always looks pretty on a summer morning—so I was having a good enough time seeing them hunt for my remainders if I only had a bite to eat. Well, then I happened to think how they always put quicksilver in loaves of bread and float them off, because they always go right to the drownded carcass and stop there. So, says I, I'll keep a lookout, and if any of them's floating around after me I'll give them a show. I changed to the Illinois edge of the island to see what luck I could have, and I warn't disappointed. A big double loaf come along, and I most got it with a long stick, but my foot slipped and she floated out further. Of course I was where the current set in the closest to the shore—I knowed enough for that. But by and by along comes another one, and this time I won. I took out the plug and shook out the little dab of quicksilver, and set my teeth in. It was "baker's bread"— what the quality eat; none of your low-down corn-pone.

I got a good place amongst the leaves, and set there on a log, munching the bread and watching the ferry-boat, and very well satisfied. And then something struck me. I says, now I reckon the widow or the parson or somebody prayed that this bread would find me, and here it has gone and done it. So there ain't no doubt but there is something in that thing—that is, there's something in it when a body like the widow or the parson prays, but it don't work for me, and I reckon it don't work for only just the right kind.

I lit a pipe and had a good long smoke, and went on watching. The ferryboat was floating with the current, and I allowed I'd have a chance to see who was aboard when she come along, because she would come in close, where the bread did. When she'd got pretty well along down towards me, I put out my pipe and went to where I fished out the bread, and laid down behind a log on the bank in a little open place. Where the log forked I could peep through.

By and by she come along, and she drifted in so close that they could a run out a plank and walked ashore. Most everybody was on the boat. Pap, and Judge Thatcher, and Bessie Thatcher, and Jo Harper, and Tom Sawyer, and his old Aunt Polly, and Sid and Mary, and plenty more. Everybody was talking about the murder, but the captain broke in and says:

"Look sharp, now; the current sets in the closest here, and maybe he's washed ashore and got tangled amongst the brush at the water's edge. I hope so, anyway."

"I didn't hope so. They all crowded up and leaned over the rails, nearly in my face, and kept still, watching with all their might. I could see them first-rate, but they couldn't see me. Then the captain sung out:

"Stand away!" and the cannon let off such a blast right before me that it made me deef with the noise and pretty near blind with the smoke, and I judged I was gone. If they'd a had some bullets in, I reckon they'd a got the corpse they was after. Well, I see

I warn't hurt, thanks to goodness. The boat floated on and went out of sight around the shoulder of the island. I could hear the booming now and then, further and further off, and by and by, after an hour, I didn't hear it no more. The island was three mile long. I judged they had got to the foot, and was giving it up. But they didn't yet a while. They turned around the foot of the island and started up the channel on the Missouri side, under steam, and booming once in a while as they went. I crossed over to that side and watched them. When they got abreast the head of the island they quit shooting and dropped over to the Missouri shore and went home to the town.

I knowed I was all right now. Nobody else would come a-hunting after me. I got my traps out of the canoe and made me a nice camp in the thick woods. I made a kind of a tent out of my blankets to put my things under so the rain couldn't get at them. I catched a catfish and haggled him open with my saw, and towards sundown I started my camp fire and had supper. Then I set out a line to catch some fish for breakfast.

When it was dark I set by my camp fire smoking, and feeling pretty well satisfied; but by and by it got sort of lonesome, and so I went and set on the bank and listened to the current swashing along, and counted the stars and drift logs and rafts that come down, and then went to bed; there ain't no better way to put in time when you are lonesome; you can't stay so, you soon get over it.

And so for three days and nights. No difference—just the same thing. But the next day I went exploring around down through the island. I was boss of it; it all belonged to me, so to say, and I wanted to know all about it; but mainly I wanted to put in the time. I found plenty strawberries, ripe and prime; and green summer grapes, and green razberries; and the green blackberries was just beginning to show. They would all come handy by and by, I judged.

Well, I went fooling along in the deep woods till I judged I warn't far from the foot of the island. I had my gun along, but I hadn't shot nothing; it was for protection; thought I would kill some game nigh home. About this time I mighty near stepped on a good-sized snake, and it went sliding off through the grass and flowers, and I after it, trying to get a shot at it. I clipped along, and all of a sudden I bounded right on to the ashes of a camp fire that was still smoking.

My heart jumped up amongst my lungs. I never waited for to look further, but uncocked my gun and went sneaking back on my tiptoes as fast as ever I could. Every now and then I stopped a second amongst the thick leaves and listened, but my breath come so hard I couldn't hear nothing else. I slunk along another piece further, then listened again; and so on, and so on. If I see a stump, I took it for a man; if I trod on a stick and broke it, it made me feel like a person had cut one of my breaths in two and I only got half, and the short half, too.

When I got to camp I warn't feeling very brash, there warn't much sand in my craw; but I says, this ain't no time to be fooling around. So I got all my traps into my canoe again so as to have them out of sight, and I put out the fire and scattered the ashes around to look like an old last year's camp, and then clumb a tree.

I reckon I was up in the tree two hours; but I didn't see nothing, I didn't hear nothing—I only THOUGHT I heard and seen as much as a thousand things. Well, I couldn't stay up there forever; so at last I got down, but I kept in the thick woods and on the lookout all the time. All I could get to eat was berries and what was left over from breakfast.

By the time it was night I was pretty hungry. So when it was good and dark I slid out from shore before moonrise and paddled over to the Illinois bank—about a quarter of a mile. I went out in the woods and cooked a supper, and I had about made up my mind I would stay there all night when I hear a PLUNKETY-PLUNK, PLUNKETY-PLUNK, and says to myself, horses coming; and next I hear people's voices. I got everything into the canoe as quick as I could, and then went creeping through the woods to see what I could find out. I hadn't got far when I hear a man say:

"We better camp here if we can find a good place; the horses is about beat out. Let's look around."

I didn't wait, but shoved out and paddled away easy. I tied up in the old place, and reckoned I would sleep in the canoe.

I didn't sleep much. I couldn't, somehow, for thinking. And every time I waked up I thought somebody had me by the neck. So the sleep didn't do me no good. By and by I says to myself, I can't live this way; I'm a-going to find out who it is that's here on the island with me; I'll find it out or bust. Well, I felt better right off.

So I took my paddle and slid out from shore just a step or two, and then let the canoe drop along down amongst the shadows. The moon was shining, and outside of the shadows it made it most as light as day. I poked along well on to an hour, everything still as rocks and sound asleep. Well, by this time I was most down to the foot of the island. A little ripply, cool breeze begun to blow, and that was as good as saying the night was about done. I give her a turn with the paddle and brung her nose to shore; then I got my gun and slipped out and into the edge of the woods. I sat down there on a log, and looked out through the leaves. I see the moon go off watch, and the darkness begin to blanket the river.

But in a little while I see a pale streak over the treetops, and knowed the day was coming. So I took my gun and slipped off towards where I had run across that camp fire, stopping every minute or two to listen. But I hadn't no luck somehow; I couldn't seem to find the place. But by and by, sure enough, I catched a glimpse of fire away through the trees. I went for it, cautious and slow. By and by I was close enough to have a look, and there laid a man on the ground. It most give me the fantods. He had a blanket around his head, and his head was nearly in the fire. I set there behind a clump of bushes in about six foot of him, and kept my eyes on him steady. It was getting gray daylight now. Pretty soon he gapped and stretched himself and hove off the blanket, and it was Miss Watson's Jim! I bet I was glad to see him. I says:

"Hello, Jim!" and skipped out.

He bounced up and stared at me wild. Then he drops down on his knees, and puts his hands together and says:

"Doan' hurt me—don't! I hain't ever done no harm to a ghos'. I alwuz liked dead people, en done all I could for 'em. You go en git in de river agin, whah you b'longs, en doan' do nuffn to Ole Jim, 'at 'uz awluz yo' fren'."

Well, I warn't long making him understand I warn't dead. I was ever so glad to see Jim. I warn't lonesome now. I told him I warn't afraid of HIM telling the people where I was. I talked along, but he only set there and looked at me; never said nothing. Then I says:

"It's good daylight. Le's get breakfast. Make up your camp fire good."

"What's de use er makin' up de camp fire to cook strawbries en sich truck? But you got a gun, hain't you? Den we kin git sumfn better den strawbries."

"Strawberries and such truck," I says. "Is that what you live on?"

"I couldn' git nuffn else," he says.

"Why, how long you been on the island, Jim?"

"I come heah de night arter you's killed."

"What, all that time?"

"Yes—indeedy."

"And ain't you had nothing but that kind of rubbage to eat?"

"No, sah—nuffn else."

"Well, you must be most starved, ain't you?"

"I reck'n I could eat a hoss. I think I could. How long you ben on de islan'?"

"Since the night I got killed."

"No! W'y, what has you lived on? But you got a gun. Oh, yes, you got a gun. Dat's good. Now you kill sumfn en I'll make up de fire."

So we went over to where the canoe was, and while he built a fire in a grassy open place amongst the trees, I fetched meal and bacon and coffee, and coffee-pot and frying-pan, and sugar and tin cups, and the nigger was set back considerable, because he reckoned it was all done with witchcraft. I catched a good big catfish, too, and Jim cleaned him with his knife, and fried him.

When breakfast was ready we lolled on the grass and eat it smoking hot. Jim laid it in with all his might, for he was most about starved. Then when we had got pretty well stuffed, we laid off and lazied. By and by Jim says:

"But looky here, Huck, who wuz it dat 'uz killed in dat shanty ef it warn't you?"

Then I told him the whole thing, and he said it was smart. He said Tom Sawyer couldn't get up no better plan than what I had. Then I says:

"How do you come to be here, Jim, and how'd you get here?"

He looked pretty uneasy, and didn't say nothing for a minute. Then he says:

"Maybe I better not tell."

"Why, Jim?"

"Well, dey's reasons. But you wouldn' tell on me ef I uz to tell you, would you, Huck?"

"Blamed if I would, Jim."

"Well, I b'lieve you, Huck. I—I RUN OFF."

"Jim!"

"But mind, you said you wouldn' tell—you know you said you wouldn' tell, Huck."

"Well, I did. I said I wouldn't, and I'll stick to it. Honest Injun, I will. People would call me a low-down Abolitionist and despise me for keeping mum—but that don't make no difference. I ain't a-going to tell, and I ain't a-going back there, anyways. So, now, le's know all about it."

"Well, you see, it 'uz dis way. Ole missus—dat's Miss Watson—she pecks on me all de time, en treats me pooty rough, but she awluz said she wouldn' sell me down to Orleans. But I noticed dey wuz a nigger trader roun' de place considable lately, en I begin to git oneasy. Well, one night I creeps to de do' pooty late, en de do' warn't quite shet, en I hear old missus tell de widder she gwyne to sell me down to Orleans, but she didn' want to, but she could git eight hund'd dollars for me, en it 'uz sich a big stack o' money she couldn' resis'. De widder she try to git her to say she wouldn' do it, but I never waited to hear de res'. I lit out mighty quick, I tell you.

"I tuck out en shin down de hill, en 'spec to steal a skift 'long de sho' som'ers 'bove de town, but dey wuz people a-stirring yit, so I hid in de ole tumble-down coo-per-shop on de bank to wait for everybody to go 'way. Well, I wuz dah all night. Dey wuz somebody roun' all de time. 'Long 'bout six in de mawnin' skifts begin to go by, en 'bout eight er nine every skift dat went 'long wuz talkin' 'bout how yo' pap come over to de town en say you's killed. Dese las' skifts wuz full o' ladies en genlmen a-goin' over for to see de place. Sometimes dey'd pull up at de sho' en take a res' b'fo' dey started acrost, so by de talk I got to know all 'bout de killin'. I 'uz powerful sorry you's killed, Huck, but I ain't no mo' now.

"I laid dah under de shavin's all day. I 'uz hungry, but I warn't afeard; bekase I knowed ole missus en de widder wuz goin' to start to de camp-meet'n' right arter breakfas' en be gone all day, en dey knows I goes off wid de cattle 'bout daylight, so dey wouldn' 'spec to see me roun' de place, en so dey wouldn' miss me tell arter dark in de evenin'. De yuther servants wouldn' miss me, kase dey'd shin out en take holi-day soon as de ole folks 'uz out'n de way.

"Well, when it come dark I tuck out up de river road, en went 'bout two mile er more to whah dey warn't no houses. I'd made up my mine 'bout what I's agwyne to do. You see, ef I kep' on tryin' to git away afoot, de dogs 'ud track me; ef I stole a skift to cross over, dey'd miss dat skift, you see, en dey'd know 'bout whah I'd lan' on de yuther side, en whah to pick up my track. So I says, a raff is what I's arter; it doan' MAKE no track.

"I see a light a-comin' roun' de p'int bymeby, so I wade' in en shove' a log ahead o' me en swum more'n half way acrost de river, en got in 'mongst de drift-wood, en kep' my head down low, en kinder swum agin de current tell de raff come along. Den I swum to de stern uv it en tuck a-holt. It clouded up en 'uz pooty dark for a little while. So I clumb up en laid down on de planks. De men 'uz all 'way yonder in de middle, whah de lantern wuz. De river wuz a-risin', en dey wuz a good current; so I reck'n'd 'at by fo' in de mawnin' I'd be twenty-five mile down de river, en den I'd slip in jis b'fo' daylight en swim asho', en take to de woods on de Illinois side.

"But I didn' have no luck. When we 'uz mos' down to de head er de islan' a man begin to come aft wid de lantern, I see it warn't no use fer to wait, so I slid overboard en struck out fer de islan'. Well, I had a notion I could lan' mos' anywhers, but I couldn't—bank too bluff. I 'uz mos' to de foot er de islan' b'fo' I found' a good place. I went into de woods en jedged I wouldn' fool wid raffs no mo', long as dey move de lantern roun' so. I had my pipe en a plug er dog-leg, en some matches in my cap, en dey warn't wet, so I 'uz all right."

"And so you ain't had no meat nor bread to eat all this time? Why didn't you get mud-turkles?"

"How you gwyne to git 'm? You can't slip up on um en grab um; en how's a body gwyne to hit um wid a rock? How could a body do it in de night? En I warn't gwyne to show mysef on de bank in de daytime."

"Well, that's so. You've had to keep in the woods all the time, of course. Did you hear 'em shooting the cannon?"

"Oh, yes. I knowed dey was arter you. I see um go by heah—watched um thoo de bushes."

Some young birds come along, flying a yard or two at a time and lighting. Jim said it was a sign it was going to rain. He said it was a sign when young chickens flew that way, and so he reckoned it was the same way when young birds done it. I was going to catch some of them, but Jim wouldn't let me. He said it was death. He said his father laid mighty sick once, and some of them catched a bird, and his old granny said his father would die, and he did.

And Jim said you mustn't count the things you are going to cook for dinner, because that would bring bad luck. The same if you shook the table-cloth after sundown. And he said if a man owned a beehive and that man died, the bees must be told about it before sun-up next morning, or else the bees would all weaken down and quit work and die. Jim said bees wouldn't sting idiots; but I didn't believe that, because I had tried them lots of times myself, and they wouldn't sting me.

I had heard about some of these things before, but not all of them. Jim knowed all kinds of signs. He said he knowed most everything. I said it looked to me like all the signs was about bad luck, and so I asked him if there warn't any good-luck signs. He says:

"Mighty few—an' DEY ain't no use to a body. What you want to know when good luck's a-comin' for? Want to keep it off?" And he said: "Ef you's got hairy arms en a hairy breas', it's a sign dat you's agwyne to be rich. Well, dey's some use in a sign like dat, 'kase it's so fur ahead. You see, maybe you's got to be po' a long time fust, en so you might git discourage' en kill yo'sef 'f you didn' know by de sign dat you gwyne to be rich bymeby."

"Have you got hairy arms and a hairy breast, Jim?"

"What's de use to ax dat question? Don't you see I has?"

"Well, are you rich?"

"No, but I ben rich wunst, and gwyne to be rich agin. Wunst I had foteen dollars, but I tuck to specalat'n', en got busted out."

"What did you speculate in, Jim?"

"Well, fust I tackled stock."

"What kind of stock?"

"Why, live stock—cattle, you know. I put ten dollars in a cow. But I ain' gwyne to resk no mo' money in stock. De cow up 'n' died on my han's."

"So you lost the ten dollars."

"No, I didn't lose it all. I on'y los' 'bout nine of it. I sole de hide en taller for a dollar en ten cents."

"You had five dollars and ten cents left. Did you speculate any more?"

"Yes. You know that one-laigged nigger dat b'longs to old Misto Bradish? Well, he sot up a bank, en say anybody dat put in a dollar would git fo' dollars mo' at de en' er de year. Well, all de niggers went in, but dey didn't have much. I wuz de on'y one dat had much. So I stuck out for mo' dan fo' dollars, en I said 'f I didn' git it I'd start a bank mysef. Well, o' course dat nigger want' to keep me out er de business, bekase he says dey warn't business 'nough for two banks, so he say I could put in my five dollars en he pay me thirty-five at de en' er de year.

"So I done it. Den I reck'n'd I'd inves' de thirty-five dollars right off en keep things a-movin'. Dey wuz a nigger name' Bob, dat had ketched a wood-flat, en his marster didn' know it; en I bought it off 'n him en told him to take de thirty-five dollars when de en' er de year come; but somebody stole de wood-flat dat night, en nex day de one-laigged nigger say de bank's busted. So dey didn' none uv us git no money."

"What did you do with the ten cents, Jim?"

"Well, I 'uz gwyne to spen' it, but I had a dream, en de dream tole me to give it to a nigger name' Balum—Balum's Ass dey call him for short; he's one er dem chuckleheads, you know. But he's lucky, dey say, en I see I warn't lucky. De dream say let Balum inves' de ten cents en he'd make a raise for me. Well, Balum he tuck de money, en when he wuz in church he hear de preacher say dat whoever give to de po' len' to de Lord, en boun' to git his money back a hund'd times. So Balum he tuck en give de ten cents to de po', en laid low to see what wuz gwyne to come of it."

"Well, what did come of it, Jim?"

"Nuffn never come of it. I couldn' manage to k'leck dat money no way; en Balum he couldn'. I ain' gwyne to len' no mo' money 'dout I see de security. Boun' to git yo' money back a hund'd times, de preacher says! Ef I could git de ten CENTS back, I'd call it squah, en be glad er de chanst."

"Well, it's all right anyway, Jim, long as you're going to be rich again some time or other."

"Yes; en I's rich now, come to look at it. I owns mysef, en I's wuth eight hund'd dollars. I wisht I had de money, I wouldn' want no mo'."

Chapter IX

I wanted to go and look at a place right about the middle of the island that I'd found when I was exploring; so we started and soon got to it, because the island was only three miles long and a quarter of a mile wide.

This place was a tolerable long, steep hill or ridge about forty foot high. We had a rough time getting to the top, the sides was so steep and the bushes so thick. We tramped and clumb around all over it, and by and by found a good big cavern in the rock, most up to the top on the side towards Illinois. The cavern was as big as two or three rooms bunched together, and Jim could stand up straight in it. It was cool in there.

Jim was for putting our traps in there right away, but I said we didn't want to be climbing up and down there all the time.

Jim said if we had the canoe hid in a good place, and had all the traps in the cavern, we could rush there if anybody was to come to the island, and they would never find us without dogs. And, besides, he said them little birds had said it was going to rain, and did I want the things to get wet?

So we went back and got the canoe, and paddled up abreast the cavern, and lugged all the traps up there. Then we hunted up a place close by to hide the canoe in, amongst the thick willows. We took some fish off of the lines and set them again, and begun to get ready for dinner.

The door of the cavern was big enough to roll a hogshead in, and on one side of the door the floor stuck out a little bit, and was flat and a good place to build a fire on. So we built it there and cooked dinner.

We spread the blankets inside for a carpet, and eat our dinner in there. We put all the other things handy at the back of the cavern. Pretty soon it darkened up, and begun to thunder and lighten; so the birds was right about it. Directly it begun to rain, and it rained like all fury, too, and I never see the wind blow so. It was one of these regular summer storms. It would get so dark that it looked all blue-black outside, and lovely; and the rain would thrash along by so thick that the trees off a little ways looked dim and spider-webby; and here would come a blast of wind that would bend the trees down and turn up the pale underside of the leaves; and then a perfect ripper of a gust would follow along and set the branches to tossing their arms as if they was just wild; and next, when it was just about the bluest and blackest—FST! it was as bright as glory, and you'd have a little glimpse of tree-tops a-plunging about away off yonder in the storm, hundreds of yards further than you could see before; dark as sin again in a second, and now you'd hear the thunder let go with an awful crash, and then go rumbling, grumbling, tumbling, down the sky towards the under side of the world, like rolling empty barrels down stairs—where it's long stairs and they bounce a good deal, you know.

"Jim, this is nice," I says. "I wouldn't want to be nowhere else but here. Pass me along another hunk of fish and some hot corn-bread."

"Well, you wouldn't a ben here 'f it hadn't a ben for Jim. You'd a ben down dah in de woods widout any dinner, en gittn' mos' drownded, too; dat you would, honey. Chickens knows when it's gwyne to rain, en so do de birds, chile."

The river went on raising and raising for ten or twelve days, till at last it was over the banks. The water was three or four foot deep on the island in the low places and on the Illinois bottom. On that side it was a good many miles wide, but on the Missouri side it was the same old distance across—a half a mile—because the Missouri shore was just a wall of high bluffs.

Daytimes we paddled all over the island in the canoe, It was mighty cool and shady in the deep woods, even if the sun was blazing outside. We went winding in and out amongst the trees, and sometimes the vines hung so thick we had to back away and go some other way. Well, on every old broken-down tree you could see rabbits and snakes and such things; and when the island had been overflowed a day or two they got so tame, on account of being hungry, that you could paddle right up and put your hand on them if you wanted to; but not the snakes and turtles—they would slide off in the water. The ridge our cavern was in was full of them. We could a had pets enough if we'd wanted them.

One night we catched a little section of a lumber raft—nice pine planks. It was twelve foot wide and about fifteen or sixteen foot long, and the top stood above water six or seven inches—a solid, level floor. We could see saw-logs go by in the daylight sometimes, but we let them go; we didn't show ourselves in daylight.

Another night when we was up at the head of the island, just before daylight, here comes a frame-house down, on the west side. She was a two-story, and tilted over considerable. We paddled out and got aboard—clumb in at an upstairs window. But it was too dark to see yet, so we made the canoe fast and set in her to wait for daylight.

The light begun to come before we got to the foot of the island. Then we looked in at the window. We could make out a bed, and a table, and two old chairs, and lots of things around about on the floor, and there was clothes hanging against the wall. There was something laying on the floor in the far corner that looked like a man. So Jim says:

"Hello, you!"

But it didn't budge. So I hollered again, and then Jim says:

"De man ain't asleep—he's dead. You hold still—I'll go en see."

He went, and bent down and looked, and says:

"It's a dead man. Yes, indeedy; naked, too. He's ben shot in de back. I reck'n he's ben dead two er three days. Come in, Huck, but doan' look at his face—it's too gashly."

I didn't look at him at all. Jim throwed some old rags over him, but he needn't done it; I didn't want to see him. There was heaps of old greasy cards scattered around over the floor, and old whisky bottles, and a couple of masks made out of black cloth; and all over the walls was the ignorantest kind of words and pictures made with charcoal. There was two old dirty calico dresses, and a sun-bonnet, and some women's underclothes hanging against the wall, and some men's clothing, too. We put the lot into the canoe—it might come good. There was a boy's old speckled straw hat on the floor; I took that, too. And there was a bottle that had had milk in it, and it had a rag stopper for a baby to suck. We would a took the bottle, but it was broke. There was a seedy old chest, and an old hair trunk with the hinges broke. They stood open, but there warn't nothing left in them that was any account. The way things was scattered about we reckoned the people left in a hurry, and warn't fixed so as to carry off most of their stuff.

We got an old tin lantern, and a butcher-knife without any handle, and a bran-new Barlow knife worth two bits in any store, and a lot of tallow candles, and a tin candlestick, and a gourd, and a tin cup, and a ratty old bedquilt off the bed, and a reticule with needles and pins and beeswax and buttons and thread and all such truck in it, and a hatchet and some nails, and a fishline as thick as my little finger with some monstrous hooks on it, and a roll of buckskin, and a leather dog-collar, and a horse-shoe, and some vials of medicine that didn't have no label on them; and just as we was leaving I found a tolerable good curry-comb, and Jim he found a ratty old fiddle-bow, and a wooden leg. The straps was broke off of it, but, barring that, it was a good enough leg, though it was too long for me and not long enough for Jim, and we couldn't find the other one, though we hunted all around.

And so, take it all around, we made a good haul. When we was ready to shove off we was a quarter of a mile below the island, and it was pretty broad day; so I made Jim lay down in the canoe and cover up with the quilt, because if he set up people could tell he was a nigger a good ways off. I paddled over to the Illinois shore, and drifted down most a half a mile doing it. I crept up the dead water under the bank, and hadn't no accidents and didn't see nobody. We got home all safe.

Chapter X

After breakfast I wanted to talk about the dead man and guess out how he come to be killed, but Jim didn't want to. He said it would fetch bad luck; and besides, he said, he might come and ha'nt us; he said a man that warn't buried was more likely to go a-ha'nting around than one that was planted and comfortable. That sounded pretty reasonable, so I didn't say no more; but I couldn't keep from studying over it and wishing I knowed who shot the man, and what they done it for.

We rummaged the clothes we'd got, and found eight dollars in silver sewed up in the lining of an old blanket overcoat. Jim said he reckoned the people in that house stole the coat, because if they'd a knowed the money was there they wouldn't a left it. I said I reckoned they killed him, too; but Jim didn't want to talk about that. I says:

"Now you think it's bad luck; but what did you say when I fetched in the snake-skin that I found on the top of the ridge day before yesterday? You said it was the worst bad luck in the world to touch a snake-skin with my hands. Well, here's your bad luck! We've raked in all this truck and eight dollars besides. I wish we could have some bad luck like this every day, Jim."

"Never you mind, honey, never you mind. Don't you git too peart. It's a-comin'. Mind I tell you, it's a-comin'."

It did come, too. It was a Tuesday that we had that talk. Well, after dinner Friday we was laying around in the grass at the upper end of the ridge, and got out of tobacco. I went to the cavern to get some, and found a rattlesnake in there. I killed him, and curled him up on the foot of Jim's blanket, ever so natural, thinking there'd be some fun when Jim found him there. Well, by night I forgot all about the snake, and when Jim flung himself down on the blanket while I struck a light the snake's mate was there, and bit him.

He jumped up yelling, and the first thing the light showed was the varmint curled up and ready for another spring. I laid him out in a second with a stick, and Jim grabbed pap's whisky-jug and begun to pour it down.

He was barefooted, and the snake bit him right on the heel. That all comes of my being such a fool as to not remember that wherever you leave a dead snake its mate always comes there and curls around it. Jim told me to chop off the snake's head and throw it away, and then skin the body and roast a piece of it. I done it, and he eat it and said it would help cure him. He made me take off the rattles and tie them around his wrist, too. He said that that would help. Then I slid out quiet and throwed the snakes clear away amongst the bushes; for I warn't going to let Jim find out it was all my fault, not if I could help it.

Jim sucked and sucked at the jug, and now and then he got out of his head and pitched around and yelled; but every time he come to himself he went to sucking at the jug again. His foot swelled up pretty big, and so did his leg; but by and by the drunk begun to come, and so I judged he was all right; but I'd druther been bit with a snake than pap's whisky.

Jim was laid up for four days and nights. Then the swelling was all gone and he was around again. I made up my mind I wouldn't ever take a-holt of a snake-skin again with my hands, now that I see what had come of it. Jim said he reckoned I would believe him next time. And he said that handling a snake-skin was such awful bad luck that maybe we hadn't got to the end of it yet. He said he druther see the new moon over his left shoulder as much as a thousand times than take up a snake-skin in his hand. Well, I was getting to feel that way myself, though I've always reckoned that looking at the new moon over your left shoulder is one of the carelessest and foolishest things a body can do. Old Hank Bunker done it once, and bragged about it; and in less than two years he got drunk and fell off of the shot-tower, and spread himself out so that he was just a kind of a layer, as you may say; and they slid him edgeways between two barn doors for a coffin, and buried him so, so they say, but I didn't see it. Pap told me. But anyway it all come of looking at the moon that way, like a fool.

Well, the days went along, and the river went down between its banks again; and about the first thing we done was to bait one of the big hooks with a skinned rabbit and set it and catch a catfish that was as big as a man, being six foot two inches long, and weighed over two hundred pounds. We couldn't handle him, of course; he would a flung us into Illinois. We just set there and watched him rip and tear around till he drownded. We found a brass button in his stomach and a round ball, and lots of rubbage. We split the ball open with the hatchet, and there was a spool in it. Jim said he'd had it there a long time, to coat it over so and make a ball of it. It was as big a fish as was ever catched in the Mississippi, I reckon. Jim said he hadn't ever seen a bigger one. He would a been worth a good deal over at the village. They peddle out such a fish as that by the pound in the market-house there; everybody buys some of him; his meat's as white as snow and makes a good fry.

Next morning I said it was getting slow and dull, and I wanted to get a stirring up some way. I said I reckoned I would slip over the river and find out what was going on. Jim liked that notion; but he said I must go in the dark and look sharp. Then he studied it over and said, couldn't I put on some of them old things and dress up like a girl? That was a good notion, too. So we shortened up one of the calico gowns, and I turned up my trouser-legs to my knees and got into it. Jim hitched it behind with the hooks, and it was a fair fit. I put on the sun-bonnet and tied it under my chin, and then for a body to look in and see my face was like looking down a joint of stove-pipe. Jim said nobody would know me, even in the daytime, hardly. I practiced around all day to get the hang of the things, and by and by I could do pretty well in them, only Jim said I didn't walk like a girl; and he said I must quit pulling up my gown to get at my britches-pocket. I took notice, and done better.

I started up the Illinois shore in the canoe just after dark.

I started across to the town from a little below the ferry-landing, and the drift of the current fetched me in at the bottom of the town. I tied up and started along the bank. There was a light burning in a little shanty that hadn't been lived in for a long time, and I wondered who had took up quarters there. I slipped up and peeped in at the window. There was a woman about forty year old in there knitting by a candle that was on a pine table. I didn't know her face; she was a stranger, for you couldn't start a face in that town that I didn't know. Now this was lucky, because I was weakening; I was getting afraid I had come; people might know my voice and find me out. But if this woman had been in such a little town two days she could tell me all I wanted to know; so I knocked at the door, and made up my mind I wouldn't forget I was a girl.

Chapter XI

"Come in," says the woman, and I did. She says: "Take a cheer."

I done it. She looked me all over with her little shiny eyes, and says:

"What might your name be?"

"Sarah Williams."

"Where 'bouts do you live? In this neighborhood?'

"No'm. In Hookerville, seven mile below. I've walked all the way and I'm all tired out."

"Hungry, too, I reckon. I'll find you something."

"No'm, I ain't hungry. I was so hungry I had to stop two miles below here at a farm; so I ain't hungry no more. It's what makes me so late. My mother's down sick, and out of money and everything, and I come to tell my uncle Abner Moore. He lives at the upper end of the town, she says. I hain't ever been here before. Do you know him?"

"No; but I don't know everybody yet. I haven't lived here quite two weeks. It's a considerable ways to the upper end of the town. You better stay here all night. Take off your bonnet."

"No," I says; "I'll rest a while, I reckon, and go on. I ain't afeared of the dark."

She said she wouldn't let me go by myself, but her husband would be in by and by, maybe in a hour and a half, and she'd send him along with me. Then she got to talking about her husband, and about her relations up the river, and her relations down the river, and about how much better off they used to was, and how they didn't know but they'd made a mistake coming to our town, instead of letting well alone—and so on and so on, till I was afeard I had made a mistake coming to her to find out what was going on in the town; but by and by she dropped on to pap and the murder, and then I was pretty willing to let her clatter right along. She told about me and Tom Sawyer finding the six thousand dollars (only she got it ten) and all about pap and what a hard lot he was, and what a hard lot I was, and at last she got down to where I was murdered. I says:

"Who done it? We've heard considerable about these goings on down in Hookerville, but we don't know who 'twas that killed Huck Finn."

"Well, I reckon there's a right smart chance of people HERE that'd like to know who killed him. Some think old Finn done it himself."

"No—is that so?"

"Most everybody thought it at first. He'll never know how nigh he come to getting lynched. But before night they changed around and judged it was done by a runaway nigger named Jim."

"Why HE—"

I stopped. I reckoned I better keep still. She run on, and never noticed I had put in at all:

"The nigger run off the very night Huck Finn was killed. So there's a reward out for him—three hundred dollars. And there's a reward out for old Finn, too—two hundred dollars. You see, he come to town the morning after the murder, and told about it, and was out with 'em on the ferryboat hunt, and right away after he up and left. Before night they wanted to lynch him, but he was gone, you see. Well, next day they found out the nigger was gone; they found out he hadn't ben seen sence ten o'clock the night the murder was done. So then they put it on him, you see; and while they was full of it, next day, back comes old Finn, and went boo-hooing to Judge Thatcher to get money to hunt for the nigger all over Illinois with. The judge gave him some, and that evening he got drunk, and was around till after midnight with a couple of mighty hard-looking strangers, and then went off with them. Well, he hain't come back sence, and they ain't looking for him back till this thing blows over a little, for people thinks now that he killed his boy and fixed things so folks would think robbers done it, and then he'd get Huck's money without having to bother a long time with a lawsuit. People do say he warn't any too good to do it. Oh, he's sly, I reckon. If he don't come back for a year he'll be all right. You can't prove anything on him, you know; everything will be quieted down then, and he'll walk in Huck's money as easy as nothing."

"Yes, I reckon so, 'm. I don't see nothing in the way of it. Has everybody quit thinking the nigger done it?"

"Oh, no, not everybody. A good many thinks he done it. But they'll get the nigger pretty soon now, and maybe they can scare it out of him."

"Why, are they after him yet?"

"Well, you're innocent, ain't you! Does three hundred dollars lay around every day for people to pick up? Some folks think the nigger ain't far from here. I'm one of them—but I hain't talked it around. A few days ago I was talking with an old couple that lives next door in the log shanty, and they happened to say hardly anybody ever goes to that island over yonder that they call Jackson's Island. Don't anybody live there? says I. No, nobody, says they. I didn't say any more, but I done some thinking. I was pretty near certain I'd seen smoke over there, about the head of the island, a day or two before that, so I says to myself, like as not that nigger's hiding over there; anyway, says I, it's worth the trouble to give the place a hunt. I hain't seen any smoke sence, so I reckon maybe he's gone, if it was him; but husband's going over to see — him and another man. He was gone up the river; but he got back to-day, and I told him as soon as he got here two hours ago."

I had got so uneasy I couldn't set still. I had to do something with my hands; so I took up a needle off of the table and went to threading it. My hands shook, and I was making a bad job of it. When the woman stopped talking I looked up, and she was looking at me pretty curious and smiling a little. I put down the needle and thread, and let on to be interested—and I was, too—and says:

"Three hundred dollars is a power of money. I wish my mother could get it. Is your husband going over there to-night?"

"Oh, yes. He went up-town with the man I was telling you of, to get a boat and see if they could borrow another gun. They'll go over after midnight."

"Couldn't they see better if they was to wait till daytime?"

"Yes. And couldn't the nigger see better, too? After midnight he'll likely be asleep, and they can slip around through the woods and hunt up his camp fire all the better for the dark, if he's got one."

"I didn't think of that."

The woman kept looking at me pretty curious, and I didn't feel a bit comfortable. Pretty soon she says,

"What did you say your name was, honey?"

"M—Mary Williams."

Somehow it didn't seem to me that I said it was Mary before, so I didn't look up— seemed to me I said it was Sarah; so I felt sort of cornered, and was afeared maybe I was looking it, too. I wished the woman would say something more; the longer she set still the uneasier I was. But now she says:

"Honey, I thought you said it was Sarah when you first come in?"

"Oh, yes'm, I did. Sarah Mary Williams. Sarah's my first name. Some calls me Sarah, some calls me Mary."

"Oh, that's the way of it?"

"Yes'm."

I was feeling better then, but I wished I was out of there, anyway. I couldn't look up yet.

Well, the woman fell to talking about how hard times was, and how poor they had to live, and how the rats was as free as if they owned the place, and so forth and so on, and then I got easy again. She was right about the rats. You'd see one stick his nose out of a hole in the corner every little while. She said she had to have things handy to throw at them when she was alone, or they wouldn't give her no peace. She showed me a bar of lead twisted up into a knot, and said she was a good shot with it generly, but she'd wrenched her arm a day or two ago, and didn't know whether she could throw true now. But she watched for a chance, and directly banged away at a rat; but she missed him wide, and said "Ouch!" it hurt her arm so. Then she told me to try for the next one. I wanted to be getting away before the old man got back, but of course I didn't let on. I got the thing, and the first rat that showed his nose I let drive, and if he'd a stayed where he was he'd a been a tolerable sick rat. She said that was first-rate, and she reckoned I would hive the next one. She went and got the lump of lead and fetched it back, and brought along a hank of yarn which she wanted me to help her with. I held up my two hands and she put the hank over them, and went on talking about her and her husband's matters. But she broke off to say:

"Keep your eye on the rats. You better have the lead in your lap, handy."

So she dropped the lump into my lap just at that moment, and I clapped my legs together on it and she went on talking. But only about a minute. Then she took off the hank and looked me straight in the face, and very pleasant, and says:

"Come, now, what's your real name?"

"Wh—what, mum?"

"What's your real name? Is it Bill, or Tom, or Bob?—or what is it?"

I reckon I shook like a leaf, and I didn't know hardly what to do. But I says:

"Please to don't poke fun at a poor girl like me, mum. If I'm in the way here, I'll—"

"No, you won't. Set down and stay where you are. I ain't going to hurt you, and I ain't going to tell on you, nuther. You just tell me your secret, and trust me. I'll keep it; and, what's more, I'll help you. So'll my old man if you want him to. You see, you're a runaway 'prentice, that's all. It ain't anything. There ain't no harm in it. You've been treated bad, and you made up your mind to cut. Bless you, child, I wouldn't tell on you. Tell me all about it now, that's a good boy."

So I said it wouldn't be no use to try to play it any longer, and I would just make a clean breast and tell her everything, but she musn't go back on her promise. Then I told her my father and mother was dead, and the law had bound me out to a mean old farmer in the country thirty mile back from the river, and he treated me so bad I couldn't stand it no longer; he went away to be gone a couple of days, and so I took my chance and stole some of his daughter's old clothes and cleared out, and I had been three nights coming the thirty miles. I traveled nights, and hid daytimes and slept, and the bag of bread and meat I carried from home lasted me all the way, and I had a-plenty. I said I believed my uncle Abner Moore would take care of me, and so that was why I struck out for this town of Goshen.

"Goshen, child? This ain't Goshen. This is St. Petersburg. Goshen's ten mile further up the river. Who told you this was Goshen?"

"Why, a man I met at daybreak this morning, just as I was going to turn into the woods for my regular sleep. He told me when the roads forked I must take the right hand, and five mile would fetch me to Goshen."

"He was drunk, I reckon. He told you just exactly wrong."

"Well, he did act like he was drunk, but it ain't no matter now. I got to be moving along. I'll fetch Goshen before daylight."

"Hold on a minute. I'll put you up a snack to eat. You might want it."

So she put me up a snack, and says:

"Say, when a cow's laying down, which end of her gets up first? Answer up prompt now—don't stop to study over it. Which end gets up first?"

"The hind end, mum."

"Well, then, a horse?"

"The for'rard end, mum."

"Which side of a tree does the moss grow on?"

"North side."

"If fifteen cows is browsing on a hillside, how many of them eats with their heads pointed the same direction?"

"The whole fifteen, mum."

"Well, I reckon you HAVE lived in the country. I thought maybe you was trying to hocus me again. What's your real name, now?"

"George Peters, mum."

"Well, try to remember it, George. Don't forget and tell me it's Elexander before you go, and then get out by saying it's George Elexander when I catch you. And don't go about women in that old calico. You do a girl tolerable poor, but you might fool men, maybe. Bless you, child, when you set out to thread a needle don't hold the thread still and fetch the needle up to it; hold the needle still and poke the thread at it; that's the way a woman most always does, but a man always does t'other way. And when you throw at a rat or anything, hitch yourself up a tiptoe and fetch your hand up over your head as awkward as you can, and miss your rat about six or seven foot. Throw stiff-armed from the shoulder, like there was a pivot there for it to turn on, like a girl; not from the wrist and elbow, with your arm out to one side, like a boy. And, mind you, when a girl tries to catch anything in her lap she throws her knees apart; she don't clap them together, the way you did when you catched the lump of lead. Why, I spotted you for a boy when you was threading the needle; and I contrived the other things just to make certain. Now trot along to your uncle, Sarah Mary Williams George Elexander Peters, and if you get into trouble you send word to Mrs. Judith Loftus, which is me, and I'll do what I can to get you out of it. Keep the river road all the way, and next time you tramp take shoes and socks with you. The river road's a rocky one, and your feet'll be in a condition when you get to Goshen, I reckon."

I went up the bank about fifty yards, and then I doubled on my tracks and slipped back to where my canoe was, a good piece below the house. I jumped in, and was off in a hurry. I went up-stream far enough to make the head of the island, and then started across. I took off the sun-bonnet, for I didn't want no blinders on then. When I was about the middle I heard the clock begin to strike, so I stops and listens; the sound come faint over the water but clear—eleven. When I struck the head of the island I never waited to blow, though I was most winded, but I shoved right into the timber where my old camp used to be, and started a good fire there on a high and dry spot.

Then I jumped in the canoe and dug out for our place, a mile and a half below, as hard as I could go. I landed, and slopped through the timber and up the ridge and into the cavern. There Jim laid, sound asleep on the ground. I roused him out and says:

"Git up and hump yourself, Jim! There ain't a minute to lose. They're after us!"

Jim never asked no questions, he never said a word; but the way he worked for the next half an hour showed about how he was scared. By that time everything we had in the world was on our raft, and she was ready to be shoved out from the willow cove where she was hid. We put out the camp fire at the cavern the first thing, and didn't show a candle outside after that.

I took the canoe out from the shore a little piece, and took a look; but if there was a boat around I couldn't see it, for stars and shadows ain't good to see by. Then we got out the raft and slipped along down in the shade, past the foot of the island dead still—never saying a word.

Chapter XII

It must a been close on to one o'clock when we got below the island at last, and the raft did seem to go mighty slow. If a boat was to come along we was going to take to the canoe and break for the Illinois shore; and it was well a boat didn't come, for we hadn't ever thought to put the gun in the canoe, or a fishing-line, or anything to eat. We was in ruther too much of a sweat to think of so many things. It warn't good judgment to put EVERYTHING on the raft.

If the men went to the island I just expect they found the camp fire I built, and watched it all night for Jim to come. Anyways, they stayed away from us, and if my building the fire never fooled them it warn't no fault of mine. I played it as low down on them as I could.

When the first streak of day began to show we tied up to a towhead in a big bend on the Illinois side, and hacked off cottonwood branches with the hatchet, and covered up the raft with them so she looked like there had been a cave-in in the bank there. A tow-head is a sandbar that has cottonwoods on it as thick as harrow-teeth.

We had mountains on the Missouri shore and heavy timber on the Illinois side, and the channel was down the Missouri shore at that place, so we warn't afraid of anybody running across us. We laid there all day, and watched the rafts and steamboats spin down the Missouri shore, and up-bound steamboats fight the big river in the middle. I told Jim all about the time I had jabbering with that woman; and Jim said she was a smart one, and if she was to start after us herself she wouldn't set down and watch a camp fire—no, sir, she'd fetch a dog. Well, then, I said, why couldn't she tell her husband to fetch a dog? Jim said he bet she did think of it by the time the men was ready to start, and he believed they must a gone up-town to get a dog and so they lost all that time, or else we wouldn't be here on a towhead sixteen or seventeen mile below the village—no, indeedy, we would be in that same old town again. So I said I didn't care what was the reason they didn't get us as long as they didn't.

When it was beginning to come on dark we poked our heads out of the cottonwood thicket, and looked up and down and across; nothing in sight; so Jim took up some of the top planks of the raft and built a snug wigwam to get under in blazing weather and rainy, and to keep the things dry. Jim made a floor for the wigwam, and raised it a foot or more above the level of the raft, so now the blankets and all the traps was out of reach of steamboat waves. Right in the middle of the wigwam we made a layer of dirt about five or six inches deep with a frame around it for to hold it to its place; this was to build a fire on in sloppy weather or chilly; the wigwam would keep it from being seen. We made an extra steering-oar, too, because one of the others might get broke on a snag or something. We fixed up a short forked stick to hang the old lantern on, because we must always light the lantern whenever we see a steamboat coming down-stream, to keep from getting run over; but we wouldn't have to light it for up-stream boats unless we see we was in what they call a "crossing"; for the river was pretty high yet, very low banks being still a little under water; so up-bound boats didn't always run the channel, but hunted easy water.

This second night we run between seven and eight hours, with a current that was making over four mile an hour. We catched fish and talked, and we took a swim now and then to keep off sleepiness. It was kind of solemn, drifting down the big, still river, laying on our backs looking up at the stars, and we didn't ever feel like talking loud, and it warn't often that we laughed—only a little kind of a low chuckle. We had mighty good weather as a general thing, and nothing ever happened to us at all—that night, nor the next, nor the next.

Every night we passed towns, some of them away up on black hillsides, nothing but just a shiny bed of lights; not a house could you see. The fifth night we passed St. Louis, and it was like the whole world lit up. In St. Petersburg they used to say there was twenty or thirty thousand people in St. Louis, but I never believed it till I see that wonderful spread of lights at two o'clock that still night. There warn't a sound there; everybody was asleep.

Every night now I used to slip ashore towards ten o'clock at some little village, and buy ten or fifteen cents' worth of meal or bacon or other stuff to eat; and sometimes I lifted a chicken that warn't roosting comfortable, and took him along. Pap always said, take a chicken when you get a chance, because if you don't want him yourself you can easy find somebody that does, and a good deed ain't ever forgot. I never see pap when he didn't want the chicken himself, but that is what he used to say, anyway.

Mornings before daylight I slipped into cornfields and borrowed a watermelon, or a mushmelon, or a punkin, or some new corn, or things of that kind. Pap always said it warn't no harm to borrow things if you was meaning to pay them back some time; but the widow said it warn't anything but a soft name for stealing, and no decent body would do it. Jim said he reckoned the widow was partly right and pap was partly right; so the best way would be for us to pick out two or three things from the list and say we wouldn't borrow them any more—then he reckoned it wouldn't be no harm to borrow the others. So we talked it over all one night, drifting along down the river, trying to make up our minds whether to drop the watermelons, or the cantelopes, or the mushmelons, or what. But towards daylight we got it all settled satisfactory, and concluded to drop crabapples and p'simmons. We warn't feeling just right before that, but it was all comfortable now. I was glad the way it come out, too, because crabapples ain't ever good, and the p'simmons wouldn't be ripe for two or three months yet.

We shot a water-fowl now and then that got up too early in the morning or didn't go to bed early enough in the evening. Take it all round, we lived pretty high.

The fifth night below St. Louis we had a big storm after midnight, with a power of thunder and lightning, and the rain poured down in a solid sheet. We stayed in the wigwam and let the raft take care of itself. When the lightning glared out we could see a big straight river ahead, and high, rocky bluffs on both sides. By and by says I, "Hel-LO, Jim, looky yonder!" It was a steamboat that had killed herself on a rock. We was drifting straight down for her. The lightning showed her very distinct. She was leaning over, with part of her upper deck above water, and you could see every little chimbly-guy clean and clear, and a chair by the big bell, with an old slouch hat hanging on the back of it, when the flashes come.

Well, it being away in the night and stormy, and all so mysterious-like, I felt just the way any other boy would a felt when I see that wreck laying there so mournful and lonesome in the middle of the river. I wanted to get aboard of her and slink around a little, and see what there was there. So I says:

"Le's land on her, Jim."

But Jim was dead against it at first. He says:

"I doan' want to go fool'n 'long er no wrack. We's doin' blame' well, en we better let blame' well alone, as de good book says. Like as not dey's a watchman on dat wrack."

"Watchman your grandmother," I says; "there ain't nothing to watch but the texas and the pilot-house; and do you reckon anybody's going to resk his life for a texas and a pilot-house such a night as this, when it's likely to break up and wash off down the river any minute?" Jim couldn't say nothing to that, so he didn't try. "And besides," I says, "we might borrow something worth having out of the captain's stateroom. Seegars, I bet you—and cost five cents apiece, solid cash. Steamboat captains is always rich, and get sixty dollars a month, and THEY don't care a cent what a thing costs, you know, long as they want it. Stick a candle in your pocket; I can't rest, Jim, till we give her a rummaging. Do you reckon Tom Sawyer would ever go by this thing? Not for pie, he wouldn't. He'd call it an adventure—that's what he'd call it; and he'd land on that wreck if it was his last act. And wouldn't he throw style into it? —wouldn't he spread himself, nor nothing? Why, you'd think it was Christopher C'lumbus discovering Kingdom-Come. I wish Tom Sawyer WAS here."

Jim he grumbled a little, but give in. He said we mustn't talk any more than we could help, and then talk mighty low. The lightning showed us the wreck again just in time, and we fetched the stabboard derrick, and made fast there.

The deck was high out here. We went sneaking down the slope of it to labboard, in the dark, towards the texas, feeling our way slow with our feet, and spreading our hands out to fend off the guys, for it was so dark we couldn't see no sign of them. Pretty soon we struck the forward end of the skylight, and clumb on to it; and the next step fetched us in front of the captain's door, which was open, and by Jimminy, away down through the texas-hall we see a light! and all in the same second we seem to hear low voices in yonder!

Jim whispered and said he was feeling powerful sick, and told me to come along. I says, all right, and was going to start for the raft; but just then I heard a voice wail out and say:

"Oh, please don't, boys; I swear I won't ever tell!"

Another voice said, pretty loud:

"It's a lie, Jim Turner. You've acted this way before. You always want more 'n your share of the truck, and you've always got it, too, because you've swore 't if you didn't you'd tell. But this time you've said it jest one time too many. You're the meanest, treacherousest hound in this country."

By this time Jim was gone for the raft. I was just a-biling with curiosity; and I says to myself, Tom Sawyer wouldn't back out now, and so I won't either; I'm a-going to see what's going on here. So I dropped on my hands and knees in the little passage, and crept aft in the dark till there warn't but one stateroom betwixt me and the cross-hall of the texas. Then in there I see a man stretched on the floor and tied hand and foot, and two men standing over him, and one of them had a dim lantern in his hand, and the other one had a pistol. This one kept pointing the pistol at the man's head on the floor, and saying:

"I'd LIKE to! And I orter, too—a mean skunk!"

The man on the floor would shrivel up and say, "Oh, please don't, Bill; I hain't ever goin' to tell."

And every time he said that the man with the lantern would laugh and say:

"'Deed you AIN'T You never said no truer thing 'n that, you bet you." And once he said: "Hear him beg! and yit if we hadn't got the best of him and tied him he'd a killed us both. And what FOR? Jist for noth'n. Jist because we stood on our RIGHTS—that's what for. But I lay you ain't a-goin' to threaten nobody any more, Jim Turner. Put UP that pistol, Bill."

Bill says:

"I don't want to, Jake Packard. I'm for killin' him—and didn't he kill old Hatfield jist the same way—and don't he deserve it?"

"But I don't WANT him killed, and I've got my reasons for it."

"Bless yo' heart for them words, Jake Packard! I'll never forget you long's I live!" says the man on the floor, sort of blubbering.

Packard didn't take no notice of that, but hung up his lantern on a nail and started towards where I was there in the dark, and motioned Bill to come. I crawfished as fast as I could about two yards, but the boat slanted so that I couldn't make very good time; so to keep from getting run over and catched I crawled into a stateroom on the upper side. The man came a-pawing along in the dark, and when Packard got to my state-room, he says:

"Here—come in here."

And in he come, and Bill after him. But before they got in I was up in the upper berth, cornered, and sorry I come. Then they stood there, with their hands on the ledge of the berth, and talked. I couldn't see them, but I could tell where they was by the whisky they'd been having. I was glad I didn't drink whisky; but it wouldn't made much difference anyway, because most of the time they couldn't a treed me because I didn't breathe. I was too scared. And, besides, a body couldn't breathe and hear such talk. They talked low and earnest. Bill wanted to kill Turner. He says:

"He's said he'll tell, and he will. If we was to give both our shares to him NOW it wouldn't make no difference after the row and the way we've served him. Shore's you're born, he'll turn State's evidence; now you hear ME. I'm for putting him out of his troubles."

"So'm I," says Packard, very quiet.

"Blame it, I'd sorter begun to think you wasn't. Well, then, that's all right. Le's go and do it."

"Hold on a minute; I hain't had my say yit. You listen to me. Shooting's good, but there's quieter ways if the thing's GOT to be done. But what I say is this: it ain't good sense to go court'n around after a halter if you can git at what you're up to in some way that's jist as good and at the same time don't bring you into no resks. Ain't that so?"

"You bet it is. But how you goin' to manage it this time?"

"Well, my idea is this: we'll rustle around and gather up whatever pickins we've overlooked in the staterooms, and shove for shore and hide the truck. Then we'll wait. Now I say it ain't a-goin' to be more'n two hours befo' this wrack breaks up and washes off down the river. See? He'll be drownded, and won't have nobody to blame for it but his own self. I reckon that's a considerble sight better 'n killin' of him. I'm unfavorable to killin' a man as long as you can git aroun' it; it ain't good sense, it ain't good morals. Ain't I right?"

"Yes, I reck'n you are. But s'pose she DON'T break up and wash off?"

"Well, we can wait the two hours anyway and see, can't we?"

"All right, then; come along."

So they started, and I lit out, all in a cold sweat, and scrambled forward. It was dark as pitch there; but I said, in a kind of a coarse whisper, "Jim!" and he answered up, right at my elbow, with a sort of a moan, and I says:

"Quick, Jim, it ain't no time for fooling around and moaning; there's a gang of murderers in yonder, and if we don't hunt up their boat and set her drifting down the river so these fellows can't get away from the wreck there's one of 'em going to be in a bad fix. But if we find their boat we can put ALL of 'em in a bad fix—for the sheriff 'll get 'em. Quick—hurry! I'll hunt the labboard side, you hunt the stabboard. You start at the raft, and—"

"Oh, my lordy, lordy! RAF'? Dey ain' no raf' no mo'; she done broke loose en gone I—en here we is!"

Chapter XIII

Well, I catched my breath and most fainted. Shut up on a wreck with such a gang as that! But it warn't no time to be sentimentering. We'd GOT to find that boat now—had to have it for ourselves. So we went a-quaking and shaking down the stabboard side, and slow work it was, too—seemed a week before we got to the stern. No sign of a boat. Jim said he didn't believe he could go any further—so scared he hadn't hardly any strength left, he said. But I said, come on, if we get left on this wreck we are in a fix, sure. So on we prowled again. We struck for the stern of the texas, and found it, and then scrabbled along forwards on the skylight, hanging on from shutter to shutter, for the edge of the skylight was in the water. When we got pretty close to the cross-hall door there was the skiff, sure enough! I could just barely see her. I felt ever so thankful. In another second I would a been aboard of her, but just then the door opened. One of the men stuck his head out only about a couple of foot from me, and I thought I was gone; but he jerked it in again, and says:

"Heave that blame lantern out o' sight, Bill!"

He flung a bag of something into the boat, and then got in himself and set down. It was Packard. Then Bill HE come out and got in. Packard says, in a low voice:

"All ready—shove off!"

I couldn't hardly hang on to the shutters, I was so weak. But Bill says:

"Hold on—'d you go through him?"

"No. Didn't you?"

"No. So he's got his share o' the cash yet."

"Well, then, come along; no use to take truck and leave money."

"Say, won't he suspicion what we're up to?"

"Maybe he won't. But we got to have it anyway. Come along."

So they got out and went in.

The door slammed to because it was on the careened side; and in a half second I was in the boat, and Jim come tumbling after me. I out with my knife and cut the rope, and away we went!

We didn't touch an oar, and we didn't speak nor whisper, nor hardly even breathe. We went gliding swift along, dead silent, past the tip of the paddle-box, and past the stern; then in a second or two more we was a hundred yards below the wreck, and the darkness soaked her up, every last sign of her, and we was safe, and knowed it.

When we was three or four hundred yards down-stream we see the lantern show like a little spark at the texas door for a second, and we knowed by that that the rascals had missed their boat, and was beginning to understand that they was in just as much trouble now as Jim Turner was.

Then Jim manned the oars, and we took out after our raft. Now was the first time that I begun to worry about the men—I reckon I hadn't had time to before. I begun to think how dreadful it was, even for murderers, to be in such a fix. I says to myself, there ain't no telling but I might come to be a murderer myself yet, and then how would I like it? So says I to Jim:

"The first light we see we'll land a hundred yards below it or above it, in a place where it's a good hiding-place for you and the skiff, and then I'll go and fix up some kind of a yarn, and get somebody to go for that gang and get them out of their scrape, so they can be hung when their time comes."

But that idea was a failure; for pretty soon it begun to storm again, and this time worse than ever. The rain poured down, and never a light showed; everybody in bed, I reckon. We boomed along down the river, watching for lights and watching for our raft. After a long time the rain let up, but the clouds stayed, and the lightning kept whimpering, and by and by a flash showed us a black thing ahead, floating, and we made for it.

It was the raft, and mighty glad was we to get aboard of it again. We seen a light now away down to the right, on shore. So I said I would go for it. The skiff was half full of plunder which that gang had stole there on the wreck. We hustled it on to the raft in a pile, and I told Jim to float along down, and show a light when he judged he had gone about two mile, and keep it burning till I come; then I manned my oars and shoved for the light. As I got down towards it three or four more showed—up on a hillside. It was a village. I closed in above the shore light, and laid on my oars and floated. As I went by I see it was a lantern hanging on the jackstaff of a double-hull ferryboat. I skimmed around for the watchman, a-wondering whereabouts he slept; and by and by I found him roosting on the bitts forward, with his head down between his knees. I gave his shoulder two or three little shoves, and begun to cry.

He stirred up in a kind of a startlish way; but when he see it was only me he took a good gap and stretch, and then he says:

"Hello, what's up? Don't cry, bub. What's the trouble?"

I says:

"Pap, and mam, and sis, and—"

Then I broke down. He says:

"Oh, dang it now, DON'T take on so; we all has to have our troubles, and this 'n 'll come out all right. What's the matter with 'em?"

"They're—they're—are you the watchman of the boat?"

"Yes," he says, kind of pretty-well-satisfied like. "I'm the captain and the owner and the mate and the pilot and watchman and head deck-hand; and sometimes I'm the freight and passengers. I ain't as rich as old Jim Hornback, and I can't be so blame' generous and good to Tom, Dick, and Harry as what he is, and slam around money the way he does; but I've told him a many a time 't I wouldn't trade places with him; for, says I, a sailor's life's the life for me, and I'm derned if I'D live two mile out o' town, where there ain't nothing ever goin' on, not for all his spondulicks and as much more on top of it. Says I—"

I broke in and says:

"They're in an awful peck of trouble, and—"

"WHO is?"

"Why, pap and mam and sis and Miss Hooker; and if you'd take your ferryboat and go up there—"

"Up where? Where are they?"

"On the wreck."

"What wreck?"

"Why, there ain't but one."

"What, you don't mean the Walter Scott?"

"Yes."

"Good land! what are they doin' THERE, for gracious sakes?"

"Well, they didn't go there a-purpose."

"I bet they didn't! Why, great goodness, there ain't no chance for 'em if they don't git off mighty quick! Why, how in the nation did they ever git into such a scrape?"

"Easy enough. Miss Hooker was a-visiting up there to the town—"

"Yes, Booth's Landing—go on."

"She was a-visiting there at Booth's Landing, and just in the edge of the evening she started over with her nigger woman in the horse-ferry to stay all night at her friend's house, Miss What-you-may-call-her I disremember her name—and they lost their steering-oar, and swung around and went a-floating down, stern first, about two mile, and saddle-baggsed on the wreck, and the ferryman and the nigger woman and the horses was all lost, but Miss Hooker she made a grab and got aboard the wreck. Well, about an hour after dark we come along down in our trading-scow, and it was so dark we didn't notice the wreck till we was right on it; and so WE saddle-baggsed; but all of us was saved but Bill Whipple—and oh, he WAS the best cretur!—I most wish 't it had been me, I do."

"My George! It's the beatenest thing I ever struck. And THEN what did you all do?"

"Well, we hollered and took on, but it's so wide there we couldn't make nobody hear. So pap said somebody got to get ashore and get help somehow. I was the only one that could swim, so I made a dash for it, and Miss Hooker she said if I didn't strike help sooner, come here and hunt up her uncle, and he'd fix the thing. I made the land about a mile below, and been fooling along ever since, trying to get people to do something, but they said, 'What, in such a night and such a current? There ain't no sense in it; go for the steam ferry.' Now if you'll go and—"

"By Jackson, I'd LIKE to, and, blame it, I don't know but I will; but who in the dingnation's a-going' to PAY for it? Do you reckon your pap—"

"Why THAT'S all right. Miss Hooker she tole me, PARTICULAR, that her uncle Hornback—"

"Great guns! is HE her uncle? Looky here, you break for that light over yonder-way, and turn out west when you git there, and about a quarter of a mile out you'll come to the tavern; tell 'em to dart you out to Jim Hornback's, and he'll foot the bill. And don't you fool around any, because he'll want to know the news. Tell him I'll have his niece all safe before he can get to town. Hump yourself, now; I'm a-going up around the corner here to roust out my engineer."

I struck for the light, but as soon as he turned the corner I went back and got into my skiff and bailed her out, and then pulled up shore in the easy water about six hundred yards, and tucked myself in among some woodboats; for I couldn't rest easy till I could see the ferryboat start. But take it all around, I was feeling ruther comfortable on accounts of taking all this trouble for that gang, for not many would a done it. I wished the widow knowed about it. I judged she would be proud of me for helping these rapscallions, because rapscallions and dead beats is the kind the widow and good people takes the most interest in.

Well, before long here comes the wreck, dim and dusky, sliding along down! A kind of cold shiver went through me, and then I struck out for her. She was very deep, and I see in a minute there warn't much chance for anybody being alive in her. I pulled all around her and hollered a little, but there wasn't any answer; all dead still. I felt a little bit heavy-hearted about the gang, but not much, for I reckoned if they could stand it I could.

Then here comes the ferryboat; so I shoved for the middle of the river on a long down-stream slant; and when I judged I was out of eye-reach I laid on my oars, and looked back and see her go and smell around the wreck for Miss Hooker's remainders, because the captain would know her uncle Hornback would want them; and then pretty soon the ferryboat give it up and went for the shore, and I laid into my work and went a-booming down the river.

It did seem a powerful long time before Jim's light showed up; and when it did show it looked like it was a thousand mile off. By the time I got there the sky was beginning to get a little gray in the east; so we struck for an island, and hid the raft, and sunk the skiff, and turned in and slept like dead people.

Chapter XIV

By and by, when we got up, we turned over the truck the gang had stole off of the wreck, and found boots, and blankets, and clothes, and all sorts of other things, and a lot of books, and a spyglass, and three boxes of seegars. We hadn't ever been this rich before in neither of our lives. The seegars was prime. We laid off all the afternoon in the woods talking, and me reading the books, and having a general good time.

I told Jim all about what happened inside the wreck and at the ferryboat, and I said these kinds of things was adventures; but he said he didn't want no more adventures. He said that when I went in the texas and he crawled back to get on the raft and found her gone he nearly died, because he judged it was all up with HIM anyway it could be fixed; for if he didn't get saved he would get drownded; and if he did get saved, whoever saved him would send him back home so as to get the reward, and then Miss Watson would sell him South, sure. Well, he was right; he was most always right; he had an uncommon level head for a nigger.

I read considerable to Jim about kings and dukes and earls and such, and how gaudy they dressed, and how much style they put on, and called each other your majesty, and your grace, and your lordship, and so on, 'stead of mister; and Jim's eyes bugged out, and he was interested. He says:

"I didn' know dey was so many un um. I hain't hearn 'bout none un um, skasely, but ole King Sollermun, onless you counts dem kings dat's in a pack er k'yards. How much do a king git?"

"Get?" I says; "why, they get a thousand dollars a month if they want it; they can have just as much as they want; everything belongs to them."

"Ain' dat gay? En what dey got to do, Huck?"

"THEY don't do nothing! Why, how you talk! They just set around."

"No; is dat so?"

"Of course it is. They just set around—except, maybe, when there's a war; then they go to the war. But other times they just lazy around; or go hawking—just hawking and sp—Sh!—d' you hear a noise?"

We skipped out and looked; but it warn't nothing but the flutter of a steamboat's wheel away down, coming around the point; so we come back.

"Yes," says I, "and other times, when things is dull, they fuss with the parlyment; and if everybody don't go just so he whacks their heads off. But mostly they hang round the harem."

"Roun' de which?"

"Harem."

"What's de harem?"

"The place where he keeps his wives. Don't you know about the harem? Solomon had one; he had about a million wives."

"Why, yes, dat's so; I—I'd done forgot it. A harem's a bo'd'n-house, I reck'n. Mos' likely dey has rackety times in de nussery. En I reck'n de wives quarrels considable; en dat 'crease de racket. Yit dey say Sollermun de wises' man dat ever live'. I doan' take no stock in dat. Bekase why: would a wise man want to live in de mids' er sich a blim-blammin' all de time? No—'deed he wouldn't. A wise man 'ud take en buil' a biler-factry; en den he could shet DOWN de biler-factry when he want to res'."

"Well, but he WAS the wisest man, anyway; because the widow she told me so, her own self.

"I doan k'yer what de widder say, he WARN'T no wise man nuther. He had some er de dad-fetchedes' ways I ever see. Does you know 'bout dat chile dat he 'uz gwyne to chop in two?"

"Yes, the widow told me all about it."

"WELL, den! Warn' dat de beatenes' notion in de worl'? You jes' take en look at it a minute. Dah's de stump, dah—dat's one er de women; heah's you—dat's de yuther one; I's Sollermun; en dish yer dollar bill's de chile. Bofe un you claims it. What does I do? Does I shin aroun' mongs' de neighbors en fine out which un you de bill DO b'long to, en han' it over to de right one, all safe en soun', de way dat anybody dat had any gumption would? No; I take en whack de bill in TWO , en give half un it to you, en de yuther half to de yuther woman. Dat's de way Sollermun was gwyne to do wid de chile. Now I want to ast you: what's de use er dat half a bill?—can't buy noth'n wid it. En what use is a half a chile? I wouldn' give a dern for a million un um."

"But hang it, Jim, you've clean missed the point—blame it, you've missed it a thousand mile."

"Who? Me? Go 'long. Doan' talk to me 'bout yo' pints. I reck'n I knows sense when I sees it; en dey ain' no sense in sich doin's as dat. De 'spute warn' 'bout a half a chile, de 'spute was 'bout a whole chile; en de man dat think he kin settle a 'spute 'bout a whole chile wid a half a chile doan' know enough to come in out'n de rain. Doan' talk to me 'bout Sollermun, Huck, I knows him by de back."

"But I tell you you don't get the point."

"Blame de point! I reck'n I knows what I knows. En mine you, de REAL pint is down furder—it's down deeper. It lays in de way Sollermun was raised. You take a man dat's got on'y one or two chillen; is dat man gwyne to be waseful o' chillen? No, he ain't; he can't 'ford it. HE know how to value 'em. But you take a man dat's got 'bout five million chillen runnin' roun' de house, en it's diffunt. HE as soon chop a chile in two as a cat. Dey's plenty mo'. A chile er two, mo' er less, warn't no consekens to Sollermun, dad fatch him!"

I never see such a nigger. If he got a notion in his head once, there warn't no getting it out again. He was the most down on Solomon of any nigger I ever see. So I went to talking about other kings, and let Solomon slide. I told about Louis Sixteenth that got his head cut off in France long time ago; and about his little boy the dolphin, that would a been a king, but they took and shut him up in jail, and some say he died there.

"Po' little chap."

"But some says he got out and got away, and come to America."

"Dat's good! But he'll be pooty lonesome—dey ain' no kings here, is dey, Huck?"

"No."

"Den he cain't git no situation. What he gwyne to do?"

"Well, I don't know. Some of them gets on the police, and some of them learns people how to talk French."

"Why, Huck, doan' de French people talk de same way we does?"

"NO, Jim; you couldn't understand a word they said—not a single word."

"Well, now, I be ding-busted! How do dat come?"

"I don't know; but it's so. I got some of their jabber out of a book. S'pose a man was to come to you and say Polly-voo-franzy—what would you think?"

"I wouldn' think nuff'n; I'd take en bust him over de head—dat is, if he warn't white. I wouldn't 'low no nigger to call me dat."

"Shucks, it ain't calling you anything. It's only saying, do you know how to talk French?"

"Well, den, why couldn't he SAY it?"

"Why, he IS a-saying it. That's a Frenchman's WAY of saying it."

"Well, it's a blame ridicklous way, en I doan' want to hear no mo' 'bout it. Dey ain' no sense in it."

"Looky here, Jim; does a cat talk like we do?"

"No, a cat don't."

"Well, does a cow?"

"No, a cow don't, nuther."

"Does a cat talk like a cow, or a cow talk like a cat?"

"No, dey don't."

"It's natural and right for 'em to talk different from each other, ain't it?"

"Course."

"And ain't it natural and right for a cat and a cow to talk different from US?"

"Why, mos' sholy it is."

"Well, then, why ain't it natural and right for a FRENCHMAN to talk different from us? You answer me that."

"Is a cat a man, Huck?"

"No."

"Well, den, dey ain't no sense in a cat talkin' like a man. Is a cow a man?—er is a cow a cat?"

"No, she ain't either of them."

"Well, den, she ain't got no business to talk like either one er the yuther of 'em. Is a Frenchman a man?"

"Yes."

"WELL, den! Dad blame it, why doan' he TALK like a man? You answer me dat!"

I see it warn't no use wasting words—you can't learn a nigger to argue. So I quit.

Chapter XV

We judged that three nights more would fetch us to Cairo, at the bottom of Illi nois, where the Ohio River comes in, and that was what we was after. We would sell the raft and get on a steamboat and go way up the Ohio amongst the free States, and then be out of trouble.

Well, the second night a fog begun to come on, and we made for a towhead to tie to, for it wouldn't do to try to run in a fog; but when I paddled ahead in the canoe, with the line to make fast, there warn't anything but little saplings to tie to. I passed the line around one of them right on the edge of the cut bank, but there was a stiff current, and the raft come booming down so lively she tore it out by the roots and away she went. I see the fog closing down, and it made me so sick and scared I couldn't budge for most a half a minute it seemed to me—and then there warn't no raft in sight; you couldn't see twenty yards. I jumped into the canoe and run back to the stern, and grabbed the paddle and set her back a stroke. But she didn't come. I was in such a hurry I hadn't untied her. I got up and tried to untie her, but I was so excited my hands shook so I couldn't hardly do anything with them.

As soon as I got started I took out after the raft, hot and heavy, right down the towhead. That was all right as far as it went, but the towhead warn't sixty yards long, and the minute I flew by the foot of it I shot out into the solid white fog, and hadn't no more idea which way I was going than a dead man.

Thinks I, it won't do to paddle; first I know I'll run into the bank or a towhead or something; I got to set still and float, and yet it's mighty fidgety business to have to hold your hands still at such a time. I whooped and listened. Away down there somewheres I hears a small whoop, and up comes my spirits. I went tearing after it, listening sharp to hear it again. The next time it come I see I warn't heading for it, but heading away to the right of it. And the next time I was heading away to the left of it—and not gaining on it much either, for I was flying around, this way and that and t'other, but it was going straight ahead all the time.

I did wish the fool would think to beat a tin pan, and beat it all the time, but he never did, and it was the still places between the whoops that was making the trouble for me. Well, I fought along, and directly I hears the whoop BEHIND me. I was tangled good now. That was somebody else's whoop, or else I was turned around.

I throwed the paddle down. I heard the whoop again; it was behind me yet, but in a different place; it kept coming, and kept changing its place, and I kept answering, till by and by it was in front of me again, and I knowed the current had swung the canoe's head down-stream, and I was all right if that was Jim and not some other raftsman hollering. I couldn't tell nothing about voices in a fog, for nothing don't look natural nor sound natural in a fog.

The whooping went on, and in about a minute I come a-booming down on a cut bank with smoky ghosts of big trees on it, and the current throwed me off to the left and shot by, amongst a lot of snags that fairly roared, the currrent was tearing by them so swift.

In another second or two it was solid white and still again. I set perfectly still then, listening to my heart thump, and I reckon I didn't draw a breath while it thumped a hundred.

I just give up then. I knowed what the matter was. That cut bank was an island, and Jim had gone down t'other side of it. It warn't no towhead that you could float by in ten minutes. It had the big timber of a regular island; it might be five or six miles long and more than half a mile wide.

I kept quiet, with my ears cocked, about fifteen minutes, I reckon. I was floating along, of course, four or five miles an hour; but you don't ever think of that. No, you FEEL like you are laying dead still on the water; and if a little glimpse of a snag slips by you don't think to yourself how fast YOU'RE going, but you catch your breath and think, my! how that snag's tearing along. If you think it ain't dismal and lonesome out in a fog that way by yourself in the night, you try it once—you'll see.

Next, for about a half an hour, I whoops now and then; at last I hears the answer a long ways off, and tries to follow it, but I couldn't do it, and directly I judged I'd got into a nest of towheads, for I had little dim glimpses of them on both sides of me— sometimes just a narrow channel between, and some that I couldn't see I knowed was there because I'd hear the wash of the current against the old dead brush and trash that hung over the banks. Well, I warn't long loosing the whoops down amongst the tow-heads; and I only tried to chase them a little while, anyway, because it was worse than chasing a Jack-o'-lantern. You never knowed a sound dodge around so, and swap places so quick and so much.

I had to claw away from the bank pretty lively four or five times, to keep from knocking the islands out of the river; and so I judged the raft must be butting into the bank every now and then, or else it would get further ahead and clear out of hearing— it was floating a little faster than what I was.

Well, I seemed to be in the open river again by and by, but I couldn't hear no sign of a whoop nowheres. I reckoned Jim had fetched up on a snag, maybe, and it was all up with him. I was good and tired, so I laid down in the canoe and said I wouldn't bother no more. I didn't want to go to sleep, of course; but I was so sleepy I couldn't help it; so I thought I would take jest one little cat-nap.

But I reckon it was more than a cat-nap, for when I waked up the stars was shining bright, the fog was all gone, and I was spinning down a big bend stern first. First I didn't know where I was; I thought I was dreaming; and when things began to come back to me they seemed to come up dim out of last week.

It was a monstrous big river here, with the tallest and the thickest kind of timber on both banks; just a solid wall, as well as I could see by the stars. I looked away down-stream, and seen a black speck on the water. I took after it; but when I got to it it warn't nothing but a couple of sawlogs made fast together. Then I see another speck, and chased that; then another, and this time I was right. It was the raft.

When I got to it Jim was setting there with his head down between his knees, asleep, with his right arm hanging over the steering-oar. The other oar was smashed off, and the raft was littered up with leaves and branches and dirt. So she'd had a rough time.

I made fast and laid down under Jim's nose on the raft, and began to gap, and stretch my fists out against Jim, and says:

"Hello, Jim, have I been asleep? Why didn't you stir me up?"

"Goodness gracious, is dat you, Huck? En you ain' dead—you ain' drownded—you's back agin? It's too good for true, honey, it's too good for true. Lemme look at you chile, lemme feel o' you. No, you ain' dead! you's back agin, 'live en soun', jis de same ole Huck—de same ole Huck, thanks to goodness!"

"What's the matter with you, Jim? You been a-drinking?"

"Drinkin'? Has I ben a-drinkin'? Has I had a chance to be a-drinkin'?"

"Well, then, what makes you talk so wild?"

"How does I talk wild?"

"HOW? Why, hain't you been talking about my coming back, and all that stuff, as if I'd been gone away?"

"Huck—Huck Finn, you look me in de eye; look me in de eye. HAIN'T you ben gone away?"

"Gone away? Why, what in the nation do you mean? I hain't been gone anywheres. Where would I go to?"

"Well, looky here, boss, dey's sumf'n wrong, dey is. Is I ME, or who IS I? Is I heah, or whah IS I? Now dat's what I wants to know."

"Well, I think you're here, plain enough, but I think you're a tangle-headed old fool, Jim."

"I is, is I? Well, you answer me dis: Didn't you tote out de line in de canoe fer to make fas' to de tow-head?"

"No, I didn't. What tow-head? I hain't see no tow-head."

"You hain't seen no towhead? Looky here, didn't de line pull loose en de raf' go a-hummin' down de river, en leave you en de canoe behine in de fog?"

"What fog?"

"Why, de fog!—de fog dat's been aroun' all night. En didn't you whoop, en didn't I whoop, tell we got mix' up in de islands en one un us got los' en t'other one was jis' as good as los', 'kase he didn' know whah he wuz? En didn't I bust up agin a lot er dem islands en have a terrible time en mos' git drownded? Now ain' dat so, boss—ain't it so? You answer me dat."

"Well, this is too many for me, Jim. I hain't seen no fog, nor no islands, nor no troubles, nor nothing. I been setting here talking with you all night till you went to sleep about ten minutes ago, and I reckon I done the same. You couldn't a got drunk in that time, so of course you've been dreaming."

"Dad fetch it, how is I gwyne to dream all dat in ten minutes?"

"Well, hang it all, you did dream it, because there didn't any of it happen."

"But, Huck, it's all jis' as plain to me as—"

"It don't make no difference how plain it is; there ain't nothing in it. I know, because I've been here all the time."

Jim didn't say nothing for about five minutes, but set there studying over it. Then he says:

"Well, den, I reck'n I did dream it, Huck; but dog my cats ef it ain't de powerfullest dream I ever see. En I hain't ever had no dream b'fo' dat's tired me like dis one."

"Oh, well, that's all right, because a dream does tire a body like everything sometimes. But this one was a staving dream; tell me all about it, Jim."

So Jim went to work and told me the whole thing right through, just as it happened, only he painted it up considerable. Then he said he must start in and "'terpret" it, because it was sent for a warning. He said the first towhead stood for a man that would try to do us some good, but the current was another man that would get us away from him. The whoops was warnings that would come to us every now and then, and if we didn't try hard to make out to understand them they'd just take us into bad luck, 'stead of keeping us out of it. The lot of towheads was troubles we was going to get into with quarrelsome people and all kinds of mean folks, but if we minded our business and didn't talk back and aggravate them, we would pull through and get out of the fog and into the big clear river, which was the free States, and wouldn't have no more trouble.

It had clouded up pretty dark just after I got on to the raft, but it was clearing up again now.

"Oh, well, that's all interpreted well enough as far as it goes, Jim," I says; "but what does THESE things stand for?"

It was the leaves and rubbish on the raft and the smashed oar. You could see them first-rate now.

Jim looked at the trash, and then looked at me, and back at the trash again. He had got the dream fixed so strong in his head that he couldn't seem to shake it loose and get the facts back into its place again right away. But when he did get the thing straightened around he looked at me steady without ever smiling, and says:

"What do dey stan' for? I'se gwyne to tell you. When I got all wore out wid work, en wid de callin' for you, en went to sleep, my heart wuz mos' broke bekase you wuz los', en I didn't k'yer no mo' what become er me en de raf'. En when I wake up en fine you back agin, all safe en soun', de tears come, en I could a got down on my knees en kiss yo' foot, I's so thankful. En all you wuz thinkin' 'bout wuz how you could make a fool uv ole Jim wid a lie. Dat truck dah is TRASH; en trash is what people is dat puts dirt on de head er dey fren's en makes 'em ashamed."

Then he got up slow and walked to the wigwam, and went in there without saying anything but that. But that was enough. It made me feel so mean I could almost kissed HIS foot to get him to take it back.

It was fifteen minutes before I could work myself up to go and humble myself to a nigger; but I done it, and I warn't ever sorry for it afterwards, neither. I didn't do him no more mean tricks, and I wouldn't done that one if I'd a knowed it would make him feel that way.

Chapter XVI

We slept most all day, and started out at night, a little ways behind a monstrous long raft that was as long going by as a procession. She had four long sweeps at each end, so we judged she carried as many as thirty men, likely. She had five big wigwams aboard, wide apart, and an open camp fire in the middle, and a tall flag-pole at each end. There was a power of style about her. It amounted to something being a raftsman onsuch a craft as that.

We went drifting down into a big bend, and the night clouded up and got hot. The river was very wide, and was walled with solid timber on both sides; you couldn't see a break in it hardly ever, or a light. We talked about Cairo, and wondered whether we would know it when we got to it. I said likely we wouldn't, because I had heard say there warn't but about a dozen houses there, and if they didn't happen to have them lit up, how was we going to know we was passing a town? Jim said if the two big rivers joined together there, that would show. But I said maybe we might think we was passing the foot of an island and coming into the same old river again. That disturbed Jim—and me too. So the question was, what to do? I said, paddle ashore the first time a light showed, and tell them pap was behind, coming along with a trading-scow, and was a green hand at the business, and wanted to know how far it was to Cairo. Jim thought it was a good idea, so we took a smoke on it and waited.

There warn't nothing to do now but to look out sharp for the town, and not pass it without seeing it. He said he'd be mighty sure to see it, because he'd be a free man the minute he seen it, but if he missed it he'd be in a slave country again and no more show for freedom. Every little while he jumps up and says:

"Dah she is?"

But it warn't. It was Jack-o'-lanterns, or lightning bugs; so he set down again, and went to watching, same as before. Jim said it made him all over trembly and feverish to be so close to freedom. Well, I can tell you it made me all over trembly and feverish, too, to hear him, because I begun to get it through my head that he WAS most free— and who was to blame for it? Why, ME. I couldn't get that out of my conscience, no how nor no way. It got to troubling me so I couldn't rest; I couldn't stay still in one place. It hadn't ever come home to me before, what this thing was that I was doing. But now it did; and it stayed with me, and scorched me more and more. I tried to make out to myself that I warn't to blame, because I didn't run Jim off from his rightful owner; but it warn't no use, conscience up and says, every time, "But you knowed he was running for his freedom, and you could a paddled ashore and told somebody." That was so—I couldn't get around that noway. That was where it pinched. Conscience says to me, "What had poor Miss Watson done to you that you could see her nigger go off right under your eyes and never say one single word? What did that poor old woman do to you that you could treat her so mean? Why, she tried to learn you your book, she tried to learn you your manners, she tried to be good to you every way she knowed how. THAT'S what she done."

I got to feeling so mean and so miserable I most wished I was dead. I fidgeted up and down the raft, abusing myself to myself, and Jim was fidgeting up and down past me. We neither of us could keep still. Every time he danced around and says, "Dah's Cairo!" it went through me like a shot, and I thought if it WAS Cairo I reckoned I would die of miserableness.

Jim talked out loud all the time while I was talking to myself. He was saying how the first thing he would do when he got to a free State he would go to saving up money and never spend a single cent, and when he got enough he would buy his wife, which was owned on a farm close to where Miss Watson lived; and then they would both work to buy the two children, and if their master wouldn't sell them, they'd get an Ab'litionist to go and steal them.

It most froze me to hear such talk. He wouldn't ever dared to talk such talk in his life before. Just see what a difference it made in him the minute he judged he was about free. It was according to the old saying, "Give a nigger an inch and he'll take an ell." Thinks I, this is what comes of my not thinking. Here was this nigger, which I had as good as helped to run away, coming right out flat-footed and saying he would steal his children—children that belonged to a man I didn't even know; a man that hadn't ever done me no harm.

I was sorry to hear Jim say that, it was such a lowering of him. My conscience got to stirring me up hotter than ever, until at last I says to it, "Let up on me—it ain't too late yet—I'll paddle ashore at the first light and tell." I felt easy and happy and light as a feather right off. All my troubles was gone. I went to looking out sharp for a light, and sort of singing to myself. By and by one showed. Jim sings out:

"We's safe, Huck, we's safe! Jump up and crack yo' heels! Dat's de good ole Cairo at las', I jis knows it!"

I says:

"I'll take the canoe and go and see, Jim. It mightn't be, you know."

He jumped and got the canoe ready, and put his old coat in the bottom for me to set on, and give me the paddle; and as I shoved off, he says:

"Pooty soon I'll be a-shout'n' for joy, en I'll say, it's all on accounts o' Huck; I's a free man, en I couldn't ever ben free ef it hadn' ben for Huck; Huck done it. Jim won't ever forget you, Huck; you's de bes' fren' Jim's ever had; en you's de ONLY fren' ole Jim's got now."

I was paddling off, all in a sweat to tell on him; but when he says this, it seemed to kind of take the tuck all out of me. I went along slow then, and I warn't right down certain whether I was glad I started or whether I warn't. When I was fifty yards off, Jim says:

"Dah you goes, de ole true Huck; de on'y white genlman dat ever kep' his promise to ole Jim."

Well, I just felt sick. But I says, I GOT to do it—I can't get OUT of it. Right then along comes a skiff with two men in it with guns, and they stopped and I stopped. One of them says:

"What's that yonder?"

"A piece of a raft," I says.

"Do you belong on it?"

"Yes, sir."

"Any men on it?"

"Only one, sir."

"Well, there's five niggers run off to-night up yonder, above the head of the bend. Is your man white or black?"

I didn't answer up prompt. I tried to, but the words wouldn't come. I tried for a second or two to brace up and out with it, but I warn't man enough—hadn't the spunk of a rabbit. I see I was weakening; so I just give up trying, and up and says:

"He's white."

"I reckon we'll go and see for ourselves."

"I wish you would," says I, "because it's pap that's there, and maybe you'd help me tow the raft ashore where the light is. He's sick—and so is mam and Mary Ann."

"Oh, the devil! we're in a hurry, boy. But I s'pose we've got to. Come, buckle to your paddle, and let's get along."

I buckled to my paddle and they laid to their oars. When we had made a stroke or two, I says:

"Pap'll be mighty much obleeged to you, I can tell you. Everybody goes away when I want them to help me tow the raft ashore, and I can't do it by myself."

"Well, that's infernal mean. Odd, too. Say, boy, what's the matter with your father?"

"It's the—a—the—well, it ain't anything much."

They stopped pulling. It warn't but a mighty little ways to the raft now. One says:

"Boy, that's a lie. What IS the matter with your pap? Answer up square now, and it'll be the better for you."

"I will, sir, I will, honest—but don't leave us, please. It's the—the —Gentlemen, if you'll only pull ahead, and let me heave you the headline, you won't have to come a-near the raft—please do."

"Set her back, John, set her back!" says one. They backed water. "Keep away, boy—keep to looard. Confound it, I just expect the wind has blowed it to us. Your pap's got the small-pox, and you know it precious well. Why didn't you come out and say so? Do you want to spread it all over?"

"Well," says I, a-blubbering, "I've told everybody before, and they just went away and left us."

"Poor devil, there's something in that. We are right down sorry for you, but we—well, hang it, we don't want the small-pox, you see. Look here, I'll tell you what to do. Don't you try to land by yourself, or you'll smash everything to pieces. You float along down about twenty miles, and you'll come to a town on the left-hand side of the river. It will be long after sun-up then, and when you ask for help you tell them your folks are all down with chills and fever. Don't be a fool again, and let people guess what is the matter. Now we're trying to do you a kindness; so you just put twenty miles between us, that's a good boy. It wouldn't do any good to land yonder where the light is—it's only a wood-yard. Say, I reckon your father's poor, and I'm bound to say he's in pretty hard luck. Here, I'll put a twenty-dollar gold piece on this board, and you get it when it floats by. I feel mighty mean to leave you; but my kingdom! it won't do to fool with small-pox, don't you see?"

"Hold on, Parker," says the other man, "here's a twenty to put on the board for me. Good-bye, boy; you do as Mr. Parker told you, and you'll be all right."

"That's so, my boy—good-bye, good-bye. If you see any runaway niggers you get help and nab them, and you can make some money by it."

"Good-bye, sir," says I; "I won't let no runaway niggers get by me if I can help it."

They went off and I got aboard the raft, feeling bad and low, because I knowed very well I had done wrong, and I see it warn't no use for me to try to learn to do right; a body that don't get STARTED right when he's little ain't got no show—when the pinch comes there ain't nothing to back him up and keep him to his work, and so he gets beat. Then I thought a minute, and says to myself, hold on; s'pose you'd a done right and give Jim up, would you felt better than what you do now? No, says I, I'd feel bad—I'd feel just the same way I do now. Well, then, says I, what's the use you learning to do right when it's troublesome to do right and ain't no trouble to do wrong, and the wages is just the same? I was stuck. I couldn't answer that. So I reckoned I wouldn't bother no more about it, but after this always do whichever come handiest at the time.

I went into the wigwam; Jim warn't there. I looked all around; he warn't anywhere. I says:

"Jim!"

"Here I is, Huck. Is dey out o' sight yit? Don't talk loud."

He was in the river under the stern oar, with just his nose out. I told him they were out of sight, so he come aboard. He says:

"I was a-listenin' to all de talk, en I slips into de river en was gwyne to shove for sho' if dey come aboard. Den I was gwyne to swim to de raf' agin when dey was gone. But lawsy, how you did fool 'em, Huck! Dat WUZ de smartes' dodge! I tell you, chile, I'spec it save' ole Jim—ole Jim ain't going to forgit you for dat, honey."

Then we talked about the money. It was a pretty good raise—twenty dollars apiece. Jim said we could take deck passage on a steamboat now, and the money would last us as far as we wanted to go in the free States. He said twenty mile more warn't far for the raft to go, but he wished we was already there.

Towards daybreak we tied up, and Jim was mighty particular about hiding the raft good. Then he worked all day fixing things in bundles, and getting all ready to quit rafting.

That night about ten we hove in sight of the lights of a town away down in a left-hand bend.

I went off in the canoe to ask about it. Pretty soon I found a man out in the river with a skiff, setting a trot-line. I ranged up and says:

"Mister, is that town Cairo?"

"Cairo? no. You must be a blame' fool."

"What town is it, mister?"

"If you want to know, go and find out. If you stay here botherin' around me for about a half a minute longer you'll get something you won't want."

I paddled to the raft. Jim was awful disappointed, but I said never mind, Cairo would be the next place, I reckoned.

We passed another town before daylight, and I was going out again; but it was high ground, so I didn't go. No high ground about Cairo, Jim said. I had forgot it. We laid up for the day on a towhead tolerable close to the left-hand bank. I begun to suspicion something. So did Jim. I says:

"Maybe we went by Cairo in the fog that night."

He says:

"Doan' le's talk about it, Huck. Po' niggers can't have no luck. I awluz 'spected dat rattlesnake-skin warn't done wid its work."

"I wish I'd never seen that snake-skin, Jim—I do wish I'd never laid eyes on it."

"It ain't yo' fault, Huck; you didn' know. Don't you blame yo'self 'bout it."

When it was daylight, here was the clear Ohio water inshore, sure enough, and outside was the old regular Muddy! So it was all up with Cairo.

We talked it all over. It wouldn't do to take to the shore; we couldn't take the raft up the stream, of course. There warn't no way but to wait for dark, and start back in the canoe and take the chances. So we slept all day amongst the cottonwood thicket, so as to be fresh for the work, and when we went back to the raft about dark the canoe was gone!

We didn't say a word for a good while. There warn't anything to say. We both knowed well enough it was some more work of the rattlesnake-skin; so what was the use to talk about it? It would only look like we was finding fault, and that would be bound to fetch more bad luck—and keep on fetching it, too, till we knowed enough to keep still.

By and by we talked about what we better do, and found there warn't no way but just to go along down with the raft till we got a chance to buy a canoe to go back in. We warn't going to borrow it when there warn't anybody around, the way pap would do, for that might set people after us.

So we shoved out after dark on the raft.

Anybody that don't believe yet that it's foolishness to handle a snake-skin, after all that that snake-skin done for us, will believe it now if they read on and see what more it done for us.

The place to buy canoes is off of rafts laying up at shore. But we didn't see no rafts laying up; so we went along during three hours and more. Well, the night got gray and ruther thick, which is the next meanest thing to fog. You can't tell the shape of the river, and you can't see no distance. It got to be very late and still, and then along comes a steamboat up the river. We lit the lantern, and judged she would see it. Up-stream boats didn't generly come close to us; they go out and follow the bars and hunt for easy water under the reefs; but nights like this they bull right up the channel against the whole river.

We could hear her pounding along, but we didn't see her good till she was close. She aimed right for us. Often they do that and try to see how close they can come without touching; sometimes the wheel bites off a sweep, and then the pilot sticks his head out and laughs, and thinks he's mighty smart. Well, here she comes, and we said she was going to try and shave us; but she didn't seem to be sheering off a bit. She was a big one, and she was coming in a hurry, too, looking like a black cloud with rows of glow-worms around it; but all of a sudden she bulged out, big and scary, with a long row of wide-open furnace doors shining like red-hot teeth, and her monstrous bows and guards hanging right over us. There was a yell at us, and a jingling of bells to stop the engines, a powwow of cussing, and whistling of steam—and as Jim went overboard on one side and I on the other, she come smashing straight through the raft.

I dived—and I aimed to find the bottom, too, for a thirty-foot wheel had got to go over me, and I wanted it to have plenty of room. I could always stay under water a minute; this time I reckon I stayed under a minute and a half. Then I bounced for the top in a hurry, for I was nearly busting. I popped out to my armpits and blowed the water out of my nose, and puffed a bit. Of course there was a booming current; and of course that boat started her engines again ten seconds after she stopped them, for they never cared much for raftsmen; so now she was churning along up the river, out of sight in the thick weather, though I could hear her.

I sung out for Jim about a dozen times, but I didn't get any answer; so I grabbed a plank that touched me while I was "treading water," and struck out for shore, shoving it ahead of me. But I made out to see that the drift of the current was towards the left-hand shore, which meant that I was in a crossing; so I changed off and went that way.

It was one of these long, slanting, two-mile crossings; so I was a good long time in getting over. I made a safe landing, and clumb up the bank. I couldn't see but a little ways, but I went poking along over rough ground for a quarter of a mile or more, and then I run across a big old-fashioned double log-house before I noticed it. I was going to rush by and get away, but a lot of dogs jumped out and went to howling and barking at me, and I knowed better than to move another peg.

Chapter XVII

In about a minute somebody spoke out of a window without putting his head out, and says:

"Be done, boys! Who's there?"

I says:

"It's me."

"Who's me?"

"George Jackson, sir."

"What do you want?"

"I don't want nothing, sir. I only want to go along by, but the dogs won't let me."

"What are you prowling around here this time of night for—hey?"

"I warn't prowling around, sir, I fell overboard off of the steamboat."

"Oh, you did, did you? Strike a light there, somebody. What did you say your name was?"

"George Jackson, sir. I'm only a boy."

"Look here, if you're telling the truth you needn't be afraid—nobody'll hurt you. But don't try to budge; stand right where you are. Rouse out Bob and Tom, some of you, and fetch the guns. George Jackson, is there anybody with you?"

"No, sir, nobody."

I heard the people stirring around in the house now, and see a light. The man sung out:

"Snatch that light away, Betsy, you old fool—ain't you got any sense? Put it on the floor behind the front door. Bob, if you and Tom are ready, take your places."

"All ready."

"Now, George Jackson, do you know the Shepherdsons?"

"No, sir; I never heard of them."

"Well, that may be so, and it mayn't. Now, all ready. Step forward, George Jackson. And mind, don't you hurry—come mighty slow. If there's anybody with you, let him keep back—if he shows himself he'll be shot. Come along now. Come slow; push the door open yourself—just enough to squeeze in, d' you hear?"

I didn't hurry; I couldn't if I'd a wanted to. I took one slow step at a time and there warn't a sound, only I thought I could hear my heart. The dogs were as still as the humans, but they followed a little behind me. When I got to the three log doorsteps I heard them unlocking and unbarring and unbolting. I put my hand on the door and pushed it a little and a little more till somebody said, "There, that's enough—put your head in." I done it, but I judged they would take it off.

The candle was on the floor, and there they all was, looking at me, and me at them, for about a quarter of a minute: Three big men with guns pointed at me, which made me wince, I tell you; the oldest, gray and about sixty, the other two thirty or more—all of them fine and handsome —and the sweetest old gray-headed lady, and back of her two young women which I couldn't see right well. The old gentleman says:

"There; I reckon it's all right. Come in."

As soon as I was in the old gentleman he locked the door and barred it and bolted it, and told the young men to come in with their guns, and they all went in a big parlor that had a new rag carpet on the floor, and got together in a corner that was out of the range of the front windows —there warn't none on the side. They held the candle, and took a good look at me, and all said, "Why, HE ain't a Shepherdson—no, there ain't any Shepherdson about him." Then the old man said he hoped I wouldn't mind being searched for arms, because he didn't mean no harm by it—it was only to make sure. So he didn't pry into my pockets, but only felt outside with his hands, and said it was all right. He told me to make myself easy and at home, and tell all about myself; but the old lady says:

"Why, bless you, Saul, the poor thing's as wet as he can be; and don't you reckon it may be he's hungry?"

"True for you, Rachel—I forgot."

So the old lady says:

"Betsy" (this was a nigger woman), "you fly around and get him something to eat as quick as you can, poor thing; and one of you girls go and wake up Buck and tell him—oh, here he is himself. Buck, take this little stranger and get the wet clothes off from him and dress him up in some of yours that's dry."

Buck looked about as old as me—thirteen or fourteen or along there, though he was a little bigger than me. He hadn't on anything but a shirt, and he was very frowzy-headed. He came in gaping and digging one fist into his eyes, and he was dragging a gun along with the other one. He says:

"Ain't they no Shepherdsons around?"

They said, no, 'twas a false alarm.

"Well," he says, "if they'd a ben some, I reckon I'd a got one."

They all laughed, and Bob says:

"Why, Buck, they might have scalped us all, you've been so slow in coming."

"Well, nobody come after me, and it ain't right I'm always kept down; I don't get no show."

"Never mind, Buck, my boy," says the old man, "you'll have show enough, all in good time, don't you fret about that. Go 'long with you now, and do as your mother told you."

When we got up-stairs to his room he got me a coarse shirt and a roundabout and pants of his, and I put them on. While I was at it he asked me what my name was, but before I could tell him he started to tell me about a bluejay and a young rabbit he had catched in the woods day before yesterday, and he asked me where Moses was when the candle went out. I said I didn't know; I hadn't heard about it before, no way.

"Well, guess," he says.

"How'm I going to guess," says I, "when I never heard tell of it before?"

"But you can guess, can't you? It's just as easy."

"WHICH candle?" I says.

"Why, any candle," he says.

"I don't know where he was," says I; "where was he?"

"Why, he was in the DARK! That's where he was!"

"Well, if you knowed where he was, what did you ask me for?"

"Why, blame it, it's a riddle, don't you see? Say, how long are you going to stay here? You got to stay always. We can just have booming times—they don't have no school now. Do you own a dog? I've got a dog—and he'll go in the river and bring out chips that you throw in. Do you like to comb up Sundays, and all that kind of foolishness? You bet I don't, but ma she makes me. Confound these ole britches! I reckon I'd better put 'em on, but I'd ruther not, it's so warm. Are you all ready? All right. Come along, old hoss."

Cold corn-pone, cold corn-beef, butter and buttermilk—that is what they had for me down there, and there ain't nothing better that ever I've come across yet. Buck and his ma and all of them smoked cob pipes, except the nigger woman, which was gone, and the two young women. They all smoked and talked, and I eat and talked. The young women had quilts around them, and their hair down their backs. They all asked me questions, and I told them how pap and me and all the family was living on a little farm down at the bottom of Arkansaw, and my sister Mary Ann run off and got married and never was heard of no more, and Bill went to hunt them and he warn't heard of no more, and Tom and Mort died, and then there warn't nobody but just me and pap left, and he was just trimmed down to nothing, on account of his troubles; so when he died I took what there was left, because the farm didn't belong to us, and started up the river, deck passage, and fell overboard; and that was how I come to be here. So they said I could have a home there as long as I wanted it. Then it was most daylight and everybody went to bed, and I went to bed with Buck, and when I waked up in the morning, drat it all, I had forgot what my name was. So I laid there about an hour trying to think, and when Buck waked up I says:

"Can you spell, Buck?"

"Yes," he says.

"I bet you can't spell my name," says I.

"I bet you what you dare I can," says he.

"All right," says I, "go ahead."

"G-e-o-r-g-e J-a-x-o-n—there now," he says.

"Well," says I, "you done it, but I didn't think you could. It ain't no slouch of a name to spell—right off without studying."

I set it down, private, because somebody might want ME to spell it next, and so I wanted to be handy with it and rattle it off like I was used to it.

It was a mighty nice family, and a mighty nice house, too. I hadn't seen no house out in the country before that was so nice and had so much style. It didn't have an iron latch on the front door, nor a wooden one with a buckskin string, but a brass knob to turn, the same as houses in town. There warn't no bed in the parlor, nor a sign of a bed; but heaps of parlors in towns has beds in them. There was a big fireplace that was bricked on the bottom, and the bricks was kept clean and red by pouring water on them and scrubbing them with another brick; sometimes they wash them over with red water-paint that they call Spanish-brown, same as they do in town. They had big brass dog-irons that could hold up a saw-log. There was a clock on the middle of the mantelpiece, with a picture of a town painted on the bottom half of the glass front, and a round place in the middle of it for the sun, and you could see the pendulum swinging behind it. It was beautiful to hear that clock tick; and sometimes when one of these peddlers had been along and scoured her up and got her in good shape, she would start in and strike a hundred and fifty before she got tuckered out. They wouldn't took any money for her.

Well, there was a big outlandish parrot on each side of the clock, made out of something like chalk, and painted up gaudy. By one of the parrots was a cat made of crockery, and a crockery dog by the other; and when you pressed down on them they squeaked, but didn't open their mouths nor look different nor interested. They squeaked through underneath. There was a couple of big wild-turkey-wing fans spread out behind those things. On the table in the middle of the room was a kind of a lovely crockery basket that had apples and oranges and peaches and grapes piled up in it, which was much redder and yellower and prettier than real ones is, but they warn't real because you could see where pieces had got chipped off and showed the white chalk, or whatever it was, underneath.

This table had a cover made out of beautiful oilcloth, with a red and blue spread-eagle painted on it, and a painted border all around. It come all the way from Philadelphia, they said. There was some books, too, piled up perfectly exact, on each corner of the table. One was a big family Bible full of pictures. One was Pilgrim's Progress, about a man that left his family, it didn't say why. I read considerable in it now and then. The statements was interesting, but tough. Another was Friendship's Offering, full of beautiful stuff and poetry; but I didn't read the poetry. Another was Henry Clay's Speeches, and another was Dr. Gunn's Family Medicine, which told you all about what to do if a body was sick or dead. There was a hymn book, and a lot of other books. And there was nice split-bottom chairs, and perfectly sound, too—not bagged down in the middle and busted, like an old basket.

They had pictures hung on the walls—mainly Washingtons and Lafayettes, and battles, and Highland Marys, and one called "Signing the Declaration." There was some that they called crayons, which one of the daughters which was dead made her own self when she was only fifteen years old. They was different from any pictures I ever see before —blacker, mostly, than is common. One was a woman in a slim black dress, belted small under the armpits, with bulges like a cabbage in the middle of the sleeves, and a large black scoop-shovel bonnet with a black veil, and white slim ankles crossed about with black tape, and very wee black slippers, like a chisel, and she was leaning pensive on a tombstone on her right elbow, under a weeping willow, and her other hand hanging down her side holding a white handkerchief and a reticule, and underneath the picture it said "Shall I Never See Thee More Alas." Another one was a young lady with her hair all combed up straight to the top of her head, and knotted there in front of a comb like a chair-back, and she was crying into a handkerchief and had a dead bird laying on its back in her other hand with its heels up, and underneath the picture it said "I Shall Never Hear Thy Sweet Chirrup More Alas." There was one where a young lady was at a window looking up at the moon, and tears running down her cheeks; and she had an open letter in one hand with black sealing wax showing on one edge of it, and she was mashing a locket with a chain to it against her mouth, and underneath the picture it said "And Art Thou Gone Yes Thou Art Gone Alas." These was all nice pictures, I reckon, but I didn't somehow seem to take to them, because if ever I was down a little they always give me the fan-tods. Everybody was sorry she died, because she had laid out a lot more of these pictures to do, and a body could see by what she had done what they had lost. But I reckoned that with her disposition she was having a better time in the graveyard. She was at work on what they said was her greatest picture when she took sick, and every day and every night it was her prayer to be allowed to live till she got it done, but she never got the chance. It was a picture of a young woman in a long white gown, standing on the rail of a bridge all ready to jump off, with her hair all down her back, and looking up to the moon, with the tears running down her face, and she had two arms folded across her breast, and two arms stretched out in front, and two more reaching up towards the moon—and the idea was to see which pair would look best, and then scratch out all the other arms; but, as I was saying, she died before she got her mind made up, and now they kept this picture over the head of the bed in her room, and every time her birthday come they hung flowers on it. Other times it was hid with a little curtain. The young woman in the picture had a kind of a nice sweet face, but there was so many arms it made her look too spidery, seemed to me.

This young girl kept a scrap-book when she was alive, and used to paste obituaries and accidents and cases of patient suffering in it out of the Presbyterian Observer, and write poetry after them out of her own head. It was very good poetry. This is what she wrote about a boy by the name of Stephen Dowling Bots that fell down a well and was drownded:

ODE TO STEPHEN DOWLING BOTS, DEC'D

And did young Stephen sicken,
And did young Stephen die?
And did the sad hearts thicken,
And did the mourners cry?

No; such was not the fate of
Young Stephen Dowling Bots;
Though sad hearts round him thickened,
'Twas not from sickness' shots.

No whooping-cough did rack his frame,
Nor measles drear with spots;
Not these impaired the sacred name
Of Stephen Dowling Bots.

Despised love struck not with woe
That head of curly knots,
Nor stomach troubles laid him low,
Young Stephen Dowling Bots.

O no. Then list with tearful eye,
Whilst I his fate do tell.
His soul did from this cold world fly
By falling down a well.

They got him out and emptied him;
Alas it was too late;
His spirit was gone for to sport aloft
In the realms of the good and great.

If Emmeline Grangerford could make poetry like that before she was fourteen, there ain't no telling what she could a done by and by. Buck said she could rattle off poetry like nothing. She didn't ever have to stop to think. He said she would slap down a line, and if she couldn't find anything to rhyme with it would just scratch it out and slap down another one, and go ahead. She warn't particular; she could write about anything you choose to give her to write about just so it was sadful.

Every time a man died, or a woman died, or a child died, she would be on hand with her "tribute" before he was cold. She called them tributes. The neighbors said it was the doctor first, then Emmeline, then the undertaker—the undertaker never got in ahead of Emmeline but once, and then she hung fire on a rhyme for the dead person's name, which was Whistler. She warn't ever the same after that; she never complained, but she kinder pined away and did not live long. Poor thing, many's the time I made myself go up to the little room that used to be hers and get out her poor old scrap-book and read in it when her pictures had been aggravating me and I had soured on her a little. I liked all that family, dead ones and all, and warn't going to let anything come between us. Poor Emmeline made poetry about all the dead people when she was alive, and it didn't seem right that there warn't nobody to make some about her now she was gone; so I tried to sweat out a verse or two myself, but I couldn't seem to make it go somehow. They kept Emmeline's room trim and nice, and all the things fixed in it just the way she liked to have them when she was alive, and nobody ever slept there. The old lady took care of the room herself, though there was plenty of niggers, and she sewed there a good deal and read her Bible there mostly.

Well, as I was saying about the parlor, there was beautiful curtains on the windows: white, with pictures painted on them of castles with vines all down the walls, and cattle coming down to drink. There was a little old piano, too, that had tin pans in it, I reckon, and nothing was ever so lovely as to hear the young ladies sing "The Last Link is Broken" and play "The Battle of Prague" on it. The walls of all the rooms was plastered, and most had carpets on the floors, and the whole house was whitewashed on the outside.

It was a double house, and the big open place betwixt them was roofed and floored, and sometimes the table was set there in the middle of the day, and it was a cool, comfortable place. Nothing couldn't be better. And warn't the cooking good, and just bushels of it too!

Chapter XVIII

Col. Grangerford was a gentleman, you see. He was a gentleman all over; and so was his family. He was well born, as the saying is, and that's worth as much in a man as it is in a horse, so the Widow Douglas said, and nobody ever denied that she was of the first aristocracy in our town; and pap he always said it, too, though he warn't no more quality than a mudcat himself. Col. Grangerford was very tall and very slim, and had a darkish-paly complexion, not a sign of red in it anywheres; he was clean shaved every morning all over his thin face, and he had the thinnest kind of lips, and the thinnest kind of nostrils, and a high nose, and heavy eyebrows, and the blackest kind of eyes, sunk so deep back that they seemed like they was looking out of caverns at you, as you may say. His forehead was high, and his hair was black and straight and hung to his shoulders. His hands was long and thin, and every day of his life he put on a clean shirt and a full suit from head to foot made out of linen so white it hurt your eyes to look at it; and on Sundays he wore a blue tail-coat with brass buttons on it. He carried a mahogany cane with a silver head to it. There warn't no frivolishness about him, not a bit, and he warn't ever loud. He was as kind as he could be—you could feel that, you know, and so you had confidence. Sometimes he smiled, and it was good to see; but when he straightened himself up like a liberty-pole, and the lightning begun to flicker out from under his eyebrows, you wanted to climb a tree first, and find out what the matter was afterwards. He didn't ever have to tell anybody to mind their manners — everybody was always good-mannered where he was. Everybody loved to have him around, too; he was sunshine most always—I mean he made it seem like good weather. When he turned into a cloudbank it was awful dark for half a minute, and that was enough; there wouldn't nothing go wrong again for a week.

When him and the old lady come down in the morning all the family got up out of their chairs and give them good-day, and didn't set down again till they had set down. Then Tom and Bob went to the sideboard where the decanter was, and mixed a glass of bitters and handed it to him, and he held it in his hand and waited till Tom's and Bob's was mixed, and then they bowed and said, "Our duty to you, sir, and madam;" and THEY bowed the least bit in the world and said thank you, and so they drank, all three, and Bob and Tom poured a spoonful of water on the sugar and the mite of whisky or apple brandy in the bottom of their tumblers, and give it to me and Buck, and we drank to the old people too.

Bob was the oldest and Tom next—tall, beautiful men with very broad shoulders and brown faces, and long black hair and black eyes. They dressed in white linen from head to foot, like the old gentleman, and wore broad Panama hats.

Then there was Miss Charlotte; she was twenty-five, and tall and proud and grand, but as good as she could be when she warn't stirred up; but when she was she had a look that would make you wilt in your tracks, like her father. She was beautiful.

So was her sister, Miss Sophia, but it was a different kind. She was gentle and sweet like a dove, and she was only twenty.

Each person had their own nigger to wait on them—Buck too. My nigger had a monstrous easy time, because I warn't used to having anybody do anything for me, but Buck's was on the jump most of the time.

This was all there was of the family now, but there used to be more —three sons; they got killed; and Emmeline that died.

The old gentleman owned a lot of farms and over a hundred niggers. Sometimes a stack of people would come there, horseback, from ten or fifteen mile around, and stay five or six days, and have such junketings round about and on the river, and dances and picnics in the woods daytimes, and balls at the house nights. These people was mostly kinfolks of the family. The men brought their guns with them. It was a handsome lot of quality, I tell you.

There was another clan of aristocracy around there—five or six families—mostly of the name of Shepherdson. They was as high-toned and well born and rich and grand as the tribe of Grangerfords. The Shepherdsons and Grangerfords used the same steamboat landing, which was about two mile above our house; so sometimes when I went up there with a lot of our folks I used to see a lot of the Shepherdsons there on their fine horses.

One day Buck and me was away out in the woods hunting, and heard a horse coming. We was crossing the road. Buck says:

"Quick! Jump for the woods!"

We done it, and then peeped down the woods through the leaves. Pretty soon a splendid young man come galloping down the road, setting his horse easy and looking like a soldier. He had his gun across his pommel. I had seen him before. It was young Harney Shepherdson. I heard Buck's gun go off at my ear, and Harney's hat tumbled off from his head. He grabbed his gun and rode straight to the place where we was hid. But we didn't wait. We started through the woods on a run. The woods warn't thick, so I looked over my shoulder to dodge the bullet, and twice I seen Harney cover Buck with his gun; and then he rode away the way he come—to get his hat, I reckon, but I couldn't see. We never stopped running till we got home. The old gentleman's eyes blazed a minute—'twas pleasure, mainly, I judged—then his face sort of smoothed down, and he says, kind of gentle:

"I don't like that shooting from behind a bush. Why didn't you step into the road, my boy?"

"The Shepherdsons don't, father. They always take advantage."

Miss Charlotte she held her head up like a queen while Buck was telling his tale, and her nostrils spread and her eyes snapped. The two young men looked dark, but never said nothing. Miss Sophia she turned pale, but the color come back when she found the man warn't hurt.

Soon as I could get Buck down by the corn-cribs under the trees by ourselves, I says:

"Did you want to kill him, Buck?"

"Well, I bet I did."

"What did he do to you?"

"Him? He never done nothing to me."

"Well, then, what did you want to kill him for?"

"Why, nothing—only it's on account of the feud."

"What's a feud?"

"Why, where was you raised? Don't you know what a feud is?"

"Never heard of it before—tell me about it."

"Well," says Buck, "a feud is this way: A man has a quarrel with another man, and kills him; then that other man's brother kills HIM; then the other brothers, on both sides, goes for one another; then the COUSINS chip in—and by and by everybody's killed off, and there ain't no more feud. But it's kind of slow, and takes a long time."

"Has this one been going on long, Buck?"

"Well, I should RECKON! It started thirty year ago, or som'ers along there. There was trouble 'bout something, and then a lawsuit to settle it; and the suit went agin one of the men, and so he up and shot the man that won the suit—which he would naturally do, of course. Anybody would."

"What was the trouble about, Buck?—land?"

"I reckon maybe—I don't know."

"Well, who done the shooting? Was it a Grangerford or a Shepherdson?"

"Laws, how do I know? It was so long ago."

"Don't anybody know?"

"Oh, yes, pa knows, I reckon, and some of the other old people; but they don't know now what the row was about in the first place."

"Has there been many killed, Buck?"

"Yes; right smart chance of funerals. But they don't always kill. Pa's got a few buckshot in him; but he don't mind it 'cuz he don't weigh much, anyway. Bob's been carved up some with a bowie, and Tom's been hurt once or twice."

"Has anybody been killed this year, Buck?"

"Yes; we got one and they got one. 'Bout three months ago my cousin Bud, four-teen year old, was riding through the woods on t'other side of the river, and didn't have no weapon with him, which was blame' foolishness, and in a lonesome place he hears a horse a-coming behind him, and sees old Baldy Shepherdson a-linkin' after him with his gun in his hand and his white hair a-flying in the wind; and 'stead of jumping off and taking to the brush, Bud 'lowed he could out-run him; so they had it, nip and tuck, for five mile or more, the old man a-gaining all the time; so at last Bud seen it warn't any use, so he stopped and faced around so as to have the bullet holes in front, you know, and the old man he rode up and shot him down. But he didn't git much chance to enjoy his luck, for inside of a week our folks laid HIM out."

"I reckon that old man was a coward, Buck."

"I reckon he WARN'T a coward. Not by a blame' sight. There ain't a coward amongst them Shepherdsons—not a one. And there ain't no cowards amongst the Grangerfords either. Why, that old man kep' up his end in a fight one day for half an hour against three Grangerfords, and come out winner. They was all a-horseback; he lit off of his horse and got behind a little woodpile, and kep' his horse before him to stop the bullets; but the Grangerfords stayed on their horses and capered around the old man, and peppered away at him, and he peppered away at them. Him and his horse both went home pretty leaky and crippled, but the Grangerfords had to be FETCHED home—and one of 'em was dead, and another died the next day. No, sir; if a body's out hunting for cowards he don't want to fool away any time amongst them Shepherdsons, becuz they don't breed any of that KIND."

Next Sunday we all went to church, about three mile, everybody a-horseback. The men took their guns along, so did Buck, and kept them between their knees or stood them handy against the wall. The Shepherdsons done the same. It was pretty ornery preaching—all about brotherly love, and such-like tiresomeness; but everybody said it was a good sermon, and they all talked it over going home, and had such a powerful lot to say about faith and good works and free grace and preforeordestination, and I don't know what all, that it did seem to me to be one of the roughest Sundays I had run across yet.

About an hour after dinner everybody was dozing around, some in their chairs and some in their rooms, and it got to be pretty dull. Buck and a dog was stretched out on the grass in the sun sound asleep. I went up to our room, and judged I would take a nap myself. I found that sweet Miss Sophia standing in her door, which was next to ours, and she took me in her room and shut the door very soft, and asked me if I liked her, and I said I did; and she asked me if I would do something for her and not tell anybody, and I said I would. Then she said she'd forgot her Testament, and left it in the seat at church between two other books, and would I slip out quiet and go there and fetch it to her, and not say nothing to nobody. I said I would. So I slid out and slipped off up the road, and there warn't anybody at the church, except maybe a hog or two, for there warn't any lock on the door, and hogs likes a puncheon floor in summer-time because it's cool. If you notice, most folks don't go to church only when they've got to; but a hog is different.

Says I to myself, something's up; it ain't natural for a girl to be in such a sweat about a Testament. So I give it a shake, and out drops a little piece of paper with "half-part-two" wrote on it with a pencil. I ransacked it, but couldn't find anything else. I couldn't make anything out of that, so I put the paper in the book again, and when I got home and upstairs there was Miss Sophia in her door waiting for me. She pulled me in and shut the door; then she looked in the Testament till she found the paper, and as soon as she read it she looked glad; and before a body could think she grabbed me and give me a squeeze, and said I was the best boy in the world, and not to tell anybody. She was mighty red in the face for a minute, and her eyes lighted up, and it made her powerful pretty. I was a good deal astonished, but when I got my breath I asked her what the paper was about, and she asked me if I had read it, and I said no, and she asked me if I could read writing, and I told her "no, only coarse-hand," and then she said the paper warn't anything but a book-mark to keep her place, and I might go and play now.

I went off down to the river, studying over this thing, and pretty soon I noticed that my nigger was following along behind. When we was out of sight of the house he looked back and around a second, and then comes a-running, and says:

"Mars Jawge, if you'll come down into de swamp I'll show you a whole stack o' water-moccasins."

Thinks I, that's mighty curious; he said that yesterday. He oughter know a body don't love water-moccasins enough to go around hunting for them. What is he up to, anyway? So I says:

"All right; trot ahead."

I followed a half a mile; then he struck out over the swamp, and waded ankle deep as much as another half-mile. We come to a little flat piece of land which was dry and very thick with trees and bushes and vines, and he says:

"You shove right in dah jist a few steps, Mars Jawge; dah's whah dey is. I's seed 'm befo'; I don't k'yer to see 'em no mo'."

Then he slopped right along and went away, and pretty soon the trees hid him. I poked into the place a-ways and come to a little open patch as big as a bedroom all hung around with vines, and found a man laying there asleep—and, by jings, it was my old Jim!

I waked him up, and I reckoned it was going to be a grand surprise to him to see me again, but it warn't. He nearly cried he was so glad, but he warn't surprised. Said he swum along behind me that night, and heard me yell every time, but dasn't answer, because he didn't want nobody to pick HIM up and take him into slavery again. Says he:

"I got hurt a little, en couldn't swim fas', so I wuz a considable ways behine you towards de las'; when you landed I reck'ned I could ketch up wid you on de lan' 'dout havin' to shout at you, but when I see dat house I begin to go slow. I 'uz off too fur to hear what dey say to you—I wuz 'fraid o' de dogs; but when it 'uz all quiet agin I knowed you's in de house, so I struck out for de woods to wait for day. Early in de mawnin' some er de niggers come along, gwyne to de fields, en dey tuk me en showed me dis place, whah de dogs can't track me on accounts o' de water, en dey brings me truck to eat every night, en tells me how you's a-gitt'n along."

"Why didn't you tell my Jack to fetch me here sooner, Jim?"

"Well, 'twarn't no use to 'sturb you, Huck, tell we could do sumfn—but we's all right now. I ben a-buyin' pots en pans en vittles, as I got a chanst, en a-patchin' up de raf' nights when—"

"WHAT raft, Jim?"

"Our ole raf'."

"You mean to say our old raft warn't smashed all to flinders?"

"No, she warn't. She was tore up a good deal—one en' of her was; but dey warn't no great harm done, on'y our traps was mos' all los'. Ef we hadn' dive' so deep en swum so fur under water, en de night hadn' ben so dark, en we warn't so sk'yerd, en ben sich punkin-heads, as de sayin' is, we'd a seed de raf'. But it's jis' as well we didn't, 'kase now she's all fixed up agin mos' as good as new, en we's got a new lot o' stuff, in de place o' what 'uz los'."

"Why, how did you get hold of the raft again, Jim—did you catch her?"

"How I gwyne to ketch her en I out in de woods? No; some er de niggers foun' her ketched on a snag along heah in de ben', en dey hid her in a crick 'mongst de willows, en dey wuz so much jawin' 'bout which un 'um she b'long to de mos' dat I come to heah 'bout it pooty soon, so I ups en settles de trouble by tellin' 'um she don't b'long to none uv um, but to you en me; en I ast 'm if dey gwyne to grab a young white genlman's propaty, en git a hid'n for it? Den I gin 'm ten cents apiece, en dey 'uz mighty well satisfied, en wisht some mo' raf's 'ud come along en make 'm rich agin. Dey's mighty good to me, dese niggers is, en whatever I wants 'm to do fur me I doan' have to ast 'm twice, honey. Dat Jack's a good nigger, en pooty smart."

"Yes, he is. He ain't ever told me you was here; told me to come, and he'd show me a lot of water-moccasins. If anything happens HE ain't mixed up in it. He can say he never seen us together, and it 'll be the truth."

I don't want to talk much about the next day. I reckon I'll cut it pretty short. I waked up about dawn, and was a-going to turn over and go to sleep again when I noticed how still it was—didn't seem to be anybody stirring. That warn't usual. Next I noticed that Buck was up and gone. Well, I gets up, a-wondering, and goes down stairs—nobody around; everything as still as a mouse. Just the same outside. Thinks I, what does it mean? Down by the wood-pile I comes across my Jack, and says:

"What's it all about?"

Says he:

"Don't you know, Mars Jawge?"

"No," says I, "I don't."

"Well, den, Miss Sophia's run off! 'deed she has. She run off in de night some time—nobody don't know jis' when; run off to get married to dat young Harney Shepherdson, you know—leastways, so dey 'spec. De fambly foun' it out 'bout half an hour ago—maybe a little mo'—en' I TELL you dey warn't no time los'. Sich another hurryin' up guns en hosses YOU never see! De women folks has gone for to stir up de relations, en ole Mars Saul en de boys tuck dey guns en rode up de river road for to try to ketch dat young man en kill him 'fo' he kin git acrost de river wid Miss Sophia. I reck'n dey's gwyne to be mighty rough times."

"Buck went off 'thout waking me up."

"Well, I reck'n he DID! Dey warn't gwyne to mix you up in it. Mars Buck he loaded up his gun en 'lowed he's gwyne to fetch home a Shepherdson or bust. Well, dey'll be plenty un 'm dah, I reck'n, en you bet you he'll fetch one ef he gits a chanst."

I took up the river road as hard as I could put. By and by I begin to hear guns a good ways off. When I came in sight of the log store and the woodpile where the steamboats lands I worked along under the trees and brush till I got to a good place, and then I clumb up into the forks of a cottonwood that was out of reach, and watched. There was a wood-rank four foot high a little ways in front of the tree, and first I was going to hide behind that; but maybe it was luckier I didn't.

There was four or five men cavorting around on their horses in the open place before the log store, cussing and yelling, and trying to get at a couple of young chaps that was behind the wood-rank alongside of the steamboat landing; but they couldn't come it. Every time one of them showed himself on the river side of the woodpile he got shot at. The two boys was squatting back to back behind the pile, so they could watch both ways.

By and by the men stopped cavorting around and yelling. They started riding towards the store; then up gets one of the boys, draws a steady bead over the wood-rank, and drops one of them out of his saddle. All the men jumped off of their horses and grabbed the hurt one and started to carry him to the store; and that minute the two boys started on the run. They got half way to the tree I was in before the men noticed. Then the men see them, and jumped on their horses and took out after them. They gained on the boys, but it didn't do no good, the boys had too good a start; they got to the woodpile that was in front of my tree, and slipped in behind it, and so they had the bulge on the men again. One of the boys was Buck, and the other was a slim young chap about nineteen years old.

The men ripped around awhile, and then rode away. As soon as they was out of sight I sung out to Buck and told him. He didn't know what to make of my voice coming out of the tree at first. He was awful surprised. He told me to watch out sharp and let him know when the men come in sight again; said they was up to some devil-ment or other —wouldn't be gone long. I wished I was out of that tree, but I dasn't come down. Buck begun to cry and rip, and 'lowed that him and his cousin Joe (that was the other young chap) would make up for this day yet. He said his father and his two brothers was killed, and two or three of the enemy. Said the Shepherdsons laid for them in ambush. Buck said his father and brothers ought to waited for their relations— the Shepherdsons was too strong for them. I asked him what was become of young Harney and Miss Sophia. He said they'd got across the river and was safe. I was glad of that; but the way Buck did take on because he didn't manage to kill Harney that day he shot at him—I hain't ever heard anything like it.

All of a sudden, bang! bang! bang! goes three or four guns—the men had slipped around through the woods and come in from behind without their horses! The boys jumped for the river—both of them hurt—and as they swum down the current the men run along the bank shooting at them and singing out, "Kill them, kill them!" It made me so sick I most fell out of the tree. I ain't a-going to tell ALL that happened— it would make me sick again if I was to do that. I wished I hadn't ever come ashore that night to see such things. I ain't ever going to get shut of them—lots of times I dream about them.

I stayed in the tree till it begun to get dark, afraid to come down. Sometimes I heard guns away off in the woods; and twice I seen little gangs of men gallop past the log store with guns; so I reckoned the trouble was still a-going on. I was mighty down-hearted; so I made up my mind I wouldn't ever go anear that house again, because I reckoned I was to blame, somehow. I judged that that piece of paper meant that Miss

Sophia was to meet Harney somewheres at half-past two and run off; and I judged I ought to told her father about that paper and the curious way she acted, and then maybe he would a locked her up, and this awful mess wouldn't ever happened.

When I got down out of the tree I crept along down the river bank a piece, and found the two bodies laying in the edge of the water, and tugged at them till I got them ashore; then I covered up their faces, and got away as quick as I could. I cried a little when I was covering up Buck's face, for he was mighty good to me.

It was just dark now. I never went near the house, but struck through the woods and made for the swamp. Jim warn't on his island, so I tramped off in a hurry for the crick, and crowded through the willows, red-hot to jump aboard and get out of that awful country. The raft was gone! My souls, but I was scared! I couldn't get my breath for most a minute. Then I raised a yell. A voice not twenty-five foot from me says:

"Good lan'! is dat you, honey? Doan' make no noise."

It was Jim's voice—nothing ever sounded so good before. I run along the bank a piece and got aboard, and Jim he grabbed me and hugged me, he was so glad to see me. He says:

"Laws bless you, chile, I 'uz right down sho' you's dead agin. Jack's been heah; he say he reck'n you's ben shot, kase you didn' come home no mo'; so I's jes' dis minute a startin' de raf' down towards de mouf er de crick, so's to be all ready for to shove out en leave soon as Jack comes agin en tells me for certain you IS dead. Lawsy, I's mighty glad to git you back again, honey."

I says:

"All right—that's mighty good; they won't find me, and they'll think I've been killed, and floated down the river—there's something up there that 'll help them think so—so don't you lose no time, Jim, but just shove off for the big water as fast as ever you can."

I never felt easy till the raft was two mile below there and out in the middle of the Mississippi. Then we hung up our signal lantern, and judged that we was free and safe once more. I hadn't had a bite to eat since yesterday, so Jim he got out some corn-dodgers and buttermilk, and pork and cabbage and greens—there ain't nothing in the world so good when it's cooked right—and whilst I eat my supper we talked and had a good time. I was powerful glad to get away from the feuds, and so was Jim to get away from the swamp. We said there warn't no home like a raft, after all. Other places do seem so cramped up and smothery, but a raft don't. You feel mighty free and easy and comfortable on a raft.

Chapter XIX

Two or three days and nights went by; I reckon I might say they swum by, they slid along so quiet and smooth and lovely. Here is the way we put in the time. It was a monstrous big river down there—sometimes a mile and a half wide; we run nights, and laid up and hid daytimes; soon as night was most gone we stopped navigating and tied up—nearly always in the dead water under a towhead; and then cut young cotton-woods and willows, and hid the raft with them. Then we set out the lines. Next we slid into the river and had a swim, so as to freshen up and cool off; then we set down on the sandy bottom where the water was about knee deep, and watched the daylight come. Not a sound anywheres— perfectly still —just like the whole world was asleep, only sometimes the bullfrogs a-cluttering, maybe. The first thing to see, looking away over the water, was a kind of dull line—that was the woods on t'other side; you couldn't make nothing else out; then a pale place in the sky; then more paleness spreading around; then the river softened up away off, and warn't black any more, but gray; you could see little dark spots drifting along ever so far away—trading scows, and such things; and long black streaks —rafts; sometimes you could hear a sweep screaking; or jumbled up voices, it was so still, and sounds come so far; and by and by you could see a streak on the water which you know by the look of the streak that there's a snag there in a swift current which breaks on it and makes that streak look that way; and you see the mist curl up off of the water, and the east reddens up, and the river, and you make out a log-cabin in the edge of the woods, away on the bank on t'other side of the river, being a woodyard, likely, and piled by them cheats so you can throw a dog through it anywheres; then the nice breeze springs up, and comes fanning you from over there, so cool and fresh and sweet to smell on account of the woods and the flowers; but sometimes not that way, because they've left dead fish laying around, gars and such, and they do get pretty rank; and next you've got the full day, and everything smiling in the sun, and the song-birds just going it!

A little smoke couldn't be noticed now, so we would take some fish off of the lines and cook up a hot breakfast. And afterwards we would watch the lonesomeness of the river, and kind of lazy along, and by and by lazy off to sleep. Wake up by and by, and look to see what done it, and maybe see a steamboat coughing along up-stream, so far off towards the other side you couldn't tell nothing about her only whether she was a stern-wheel or side-wheel; then for about an hour there wouldn't be nothing to hear nor nothing to see—just solid lonesomeness. Next you'd see a raft sliding by, away off yonder, and maybe a galoot on it chopping, because they're most always doing it on a raft; you'd see the axe flash and come down—you don't hear nothing; you see that axe go up again, and by the time it's above the man's head then you hear the K'CHUCK!—

it had took all that time to come over the water. So we would put in the day, lazying around, listening to the stillness. Once there was a thick fog, and the rafts and things that went by was beating tin pans so the steamboats wouldn't run over them. A scow or a raft went by so close we could hear them talking and cussing and laughing—heard them plain; but we couldn't see no sign of them; it made you feel crawly; it was like spirits carrying on that way in the air. Jim said he believed it was spirits; but I says:

"No; spirits wouldn't say, 'Dern the dern fog.'"

Soon as it was night out we shoved; when we got her out to about the middle we let her alone, and let her float wherever the current wanted her to; then we lit the pipes, and dangled our legs in the water, and talked about all kinds of things—we was always naked, day and night, whenever the mosquitoes would let us—the new clothes Buck's folks made for me was too good to be comfortable, and besides I didn't go much on clothes, nohow.

Sometimes we'd have that whole river all to ourselves for the longest time. Yonder was the banks and the islands, across the water; and maybe a spark—which was a candle in a cabin window; and sometimes on the water you could see a spark or two—on a raft or a scow, you know; and maybe you could hear a fiddle or a song coming over from one of them crafts. It's lovely to live on a raft. We had the sky up there, all speckled with stars, and we used to lay on our backs and look up at them, and discuss about whether they was made or only just happened. Jim he allowed they was made, but I allowed they happened; I judged it would have took too long to MAKE so many. Jim said the moon could a LAID them; well, that looked kind of reasonable, so I didn't say nothing against it, because I've seen a frog lay most as many, so of course it could be done. We used to watch the stars that fell, too, and see them streak down. Jim allowed they'd got spoiled and was hove out of the nest.

Once or twice of a night we would see a steamboat slipping along in the dark, and now and then she would belch a whole world of sparks up out of her chimbleys, and they would rain down in the river and look awful pretty; then she would turn a corner and her lights would wink out and her powwow shut off and leave the river still again; and by and by her waves would get to us, a long time after she was gone, and joggle the raft a bit, and after that you wouldn't hear nothing for you couldn't tell how long, except maybe frogs or something.

After midnight the people on shore went to bed, and then for two or three hours the shores was black—no more sparks in the cabin windows. These sparks was our clock—the first one that showed again meant morning was coming, so we hunted a place to hide and tie up right away.

One morning about daybreak I found a canoe and crossed over a chute to the main shore—it was only two hundred yards—and paddled about a mile up a crick amongst the cypress woods, to see if I couldn't get some berries. Just as I was passing a place where a kind of a cowpath crossed the crick, here comes a couple of men tearing up the path as tight as they could foot it. I thought I was a goner, for whenever anybody was after anybody I judged it was ME—or maybe Jim. I was about to dig out from there in a hurry, but they was pretty close to me then, and sung out and begged me to save their lives—said they hadn't been doing nothing, and was being chased for it—said there was men and dogs a-coming. They wanted to jump right in, but I says:

"Don't you do it. I don't hear the dogs and horses yet; you've got time to crowd through the brush and get up the crick a little ways; then you take to the water and wade down to me and get in—that'll throw the dogs off the scent."

They done it, and soon as they was aboard I lit out for our towhead, and in about five or ten minutes we heard the dogs and the men away off, shouting. We heard them come along towards the crick, but couldn't see them; they seemed to stop and fool around a while; then, as we got further and further away all the time, we couldn't hardly hear them at all; by the time we had left a mile of woods behind us and struck the river, everything was quiet, and we paddled over to the towhead and hid in the cottonwoods and was safe.

One of these fellows was about seventy or upwards, and had a bald head and very gray whiskers. He had an old battered-up slouch hat on, and a greasy blue woollen shirt, and ragged old blue jeans britches stuffed into his boot-tops, and home-knit galluses— no, he only had one. He had an old long-tailed blue jeans coat with slick brass buttons flung over his arm, and both of them had big, fat, ratty-looking carpet-bags.

The other fellow was about thirty, and dressed about as ornery. After breakfast we all laid off and talked, and the first thing that come out was that these chaps didn't know one another.

"What got you into trouble?" says the baldhead to t'other chap.

"Well, I'd been selling an article to take the tartar off the teeth—and it does take it off, too, and generly the enamel along with it—but I stayed about one night longer than I ought to, and was just in the act of sliding out when I ran across you on the trail this side of town, and you told me they were coming, and begged me to help you to get off. So I told you I was expecting trouble myself, and would scatter out WITH you. That's the whole yarn—what's yourn?"

"Well, I'd ben a-runnin' a little temperance revival thar 'bout a week, and was the pet of the women folks, big and little, for I was makin' it mighty warm for the rummies, I TELL you, and takin' as much as five or six dollars a night—ten cents a head, children and niggers free—and business a-growin' all the time, when somehow or another a little report got around last night that I had a way of puttin' in my time with a private jug on the sly. A nigger rousted me out this mornin', and told me the people was getherin' on the quiet with their dogs and horses, and they'd be along pretty soon and give me 'bout half an hour's start, and then run me down if they could; and if they got me they'd tar and feather me and ride me on a rail, sure. I didn't wait for no breakfast—I warn't hungry."

"Old man," said the young one, "I reckon we might double-team it together; what do you think?"

"I ain't undisposed. What's your line—mainly?"

"Jour printer by trade; do a little in patent medicines; theater-actor —tragedy, you know; take a turn to mesmerism and phrenology when there's a chance; teach singing-geography school for a change; sling a lecture sometimes—oh, I do lots of things—most anything that comes handy, so it ain't work. What's your lay?"

"I've done considerble in the doctoring way in my time. Layin' on o' hands is my best holt—for cancer and paralysis, and sich things; and I k'n tell a fortune pretty good when I've got somebody along to find out the facts for me. Preachin's my line, too, and workin' camp-meetin's, and missionaryin' around."

Nobody never said anything for a while; then the young man hove a sigh and says: "Alas!"

"What 're you alassin' about?" says the bald-head.

"To think I should have lived to be leading such a life, and be degraded down into such company." And he begun to wipe the corner of his eye with a rag.

"Dern your skin, ain't the company good enough for you?" says the baldhead, pretty pert and uppish.

"Yes, it IS good enough for me; it's as good as I deserve; for who fetched me so low when I was so high? I did myself. I don't blame YOU, gentlemen—far from it; I don't blame anybody. I deserve it all. Let the cold world do its worst; one thing I know—there's a grave somewhere for me. The world may go on just as it's always done, and take everything from me—loved ones, property, everything; but it can't take that. Some day I'll lie down in it and forget it all, and my poor broken heart will be at rest." He went on a-wiping.

"Drot your pore broken heart," says the baldhead; "what are you heaving your pore broken heart at US f'r? WE hain't done nothing."

"No, I know you haven't. I ain't blaming you, gentlemen. I brought myself down— yes, I did it myself. It's right I should suffer—perfectly right—I don't make any moan."

"Brought you down from whar? Whar was you brought down from?"

"Ah, you would not believe me; the world never believes—let it pass —'tis no matter. The secret of my birth—"

"The secret of your birth! Do you mean to say—"

"Gentlemen," says the young man, very solemn, "I will reveal it to you, for I feel I may have confidence in you. By rights I am a duke!"

Jim's eyes bugged out when he heard that; and I reckon mine did, too. Then the baldhead says: "No! you can't mean it?"

"Yes. My great-grandfather, eldest son of the Duke of Bridgewater, fled to this country about the end of the last century, to breathe the pure air of freedom; married here, and died, leaving a son, his own father dying about the same time. The second son of the late duke seized the titles and estates—the infant real duke was ignored. I am the lineal descendant of that infant—I am the rightful Duke of Bridgewater; and here am I, forlorn, torn from my high estate, hunted of men, despised by the cold world, ragged, worn, heart-broken, and degraded to the companionship of felons on a raft!"

Jim pitied him ever so much, and so did I. We tried to comfort him, but he said it warn't much use, he couldn't be much comforted; said if we was a mind to acknowledge him, that would do him more good than most anything else; so we said we would, if he would tell us how. He said we ought to bow when we spoke to him, and say "Your Grace," or "My Lord," or "Your Lordship"—and he wouldn't mind it if we called him plain "Bridgewater," which, he said, was a title anyway, and not a name; and one of us ought to wait on him at dinner, and do any little thing for him he wanted done.

Well, that was all easy, so we done it. All through dinner Jim stood around and waited on him, and says, "Will yo' Grace have some o' dis or some o' dat?" and so on, and a body could see it was mighty pleasing to him.

But the old man got pretty silent by and by—didn't have much to say, and didn't look pretty comfortable over all that petting that was going on around that duke. He seemed to have something on his mind. So, along in the afternoon, he says:

"Looky here, Bilgewater," he says, "I'm nation sorry for you, but you ain't the only person that's had troubles like that."

"No?"

"No you ain't. You ain't the only person that's ben snaked down wrongfully out'n a high place."

"Alas!"

"No, you ain't the only person that's had a secret of his birth." And, by jings, HE begins to cry.

"Hold! What do you mean?"

"Bilgewater, kin I trust you?" says the old man, still sort of sobbing.

"To the bitter death!" He took the old man by the hand and squeezed it, and says, "That secret of your being: speak!"

"Bilgewater, I am the late Dauphin!"

You bet you, Jim and me stared this time. Then the duke says:

"You are what?"

"Yes, my friend, it is too true—your eyes is lookin' at this very moment on the pore disappeared Dauphin, Looy the Seventeen, son of Looy the Sixteen and Marry Antonette."

"You! At your age! No! You mean you're the late Charlemagne; you must be six or seven hundred years old, at the very least."

"Trouble has done it, Bilgewater, trouble has done it; trouble has brung these gray hairs and this premature balditude. Yes, gentlemen, you see before you, in blue jeans and misery, the wanderin', exiled, trampled-on, and sufferin' rightful King of France."

Well, he cried and took on so that me and Jim didn't know hardly what to do, we was so sorry—and so glad and proud we'd got him with us, too. So we set in, like we done before with the duke, and tried to comfort HIM. But he said it warn't no use, nothing but to be dead and done with it all could do him any good; though he said it often made him feel easier and better for a while if people treated him according to his rights, and got down on one knee to speak to him, and always called him "Your Majesty," and waited on him first at meals, and didn't set down in his presence till he asked them. So Jim and me set to majestying him, and doing this and that and t'other for him, and standing up till he told us we might set down. This done him heaps of good, and so he got cheerful and comfortable. But the duke kind of soured on him, and didn't look a bit satisfied with the way things was going; still, the king acted real friendly towards him, and said the duke's great-grandfather and all the other Dukes of Bilgewater was a good deal thought of by HIS father, and was allowed to come to the palace considerable; but the duke stayed huffy a good while, till by and by the king says:

"Like as not we got to be together a blamed long time on this h-yer raft, Bilgewater, and so what's the use o' your bein' sour? It 'll only make things oncomfortable. It ain't my fault I warn't born a duke, it ain't your fault you warn't born a king—so what's the use to worry? Make the best o' things the way you find 'em, says I—that's my motto. This ain't no bad thing that we've struck here—plenty grub and an easy life—come, give us your hand, duke, and le's all be friends."

The duke done it, and Jim and me was pretty glad to see it. It took away all the uncomfortableness and we felt mighty good over it, because it would a been a miserable business to have any unfriendliness on the raft; for what you want, above all things, on a raft, is for everybody to be satisfied, and feel right and kind towards the others.

It didn't take me long to make up my mind that these liars warn't no kings nor dukes at all, but just low-down humbugs and frauds. But I never said nothing, never let on; kept it to myself; it's the best way; then you don't have no quarrels, and don't get into no trouble. If they wanted us to call them kings and dukes, I hadn't no objections, 'long as it would keep peace in the family; and it warn't no use to tell Jim, so I didn't tell him. If I never learnt nothing else out of pap, I learnt that the best way to get along with his kind of people is to let them have their own way.

Chapter XX

They asked us considerable many questions; wanted to know what we covered up the raft that way for, and laid by in the daytime instead of running—was Jim a runaway nigger? Says I:

"Goodness sakes! would a runaway nigger run SOUTH?"

No, they allowed he wouldn't. I had to account for things some way, so I says:

"My folks was living in Pike County, in Missouri, where I was born, and they all died off but me and pa and my brother Ike. Pa, he 'lowed he'd break up and go down and live with Uncle Ben, who's got a little one-horse place on the river, forty-four mile below Orleans. Pa was pretty poor, and had some debts; so when he'd squared up there warn't nothing left but sixteen dollars and our nigger, Jim. That warn't enough to take us fourteen hundred mile, deck passage nor no other way. Well, when the river rose pa had a streak of luck one day; he ketched this piece of a raft; so we reckoned we'd go down to Orleans on it. Pa's luck didn't hold out; a steamboat run over the forrard corner of the raft one night, and we all went overboard and dove under the wheel; Jim and me come up all right, but pa was drunk, and Ike was only four years old, so they never come up no more. Well, for the next day or two we had considerable trouble, because people was always coming out in skiffs and trying to take Jim away from me, saying they believed he was a runaway nigger. We don't run daytimes no more now; nights they don't bother us."

The duke says:

"Leave me alone to cipher out a way so we can run in the daytime if we want to. I'll think the thing over—I'll invent a plan that'll fix it. We'll let it alone for to-day, because of course we don't want to go by that town yonder in daylight—it mightn't be healthy."

Towards night it begun to darken up and look like rain; the heat lightning was squirting around low down in the sky, and the leaves was beginning to shiver—it was going to be pretty ugly, it was easy to see that. So the duke and the king went to over-hauling our wigwam, to see what the beds was like. My bed was a straw tick better than Jim's, which was a corn-shuck tick; there's always cobs around about in a shuck tick, and they poke into you and hurt; and when you roll over the dry shucks sound like you was rolling over in a pile of dead leaves; it makes such a rustling that you wake up. Well, the duke allowed he would take my bed; but the king allowed he wouldn't. He says:

"I should a reckoned the difference in rank would a sejested to you that a corn-shuck bed warn't just fitten for me to sleep on. Your Grace 'll take the shuck bed yourself."

Jim and me was in a sweat again for a minute, being afraid there was going to be some more trouble amongst them; so we was pretty glad when the duke says:

"'Tis my fate to be always ground into the mire under the iron heel of oppression. Misfortune has broken my once haughty spirit; I yield, I submit; 'tis my fate. I am alone in the world—let me suffer; can bear it."

We got away as soon as it was good and dark. The king told us to stand well out towards the middle of the river, and not show a light till we got a long ways below the town. We come in sight of the little bunch of lights by and by—that was the town, you know—and slid by, about a half a mile out, all right. When we was three-quarters of a mile below we hoisted up our signal lantern; and about ten o'clock it come on to rain and blow and thunder and lighten like everything; so the king told us to both stay on watch till the weather got better; then him and the duke crawled into the wigwam and turned in for the night. It was my watch below till twelve, but I wouldn't a turned in anyway if I'd had a bed, because a body don't see such a storm as that every day in the week, not by a long sight. My souls, how the wind did scream along! And every second or two there'd come a glare that lit up the white-caps for a half a mile around, and you'd see the islands looking dusty through the rain, and the trees thrashing around in the wind; then comes a HWACK!—BUM! BUM! BUMBLE-UMBLE-UM-BUM-BUM-BUM-BUM—and the thunder would go rumbling and grumbling away, and quit—and then RIP! comes another flash and another sockdolager. The waves most washed me off the raft sometimes, but I hadn't any clothes on, and didn't mind. We didn't have no trouble about snags; the lightning was glaring and flittering around so constant that we could see them plenty soon enough to throw her head this way or that and miss them.

I had the middle watch, you know, but I was pretty sleepy by that time, so Jim he said he would stand the first half of it for me; he was always mighty good that way, Jim was. I crawled into the wigwam, but the king and the duke had their legs sprawled around so there warn't no show for me; so I laid outside—I didn't mind the rain, because it was warm, and the waves warn't running so high now. About two they come up again, though, and Jim was going to call me; but he changed his mind, because he reckoned they warn't high enough yet to do any harm; but he was mistaken about that, for pretty soon all of a sudden along comes a regular ripper and washed me overboard. It most killed Jim a-laughing. He was the easiest nigger to laugh that ever was, anyway.

I took the watch, and Jim he laid down and snored away; and by and by the storm let up for good and all; and the first cabin-light that showed I rousted him out, and we slid the raft into hiding quarters for the day.

The king got out an old ratty deck of cards after breakfast, and him and the duke played seven-up a while, five cents a game. Then they got tired of it, and allowed they would "lay out a campaign," as they called it. The duke went down into his carpet-bag, and fetched up a lot of little printed bills and read them out loud. One bill said, "The celebrated Dr. Armand de Montalban, of Paris," would "lecture on the Science of Phrenology" at such and such a place, on the blank day of blank, at ten cents admission, and "furnish charts of character at twenty-five cents apiece." The duke said that was HIM. In another bill he was the "world-renowned Shakespearian tragedian, Garrick the Younger, of Drury Lane, London." In other bills he had a lot of other names and done other wonderful things, like finding water and gold with a "divining-rod," "dissipating witch spells," and so on. By and by he says:

"But the histrionic muse is the darling. Have you ever trod the boards, Royalty?"

"No," says the king.

"You shall, then, before you're three days older, Fallen Grandeur," says the duke. "The first good town we come to we'll hire a hall and do the sword fight in Richard III. and the balcony scene in Romeo and Juliet. How does that strike you?"

"I'm in, up to the hub, for anything that will pay, Bilgewater; but, you see, I don't know nothing about play-actin', and hain't ever seen much of it. I was too small when pap used to have 'em at the palace. Do you reckon you can learn me?"

"Easy!"

"All right. I'm jist a-freezn' for something fresh, anyway. Le's commence right away."

So the duke he told him all about who Romeo was and who Juliet was, and said he was used to being Romeo, so the king could be Juliet.

"But if Juliet's such a young gal, duke, my peeled head and my white whiskers is goin' to look oncommon odd on her, maybe."

"No, don't you worry; these country jakes won't ever think of that. Besides, you know, you'll be in costume, and that makes all the difference in the world; Juliet's in a balcony, enjoying the moonlight before she goes to bed, and she's got on her night-gown and her ruffled nightcap. Here are the costumes for the parts."

He got out two or three curtain-calico suits, which he said was meedyevil armor for Richard III. and t'other chap, and a long white cotton nightshirt and a ruffled nightcap to match. The king was satisfied; so the duke got out his book and read the parts over in the most splendid spread-eagle way, prancing around and acting at the same time, to show how it had got to be done; then he give the book to the king and told him to get his part by heart.

There was a little one-horse town about three mile down the bend, and after dinner the duke said he had ciphered out his idea about how to run in daylight without it being dangersome for Jim; so he allowed he would go down to the town and fix that thing. The king allowed he would go, too, and see if he couldn't strike something. We was out of coffee, so Jim said I better go along with them in the canoe and get some.

When we got there there warn't nobody stirring; streets empty, and perfectly dead and still, like Sunday. We found a sick nigger sunning himself in a back yard, and he said everybody that warn't too young or too sick or too old was gone to camp-meeting, about two mile back in the woods. The king got the directions, and allowed he'd go and work that camp-meeting for all it was worth, and I might go, too.

The duke said what he was after was a printing-office. We found it; a little bit of a concern, up over a carpenter shop—carpenters and printers all gone to the meeting, and no doors locked. It was a dirty, littered-up place, and had ink marks, and handbills with pictures of horses and runaway niggers on them, all over the walls. The duke shed his coat and said he was all right now. So me and the king lit out for the camp-meeting.

We got there in about a half an hour fairly dripping, for it was a most awful hot day. There was as much as a thousand people there from twenty mile around. The woods was full of teams and wagons, hitched everywheres, feeding out of the wagon-troughs and stomping to keep off the flies. There was sheds made out of poles and roofed over with branches, where they had lemonade and gingerbread to sell, and piles of watermelons and green corn and such-like truck.

The preaching was going on under the same kinds of sheds, only they was bigger and held crowds of people. The benches was made out of outside slabs of logs, with holes bored in the round side to drive sticks into for legs. They didn't have no backs. The preachers had high platforms to stand on at one end of the sheds. The women had on sun-bonnets; and some had linsey-woolsey frocks, some gingham ones, and a few of the young ones had on calico. Some of the young men was barefooted, and some of the children didn't have on any clothes but just a tow-linen shirt. Some of the old women was knitting, and some of the young folks was courting on the sly.

The first shed we come to the preacher was lining out a hymn. He lined out two lines, everybody sung it, and it was kind of grand to hear it, there was so many of them and they done it in such a rousing way; then he lined out two more for them to sing—and so on. The people woke up more and more, and sung louder and louder; and towards the end some begun to groan, and some begun to shout. Then the preacher begun to preach, and begun in earnest, too; and went weaving first to one side of the platform and then the other, and then a-leaning down over the front of it, with his arms and his body going all the time, and shouting his words out with all his might; and every now and then he would hold up his Bible and spread it open, and kind of pass it around this way and that, shouting, "It's the brazen serpent in the wilderness! Look upon it and live!" And people would shout out, "Glory!—A-a-MEN!" And so he went on, and the people groaning and crying and saying amen:

"Oh, come to the mourners' bench! come, black with sin! (AMEN!) come, sick and sore! (AMEN!) come, lame and halt and blind! (AMEN!) come, pore and needy, sunk in shame! (A-A-MEN!) come, all that's worn and soiled and suffering!—come with a broken spirit! come with a contrite heart! Come in your rags and sin and dirt! the waters that cleanse is free, the door of heaven stands open—oh, enter in and be at rest!" (A-A-MEN! GLORY, GLORY HALLELUJAH!)

And so on. You couldn't make out what the preacher said any more, on account of the shouting and crying. Folks got up everywheres in the crowd, and worked their way just by main strength to the mourners' bench, with the tears running down their faces; and when all the mourners had got up there to the front benches in a crowd, they sung and shouted and flung themselves down on the straw, just crazy and wild.

Well, the first I knowed the king got a-going, and you could hear him over every-body; and next he went a-charging up on to the platform, and the preacher he begged him to speak to the people, and he done it. He told them he was a pirate—been a pirate for thirty years out in the Indian Ocean—and his crew was thinned out considerable last spring in a fight, and he was home now to take out some fresh men, and thanks to goodness he'd been robbed last night and put ashore off of a steamboat without a cent, and he was glad of it; it was the blessedest thing that ever happened to him, because he was a changed man now, and happy for the first time in his life; and, poor as he was, he was going to start right off and work his way back to the Indian Ocean, and put in the rest of his life trying to turn the pirates into the true path; for he could do it better than anybody else, being acquainted with all pirate crews in that ocean; and though it would take him a long time to get there without money, he would get there anyway, and every time he convinced a pirate he would say to him, "Don't you thank me, don't you give me no credit; it all belongs to them dear people in Pokeville camp-meeting, natural brothers and benefactors of the race, and that dear preacher there, the truest friend a pirate ever had!"

And then he busted into tears, and so did everybody. Then somebody sings out, "Take up a collection for him, take up a collection!" Well, a half a dozen made a jump to do it, but somebody sings out, "Let HIM pass the hat around!" Then everybody said it, the preacher too.

So the king went all through the crowd with his hat swabbing his eyes, and bless-ing the people and praising them and thanking them for being so good to the poor pirates away off there; and every little while the prettiest kind of girls, with the tears running down their cheeks, would up and ask him would he let them kiss him for to remember him by; and he always done it; and some of them he hugged and kissed as many as five or six times—and he was invited to stay a week; and everybody wanted him to live in their houses, and said they'd think it was an honor; but he said as this was the last day of the camp-meeting he couldn't do no good, and besides he was in a sweat to get to the Indian Ocean right off and go to work on the pirates.

When we got back to the raft and he come to count up he found he had collected eighty-seven dollars and seventy-five cents. And then he had fetched away a three-gallon jug of whisky, too, that he found under a wagon when he was starting home through the woods. The king said, take it all around, it laid over any day he'd ever put in in the missionarying line. He said it warn't no use talking, heathens don't amount to shucks alongside of pirates to work a camp-meeting with.

The duke was thinking he'd been doing pretty well till the king come to show up, but after that he didn't think so so much. He had set up and printed off two little jobs for farmers in that printing-office—horse bills—and took the money, four dollars. And he had got in ten dollars' worth of advertisements for the paper, which he said he would put in for four dollars if they would pay in advance—so they done it.

The price of the paper was two dollars a year, but he took in three subscriptions for half a dollar apiece on condition of them paying him in advance; they were going to pay in cordwood and onions as usual, but he said he had just bought the concern and knocked down the price as low as he could afford it, and was going to run it for cash. He set up a little piece of poetry, which he made, himself, out of his own head—three verses—kind of sweet and saddish—the name of it was, "Yes, crush, cold world, this breaking heart"—and he left that all set up and ready to print in the paper, and didn't charge nothing for it. Well, he took in nine dollars and a half, and said he'd done a pretty square day's work for it.

Then he showed us another little job he'd printed and hadn't charged for, because it was for us. It had a picture of a runaway nigger with a bundle on a stick over his shoulder, and "$200 reward" under it. The reading was all about Jim, and just described him to a dot. It said he run away from St. Jacques' plantation, forty mile below New Orleans, last winter, and likely went north, and whoever would catch him and send him back he could have the reward and expenses.

"Now," says the duke, "after to-night we can run in the daytime if we want to. Whenever we see anybody coming we can tie Jim hand and foot with a rope, and lay him in the wigwam and show this handbill and say we captured him up the river, and were too poor to travel on a steamboat, so we got this little raft on credit from our friends and are going down to get the reward. Handcuffs and chains would look still better on Jim, but it wouldn't go well with the story of us being so poor. Too much like jewelry. Ropes are the correct thing—we must preserve the unities, as we say on the boards."

We all said the duke was pretty smart, and there couldn't be no trouble about running daytimes. We judged we could make miles enough that night to get out of the reach of the powwow we reckoned the duke's work in the printing office was going to make in that little town; then we could boom right along if we wanted to.

We laid low and kept still, and never shoved out till nearly ten o'clock; then we slid by, pretty wide away from the town, and didn't hoist our lantern till we was clear out of sight of it.

When Jim called me to take the watch at four in the morning, he says:

"Huck, does you reck'n we gwyne to run acrost any mo' kings on dis trip?"

"No," I says, "I reckon not."

"Well," says he, "dat's all right, den. I doan' mine one er two kings, but dat's enough. Dis one's powerful drunk, en de duke ain' much better."

I found Jim had been trying to get him to talk French, so he could hear what it was like; but he said he had been in this country so long, and had so much trouble, he'd forgot it.

Chapter XXI

It was after sun-up now, but we went right on and didn't tie up. The king and the duke turned out by and by looking pretty rusty; but after they'd jumped overboard and took a swim it chippered them up a good deal. After breakfast the king he took a seat on the corner of the raft, and pulled off his boots and rolled up his britches, and let his legs dangle in the water, so as to be comfortable, and lit his pipe, and went to getting his Romeo and Juliet by heart. When he had got it pretty good him and the duke begun to practice it together. The duke had to learn him over and over again how to say every speech; and he made him sigh, and put his hand on his heart, and after a while he said he done it pretty well; "only," he says, "you mustn't bellow out ROMEO! that way, like a bull—you must say it soft and sick and languishy, so—R-O-O-MEO! that is the idea; for Juliet's a dear sweet mere child of a girl, you know, and she doesn't bray like a jackass."

Well, next they got out a couple of long swords that the duke made out of oak laths, and begun to practice the sword fight—the duke called himself Richard III.; and the way they laid on and pranced around the raft was grand to see. But by and by the king tripped and fell overboard, and after that they took a rest, and had a talk about all kinds of adventures they'd had in other times along the river.

After dinner the duke says:

"Well, Capet, we'll want to make this a first-class show, you know, so I guess we'll add a little more to it. We want a little something to answer encores with, anyway."

"What's onkores, Bilgewater?"

The duke told him, and then says:

"I'll answer by doing the Highland fling or the sailor's hornpipe; and you—well, let me see—oh, I've got it—you can do Hamlet's soliloquy."

"Hamlet's which?"

"Hamlet's soliloquy, you know; the most celebrated thing in Shakespeare. Ah, it's sublime, sublime! Always fetches the house. I haven't got it in the book—I've only got one volume—but I reckon I can piece it out from memory. I'll just walk up and down a minute, and see if I can call it back from recollection's vaults."

So he went to marching up and down, thinking, and frowning horrible every now and then; then he would hoist up his eyebrows; next he would squeeze his hand on his forehead and stagger back and kind of moan; next he would sigh, and next he'd let on to drop a tear. It was beautiful to see him. By and by he got it. He told us to give attention. Then he strikes a most noble attitude, with one leg shoved forwards, and his arms stretched away up, and his head tilted back, looking up at the sky; and then he begins to rip and rave and grit his teeth; and after that, all through his speech, he howled, and spread around, and swelled up his chest, and just knocked the spots out of any acting ever I see before. This is the speech—I learned it, easy enough, while he was learning it to the king:

"To be, or not to be; that is the bare bodkin that makes calamity of so long life; for who would fardels bear, till Birnam Wood do come to Dunsinane, but that the fear of something after death murders the innocent sleep, great nature's second course, and makes us rather sling the arrows of outrageous fortune than fly to others that we know not of. There's the respect must give us pause: wake Duncan with thy knocking! I would thou couldst; for who would bear the whips and scorns of time, the oppressor's wrong, the proud man's contumely, the law's delay, and the quietus which his pangs might take, In the dead waste and middle of the night, when churchyards yawn in customary suits of solemn black, but that the undiscovered country from whose bourne no traveler returns, breathes forth contagion on the world, and thus the native hue of resolution, like the poor cat i' the adage, is sicklied o'er with care, and all the clouds that lowered o'er our housetops, with this regard their currents turn awry, and lose the name of action. 'Tis a consummation devoutly to be wished. But soft you, the fair Ophelia: Ope not thy ponderous and marble jaws, but get thee to a nunnery—go!"

Well, the old man he liked that speech, and he mighty soon got it so he could do it first-rate. It seemed like he was just born for it; and when he had his hand in and was excited, it was perfectly lovely the way he would rip and tear and rair up behind when he was getting it off.

The first chance we got the duke he had some showbills printed; and after that, for two or three days as we floated along, the raft was a most uncommon lively place, for there warn't nothing but sword fighting and rehearsing—as the duke called it—going on all the time. One morning, when we was pretty well down the State of Arkansaw, we come in sight of a little one-horse town in a big bend; so we tied up about three-quarters of a mile above it, in the mouth of a crick which was shut in like a tunnel by the cypress trees, and all of us but Jim took the canoe and went down there to see if there was any chance in that place for our show.

We struck it mighty lucky; there was going to be a circus there that afternoon, and the country people was already beginning to come in, in all kinds of old shackly wagons, and on horses. The circus would leave before night, so our show would have a pretty good chance. The duke he hired the courthouse, and we went around and stuck up our bills. They read like this:

Shaksperean Revival ! ! !
Wonderful Attraction!
For One Night Only!

The world renowned tragedians, David Garrick the Younger, of Drury Lane Theatre London,
and Edmund Kean the elder, of the Royal Haymarket Theatre, Whitechapel,
Pudding Lane, Piccadilly, London, and the Royal Continental Theatres,
in their sublime Shaksperean Spectacle entitled

The Balcony Scene in Romeo and Juliet ! ! !

Romeo...................Mr. Garrick
Juliet..................Mr. Kean

Assisted by the whole strength of the company!
New costumes, new scenes, new appointments!
Also: The thrilling, masterly, and blood-curdling
Broad-sword conflict In Richard III ! ! !

Richard III..................Mr. Garrick
Richmond............Mr. Kean

Also: By special request: Hamlet's Immortal Soliloquy ! !
By The Illustrious Kean! Done by him 300 consecutive nights in Paris!
For One Night Only, On account of imperative European engagements!
Admission 25 cents; children and servants, 10 cents.

Then we went loafing around town. The stores and houses was most all old, shackly, dried up frame concerns that hadn't ever been painted; they was set up three or four foot above ground on stilts, so as to be out of reach of the water when the river was over-flowed. The houses had little gardens around them, but they didn't seem to raise hardly anything in them but jimpson-weeds, and sunflowers, and ash piles, and old curled-up boots and shoes, and pieces of bottles, and rags, and played-out tinware. The fences was made of different kinds of boards, nailed on at different times; and they leaned every which way, and had gates that didn't generly have but one hinge— a leather one. Some of the fences had been white-washed some time or another, but the duke said it was in Clumbus' time, like enough. There was generly hogs in the garden, and people driving them out.

All the stores was along one street. They had white domestic awnings in front, and the country people hitched their horses to the awning-posts. There was empty drygoods boxes under the awnings, and loafers roosting on them all day long, whittling them with their Barlow knives; and chawing tobacco, and gaping and yawning and stretching—a mighty ornery lot. They generly had on yellow straw hats most as wide as an umbrella, but didn't wear no coats nor waistcoats, they called one another Bill, and Buck, and Hank, and Joe, and Andy, and talked lazy and drawly, and used considerable many cuss words. There was as many as one loafer leaning up against every awning-post, and he most always had his hands in his britches-pockets, except when he fetched them out to lend a chaw of tobacco or scratch. What a body was hearing amongst them all the time was:

"Gimme a chaw 'v tobacker, Hank."

"Cain't; I hain't got but one chaw left. Ask Bill."

Maybe Bill he gives him a chaw; maybe he lies and says he ain't got none. Some of them kinds of loafers never has a cent in the world, nor a chaw of tobacco of their own. They get all their chawing by borrowing; they say to a fellow, "I wisht you'd len' me a chaw, Jack, I jist this minute give Ben Thompson the last chaw I had"—which is a lie pretty much everytime; it don't fool nobody but a stranger; but Jack ain't no stranger, so he says:

"YOU give him a chaw, did you? So did your sister's cat's grandmother. You pay me back the chaws you've awready borry'd off 'n me, Lafe Buckner, then I'll loan you one or two ton of it, and won't charge you no back intrust, nuther."

"Well, I DID pay you back some of it wunst."

"Yes, you did—'bout six chaws. You borry'd store tobacker and paid back nigger-head."

Store tobacco is flat black plug, but these fellows mostly chaws the natural leaf twisted. When they borrow a chaw they don't generly cut it off with a knife, but set the plug in between their teeth, and gnaw with their teeth and tug at the plug with their hands till they get it in two; then sometimes the one that owns the tobacco looks mournful at it when it's handed back, and says, sarcastic:

"Here, gimme the CHAW, and you take the PLUG."

All the streets and lanes was just mud; they warn't nothing else BUT mud —mud as black as tar and nigh about a foot deep in some places, and two or three inches deep in ALL the places. The hogs loafed and grunted around everywheres. You'd see a muddy sow and a litter of pigs come lazying along the street and whollop herself right down in the way, where folks had to walk around her, and she'd stretch out and shut her eyes and wave her ears whilst the pigs was milking her, and look as happy as if she was on salary. And pretty soon you'd hear a loafer sing out, "Hi! SO boy! sick him, Tige!" and away the sow would go, squealing most horrible, with a dog or two swinging to each ear, and three or four dozen more a-coming; and then you would see all the loafers get up and watch the thing out of sight, and laugh at the fun and look grateful for the noise. Then they'd settle back again till there was a dog fight. There couldn't anything wake them up all over, and make them happy all over, like a dog fight—unless it might be putting turpentine on a stray dog and setting fire to him, or tying a tin pan to his tail and see him run himself to death.

On the river front some of the houses was sticking out over the bank, and they was bowed and bent, and about ready to tumble in, The people had moved out of them. The bank was caved away under one corner of some others, and that corner was hanging over. People lived in them yet, but it was dangersome, because sometimes a strip of land as wide as a house caves in at a time. Sometimes a belt of land a quarter of a mile deep will start in and cave along and cave along till it all caves into the river in one summer. Such a town as that has to be always moving back, and back, and back, because the river's always gnawing at it.

The nearer it got to noon that day the thicker and thicker was the wagons and horses in the streets, and more coming all the time. Families fetched their dinners with them from the country, and eat them in the wagons. There was considerable whisky drinking going on, and I seen three fights. By and by somebody sings out:

"Here comes old Boggs!—in from the country for his little old monthly drunk; here he comes, boys!"

All the loafers looked glad; I reckoned they was used to having fun out of Boggs. One of them says: "Wonder who he's a-gwyne to chaw up this time. If he'd a-chawed up all the men he's ben a-gwyne to chaw up in the last twenty year he'd have considerable ruputation now."

Another one says, "I wisht old Boggs 'd threaten me, 'cuz then I'd know I warn't gwyne to die for a thousan' year."

Boggs comes a-tearing along on his horse, whooping and yelling like an Injun, and singing out:

"Cler the track, thar. I'm on the waw-path, and the price uv coffins is a-gwyne to raise."

He was drunk, and weaving about in his saddle; he was over fifty year old, and had a very red face. Everybody yelled at him and laughed at him and sassed him, and he sassed back, and said he'd attend to them and lay them out in their regular turns, but he couldn't wait now because he'd come to town to kill old Colonel Sherburn, and his motto was, "Meat first, and spoon vittles to top off on."

He see me, and rode up and says:

"Whar'd you come f'm, boy? You prepared to die?"

Then he rode on. I was scared, but a man says:

"He don't mean nothing; he's always a-carryin' on like that when he's drunk. He's the best naturedest old fool in Arkansaw—never hurt nobody, drunk nor sober."

Boggs rode up before the biggest store in town, and bent his head down so he could see under the curtain of the awning and yells:

"Come out here, Sherburn! Come out and meet the man you've swindled. You're the houn' I'm after, and I'm a-gwyne to have you, too!"

And so he went on, calling Sherburn everything he could lay his tongue to, and the whole street packed with people listening and laughing and going on. By and by a proud-looking man about fifty-five—and he was a heap the best dressed man in that town, too—steps out of the store, and the crowd drops back on each side to let him come. He says to Boggs, mighty ca'm and slow—he says:

"I'm tired of this, but I'll endure it till one o'clock. Till one o'clock, mind—no longer. If you open your mouth against me only once after that time you can't travel so far but I will find you."

Then he turns and goes in. The crowd looked mighty sober; nobody stirred, and there warn't no more laughing. Boggs rode off blackguarding Sherburn as loud as he could yell, all down the street; and pretty soon back he comes and stops before the store, still keeping it up. Some men crowded around him and tried to get him to shut up, but he wouldn't; they told him it would be one o'clock in about fifteen minutes, and so he MUST go home—he must go right away. But it didn't do no good. He cussed away with all his might, and throwed his hat down in the mud and rode over it, and pretty soon away he went a-raging down the street again, with his gray hair a-flying. Everybody that could get a chance at him tried their best to coax him off of his horse so they could lock him up and get him sober; but it warn't no use—up the street he would tear again, and give Sherburn another cussing. By and by somebody says:

"Go for his daughter!—quick, go for his daughter; sometimes he'll listen to her. If anybody can persuade him, she can."

So somebody started on a run. I walked down street a ways and stopped. In about five or ten minutes here comes Boggs again, but not on his horse. He was a-reeling across the street towards me, bare-headed, with a friend on both sides of him a-holt of his arms and hurrying him along. He was quiet, and looked uneasy; and he warn't hanging back any, but was doing some of the hurrying himself. Somebody sings out:

"Boggs!"

I looked over there to see who said it, and it was that Colonel Sherburn. He was standing perfectly still in the street, and had a pistol raised in his right hand—not aiming it, but holding it out with the barrel tilted up towards the sky. The same second I see a young girl coming on the run, and two men with her. Boggs and the men turned round to see who called him, and when they see the pistol the men jumped to one side, and the pistol-barrel come down slow and steady to a level—both barrels cocked. Boggs throws up both of his hands and says, "O Lord, don't shoot!" Bang! goes the first shot, and he staggers back, clawing at the air—bang! goes the second one, and he tumbles backwards on to the ground, heavy and solid, with his arms spread out. That young girl screamed out and comes rushing, and down she throws herself on her father, crying, and saying, "Oh, he's killed him, he's killed him!" The crowd closed up around them, and shouldered and jammed one another, with their necks stretched, trying to see, and people on the inside trying to shove them back and shouting, "Back, back! give him air, give him air!"

Colonel Sherburn he tossed his pistol on to the ground, and turned around on his heels and walked off.

They took Boggs to a little drug store, the crowd pressing around just the same, and the whole town following, and I rushed and got a good place at the window, where I was close to him and could see in. They laid him on the floor and put one large Bible under his head, and opened another one and spread it on his breast; but they tore open his shirt first, and I seen where one of the bullets went in. He made about a dozen long gasps, his breast lifting the Bible up when he drawed in his breath, and letting it down again when he breathed it out—and after that he laid still; he was dead. Then they pulled his daughter away from him, screaming and crying, and took her off. She was about sixteen, and very sweet and gentle looking, but awful pale and scared.

Well, pretty soon the whole town was there, squirming and scrouging and pushing and shoving to get at the window and have a look, but people that had the places wouldn't give them up, and folks behind them was saying all the time, "Say, now, you've looked enough, you fellows; 'tain't right and 'tain't fair for you to stay thar all the time, and never give nobody a chance; other folks has their rights as well as you."

There was considerable jawing back, so I slid out, thinking maybe there was going to be trouble. The streets was full, and everybody was excited. Everybody that seen the shooting was telling how it happened, and there was a big crowd packed around each one of these fellows, stretching their necks and listening. One long, lanky man, with long hair and a big white fur stovepipe hat on the back of his head, and a crooked-handled cane, marked out the places on the ground where Boggs stood and where Sherburn stood, and the people following him around from one place to t'other and watching everything he done, and bobbing their heads to show they understood, and stooping a little and resting their hands on their thighs to watch him mark the places on the ground with his cane; and then he stood up straight and stiff where Sherburn had stood, frowning and having his hat-brim down over his eyes, and sung out, "Boggs!" and then fetched his cane down slow to a level, and says "Bang!" staggered backwards, says "Bang!" again, and fell down flat on his back. The people that had seen the thing said he done it perfect; said it was just exactly the way it all happened. Then as much as a dozen people got out their bottles and treated him.

Well, by and by somebody said Sherburn ought to be lynched. In about a minute everybody was saying it; so away they went, mad and yelling, and snatching down every clothes-line they come to to do the hanging with.

Chapter XXII

They swarmed up towards Sherburn's house, a-whooping and raging like Injuns, and everything had to clear the way or get run over and tromped to mush, and it was awful to see. Children was heeling it ahead of the mob, screaming and trying to get out of the way; and every window along the road was full of women's heads, and there was nigger boys in every tree, and bucks and wenches looking over every fence; and as soon as the mob would get nearly to them they would break and skaddle back out of reach. Lots of the women and girls was crying and taking on, scared most to death.

They swarmed up in front of Sherburn's palings as thick as they could jam together, and you couldn't hear yourself think for the noise. It was a little twenty-foot yard. Some sung out "Tear down the fence! tear down the fence!" Then there was a racket of ripping and tearing and smashing, and down she goes, and the front wall of the crowd begins to roll in like a wave.

Just then Sherburn steps out on to the roof of his little front porch, with a double-barrel gun in his hand, and takes his stand, perfectly ca'm and deliberate, not saying a word. The racket stopped, and the wave sucked back.

Sherburn never said a word—just stood there, looking down. The stillness was awful creepy and uncomfortable. Sherburn run his eye slow along the crowd; and wherever it struck the people tried a little to out-gaze him, but they couldn't; they dropped their eyes and looked sneaky. Then pretty soon Sherburn sort of laughed; not the pleasant kind, but the kind that makes you feel like when you are eating bread that's got sand in it.

Then he says, slow and scornful:

"The idea of YOU lynching anybody! It's amusing. The idea of you thinking you had pluck enough to lynch a MAN! Because you're brave enough to tar and feather poor friendless cast-out women that come along here, did that make you think you had grit enough to lay your hands on a MAN? Why, a MAN'S safe in the hands of ten thousand of your kind—as long as it's daytime and you're not behind him.

"Do I know you? I know you clear through was born and raised in the South, and I've lived in the North; so I know the average all around. The average man's a coward. In the North he lets anybody walk over him that wants to, and goes home and prays for a humble spirit to bear it. In the South one man all by himself, has stopped a stage full of men in the daytime, and robbed the lot. Your newspapers call you a brave people so much that you think you are braver than any other people—whereas you're just AS brave, and no braver. Why don't your juries hang murderers? Because they're afraid the man's friends will shoot them in the back, in the dark—and it's just what they WOULD do.

"So they always acquit; and then a MAN goes in the night, with a hundred masked cowards at his back and lynches the rascal. Your mistake is, that you didn't bring a man with you; that's one mistake, and the other is that you didn't come in the dark and fetch your masks. You brought PART of a man—Buck Harkness, there—and if you hadn't had him to start you, you'd a taken it out in blowing.

"You didn't want to come. The average man don't like trouble and danger. YOU don't like trouble and danger. But if only HALF a man—like Buck Harkness, there—shouts 'Lynch him! lynch him!' you're afraid to back down—afraid you'll be found out to be what you are—COWARDS—and so you raise a yell, and hang yourselves on to that half-a-man's coat-tail, and come raging up here, swearing what big things you're going to do. The pitifulest thing out is a mob; that's what an army is—a mob; they don't fight with courage that's born in them, but with courage that's borrowed from their mass, and from their officers. But a mob without any MAN at the head of it is BENEATH pitifulness. Now the thing for YOU to do is to droop your tails and go home and crawl in a hole. If any real lynching's going to be done it will be done in the dark, Southern fashion; and when they come they'll bring their masks, and fetch a MAN along. Now LEAVE—and take your half-a-man with you"—tossing his gun up across his left arm and cocking it when he says this.

The crowd washed back sudden, and then broke all apart, and went tearing off every which way, and Buck Harkness he heeled it after them, looking tolerable cheap. I could a stayed if I wanted to, but I didn't want to.

I went to the circus and loafed around the back side till the watchman went by, and then dived in under the tent. I had my twenty-dollar gold piece and some other money, but I reckoned I better save it, because there ain't no telling how soon you are going to need it, away from home and amongst strangers that way. You can't be too careful. I ain't opposed to spending money on circuses when there ain't no other way, but there ain't no use in WASTING it on them.

It was a real bully circus. It was the splendidest sight that ever was when they all come riding in, two and two, a gentleman and lady, side by side, the men just in their drawers and undershirts, and no shoes nor stirrups, and resting their hands on their thighs easy and comfortable—there must a been twenty of them—and every lady with a lovely complexion, and perfectly beautiful, and looking just like a gang of real sure-enough queens, and dressed in clothes that cost millions of dollars, and just littered with diamonds. It was a powerful fine sight; I never see anything so lovely. And then one by one they got up and stood, and went a-weaving around the ring so gentle and wavy and graceful, the men looking ever so tall and airy and straight, with their heads bobbing and skimming along, away up there under the tent-roof, and every lady's rose-leafy dress flapping soft and silky around her hips, and she looking like the most loveliest parasol.

And then faster and faster they went, all of them dancing, first one foot out in the air and then the other, the horses leaning more and more, and the ringmaster going round and round the center-pole, cracking his whip and shouting "Hi!—hi!" and the clown cracking jokes behind him; and by and by all hands dropped the reins, and every lady put her knuckles on her hips and every gentleman folded his arms, and then how the horses did lean over and hump themselves! And so one after the other they all skipped off into the ring, and made the sweetest bow I ever see, and then scampered out, and everybody clapped their hands and went just about wild.

Well, all through the circus they done the most astonishing things; and all the time that clown carried on so it most killed the people. The ringmaster couldn't ever say a word to him but he was back at him quick as a wink with the funniest things a body ever said; and how he ever COULD think of so many of them, and so sudden and so pat, was what I couldn't noway understand. Why, I couldn't a thought of them in a year. And by and by a drunk man tried to get into the ring—said he wanted to ride; said he could ride as well as anybody that ever was. They argued and tried to keep him out, but he wouldn't listen, and the whole show come to a standstill. Then the people begun to holler at him and make fun of him, and that made him mad, and he begun to rip and tear; so that stirred up the people, and a lot of men begun to pile down off of the benches and swarm towards the ring, saying, "Knock him down! throw him out!" and one or two women begun to scream. So, then, the ringmaster he made a little speech, and said he hoped there wouldn't be no disturbance, and if the man would promise he wouldn't make no more trouble he would let him ride if he thought he could stay on the horse. So everybody laughed and said all right, and the man got on. The minute he was on, the horse begun to rip and tear and jump and cavort around, with two circus men hanging on to his bridle trying to hold him, and the drunk man hanging on to his neck, and his heels flying in the air every jump, and the whole crowd of people standing up shouting and laughing till tears rolled down. And at last, sure enough, all the circus men could do, the horse broke loose, and away he went like the very nation, round and round the ring, with that sot laying down on him and hanging to his neck, with first one leg hanging most to the ground on one side, and then t'other one on t'other side, and the people just crazy. It warn't funny to me, though; I was all of a tremble to see his danger. But pretty soon he struggled up astraddle and grabbed the bridle, a-reeling this way and that; and the next minute he sprung up and dropped the bridle and stood! and the horse a-going like a house afire too. He just stood up there, a-sailing around as easy and comfortable as if he warn't ever drunk in his life— and then he begun to pull off his clothes and sling them. He shed them so thick they kind of clogged up the air, and altogether he shed seventeen suits. And, then, there he was, slim and handsome, and dressed the gaudiest and prettiest you ever saw, and he lit into that horse with his whip and made him fairly hum—and finally skipped off, and made his bow and danced off to the dressing-room, and everybody just a-howling with pleasure and astonishment.

Then the ringmaster he see how he had been fooled, and he WAS the sickest ring-master you ever see, I reckon. Why, it was one of his own men! He had got up that joke all out of his own head, and never let on to nobody. Well, I felt sheepish enough to be took in so, but I wouldn't a been in that ringmaster's place, not for a thousand dollars. I don't know; there may be bullier circuses than what that one was, but I never struck them yet. Anyways, it was plenty good enough for ME; and wherever I run across it, it can have all of MY custom every time.

Well, that night we had OUR show; but there warn't only about twelve people there—just enough to pay expenses. And they laughed all the time, and that made the duke mad; and everybody left, anyway, before the show was over, but one boy which was asleep. So the duke said these Arkansaw lunkheads couldn't come up to Shakespeare; what they wanted was low comedy—and maybe something ruther worse than low comedy, he reckoned. He said he could size their style. So next morning he got some big sheets of wrapping paper and some black paint, and drawed off some handbills, and stuck them up all over the village. The bills said:

AT THE COURT HOUSE! FOR 3 NIGHTS ONLY!
The World-Renowned Tragedians
DAVID GARRICK THE YOUNGER!
AND EDMUND KEAN THE ELDER!
Of the London and
Continental Theatres,
In their Thrilling Tragedy of
THE KING'S CAMELEOPARD,
OR THE ROYAL NONESUCH ! ! !
Admission 50 cents.

Then at the bottom was the biggest line of all, which said:

LADIES AND CHILDREN NOT ADMITTED

"There," says he, "if that line don't fetch them, I don't know Arkansaw!"

Chapter XXIII

Well, all day him and the king was hard at it, rigging up a stage and a curtain and a row of candles for footlights; and that night the house was jam full of men in no time. When the place couldn't hold no more, the duke he quit tending door and went around the back way and come on to the stage and stood up before the curtain and made a little speech, and praised up this tragedy, and said it was the most thrillingest one that ever was; and so he went on a-bragging about the tragedy, and about Edmund Kean the Elder, which was to play the main principal part in it; and at last when he'd got everybody's expectations up high enough, he rolled up the curtain, and the next minute the king come a-prancing out on all fours, naked; and he was painted all over, ring-streaked-and- striped, all sorts of colors, as splendid as a rainbow. And—but never mind the rest of his outfit; it was just wild, but it was awful funny. The people most killed themselves laughing; and when the king got done capering and capered off behind the scenes, they roared and clapped and stormed and haw-hawed till he come back and done it over again, and after that they made him do it another time. Well, it would make a cow laugh to see the shines that old idiot cut.

Then the duke he lets the curtain down, and bows to the people, and says the great tragedy will be performed only two nights more, on accounts of pressing London engagements, where the seats is all sold already for it in Drury Lane; and then he makes them another bow, and says if he has succeeded in pleasing them and instructing them, he will be deeply obleeged if they will mention it to their friends and get them to come and see it.

Twenty people sings out:

"What, is it over? Is that ALL?"

The duke says yes. Then there was a fine time. Everybody sings out, "Sold!" and rose up mad, and was a-going for that stage and them tragedians. But a big, fine looking man jumps up on a bench and shouts:

"Hold on! Just a word, gentlemen." They stopped to listen. "We are sold—mighty badly sold. But we don't want to be the laughing stock of this whole town, I reckon, and never hear the last of this thing as long as we live. NO. What we want is to go out of here quiet, and talk this show up, and sell the REST of the town! Then we'll all be in the same boat. Ain't that sensible?" ("You bet it is!—the jedge is right!" everybody sings out.) "All right, then—not a word about any sell. Go along home, and advise everybody to come and see the tragedy."

Next day you couldn't hear nothing around that town but how splendid that show was. House was jammed again that night, and we sold this crowd the same way. When me and the king and the duke got home to the raft we all had a supper; and by and by, about midnight, they made Jim and me back her out and float her down the middle of the river, and fetch her in and hide her about two mile below town.

The third night the house was crammed again—and they warn't new-comers this time, but people that was at the show the other two nights. I stood by the duke at the door, and I see that every man that went in had his pockets bulging, or something muffled up under his coat—and I see it warn't no perfumery, neither, not by a long sight. I smelt sickly eggs by the barrel, and rotten cabbages, and such things; and if I know the signs of a dead cat being around, and I bet I do, there was sixty-four of them went in. I shoved in there for a minute, but it was too various for me; I couldn't stand it. Well, when the place couldn't hold no more people the duke he give a fellow a quarter and told him to tend door for him a minute, and then he started around for the stage door, I after him; but the minute we turned the corner and was in the dark he says:

"Walk fast now till you get away from the houses, and then shin for the raft like the dickens was after you!"

I done it, and he done the same. We struck the raft at the same time, and in less than two seconds we was gliding down stream, all dark and still, and edging towards the middle of the river, nobody saying a word. I reckoned the poor king was in for a gaudy time of it with the audience, but nothing of the sort; pretty soon he crawls out from under the wigwam, and says:

"Well, how'd the old thing pan out this time, duke?" He hadn't been up-town at all.

We never showed a light till we was about ten mile below the village. Then we lit up and had a supper, and the king and the duke fairly laughed their bones loose over the way they'd served them people. The duke says:

"Greenhorns, flatheads! I knew the first house would keep mum and let the rest of the town get roped in; and I knew they'd lay for us the third night, and consider it was THEIR turn now. Well, it IS their turn, and I'd give something to know how much they'd take for it. I WOULD just like to know how they're putting in their opportunity. They can turn it into a picnic if they want to—they brought plenty provisions."

Them rapscallions took in four hundred and sixty-five dollars in that three nights. I never see money hauled in by the wagon-load like that before. By and by, when they was asleep and snoring, Jim says:

"Don't it s'prise you de way dem kings carries on, Huck?"

"No," I says, "it don't."

"Why don't it, Huck?"

"Well, it don't, because it's in the breed. I reckon they're all alike,"

"But, Huck, dese kings o' ourn is reglar rapscallions; dat's jist what dey is; dey's reglar rapscallions."

"Well, that's what I'm a-saying; all kings is mostly rapscallions, as fur as I can make out."

"Is dat so?"

"You read about them once—you'll see. Look at Henry the Eight; this 'n 's a Sunday-school Superintendent to HIM. And look at Charles Second, and Louis Fourteen, and Louis Fifteen, and James Second, and Edward Second, and Richard Third, and forty more; besides all them Saxon heptarchies that used to rip around so in old times and raise Cain. My, you ought to seen old Henry the Eight when he was in bloom. He WAS a blossom. He used to marry a new wife every day, and chop off her head next morning. And he would do it just as indifferent as if he was ordering up eggs. 'Fetch up Nell Gwynn,' he says. They fetch her up. Next morning, 'Chop off her head!' And they chop it off. 'Fetch up Jane Shore,' he says; and up she comes, Next morning, 'Chop off her head'—and they chop it off. 'Ring up Fair Rosamun.' Fair Rosamun answers the bell. Next morning, 'Chop off her head.' And he made every one of them tell him a tale every night; and he kept that up till he had hogged a thousand and one tales that way, and then he put them all in a book, and called it Domesday Book—which was a good name and stated the case. You don't know kings, Jim, but I know them; and this old rip of ourn is one of the cleanest I've struck in history. Well, Henry he takes a notion he wants to get up some trouble with this country. How does he go at it—give notice?—give the country a show? No. All of a sudden he heaves all the tea in Boston Harbor overboard, and whacks out a declaration of independence, and dares them to come on. That was HIS style—he never give anybody a chance. He had suspicions of his father, the Duke of Wellington. Well, what did he do? Ask him to show up? No—drownded him in a butt of mamsey, like a cat. S'pose people left money laying around where he was—what did he do? He collared it. S'pose he contracted to do a thing, and you paid him, and didn't set down there and see that he done it—what did he do? He always done the other thing. S'pose he opened his mouth—what then? If he didn't shut it up powerful quick he'd lose a lie every time. That's the kind of a bug Henry was; and if we'd a had him along 'stead of our kings he'd a fooled that town a heap worse than ourn done. I don't say that ourn is lambs, because they ain't, when you come right down to the cold facts; but they ain't nothing to THAT old ram, anyway. All I say is, kings is kings, and you got to make allowances. Take them all around, they're a mighty ornery lot. It's the way they're raised."

"But dis one do SMELL so like de nation, Huck."

"Well, they all do, Jim. We can't help the way a king smells; history don't tell no way."

"Now de duke, he's a tolerble likely man in some ways."

"Yes, a duke's different. But not very different. This one's a middling hard lot for a duke. When he's drunk there ain't no near-sighted man could tell him from a king."

"Well, anyways, I doan' hanker for no mo' un um, Huck. Dese is all I kin stan'."

"It's the way I feel, too, Jim. But we've got them on our hands, and we got to remember what they are, and make allowances. Sometimes I wish we could hear of a country that's out of kings."

What was the use to tell Jim these warn't real kings and dukes? It wouldn't a done no good; and, besides, it was just as I said: you couldn't tell them from the real kind.

I went to sleep, and Jim didn't call me when it was my turn. He often done that. When I waked up just at daybreak he was sitting there with his head down betwixt his knees, moaning and mourning to himself. I didn't take notice nor let on. I knowed what it was about. He was thinking about his wife and his children, away up yonder, and he was low and homesick; because he hadn't ever been away from home before in his life; and I do believe he cared just as much for his people as white folks does for their'n. It don't seem natural, but I reckon it's so. He was often moaning and mourning that way nights, when he judged I was asleep, and saying, "Po' little 'Lizabeth! po' little Johnny! it's mighty hard; I spec' I ain't ever gwyne to see you no mo', no mo'!" He was a mighty good nigger, Jim was.

But this time I somehow got to talking to him about his wife and young ones; and by and by he says:

"What makes me feel so bad dis time 'uz bekase I hear sumpn over yonder on de bank like a whack, er a slam, while ago, en it mine me er de time I treat my little 'Lizabeth so ornery. She warn't on'y 'bout fo' year ole, en she tuck de sk'yarlet fever, en had a powful rough spell; but she got well, en one day she was a-stannin' aroun', en I says to her, I says: 'Shet de do'.'

"She never done it; jis' stood dah, kiner smilin' up at me. It make me mad; en I says agin, mighty loud, I says:

"'Doan' you hear me? Shet de do'!'

"She jis stood de same way, kiner smilin' up. I was a-bilin'! I says:

"'I lay I MAKE you mine!'

"En wid dat I fetch' her a slap side de head dat sont her a-sprawlin'. Den I went into de yuther room, en 'uz gone 'bout ten minutes; en when I come back dah was dat do' a-stannin' open yit, en dat chile stannin' mos' right in it, a-lookin' down and mournin', en de tears runnin' down. My, but I wuz mad! I was a-gwyne for de chile, but jis' den—it was a do' dat open innerds—jis' den, 'long come de wind en slam it to, behine de chile, ker-blam!—en my lan', de chile never move'! My breff mos' hop outer me; en I feel so—so—I doan' know HOW I feel. I crope out, all a-tremblin', en crope aroun' en open de do' easy en slow, en poke my head in behine de chile, sof' en still, en all uv a sudden I says POW! jis' as loud as I could yell. SHE NEVER BUDGE! Oh, Huck, I bust out a-cryin' en grab her up in my arms, en say, 'Oh, de po' little thing! De Lord God Amighty fogive po' ole Jim, kaze he never gwyne to fogive hisself as long's he live!' Oh, she was plumb deef en dumb, Huck, plumb deef en dumb—en I'd ben a-treat'n her so!"

Chapter XXIV

Next day, towards night, we laid up under a little willow towhead out in the middle, where there was a village on each side of the river, and the duke and the king begun to lay out a plan for working them towns. Jim he spoke to the duke, and said he hoped it wouldn't take but a few hours, because it got mighty heavy and tiresome to him when he had to lay all day in the wigwam tied with the rope. You see, when we left him all alone we had to tie him, because if anybody happened on to him all by himself and not tied it wouldn't look much like he was a runaway nigger, you know. So the duke said it kind of hard to have to lay roped all day, and he'd cipher out some way to get around it.

He was uncommon bright, the duke was, and he soon struck it. He dressed Jim up in King Lear's outfit—it was a long curtain-calico gown, and a white horse-hair wig and whiskers; and then he took his theater paint and painted Jim's face and hands and ears and neck all over a dead, dull, solid blue, like a man that's been drownded nine days. Blamed if he warn't the horriblest looking outrage I ever see. Then the duke took and wrote out a sign on a shingle so:

Sick Arab
—but harmless when not
out of his head.

And he nailed that shingle to a lath, and stood the lath up four or five foot in front of the wigwam. Jim was satisfied. He said it was a sight better than lying tied a couple of years every day, and trembling all over every time there was a sound. The duke told him to make himself free and easy, and if anybody ever come meddling around, he must hop out of the wigwam, and carry on a little, and fetch a howl or two like a wild beast, and he reckoned they would light out and leave him alone. Which was sound enough judgment; but you take the average man, and he wouldn't wait for him to howl. Why, he didn't only look like he was dead, he looked considerable more than that.

These rapscallions wanted to try the Nonesuch again, because there was so much money in it, but they judged it wouldn't be safe, because maybe the news might a worked along down by this time. They couldn't hit no project that suited exactly; so at last the duke said he reckoned he'd lay off and work his brains an hour or two and see if he couldn't put up something on the Arkansaw village; and the king he allowed he would drop over to t'other village without any plan, but just trust in Providence to lead him the profitable way—meaning the devil, I reckon. We had all bought store clothes where we stopped last; and now the king put his'n on, and he told me to put mine on. I done it, of course. The king's duds was all black, and he did look real swell and starchy. I never knowed how clothes could change a body before. Why, before, he looked like the orneriest old rip that ever was; but now, when he'd take off his new white beaver and make a bow and do a smile, he looked that grand and good and pious that you'd say he had walked right out of the ark, and maybe was old Leviticus himself. Jim cleaned up the canoe, and I got my paddle ready. There was a big steamboat laying at the shore away up under the point, about three mile above the town—been there a couple of hours, taking on freight. Says the king:

"Seein' how I'm dressed, I reckon maybe I better arrive down from St. Louis or Cincinnati, or some other big place. Go for the steamboat, Huckleberry; we'll come down to the village on her."

I didn't have to be ordered twice to go and take a steamboat ride. I fetched the shore a half a mile above the village, and then went scooting along the bluff bank in the easy water. Pretty soon we come to a nice innocent-looking young country jake setting on a log swabbing the sweat off of his face, for it was powerful warm weather; and he had a couple of big carpet-bags by him.

"Run her nose in shore," says the king. I done it. "Wher' you bound for, young man?"

"For the steamboat; going to Orleans."

"Git aboard," says the king. "Hold on a minute, my servant 'll he'p you with them bags. Jump out and he'p the gentleman, Adolphus"—meaning me, I see.

I done so, and then we all three started on again. The young chap was mighty thankful; said it was tough work toting his baggage such weather. He asked the king where he was going, and the king told him he'd come down the river and landed at the other village this morning, and now he was going up a few mile to see an old friend on a farm up there. The young fellow says:

"When I first see you I says to myself, 'It's Mr. Wilks, sure, and he come mighty near getting here in time.' But then I says again, 'No, I reckon it ain't him, or else he wouldn't be paddling up the river.' You AIN'T him, are you?"

"No, my name's Blodgett—Elexander Blodgett—REVEREND Elexander Blodgett, I s'pose I must say, as I'm one o' the Lord's poor servants. But still I'm jist as able to be sorry for Mr. Wilks for not arriving in time, all the same, if he's missed anything by it—which I hope he hasn't."

"Well, he don't miss any property by it, because he'll get that all right; but he's missed seeing his brother Peter die—which he mayn't mind, nobody can tell as to that—but his brother would a give anything in this world to see HIM before he died; never talked about nothing else all these three weeks; hadn't seen him since they was boys together—and hadn't ever seen his brother William at all—that's the deef and dumb one—William ain't more than thirty or thirty-five. Peter and George were the only ones that come out here; George was the married brother; him and his wife both died last year. Harvey and William's the only ones that's left now; and, as I was saying, they haven't got here in time."

"Did anybody send 'em word?"

"Oh, yes; a month or two ago, when Peter was first took; because Peter said then that he sorter felt like he warn't going to get well this time. You see, he was pretty old, and George's g'yirls was too young to be much company for him, except Mary Jane, the red-headed one; and so he was kinder lonesome after George and his wife died, and didn't seem to care much to live. He most desperately wanted to see Harvey—and William, too, for that matter—because he was one of them kind that can't bear to make a will. He left a letter behind for Harvey, and said he'd told in it where his money was hid, and how he wanted the rest of the property divided up so George's g'yirls would be all right—for George didn't leave nothing. And that letter was all they could get him to put a pen to."

"Why do you reckon Harvey don't come? Wher' does he live?"

"Oh, he lives in England—Sheffield—preaches there—hasn't ever been in this country. He hasn't had any too much time—and besides he mightn't a got the letter at all, you know."

"Too bad, too bad he couldn't a lived to see his brothers, poor soul. You going to Orleans, you say?"

"Yes, but that ain't only a part of it. I'm going in a ship, next Wednesday, for Ryo Janeero, where my uncle lives."

"It's a pretty long journey. But it'll be lovely; wisht I was a-going. Is Mary Jane the oldest? How old is the others?"

"Mary Jane's nineteen, Susan's fifteen, and Joanna's about fourteen —that's the one that gives herself to good works and has a hare-lip."

"Poor things! to be left alone in the cold world so."

"Well, they could be worse off. Old Peter had friends, and they ain't going to let them come to no harm. There's Hobson, the Babtis' preacher; and Deacon Lot Hovey, and Ben Rucker, and Abner Shackleford, and Levi Bell, the lawyer; and Dr. Robinson, and their wives, and the widow Bartley, and—well, there's a lot of them; but these are the ones that Peter was thickest with, and used to write about sometimes, when he wrote home; so Harvey 'll know where to look for friends when he gets here."

Well, the old man went on asking questions till he just fairly emptied that young fellow. Blamed if he didn't inquire about everybody and everything in that blessed town, and all about the Wilkses; and about Peter's business—which was a tanner; and about George's—which was a carpenter; and about Harvey's—which was a dissentering minister; and so on, and so on. Then he says:

"What did you want to walk all the way up to the steamboat for?"

"Because she's a big Orleans boat, and I was afeard she mightn't stop there. When they're deep they won't stop for a hail. A Cincinnati boat will, but this is a St. Louis one."

"Was Peter Wilks well off?"

"Oh, yes, pretty well off. He had houses and land, and it's reckoned he left three or four thousand in cash hid up som'ers."

"When did you say he died?"

"I didn't say, but it was last night."

"Funeral to-morrow, likely?"

"Yes, 'bout the middle of the day."

"Well, it's all terrible sad; but we've all got to go, one time or another. So what we want to do is to be prepared; then we're all right."

"Yes, sir, it's the best way. Ma used to always say that."

When we struck the boat she was about done loading, and pretty soon she got off. The king never said nothing about going aboard, so I lost my ride, after all. When the boat was gone the king made me paddle up another mile to a lonesome place, and then he got ashore and says:

"Now hustle back, right off, and fetch the duke up here, and the new carpet-bags. And if he's gone over to t'other side, go over there and git him. And tell him to git himself up regardless. Shove along, now."

I see what HE was up to; but I never said nothing, of course. When I got back with the duke we hid the canoe, and then they set down on a log, and the king told him everything, just like the young fellow had said it —every last word of it. And all the time he was a-doing it he tried to talk like an Englishman; and he done it pretty well, too, for a slouch. I can't imitate him, and so I ain't a-going to try to; but he really done it pretty good. Then he says:

"How are you on the deef and dumb, Bilgewater?"

The duke said, leave him alone for that; said he had played a deef and dumb person on the histronic boards. So then they waited for a steamboat.

About the middle of the afternoon a couple of little boats come along, but they didn't come from high enough up the river; but at last there was a big one, and they hailed her. She sent out her yawl, and we went aboard, and she was from Cincinnati; and when they found we only wanted to go four or five mile they was booming mad, and gave us a cussing, and said they wouldn't land us. But the king was ca'm. He says:

"If gentlemen kin afford to pay a dollar a mile apiece to be took on and put off in a yawl, a steamboat kin afford to carry 'em, can't it?"

So they softened down and said it was all right; and when we got to the village they yawled us ashore. About two dozen men flocked down when they see the yawl a-coming, and when the king says:

"Kin any of you gentlemen tell me wher' Mr. Peter Wilks lives?" they give a glance at one another, and nodded their heads, as much as to say, "What d' I tell you?"

Then one of them says, kind of soft and gentle:

"I'm sorry sir, but the best we can do is to tell you where he DID live yesterday evening."

Sudden as winking the ornery old cretur went an to smash, and fell up against the man, and put his chin on his shoulder, and cried down his back, and says:

"Alas, alas, our poor brother—gone, and we never got to see him; oh, it's too, too hard!"

Then he turns around, blubbering, and makes a lot of idiotic signs to the duke on his hands, and blamed if he didn't drop a carpet-bag and bust out a-crying. If they warn't the beatenest lot, them two frauds, that ever I struck.

Well, the men gathered around and sympathized with them, and said all sorts of kind things to them, and carried their carpet-bags up the hill for them, and let them lean on them and cry, and told the king all about his brother's last moments, and the king he told it all over again on his hands to the duke, and both of them took on about that dead tanner like they'd lost the twelve disciples. Well, if ever I struck anything like it, I'm a nigger. It was enough to make a body ashamed of the human race.

Chapter XXV

The news was all over town in two minutes, and you could see the people tearing down on the run from every which way, some of them putting on their coats as they come. Pretty soon we was in the middle of a crowd, and the noise of the tramping was like a soldier march. The windows and dooryards was full; and every minute somebody would say, over a fence:

"Is it THEM?"

And somebody trotting along with the gang would answer back and say:

"You bet it is."

When we got to the house the street in front of it was packed, and the three girls was standing in the door. Mary Jane WAS red-headed, but that don't make no difference, she was most awful beautiful, and her face and her eyes was all lit up like glory, she was so glad her uncles was come. The king he spread his arms, and Mary Jane she jumped for them, and the hare-lip jumped for the duke, and there they HAD it! Everybody most, leastways women, cried for joy to see them meet again at last and have such good times.

Then the king he hunched the duke private—I see him do it—and then he looked around and see the coffin, over in the corner on two chairs; so then him and the duke, with a hand across each other's shoulder, and t'other hand to their eyes, walked slow and solemn over there, everybody dropping back to give them room, and all the talk and noise stopping, people saying "Sh!" and all the men taking their hats off and drooping their heads, so you could a heard a pin fall. And when they got there they bent over and looked in the coffin, and took one sight, and then they bust out a-crying so you could a heard them to Orleans, most; and then they put their arms around each other's necks, and hung their chins over each other's shoulders; and then for three minutes, or maybe four, I never see two men leak the way they done. And, mind you, everybody was doing the same; and the place was that damp I never see anything like it. Then one of them got on one side of the coffin, and t'other on t'other side, and they kneeled down and rested their foreheads on the coffin, and let on to pray all to themselves. Well, when it come to that it worked the crowd like you never see anything like it, and everybody broke down and went to sobbing right out loud—the poor girls, too; and every woman, nearly, went up to the girls, without saying a word, and kissed them, solemn, on the forehead, and then put their hand on their head, and looked up towards the sky, with the tears running down, and then busted out and went off sobbing and swabbing, and give the next woman a show. I never see anything so disgusting.

Well, by and by the king he gets up and comes forward a little, and works himself up and slobbers out a speech, all full of tears and flapdoodle about its being a sore trial for him and his poor brother to lose the diseased, and to miss seeing diseased alive after the long journey of four thousand mile, but it's a trial that's sweetened and sanctified to us by this dear sympathy and these holy tears, and so he thanks them out of his heart and out of his brother's heart, because out of their mouths they can't, words being too weak and cold, and all that kind of rot and slush, till it was just sickening; and then he blubbers out a pious goody-goody Amen, and turns himself loose and goes to crying fit to bust.

And the minute the words were out of his mouth somebody over in the crowd struck up the doxolojer, and everybody joined in with all their might, and it just warmed you up and made you feel as good as church letting out. Music is a good thing; and after all that soul-butter and hogwash I never see it freshen up things so, and sound so honest and bully.

Then the king begins to work his jaw again, and says how him and his nieces would be glad if a few of the main principal friends of the family would take supper here with them this evening, and help set up with the ashes of the diseased; and says if his poor brother laying yonder could speak he knows who he would name, for they was names that was very dear to him, and mentioned often in his letters; and so he will name the same, to wit, as follows, vizz.:—Rev. Mr. Hobson, and Deacon Lot Hovey, and Mr. Ben Rucker, and Abner Shackleford, and Levi Bell, and Dr. Robinson, and their wives, and the widow Bartley.

Rev. Hobson and Dr. Robinson was down to the end of the town a-hunting together—that is, I mean the doctor was shipping a sick man to t'other world, and the preacher was pinting him right. Lawyer Bell was away up to Louisville on business. But the rest was on hand, and so they all come and shook hands with the king and thanked him and talked to him; and then they shook hands with the duke and didn't say nothing, but just kept a-smiling and bobbing their heads like a passel of sapheads whilst he made all sorts of signs with his hands and said "Goo-goo—goo-goo-goo" all the time, like a baby that can't talk.

So the king he blattered along, and managed to inquire about pretty much everybody and dog in town, by his name, and mentioned all sorts of little things that happened one time or another in the town, or to George's family, or to Peter. And he always let on that Peter wrote him the things; but that was a lie: he got every blessed one of them out of that young flathead that we canoed up to the steamboat.

Then Mary Jane she fetched the letter her father left behind, and the king he read it out loud and cried over it. It give the dwelling-house and three thousand dollars, gold, to the girls; and it give the tanyard (which was doing a good business), along with some other houses and land (worth about seven thousand), and three thousand dollars in gold to Harvey and William, and told where the six thousand cash was hid down cellar. So these two frauds said they'd go and fetch it up, and have everything square and above-board; and told me to come with a candle. We shut the cellar door behind us, and when they found the bag they spilt it out on the floor, and it was a lovely sight, all them yaller-boys. My, the way the king's eyes did shine! He slaps the duke on the shoulder and says:

"Oh, THIS ain't bully nor noth'n! Oh, no, I reckon not! Why, Billy, it beats the Nonesuch, DON'T it?"

The duke allowed it did. They pawed the yaller-boys, and sifted them through their fingers and let them jingle down on the floor; and the king says:

"It ain't no use talkin'; bein' brothers to a rich dead man and representatives of furrin heirs that's got left is the line for you and me, Bilge. Thish yer comes of trust'n to Providence. It's the best way, in the long run. I've tried 'em all, and ther' ain't no better way."

Most everybody would a been satisfied with the pile, and took it on trust; but no, they must count it. So they counts it, and it comes out four hundred and fifteen dollars short. Says the king:

"Dern him, I wonder what he done with that four hundred and fifteen dollars?"

They worried over that awhile, and ransacked all around for it. Then the duke says:

"Well, he was a pretty sick man, and likely he made a mistake—I reckon that's the way of it. The best way's to let it go, and keep still about it. We can spare it."

"Oh, shucks, yes, we can SPARE it. I don't k'yer noth'n 'bout that—it's the COUNT I'm thinkin' about. We want to be awful square and open and above-board here, you know. We want to lug this h-yer money up stairs and count it before everybody—then ther' ain't noth'n suspicious. But when the dead man says ther's six thous'n dollars, you know, we don't want to—"

"Hold on," says the duke. "Le's make up the deffisit," and he begun to haul out yaller-boys out of his pocket.

"It's a most amaz'n' good idea, duke—you HAVE got a rattlin' clever head on you," says the king. "Blest if the old Nonesuch ain't a heppin' us out agin," and HE begun to haul out yaller-jackets and stack them up.

It most busted them, but they made up the six thousand clean and clear.

"Say," says the duke, "I got another idea. Le's go up stairs and count this money, and then take and GIVE IT TO THE GIRLS."

"Good land, duke, lemme hug you! It's the most dazzling idea 'at ever a man struck. You have cert'nly got the most astonishin' head I ever see. Oh, this is the boss dodge, ther' ain't no mistake 'bout it. Let 'em fetch along their suspicions now if they want to—this 'll lay 'em out."

When we got up-stairs everybody gethered around the table, and the king he counted it and stacked it up, three hundred dollars in a pile—twenty elegant little piles. Everybody looked hungry at it, and licked their chops. Then they raked it into the bag again, and I see the king begin to swell himself up for another speech. He says:

"Friends all, my poor brother that lays yonder has done generous by them that's left behind in the vale of sorrers. He has done generous by these yer poor little lambs that he loved and sheltered, and that's left fatherless and motherless. Yes, and we that knowed him knows that he would a done MORE generous by 'em if he hadn't ben afeard o' woundin' his dear William and me. Now, WOULDN'T he? Ther' ain't no question 'bout it in MY mind. Well, then, what kind o' brothers would it be that 'd stand in his way at sech a time? And what kind o' uncles would it be that 'd rob—yes, ROB—sech poor sweet lambs as these 'at he loved so at sech a time? If I know William—and I THINK I do—he—well, I'll jest ask him."

He turns around and begins to make a lot of signs to the duke with his hands, and the duke he looks at him stupid and leather-headed a while; then all of a sudden he seems to catch his meaning, and jumps for the king, goo-gooing with all his might for joy, and hugs him about fifteen times before he lets up. Then the king says, "I knowed it; I reckon THAT'LL convince anybody the way HE feels about it. Here, Mary Jane, Susan, Joanner, take the money—take it ALL. It's the gift of him that lays yonder, cold but joyful."

Mary Jane she went for him, Susan and the hare-lip went for the duke, and then such another hugging and kissing I never see yet. And everybody crowded up with the tears in their eyes, and most shook the hands off of them frauds, saying all the time:

"You DEAR good souls!—how LOVELY!—how COULD you!"

Well, then, pretty soon all hands got to talking about the diseased again, and how good he was, and what a loss he was, and all that; and before long a big iron-jawed man worked himself in there from outside, and stood a-listening and looking, and not saying anything; and nobody saying anything to him either, because the king was talking and they was all busy listening. The king was saying—in the middle of something he'd started in on—

"—they bein' partickler friends o' the diseased. That's why they're invited here this evenin'; but tomorrow we want ALL to come—everybody; for he respected everybody, he liked everybody, and so it's fitten that his funeral orgies sh'd be public."

And so he went a-mooning on and on, liking to hear himself talk, and every little while he fetched in his funeral orgies again, till the duke he couldn't stand it no more; so he writes on a little scrap of paper, "OBSEQUIES, you old fool," and folds it up, and goes to goo-gooing and reaching it over people's heads to him. The king he reads it and puts it in his pocket, and says:

"Poor William, afflicted as he is, his HEART'S aluz right. Asks me to invite everybody to come to the funeral—wants me to make 'em all welcome. But he needn't a worried—it was jest what I was at."

Then he weaves along again, perfectly ca'm, and goes to dropping in his funeral orgies again every now and then, just like he done before. And when he done it the third time he says:

"I say orgies, not because it's the common term, because it ain't —obsequies bein' the common term—but because orgies is the right term. Obsequies ain't used in England no more now—it's gone out. We say orgies now in England. Orgies is better, because it means the thing you're after more exact. It's a word that's made up out'n the Greek ORGO, outside, open, abroad; and the Hebrew JEESUM, to plant, cover up; hence inTER. So, you see, funeral orgies is an open er public funeral."

He was the WORST I ever struck. Well, the iron-jawed man he laughed right in his face. Everybody was shocked. Everybody says, "Why, DOCTOR!" and Abner Shackleford says:

"Why, Robinson, hain't you heard the news? This is Harvey Wilks."

The king he smiled eager, and shoved out his flapper, and says:

"Is it my poor brother's dear good friend and physician? I—"

"Keep your hands off of me!" says the doctor. "YOU talk like an Englishman, DON'T you? It's the worst imitation I ever heard. YOU Peter Wilks's brother! You're a fraud, that's what you are!"

Well, how they all took on! They crowded around the doctor and tried to quiet him down, and tried to explain to him and tell him how Harvey 'd showed in forty ways that he WAS Harvey, and knowed everybody by name, and the names of the very dogs, and begged and BEGGED him not to hurt Harvey's feelings and the poor girl's feelings, and all that. But it warn't no use; he stormed right along, and said any man that pretended to be an Englishman and couldn't imitate the lingo no better than what he did was a fraud and a liar. The poor girls was hanging to the king and crying; and all of a sudden the doctor ups and turns on THEM. He says:

"I was your father's friend, and I'm your friend; and I warn you as a friend, and an honest one that wants to protect you and keep you out of harm and trouble, to turn your backs on that scoundrel and have nothing to do with him, the ignorant tramp, with his idiotic Greek and Hebrew, as he calls it. He is the thinnest kind of an impostor—has come here with a lot of empty names and facts which he picked up somewheres, and you take them for PROOFS, and are helped to fool yourselves by these foolish friends here, who ought to know better. Mary Jane Wilks, you know me for your friend, and for your unselfish friend, too. Now listen to me; turn this pitiful rascal out—I BEG you to do it. Will you?"

Mary Jane straightened herself up, and my, but she was handsome! She says:

"HERE is my answer." She hove up the bag of money and put it in the king's hands, and says, "Take this six thousand dollars, and invest for me and my sisters any way you want to, and don't give us no receipt for it."

Then she put her arm around the king on one side, and Susan and the hare-lip done the same on the other. Everybody clapped their hands and stomped on the floor like a perfect storm, whilst the king held up his head and smiled proud. The doctor says:

"All right; I wash MY hands of the matter. But I warn you all that a time 's coming when you're going to feel sick whenever you think of this day." And away he went.

"All right, doctor," says the king, kinder mocking him; "we'll try and get 'em to send for you;" which made them all laugh, and they said it was a prime good hit.

Chapter XXVI

Well, when they was all gone the king he asks Mary Jane how they was off for spare rooms, and she said she had one spare room, which would do for Uncle William, and she'd give her own room to Uncle Harvey, which was a little bigger, and she would turn into the room with her sisters and sleep on a cot; and up garret was a little cubby, with a pallet in it. The king said the cubby would do for his valley— meaning me.

So Mary Jane took us up, and she showed them their rooms, which was plain but nice. She said she'd have her frocks and a lot of other traps took out of her room if they was in Uncle Harvey's way, but he said they warn't. The frocks was hung along the wall, and before them was a curtain made out of calico that hung down to the floor. There was an old hair trunk in one corner, and a guitar-box in another, and all sorts of little knickknacks and jimcracks around, like girls brisken up a room with. The king said it was all the more homely and more pleasanter fo these fixings, and so don't disturb them. The duke's room was pretty small, but plenty good enough, and so was my cubby.

That night they had a big supper, and all them men and women was there, and I stood behind the king and the duke's chairs and waited on them, and the niggers waited on the rest. Mary Jane she set at the head of the table, with Susan alongside of her, and said how bad the biscuits was, and how mean the preserves was, and how ornery and tough the fried chickens was—and all that kind of rot, the way women always do for to force out compliments; and the people all knowed everything was tiptop, and said so—said "How DO you get biscuits to brown so nice?" and "Where, for the land's sake, DID you get these amaz'n pickles?" and all that kind of humbug talky-talk, just the way people always does at a supper, you know.

And when it was all done me and the hare-lip had supper in the kitchen off of the leavings, whilst the others was helping the niggers clean up the things. The hare-lip she got to pumping me about England, and blest if I didn't think the ice was getting mighty thin sometimes. She says:

"Did you ever see the king?"

"Who? William Fourth? Well, I bet I have—he goes to our church." I knowed he was dead years ago, but I never let on. So when I says he goes to our church, she says:

"What—regular?"

"Yes—regular. His pew's right over opposite ourn—on t'other side the pulpit."

"I thought he lived in London?"

"Well, he does. Where WOULD he live?"

"But I thought YOU lived in Sheffield?"

I see I was up a stump. I had to let on to get choked with a chicken bone, so as to get time to think how to get down again. Then I says:

"I mean he goes to our church regular when he's in Sheffield. That's only in the summer time, when he comes there to take the sea baths."

"Why, how you talk—Sheffield ain't on the sea."

"Well, who said it was?"

"Why, you did."

"I DIDN'T nuther."

"You did!"

"I didn't."

"You did."

"I never said nothing of the kind."

"Well, what DID you say, then?"

"Said he come to take the sea BATHS—that's what I said."

"Well, then, how's he going to take the sea baths if it ain't on the sea?"

"Looky here," I says; "did you ever see any Congress-water?"

"Yes."

"Well, did you have to go to Congress to get it?"

"Why, no."

"Well, neither does William Fourth have to go to the sea to get a sea bath."

"How does he get it, then?"

"Gets it the way people down here gets Congress-water—in barrels. There in the palace at Sheffield they've got furnaces, and he wants his water hot. They can't bile that amount of water away off there at the sea. They haven't got no conveniences for it."

"Oh, I see, now. You might a said that in the first place and saved time."

When she said that I see I was out of the woods again, and so I was comfortable and glad. Next, she says:

"Do you go to church, too?"

"Yes—regular."

"Where do you set?"

"Why, in our pew."

"WHOSE pew?"

"Why, OURN—your Uncle Harvey's."

"His'n? What does HE want with a pew?"

"Wants it to set in. What did you RECKON he wanted with it?"

"Why, I thought he'd be in the pulpit."

Rot him, I forgot he was a preacher. I see I was up a stump again, so I played another chicken bone and got another think. Then I says:

"Blame it, do you suppose there ain't but one preacher to a church?"

"Why, what do they want with more?"

"What!—to preach before a king? I never did see such a girl as you. They don't have no less than seventeen."

"Seventeen! My land! Why, I wouldn't set out such a string as that, not if I NEVER got to glory. It must take 'em a week."

"Shucks, they don't ALL of 'em preach the same day—only ONE of 'em."

"Well, then, what does the rest of 'em do?"

"Oh, nothing much. Loll around, pass the plate—and one thing or another. But mainly they don't do nothing."

"Well, then, what are they FOR?"

"Why, they're for STYLE. Don't you know nothing?"

"Well, I don't WANT to know no such foolishness as that. How is servants treated in England? Do they treat 'em better 'n we treat our niggers?"

"NO! A servant ain't nobody there. They treat them worse than dogs."

"Don't they give 'em holidays, the way we do, Christmas and New Year's week, and Fourth of July?"

"Oh, just listen! A body could tell YOU hain't ever been to England by that. Why, Hare-l—why, Joanna, they never see a holiday from year's end to year's end; never go to the circus, nor theater, nor nigger shows, nor nowheres."

"Nor church?"

"Nor church."

"But YOU always went to church."

Well, I was gone up again. I forgot I was the old man's servant. But next minute I whirled in on a kind of an explanation how a valley was different from a common servant and HAD to go to church whether he wanted to or not, and set with the family, on account of its being the law. But I didn't do it pretty good, and when I got done I see she warn't satisfied. She says:

"Honest injun, now, hain't you been telling me a lot of lies?"

"Honest injun," says I.

"None of it at all?"

"None of it at all. Not a lie in it," says I.

"Lay your hand on this book and say it."

I see it warn't nothing but a dictionary, so I laid my hand on it and said it. So then she looked a little better satisfied, and says:

"Well, then, I'll believe some of it; but I hope to gracious if I'll believe the rest."

"What is it you won't believe, Joe?" says Mary Jane, stepping in with Susan behind her. "It ain't right nor kind for you to talk so to him, and him a stranger and so far from his people. How would you like to be treated so?"

"That's always your way, Maim—always sailing in to help somebody before they're hurt. I hain't done nothing to him. He's told some stretchers, I reckon, and I said I wouldn't swallow it all; and that's every bit and grain I DID say. I reckon he can stand a little thing like that, can't he?"

"I don't care whether 'twas little or whether 'twas big; he's here in our house and a stranger, and it wasn't good of you to say it. If you was in his place it would make you feel ashamed; and so you oughtn't to say a thing to another person that will make THEM feel ashamed."

"Why, Maim, he said—"

"It don't make no difference what he SAID—that ain't the thing. The thing is for you to treat him KIND, and not be saying things to make him remember he ain't in his own country and amongst his own folks."

I says to myself, THIS is a girl that I'm letting that old reptle rob her of her money!

Then Susan SHE waltzed in; and if you'll believe me, she did give Hare-lip hark from the tomb!

Says I to myself, and this is ANOTHER one that I'm letting him rob her of her money!

Then Mary Jane she took another inning, and went in sweet and lovely again—which was her way; but when she got done there warn't hardly anything left o' poor Hare-lip. So she hollered.

"All right, then," says the other girls; "you just ask his pardon."

She done it, too; and she done it beautiful. She done it so beautiful it was good to hear; and I wished I could tell her a thousand lies, so she could do it again.

I says to myself, this is ANOTHER one that I'm letting him rob her of her money. And when she got through they all jest laid theirselves out to make me feel at home and know I was amongst friends. I felt so ornery and low down and mean that I says to myself, my mind's made up; I'll hive that money for them or bust.

So then I lit out—for bed, I said, meaning some time or another. When I got by myself I went to thinking the thing over. I says to myself, shall I go to that doctor, private, and blow on these frauds? No—that won't do. He might tell who told him; then the king and the duke would make it warm for me. Shall I go, private, and tell Mary Jane? No—I dasn't do it. Her face would give them a hint, sure; they've got the money, and they'd slide right out and get away with it. If she was to fetch in help I'd get mixed up in the business before it was done with, I judge. No; there ain't no good way but one. I got to steal that money, somehow; and I got to steal it some way that they won't suspicion that I done it. They've got a good thing here, and they ain't a-going to leave till they've played this family and this town for all they're worth, so I'll find a chance time enough. I'll steal it and hide it; and by and by, when I'm away down the river, I'll write a letter and tell Mary Jane where it's hid. But I better hive it tonight if I can, because the doctor maybe hasn't let up as much as he lets on he has; he might scare them out of here yet.

So, thinks I, I'll go and search them rooms. Upstairs the hall was dark, but I found the duke's room, and started to paw around it with my hands; but I recollected it wouldn't be much like the king to let anybody else take care of that money but his own self; so then I went to his room and begun to paw around there. But I see I couldn't do nothing without a candle, and I dasn't light one, of course. So I judged I'd got to do the other thing—lay for them and eavesdrop. About that time I hears their footsteps coming, and was going to skip under the bed; I reached for it, but it wasn't where I thought it would be; but I touched the curtain that hid Mary Jane's frocks, so I jumped in behind that and snuggled in amongst the gowns, and stood there perfectly still.

They come in and shut the door; and the first thing the duke done was to get down and look under the bed. Then I was glad I hadn't found the bed when I wanted it. And yet, you know, it's kind of natural to hide under the bed when you are up to anything private. They sets down then, and the king says:

"Well, what is it? And cut it middlin' short, because it's better for us to be down there a-whoopin' up the mournin' than up here givin' 'em a chance to talk us over."

"Well, this is it, Capet. I ain't easy; I ain't comfortable. That doctor lays on my mind. I wanted to know your plans. I've got a notion, and I think it's a sound one."

"What is it, duke?"

"That we better glide out of this before three in the morning, and clip it down the river with what we've got. Specially, seeing we got it so easy—GIVEN back to us, flung at our heads, as you may say, when of course we allowed to have to steal it back. I'm for knocking off and lighting out."

That made me feel pretty bad. About an hour or two ago it would a been a little different, but now it made me feel bad and disappointed, The king rips out and says:

"What! And not sell out the rest o' the property? March off like a passel of fools and leave eight or nine thous'n' dollars' worth o' property layin' around jest sufferin' to be scooped in?—and all good, salable stuff, too."

The duke he grumbled; said the bag of gold was enough, and he didn't want to go no deeper—didn't want to rob a lot of orphans of EVERYTHING they had.

"Why, how you talk!" says the king. "We sha'n't rob 'em of nothing at all but jest this money. The people that BUYS the property is the suff'rers; because as soon 's it's found out 'at we didn't own it—which won't be long after we've slid—the sale won't be valid, and it 'll all go back to the estate. These yer orphans 'll git their house back agin, and that's enough for THEM; they're young and spry, and k'n easy earn a livin'. THEY ain't a-goin to suffer. Why, jest think—there's thous'n's and thous'n's that ain't nigh so well off. Bless you, THEY ain't got noth'n' to complain of."

Well, the king he talked him blind; so at last he give in, and said all right, but said he believed it was blamed foolishness to stay, and that doctor hanging over them. But the king says:

"Cuss the doctor! What do we k'yer for HIM? Hain't we got all the fools in town on our side? And ain't that a big enough majority in any town?"

So they got ready to go down stairs again. The duke says:

"I don't think we put that money in a good place."

That cheered me up. I'd begun to think I warn't going to get a hint of no kind to help me. The king says:

"Why?"

"Because Mary Jane 'll be in mourning from this out; and first you know the nigger that does up the rooms will get an order to box these duds up and put 'em away; and do you reckon a nigger can run across money and not borrow some of it?"

"Your head's level agin, duke," says the king; and he comes a-fumbling under the curtain two or three foot from where I was. I stuck tight to the wall and kept mighty still, though quivery; and I wondered what them fellows would say to me if they catched me; and I tried to think what I'd better do if they did catch me. But the king he got the bag before I could think more than about a half a thought, and he never suspicioned I was around. They took and shoved the bag through a rip in the straw tick that was under the feather-bed, and crammed it in a foot or two amongst the straw and said it was all right now, because a nigger only makes up the feather-bed, and don't turn over the straw tick only about twice a year, and so it warn't in no danger of getting stole now.

But I knowed better. I had it out of there before they was half-way down stairs. I groped along up to my cubby, and hid it there till I could get a chance to do better. I judged I better hide it outside of the house somewheres, because if they missed it they would give the house a good ransacking: I knowed that very well. Then I turned in, with my clothes all on; but I couldn't a gone to sleep if I'd a wanted to, I was in such a sweat to get through with the business. By and by I heard the king and the duke come up; so I rolled off my pallet and laid with my chin at the top of my ladder, and waited to see if anything was going to happen. But nothing did.

So I held on till all the late sounds had quit and the early ones hadn't begun yet; and then I slipped down the ladder.

Chapter XXVII

I crept to their doors and listened; they was snoring. So I tiptoed along, and got down stairs all right. There warn't a sound anywheres. I peeped through a crack of the dining-room door, and see the men that was watching the corpse all sound asleep on their chairs. The door was open into the parlor, where the corpse was laying, and there was a candle in both rooms. I passed along, and the parlor door was open; but I see there warn't nobody in there but the remainders of Peter; so I shoved on by; but the front door was locked, and the key wasn't there. Just then I heard somebody coming down the stairs, back behind me. I run in the parlor and took a swift look around, and the only place I see to hide the bag was in the coffin. The lid was shoved along about a foot, showing the dead man's face down in there, with a wet cloth over it, and his shroud on. I tucked the money-bag in under the lid, just down beyond where his hands was crossed, which made me creep, they was so cold, and then I run back across the room and in behind the door.

The person coming was Mary Jane. She went to the coffin, very soft, and kneeled down and looked in; then she put up her handkerchief, and I see she begun to cry, though I couldn't hear her, and her back was to me. I slid out, and as I passed the dining-room I thought I'd make sure them watchers hadn't seen me; so I looked through the crack, and everything was all right. They hadn't stirred.

I slipped up to bed, feeling ruther blue, on accounts of the thing playing out that way after I had took so much trouble and run so much resk about it. Says I, if it could stay where it is, all right; because when we get down the river a hundred mile or two I could write back to Mary Jane, and she could dig him up again and get it; but that ain't the thing that's going to happen; the thing that's going to happen is, the money 'll be found when they come to screw on the lid. Then the king 'll get it again, and it 'll be a long day before he gives anybody another chance to smouch it from him. Of course I WANTED to slide down and get it out of there, but I dasn't try it. Every minute it was getting earlier now, and pretty soon some of them watchers would begin to stir, and I might get catched—catched with six thousand dollars in my hands that nobody hadn't hired me to take care of. I don't wish to be mixed up in no such business as that, I says to myself.

When I got down stairs in the morning the parlor was shut up, and the watchers was gone. There warn't nobody around but the family and the widow Bartley and our tribe. I watched their faces to see if anything had been happening, but I couldn't tell.

Towards the middle of the day the undertaker come with his man, and they set the coffin in the middle of the room on a couple of chairs, and then set all our chairs in rows, and borrowed more from the neighbors till the hall and the parlor and the dining-room was full. I see the coffin lid was the way it was before, but I dasn't go to look in under it, with folks around.

Then the people begun to flock in, and the beats and the girls took seats in the front row at the head of the coffin, and for a half an hour the people filed around slow, in single rank, and looked down at the dead man's face a minute, and some dropped in a tear, and it was all very still and solemn, only the girls and the beats holding handkerchiefs to their eyes and keeping their heads bent, and sobbing a little. There warn't no other sound but the scraping of the feet on the floor and blowing noses—because people always blows them more at a funeral than they do at other places except church.

When the place was packed full the undertaker he slid around in his black gloves with his softy soothering ways, putting on the last touches, and getting people and things all ship-shape and comfortable, and making no more sound than a cat. He never spoke; he moved people around, he squeezed in late ones, he opened up passageways, and done it with nods, and signs with his hands. Then he took his place over against the wall. He was the softest, glidingest, stealthiest man I ever see; and there warn't no more smile to him than there is to a ham.

They had borrowed a melodeum—a sick one; and when everything was ready a young woman set down and worked it, and it was pretty skreeky and colicky, and everybody joined in and sung, and Peter was the only one that had a good thing, according to my notion. Then the Reverend Hobson opened up, slow and solemn, and begun to talk; and straight off the most outrageous row busted out in the cellar a body ever heard; it was only one dog, but he made a most powerful racket, and he kept it up right along; the parson he had to stand there, over the coffin, and wait—you couldn't hear yourself think. It was right down awkward, and nobody didn't seem to know what to do. But pretty soon they see that long-legged undertaker make a sign to the preacher as much as to say, "Don't you worry—just depend on me." Then he stooped down and begun to glide along the wall, just his shoulders showing over the people's heads. So he glided along, and the powwow and racket getting more and more outrageous all the time; and at last, when he had gone around two sides of the room, he disappears down cellar. Then in about two seconds we heard a whack, and the dog he finished up with a most amazing howl or two, and then everything was dead still, and the parson begun his solemn talk where he left off. In a minute or two here comes this undertaker's back and shoulders gliding along the wall again; and so he glided and glided around three sides of the room, and then rose up, and shaded his mouth with his hands, and stretched his neck out towards the preacher, over the people's heads, and says, in a kind of a coarse whisper, "HE HAD A RAT!" Then he drooped down and glided along the wall again to his place. You could see it was a great satisfaction to the people, because naturally they wanted to know. A little thing like that don't cost nothing, and it's just the little things that makes a man to be looked up to and liked. There warn't no more popular man in town than what that undertaker was.

Well, the funeral sermon was very good, but pison long and tiresome; and then the king he shoved in and got off some of his usual rubbage, and at last the job was through, and the undertaker begun to sneak up on the coffin with his screw-driver. I was in a sweat then, and watched him pretty keen. But he never meddled at all; just slid the lid along as soft as mush, and screwed it down tight and fast. So there I was! I didn't know whether the money was in there or not. So, says I, s'pose somebody has hogged that bag on the sly?—now how do I know whether to write to Mary Jane or not? S'pose she dug him up and didn't find nothing, what would she think of me? Blame it, I says, I might get hunted up and jailed; I'd better lay low and keep dark, and not write at all; the thing's awful mixed now; trying to better it, I've worsened it a hundred times, and I wish to goodness I'd just let it alone, dad fetch the whole business!

They buried him, and we come back home, and I went to watching faces again—I couldn't help it, and I couldn't rest easy. But nothing come of it; the faces didn't tell me nothing.

The king he visited around in the evening, and sweetened everybody up, and made himself ever so friendly; and he give out the idea that his congregation over in England would be in a sweat about him, so he must hurry and settle up the estate right away and leave for home. He was very sorry he was so pushed, and so was everybody; they wished he could stay longer, but they said they could see it couldn't be done. And he said of course him and William would take the girls home with them; and that pleased everybody too, because then the girls would be well fixed and amongst their own relations; and it pleased the girls, too—tickled them so they clean forgot they ever had a trouble in the world; and told him to sell out as quick as he wanted to, they would be ready. Them poor things was that glad and happy it made my heart ache to see them getting fooled and lied to so, but I didn't see no safe way for me to chip in and change the general tune.

Well, blamed if the king didn't bill the house and the niggers and all the property for auction straight off—sale two days after the funeral; but anybody could buy private beforehand if they wanted to.

So the next day after the funeral, along about noon-time, the girls' joy got the first jolt. A couple of nigger traders come along, and the king sold them the niggers reasonable, for three-day drafts as they called it, and away they went, the two sons up the river to Memphis, and their mother down the river to Orleans. I thought them poor girls and them niggers would break their hearts for grief; they cried around each other, and took on so it most made me down sick to see it. The girls said they hadn't ever dreamed of seeing the family separated or sold away from the town. I can't ever get it out of my memory, the sight of them poor miserable girls and niggers hanging around each other's necks and crying; and I reckon I couldn't a stood it all, but would a had to bust out and tell on our gang if I hadn't knowed the sale warn't no account and the niggers would be back home in a week or two.

The thing made a big stir in the town, too, and a good many come out flatfooted and said it was scandalous to separate the mother and the children that way. It injured the frauds some; but the old fool he bulled right along, spite of all the duke could say or do, and I tell you the duke was powerful uneasy.

Next day was auction day. About broad day in the morning the king and the duke come up in the garret and woke me up, and I see by their look that there was trouble. The king says:

"Was you in my room night before last?"

"No, your majesty"—which was the way I always called him when nobody but our gang warn't around.

"Was you in there yisterday er last night?"

"No, your majesty."

"Honor bright, now—no lies."

"Honor bright, your majesty, I'm telling you the truth. I hain't been a-near your room since Miss Mary Jane took you and the duke and showed it to you."

The duke says:

"Have you seen anybody else go in there?"

"No, your grace, not as I remember, I believe."

"Stop and think."

I studied awhile and see my chance; then I says:

"Well, I see the niggers go in there several times."

Both of them gave a little jump, and looked like they hadn't ever expected it, and then like they HAD. Then the duke says:

"What, all of them?"

"No—leastways, not all at once—that is, I don't think I ever see them all come OUT at once but just one time."

"Hello! When was that?"

"It was the day we had the funeral. In the morning. It warn't early, because I overslept. I was just starting down the ladder, and I see them."

"Well, go on, GO on! What did they do? How'd they act?"

"They didn't do nothing. And they didn't act anyway much, as fur as I see. They tiptoed away; so I seen, easy enough, that they'd shoved in there to do up your majesty's room, or something, s'posing you was up; and found you WARN'T up, and so they was hoping to slide out of the way of trouble without waking you up, if they hadn't already waked you up."

"Great guns, THIS is a go!" says the king; and both of them looked pretty sick and tolerable silly. They stood there a-thinking and scratching their heads a minute, and the duke he bust into a kind of a little raspy chuckle, and says:

"It does beat all how neat the niggers played their hand. They let on to be SORRY they was going out of this region! And I believed they WAS sorry, and so did you, and so did everybody. Don't ever tell ME any more that a nigger ain't got any histrionic talent. Why, the way they played that thing it would fool ANYBODY. In my opinion, there's a fortune in 'em. If I had capital and a theater, I wouldn't want a better lay-out than that—and here we've gone and sold 'em for a song. Yes, and ain't privileged to sing the song yet. Say, where IS that song—that draft?"

"In the bank for to be collected. Where WOULD it be?"

"Well, THAT'S all right then, thank goodness."

Says I, kind of timid-like:

"Is something gone wrong?"

The king whirls on me and rips out:

"None o' your business! You keep your head shet, and mind y'r own affairs—if you got any. Long as you're in this town don't you forget THAT—you hear?" Then he says to the duke, "We got to jest swaller it and say noth'n': mum's the word for US."

As they was starting down the ladder the duke he chuckles again, and says:

"Quick sales AND small profits! It's a good business—yes."

The king snarls around on him and says:

"I was trying to do for the best in sellin' 'em out so quick. If the profits has turned out to be none, lackin' considable, and none to carry, is it my fault any more'n it's yourn?"

"Well, THEY'D be in this house yet and we WOULDN'T if I could a got my advice listened to."

The king sassed back as much as was safe for him, and then swapped around and lit into ME again. He give me down the banks for not coming and TELLING him I see the niggers come out of his room acting that way—said any fool would a KNOWED something was up. And then waltzed in and cussed HIMSELF awhile, and said it all come of him not laying late and taking his natural rest that morning, and he'd be blamed if he'd ever do it again. So they went off a-jawing; and I felt dreadful glad I'd worked it all off on to the niggers, and yet hadn't done the niggers no harm by it.

Chapter XXVIII

By and by it was getting-up time. So I come down the ladder and started for downstairs; but as I come to the girls' room the door was open, and I see Mary Jane setting by her old hair trunk, which was open and she'd been packing things in it—getting ready to go to England. But she had stopped now with a folded gown in her lap, and had her face in her hands, crying. I felt awful bad to see it; of course anybody would. I went in there and says:

"Miss Mary Jane, you can't a-bear to see people in trouble, and I can't —most always. Tell me about it."

So she done it. And it was the niggers—I just expected it. She said the beautiful trip to England was most about spoiled for her; she didn't know HOW she was ever going to be happy there, knowing the mother and the children warn't ever going to see each other no more—and then busted out bitterer than ever, and flung up her hands, and says:

"Oh, dear, dear, to think they ain't EVER going to see each other any more!"

"But they WILL—and inside of two weeks—and I KNOW it!" says I.

Laws, it was out before I could think! And before I could budge she throws her arms around my neck and told me to say it AGAIN, say it AGAIN, say it AGAIN!

I see I had spoke too sudden and said too much, and was in a close place. I asked her to let me think a minute; and she set there, very impatient and excited and handsome, but looking kind of happy and eased-up, like a person that's had a tooth pulled out. So I went to studying it out. I says to myself, I reckon a body that ups and tells the truth when he is in a tight place is taking considerable many resks, though I ain't had no experience, and can't say for certain; but it looks so to me, anyway; and yet here's a case where I'm blest if it don't look to me like the truth is better and actly SAFER than a lie. I must lay it by in my mind, and think it over some time or other, it's so kind of strange and unregular. I never see nothing like it. Well, I says to myself at last, I'm a-going to chance it; I'll up and tell the truth this time, though it does seem most like setting down on a kag of powder and touching it off just to see where you'll go to. Then I says:

"Miss Mary Jane, is there any place out of town a little ways where you could go and stay three or four days?"

"Yes; Mr. Lothrop's. Why?"

"Never mind why yet. If I'll tell you how I know the niggers will see each other again inside of two weeks—here in this house—and PROVE how I know it—will you go to Mr. Lothrop's and stay four days?"

"Four days!" she says; "I'll stay a year!"

"All right," I says, "I don't want nothing more out of YOU than just your word—I druther have it than another man's kiss-the-Bible." She smiled and reddened up very sweet, and I says, "If you don't mind it, I'll shut the door—and bolt it."

Then I come back and set down again, and says:

"Don't you holler. Just set still and take it like a man. I got to tell the truth, and you want to brace up, Miss Mary, because it's a bad kind, and going to be hard to take, but there ain't no help for it. These uncles of yourn ain't no uncles at all; they're a couple of frauds—regular dead-beats. There, now we're over the worst of it, you can stand the rest middling easy."

It jolted her up like everything, of course; but I was over the shoal water now, so I went right along, her eyes a-blazing higher and higher all the time, and told her every blame thing, from where we first struck that young fool going up to the steamboat, clear through to where she flung herself on to the king's breast at the front door and he kissed her sixteen or seventeen times—and then up she jumps, with her face afire like sunset, and says:

"The brute! Come, don't waste a minute—not a SECOND—we'll have them tarred and feathered, and flung in the river!"

Says I:

"Cert'nly. But do you mean BEFORE you go to Mr. Lothrop's, or—"

"Oh," she says, "what am I THINKING about!" she says, and set right down again. "Don't mind what I said—please don't—you WON'T, now, WILL you?" Laying her silky hand on mine in that kind of a way that I said I would die first. "I never thought, I was so stirred up," she says; "now go on, and I won't do so any more. You tell me what to do, and whatever you say I'll do it."

"Well," I says, "it's a rough gang, them two frauds, and I'm fixed so I got to travel with them a while longer, whether I want to or not—I druther not tell you why; and if you was to blow on them this town would get me out of their claws, and I'd be all right; but there'd be another person that you don't know about who'd be in big trouble. Well, we got to save HIM, hain't we? Of course. Well, then, we won't blow on them."

Saying them words put a good idea in my head. I see how maybe I could get me and Jim rid of the frauds; get them jailed here, and then leave.

But I didn't want to run the raft in the daytime without anybody aboard to answer questions but me; so I didn't want the plan to begin working till pretty late to-night. I says:

"Miss Mary Jane, I'll tell you what we'll do, and you won't have to stay at Mr. Lothrop's so long, nuther. How fur is it?"

"A little short of four miles—right out in the country, back here."

"Well, that'll answer. Now you go along out there, and lay low till nine or half-past to-night, and then get them to fetch you home again —tell them you've thought of something. If you get here before eleven put a candle in this window, and if I don't turn up wait TILL eleven, and THEN if I don't turn up it means I'm gone, and out of the way, and safe. Then you come out and spread the news around, and get these beats jailed."

"Good," she says, "I'll do it."

"And if it just happens so that I don't get away, but get took up along with them, you must up and say I told you the whole thing beforehand, and you must stand by me all you can."

"Stand by you! indeed I will. They sha'n't touch a hair of your head!" she says, and I see her nostrils spread and her eyes snap when she said it, too.

"If I get away I sha'n't be here," I says, "to prove these rapscallions ain't your uncles, and I couldn't do it if I WAS here. I could swear they was beats and bummers, that's all, though that's worth something. Well, there's others can do that better than what I can, and they're people that ain't going to be doubted as quick as I'd be. I'll tell you how to find them. Gimme a pencil and a piece of paper. There—'Royal Nonesuch, Bricksville.' Put it away, and don't lose it. When the court wants to find out something about these two, let them send up to Bricksville and say they've got the men that played the Royal Nonesuch, and ask for some witnesses—why, you'll have that entire town down here before you can hardly wink, Miss Mary. And they'll come a-biling, too."

I judged we had got everything fixed about right now. So I says:

"Just let the auction go right along, and don't worry. Nobody don't have to pay for the things they buy till a whole day after the auction on accounts of the short notice, and they ain't going out of this till they get that money; and the way we've fixed it the sale ain't going to count, and they ain't going to get no money. It's just like the way it was with the niggers—it warn't no sale, and the niggers will be back before long. Why, they can't collect the money for the NIGGERS yet—they're in the worst kind of a fix, Miss Mary."

"Well," she says, "I'll run down to breakfast now, and then I'll start straight for Mr. Lothrop's."

"'Deed, THAT ain't the ticket, Miss Mary Jane," I says, "by no manner of means; go BEFORE breakfast."

"Why?"

"What did you reckon I wanted you to go at all for, Miss Mary?"

"Well, I never thought—and come to think, I don't know. What was it?"

"Why, it's because you ain't one of these leather-face people. I don't want no better book than what your face is. A body can set down and read it off like coarse print. Do you reckon you can go and face your uncles when they come to kiss you good-morning, and never—"

"There, there, don't! Yes, I'll go before breakfast—I'll be glad to. And leave my sisters with them?"

"Yes; never mind about them. They've got to stand it yet a while. They might suspicion something if all of you was to go. I don't want you to see them, nor your sisters, nor nobody in this town; if a neighbor was to ask how is your uncles this morning your face would tell something. No, you go right along, Miss Mary Jane, and I'll fix it with all of them. I'll tell Miss Susan to give your love to your uncles and say you've went away for a few hours for to get a little rest and change, or to see a friend, and you'll be back to-night or early in the morning."

"Gone to see a friend is all right, but I won't have my love given to them."

"Well, then, it sha'n't be." It was well enough to tell HER so—no harm in it. It was only a little thing to do, and no trouble; and it's the little things that smooths people's roads the most, down here below; it would make Mary Jane comfortable, and it wouldn't cost nothing. Then I says: "There's one more thing—that bag of money."

"Well, they've got that; and it makes me feel pretty silly to think HOW they got it."

"No, you're out, there. They hain't got it."

"Why, who's got it?"

"I wish I knowed, but I don't. I HAD it, because I stole it from them; and I stole it to give to you; and I know where I hid it, but I'm afraid it ain't there no more. I'm awful sorry, Miss Mary Jane, I'm just as sorry as I can be; but I done the best I could; I did honest. I come nigh getting caught, and I had to shove it into the first place I come to, and run—and it warn't a good place."

"Oh, stop blaming yourself—it's too bad to do it, and I won't allow it —you couldn't help it; it wasn't your fault. Where did you hide it?"

I didn't want to set her to thinking about her troubles again; and I couldn't seem to get my mouth to tell her what would make her see that corpse laying in the coffin with that bag of money on his stomach. So for a minute I didn't say nothing; then I says:

"I'd ruther not TELL you where I put it, Miss Mary Jane, if you don't mind letting me off; but I'll write it for you on a piece of paper, and you can read it along the road to Mr. Lothrop's, if you want to. Do you reckon that 'll do?"

"Oh, yes."

So I wrote: "I put it in the coffin. It was in there when you was crying there, away in the night. I was behind the door, and I was mighty sorry for you, Miss Mary Jane."

It made my eyes water a little to remember her crying there all by herself in the night, and them devils laying there right under her own roof, shaming her and robbing her; and when I folded it up and give it to her I see the water come into her eyes, too; and she shook me by the hand, hard, and says:

"Good-bye. I'm going to do everything just as you've told me; and if I don't ever see you again, I sha'n't ever forget you and I'll think of you a many and a many a time, and I'll PRAY for you, too!"—and she was gone.

Pray for me! I reckoned if she knowed me she'd take a job that was more nearer her size. But I bet she done it, just the same—she was just that kind. She had the grit to pray for Judus if she took the notion—there warn't no back-down to her, I judge. You may say what you want to, but in my opinion she had more sand in her than any girl I ever see; in my opinion she was just full of sand. It sounds like flattery, but it ain't no flattery. And when it comes to beauty—and goodness, too—she lays over them all. I hain't ever seen her since that time that I see her go out of that door; no, I hain't ever seen her since, but I reckon I've thought of her a many and a many a million times, and of her saying she would pray for me; and if ever I'd a thought it would do any good for me to pray for HER, blamed if I wouldn't a done it or bust.

Well, Mary Jane she lit out the back way, I reckon; because nobody see her go. When I struck Susan and the hare-lip, I says:

"What's the name of them people over on t'other side of the river that you all goes to see sometimes?"

They says:

"There's several; but it's the Proctors, mainly."

"That's the name," I says; "I most forgot it. Well, Miss Mary Jane sh told me to tell you she's gone over there in a dreadful hurry—one of them's sick."

"Which one?"

"I don't know; leastways, I kinder forget; but I thinks it's—"

"Sakes alive, I hope it ain't HANNER?"

"I'm sorry to say it," I says, "but Hanner's the very one."

"My goodness, and she so well only last week! Is she took bad?"

"It ain't no name for it. They set up with her all night, Miss Mary Jane said, and they don't think she'll last many hours."

"Only think of that, now! What's the matter with her?"

I couldn't think of anything reasonable, right off that way, so I says:

"Mumps."

"Mumps your granny! They don't set up with people that's got the mumps."

"They don't, don't they? You better bet they do with THESE mumps. These mumps is different. It's a new kind, Miss Mary Jane said."

"How's it a new kind?"

"Because it's mixed up with other things."

"What other things?"

"Well, measles, and whooping-cough, and erysiplas, and consumption, and yaller janders, and brain-fever, and I don't know what all."

"My land! And they call it the MUMPS?"

"That's what Miss Mary Jane said."

"Well, what in the nation do they call it the MUMPS for?"

"Why, because it IS the mumps. That's what it starts with."

"Well, ther' ain't no sense in it. A body might stump his toe, and take pison, and fall down the well, and break his neck, and bust his brains out, and somebody come along and ask what killed him, and some numskull up and say, 'Why, he stumped his TOE.' Would ther' be any sense in that? NO. And ther' ain't no sense in THIS, nuther. Is it ketching?"

"Is it KETCHING? Why, how you talk. Is a HARROW catching—in the dark? If you don't hitch on to one tooth, you're bound to on another, ain't you? And you can't get away with that tooth without fetching the whole harrow along, can you? Well, these kind of mumps is a kind of a harrow, as you may say—and it ain't no slouch of a harrow, nuther, you come to get it hitched on good."

"Well, it's awful, I think," says the hare-lip. "I'll go to Uncle Harvey and—"

"Oh, yes," I says, "I WOULD. OF COURSE I would. I wouldn't lose no time."

"Well, why wouldn't you?"

"Just look at it a minute, and maybe you can see. Hain't your uncles obleegd to get along home to England as fast as they can? And do you reckon they'd be mean enough to go off and leave you to go all that journey by yourselves? YOU know they'll wait for you. So fur, so good. Your uncle Harvey's a preacher, ain't he? Very well, then; is a PREACHER going to deceive a steamboat clerk? is he going to deceive a SHIP CLERK? —so as to get them to let Miss Mary Jane go aboard? Now YOU know he ain't. What WILL he do, then? Why, he'll say, 'It's a great pity, but my church matters has got to get along the best way they can; for my niece has been ex-posed to the dreadful pluribus-unum mumps, and so it's my bounden duty to set down here and wait the three months it takes to show on her if she's got it.' But never mind, if you think it's best to tell your uncle Harvey——"

"Shucks, and stay fooling around here when we could all be having good times in England whilst we was waiting to find out whether Mary Jane's got it or not? Why, you talk like a muggins."

"Well, anyway, maybe you'd better tell some of the neighbors."

"Listen at that, now. You do beat all for natural stupidness. Can't you SEE that THEY'D go and tell? Ther' ain't no way but just to not tell anybody at ALL."

"Well, maybe you're right—yes, I judge you ARE right."

"But I reckon we ought to tell Uncle Harvey she's gone out a while, anyway, so he won't be uneasy about her?"

"Yes, Miss Mary Jane she wanted you to do that. She says, 'Tell them to give Uncle Harvey and William my love and a kiss, and say I've run over the river to see Mr.'—Mr.—what IS the name of that rich family your uncle Peter used to think so much of?—I mean the one that——"

"Why, you must mean the Apthorps, ain't it?"

"Of course; bother them kind of names, a body can't ever seem to remember them, half the time, somehow. Yes, she said, say she has run over for to ask the Apthorps to be sure and come to the auction and buy this house, because she allowed her uncle Peter would ruther they had it than anybody else; and she's going to stick to them till they say they'll come, and then, if she ain't too tired, she's coming home; and if she is, she'll be home in the morning anyway. She said, don't say nothing about the Proctors, but only about the Apthorps—which 'll be perfectly true, because she is going there to speak about their buying the house; I know it, because she told me so herself."

"All right," they said, and cleared out to lay for their uncles, and give them the love and the kisses, and tell them the message.

Everything was all right now. The girls wouldn't say nothing because they wanted to go to England; and the king and the duke would ruther Mary Jane was off working for the auction than around in reach of Doctor Robinson. I felt very good; I judged I had done it pretty neat—I reckoned Tom Sawyer couldn't a done it no neater himself. Of course he would a throwed more style into it, but I can't do that very handy, not being brung up to it.

Well, they held the auction in the public square, along towards the end of the afternoon, and it strung along, and strung along, and the old man he was on hand and looking his level pisonest, up there longside of the auctioneer, and chipping in a little Scripture now and then, or a little goody-goody saying of some kind, and the duke he was around goo-gooing for sympathy all he knowed how, and just spreading himself generly.

But by and by the thing dragged through, and everything was sold—everything but a little old trifling lot in the graveyard. So they'd got to work that off—I never see such a giraff as the king was for wanting to swallow EVERYTHING. Well, whilst they was at it a steamboat landed, and in about two minutes up comes a crowd a-whooping and yelling and laughing and carrying on, and singing out:

"HERE'S your opposition line! here's your two sets o' heirs to old Peter Wilks—and you pays your money and you takes your choice!"

Chapter XXIX

They was fetching a very nice-looking old gentleman along, and a nice-looking younger one, with his right arm in a sling. And, my souls, how the people yelled and laughed, and kept it up. But I didn't see no joke about it, and I judged it would strain the duke and the king some to see any. I reckoned they'd turn pale. But no, nary a pale did THEY turn. The duke he never let on he suspicioned what was up, but just went a goo-gooing around, happy and satisfied, like a jug that's googling out buttermilk; and as for the king, he just gazed and gazed down sorrowful on them new-comers like it give him the stomach-ache in his very heart to think there could be such frauds and rascals in the world. Oh, he done it admirable. Lots of the principal people gethered around the king, to let him see they was on his side. That old gentleman that had just come looked all puzzled to death. Pretty soon he begun to speak, and I see straight off he pronounced LIKE an Englishman—not the king's way, though the king's WAS pretty good for an imitation. I can't give the old gent's words, nor I can't imitate him; but he turned around to the crowd, and says, about like this:

"This is a surprise to me which I wasn't looking for; and I'll acknowledge, candid and frank, I ain't very well fixed to meet it and answer it; for my brother and me has had misfortunes; he's broke his arm, and our baggage got put off at a town above here last night in the night by a mistake. I am Peter Wilks' brother Harvey, and this is his brother William, which can't hear nor speak—and can't even make signs to amount to much, now't he's only got one hand to work them with. We are who we say we are; and in a day or two, when I get the baggage, I can prove it. But up till then I won't say nothing more, but go to the hotel and wait."

So him and the new dummy started off; and the king he laughs, and blethers out:

"Broke his arm—VERY likely, AIN'T it?—and very convenient, too, for a fraud that's got to make signs, and ain't learnt how. Lost their baggage! That's MIGHTY good!—and mighty ingenious—under the CIRCUMSTANCES!"

So he laughed again; and so did everybody else, except three or four, or maybe half a dozen. One of these was that doctor; another one was a sharp-looking gentleman, with a carpet-bag of the old-fashioned kind made out of carpet-stuff, that had just come off of the steamboat and was talking to him in a low voice, and glancing towards the king now and then and nodding their heads—it was Levi Bell, the lawyer that was gone up to Louisville; and another one was a big rough husky that come along and listened to all the old gentleman said, and was listening to the king now. And when the king got done this husky up and says:

"Say, looky here; if you are Harvey Wilks, when'd you come to this town?"

"The day before the funeral, friend," says the king.

"But what time o' day?"

"In the evenin'—'bout an hour er two before sundown."

"HOW'D you come?"

"I come down on the Susan Powell from Cincinnati."

"Well, then, how'd you come to be up at the Pint in the MORNIN'—in a canoe?"

"I warn't up at the Pint in the mornin'."

"It's a lie."

Several of them jumped for him and begged him not to talk that way to an old man and a preacher.

"Preacher be hanged, he's a fraud and a liar. He was up at the Pint that mornin'. I live up there, don't I? Well, I was up there, and he was up there. I see him there. He come in a canoe, along with Tim Collins and a boy."

The doctor he up and says:

"Would you know the boy again if you was to see him, Hines?"

"I reckon I would, but I don't know. Why, yonder he is, now. I know him perfectly easy."

It was me he pointed at. The doctor says:

"Neighbors, I don't know whether the new couple is frauds or not; but if THESE two ain't frauds, I am an idiot, that's all. I think it's our duty to see that they don't get away from here till we've looked into this thing. Come along, Hines; come along, the rest of you. We'll take these fellows to the tavern and affront them with t'other couple, and I reckon we'll find out SOMETHING before we get through."

It was nuts for the crowd, though maybe not for the king's friends; so we all started. It was about sundown. The doctor he led me along by the hand, and was plenty kind enough, but he never let go my hand.

We all got in a big room in the hotel, and lit up some candles, and fetched in the new couple. First, the doctor says:

"I don't wish to be too hard on these two men, but I think they're frauds, and they may have complices that we don't know nothing about. If they have, won't the complices get away with that bag of gold Peter Wilks left? It ain't unlikely. If these men ain't frauds, they won't object to sending for that money and letting us keep it till they prove they're all right—ain't that so?"

Everybody agreed to that. So I judged they had our gang in a pretty tight place right at the outstart. But the king he only looked sorrowful, and says:

"Gentlemen, I wish the money was there, for I ain't got no disposition to throw anything in the way of a fair, open, out-and-out investigation o' this misable business; but, alas, the money ain't there; you k'n send and see, if you want to."

"Where is it, then?"

"Well, when my niece give it to me to keep for her I took and hid it inside o' the straw tick o' my bed, not wishin' to bank it for the few days we'd be here, and considerin' the bed a safe place, we not bein' used to niggers, and suppos'n' 'em honest, like servants in England. The niggers stole it the very next mornin' after I had went down stairs; and when I sold 'em I hadn't missed the money yit, so they got clean away with it. My servant here k'n tell you 'bout it, gentlemen."

The doctor and several said "Shucks!" and I see nobody didn't altogether believe him. One man asked me if I see the niggers steal it. I said no, but I see them sneaking out of the room and hustling away, and I never thought nothing, only I reckoned they was afraid they had waked up my master and was trying to get away before he made trouble with them. That was all they asked me. Then the doctor whirls on me and says:

"Are YOU English, too?"

I says yes; and him and some others laughed, and said, "Stuff!"

Well, then they sailed in on the general investigation, and there we had it, up and down, hour in, hour out, and nobody never said a word about supper, nor ever seemed to think about it—and so they kept it up, and kept it up; and it WAS the worst mixed-up thing you ever see. They made the king tell his yarn, and they made the old gentleman tell his'n; and anybody but a lot of prejudiced chuckleheads would a SEEN that the old gentleman was spinning truth and t'other one lies. And by and by they had me up to tell what I knowed. The king he give me a left-handed look out of the corner of his eye, and so I knowed enough to talk on the right side. I begun to tell about Sheffield, and how we lived there, and all about the English Wilkses, and so on; but I didn't get pretty fur till the doctor begun to laugh; and Levi Bell, the lawyer, says:

"Set down, my boy; I wouldn't strain myself if I was you. I reckon you ain't used to lying, it don't seem to come handy; what you want is practice. You do it pretty awkward."

I didn't care nothing for the compliment, but I was glad to be let off, anyway.

The doctor he started to say something, and turns and says:

"If you'd been in town at first, Levi Bell—" The king broke in and reached out his hand, and says:

"Why, is this my poor dead brother's old friend that he's wrote so often about?"

The lawyer and him shook hands, and the lawyer smiled and looked pleased, and they talked right along awhile, and then got to one side and talked low; and at last the lawyer speaks up and says:

"That 'll fix it. I'll take the order and send it, along with your brother's, and then they'll know it's all right."

So they got some paper and a pen, and the king he set down and twisted his head to one side, and chawed his tongue, and scrawled off something; and then they give the pen to the duke—and then for the first time the duke looked sick. But he took the pen and wrote. So then the lawyer turns to the new old gentleman and says:

"You and your brother please write a line or two and sign your names."

The old gentleman wrote, but nobody couldn't read it. The lawyer looked powerful astonished, and says:

"Well, it beats ME"—and snaked a lot of old letters out of his pocket, and examined them, and then examined the old man's writing, and then THEM again; and then says: "These old letters is from Harvey Wilks; and here's THESE two handwritings, and anybody can see they didn't write them" (the king and the duke looked sold and foolish, I tell you, to see how the lawyer had took them in), "and here's THIS old gentleman's hand writing, and anybody can tell, easy enough, HE didn't write them— fact is, the scratches he makes ain't properly WRITING at all. Now, here's some letters from—"

The new old gentleman says:

"If you please, let me explain. Nobody can read my hand but my brother there— so he copies for me. It's HIS hand you've got there, not mine."

"WELL!" says the lawyer, "this IS a state of things. I've got some of William's letters, too; so if you'll get him to write a line or so we can com—"

"He CAN'T write with his left hand," says the old gentleman. "If he could use his right hand, you would see that he wrote his own letters and mine too. Look at both, please—they're by the same hand."

The lawyer done it, and says:

"I believe it's so—and if it ain't so, there's a heap stronger resemblance than I'd noticed before, anyway. Well, well, well! I thought we was right on the track of a solution, but it's gone to grass, partly. But anyway, one thing is proved—THESE two ain't either of 'em Wilkses"—and he wagged his head towards the king and the duke.

Well, what do you think? That muleheaded old fool wouldn't give in THEN! Indeed he wouldn't. Said it warn't no fair test. Said his brother William was the cussedest joker in the world, and hadn't tried to write —HE see William was going to play one of his jokes the minute he put the pen to paper. And so he warmed up and went warbling right along till he was actuly beginning to believe what he was saying HIMSELF; but pretty soon the new gentleman broke in, and says:

"I've thought of something. Is there anybody here that helped to lay out my br— helped to lay out the late Peter Wilks for burying?"

"Yes," says somebody, "me and Ab Turner done it. We're both here."

Then the old man turns towards the king, and says: "Perhaps this gentleman can tell me what was tattooed on his breast?"

Blamed if the king didn't have to brace up mighty quick, or he'd a squshed down like a bluff bank that the river has cut under, it took him so sudden; and, mind you, it was a thing that was calculated to make most ANYBODY sqush to get fetched such a solid one as that without any notice, because how was HE going to know what was tattooed on the man? He whitened a little; he couldn't help it; and it was mighty still in there, and everybody bending a little forwards and gazing at him. Says I to myself, NOW he'll throw up the sponge—there ain't no more use. Well, did he? A body can't hardly believe it, but he didn't. I reckon he thought he'd keep the thing up till he tired them people out, so they'd thin out, and him and the duke could break loose and get away. Anyway, he set there, and pretty soon he begun to smile, and says:

"Mf! It's a VERY tough question, AIN'T it! YES, sir, I k'n tell you what's tattooed on his breast. It's jest a small, thin, blue arrow —that's what it is; and if you don't look clost, you can't see it. NOW what do you say—hey?"

Well, I never see anything like that old blister for clean out-and-out cheek.

The new old gentleman turns brisk towards Ab Turner and his pard, and his eye lights up like he judged he'd got the king THIS time, and says:

"There—you've heard what he said! Was there any such mark on Peter Wilks' breast?"

Both of them spoke up and says:

"We didn't see no such mark."

"Good!" says the old gentleman. "Now, what you DID see on his breast was a small dim P, and a B (which is an initial he dropped when he was young), and a W, with dashes between them, so: P—B—W"—and he marked them that way on a piece of paper. "Come, ain't that what you saw?"

Both of them spoke up again, and says:

"No, we DIDN'T. We never seen any marks at all."

Well, everybody WAS in a state of mind now, and they sings out:

"The whole BILIN' of 'm 's frauds! Le's duck 'em! le's drown 'em! le's ride 'em on a rail!" and everybody was whooping at once, and there was a rattling powwow. But the lawyer he jumps on the table and yells, and says:

"Gentlemen—gentleMEN! Hear me just a word—just a SINGLE word—if you PLEASE! There's one way yet—let's go and dig up the corpse and look."

That took them.

"Hooray!" they all shouted, and was starting right off; but the lawyer and the doctor sung out:

"Hold on, hold on! Collar all these four men and the boy, and fetch THEM along, too!"

"We'll do it!" they all shouted; "and if we don't find them marks we'll lynch the whole gang!"

I WAS scared, now, I tell you. But there warn't no getting away, you know. They gripped us all, and marched us right along, straight for the graveyard, which was a mile and a half down the river, and the whole town at our heels, for we made noise enough, and it was only nine in the evening.

As we went by our house I wished I hadn't sent Mary Jane out of town; because now if I could tip her the wink she'd light out and save me, and blow on our dead-beats.

Well, we swarmed along down the river road, just carrying on like wildcats; and to make it more scary the sky was darking up, and the lightning beginning to wink and flitter, and the wind to shiver amongst the leaves. This was the most awful trouble and most dangersome I ever was in; and I was kinder stunned; everything was going so different from what I had allowed for; stead of being fixed so I could take my own time if I wanted to, and see all the fun, and have Mary Jane at my back to save me and set me free when the close-fit come, here was nothing in the world betwixt me and sudden death but just them tattoo-marks. If they didn't find them—

I couldn't bear to think about it; and yet, somehow, I couldn't think about nothing else. It got darker and darker, and it was a beautiful time to give the crowd the slip; but that big husky had me by the wrist —Hines—and a body might as well try to give Goliar the slip. He dragged me right along, he was so excited, and I had to run to keep up.

When they got there they swarmed into the graveyard and washed over it like an overflow. And when they got to the grave they found they had about a hundred times as many shovels as they wanted, but nobody hadn't thought to fetch a lantern. But they sailed into digging anyway by the flicker of the lightning, and sent a man to the nearest house, a half a mile off, to borrow one.

So they dug and dug like everything; and it got awful dark, and the rain started, and the wind swished and swushed along, and the lightning come brisker and brisker, and the thunder boomed; but them people never took no notice of it, they was so full of this business; and one minute you could see everything and every face in that big crowd, and the shovelfuls of dirt sailing up out of the grave, and the next second the dark wiped it all out, and you couldn't see nothing at all.

At last they got out the coffin and begun to unscrew the lid, and then such another crowding and shouldering and shoving as there was, to scrouge in and get a sight, you never see; and in the dark, that way, it was awful. Hines he hurt my wrist dreadful pulling and tugging so, and I reckon he clean forgot I was in the world, he was so excited and panting.

All of a sudden the lightning let go a perfect sluice of white glare, and somebody sings out:

"By the living jingo, here's the bag of gold on his breast!"

Hines let out a whoop, like everybody else, and dropped my wrist and give a big surge to bust his way in and get a look, and the way I lit out and shinned for the road in the dark there ain't nobody can tell.

I had the road all to myself, and I fairly flew—leastways, I had it all to myself except the solid dark, and the now-and-then glares, and the buzzing of the rain, and the thrashing of the wind, and the splitting of the thunder; and sure as you are born I did clip it along!

When I struck the town I see there warn't nobody out in the storm, so I never hunted for no back streets, but humped it straight through the main one; and when I begun to get towards our house I aimed my eye and set it. No light there; the house all dark—which made me feel sorry and disappointed, I didn't know why. But at last, just as I was sailing by, FLASH comes the light in Mary Jane's window! and my heart swelled up sudden, like to bust; and the same second the house and all was behind me in the dark, and wasn't ever going to be before me no more in this world. She WAS the best girl I ever see, and had the most sand.

The minute I was far enough above the town to see I could make the towhead, I begun to look sharp for a boat to borrow, and the first time the lightning showed me one that wasn't chained I snatched it and shoved. It was a canoe, and warn't fastened with nothing but a rope. The towhead was a rattling big distance off, away out there in the middle of the river, but I didn't lose no time; and when I struck the raft at last I was so fagged I would a just laid down to blow and gasp if I could afforded it. But I didn't. As I sprung aboard I sung out:

"Out with you, Jim, and set her loose! Glory be to goodness, we're shut of them!"

Jim lit out, and was a-coming for me with both arms spread, he was so full of joy; but when I glimpsed him in the lightning my heart shot up in my mouth and I went overboard backwards; for I forgot he was old King Lear and a drownded A-rab all in one, and it most scared the livers and lights out of me. But Jim fished me out, and was going to hug me and bless me, and so on, he was so glad I was back and we was shut of the king and the duke, but I says:

"Not now; have it for breakfast, have it for breakfast! Cut loose and let her slide!"

So in two seconds away we went a-sliding down the river, and it DID seem so good to be free again and all by ourselves on the big river, and nobody to bother us. I had to skip around a bit, and jump up and crack my heels a few times—I couldn't help it; but about the third crack I noticed a sound that I knowed mighty well, and held my breath and listened and waited; and sure enough, when the next flash busted out over the water, here they come!—and just a-laying to their oars and making their skiff hum! It was the king and the duke.

So I wilted right down on to the planks then, and give up; and it was all I could do to keep from crying.

Chapter XXX

When they got aboard the king went for me, and shook me by the collar, and says:

"Tryin' to give us the slip, was ye, you pup! Tired of our company, hey?"

I says:

"No, your majesty, we warn't—PLEASE don't, your majesty!"

"Quick, then, and tell us what WAS your idea, or I'll shake the insides out o' you!"

"Honest, I'll tell you everything just as it happened, your majesty. The man that had a-holt of me was very good to me, and kept saying he had a boy about as big as me that died last year, and he was sorry to see a boy in such a dangerous fix; and when they was all took by surprise by finding the gold, and made a rush for the coffin, he lets go of me and whispers, 'Heel it now, or they'll hang ye, sure!' and I lit out. It didn't seem no good for ME to stay—I couldn't do nothing, and I didn't want to be hung if I could get away. So I never stopped running till I found the canoe; and when I got here I told Jim to hurry, or they'd catch me and hang me yet, and said I was afeard you and the duke wasn't alive now, and I was awful sorry, and so was Jim, and was awful glad when we see you coming; you may ask Jim if I didn't."

Jim said it was so; and the king told him to shut up, and said, "Oh, yes, it's MIGHTY likely!" and shook me up again, and said he reckoned he'd drownd me. But the duke says:

"Leggo the boy, you old idiot! Would YOU a done any different? Did you inquire around for HIM when you got loose? I don't remember it."

So the king let go of me, and begun to cuss that town and everybody in it. But the duke says:

"You better a blame' sight give YOURSELF a good cussing, for you're the one that's entitled to it most. You hain't done a thing from the start that had any sense in it, except coming out so cool and cheeky with that imaginary blue-arrow mark. That WAS bright—it was right down bully; and it was the thing that saved us. For if it hadn't been for that they'd a jailed us till them Englishmen's baggage come—and then—the penitentiary, you bet! But that trick took 'em to the graveyard, and the gold done us a still bigger kindness; for if the excited fools hadn't let go all holts and made that rush to get a look we'd a slept in our cravats to-night—cravats warranted to WEAR, too—longer than WE'D need 'em."

They was still a minute—thinking; then the king says, kind of absent-minded like:
"Mf! And we reckoned the NIGGERS stole it!"
That made me squirm!
"Yes," says the duke, kinder slow and deliberate and sarcastic, "WE did."
After about a half a minute the king drawls out:
"Leastways, I did."
The duke says, the same way:
"On the contrary, I did."
The king kind of ruffles up, and says:
"Looky here, Bilgewater, what'r you referrin' to?"
The duke says, pretty brisk:
"When it comes to that, maybe you'll let me ask, what was YOU referring to?"
"Shucks!" says the king, very sarcastic; "but I don't know—maybe you was asleep,

and didn't know what you was about."

The duke bristles up now, and says:

"Oh, let UP on this cussed nonsense; do you take me for a blame' fool? Don't you reckon I know who hid that money in that coffin?"

"YES, sir! I know you DO know, because you done it yourself!"

"It's a lie!"—and the duke went for him. The king sings out:

"Take y'r hands off!—leggo my throat!—I take it all back!"

The duke says:

"Well, you just own up, first, that you DID hide that money there, intending to give me the slip one of these days, and come back and dig it up, and have it all to yourself."

"Wait jest a minute, duke—answer me this one question, honest and fair; if you didn't put the money there, say it, and I'll b'lieve you, and take back everything I said."

"You old scoundrel, I didn't, and you know I didn't. There, now!"

"Well, then, I b'lieve you. But answer me only jest this one more—now DON'T git mad; didn't you have it in your mind to hook the money and hide it?"

The duke never said nothing for a little bit; then he says:

"Well, I don't care if I DID, I didn't DO it, anyway. But you not only had it in mind to do it, but you DONE it."

"I wisht I never die if I done it, duke, and that's honest. I won't say I warn't goin' to do it, because I WAS; but you—I mean somebody—got in ahead o' me."

"It's a lie! You done it, and you got to SAY you done it, or—"

The king began to gurgle, and then he gasps out:

"'Nough!—I OWN UP!"

I was very glad to hear him say that; it made me feel much more easier than what I was feeling before. So the duke took his hands off and says:

"If you ever deny it again I'll drown you. It's WELL for you to set there and blubber like a baby—it's fitten for you, after the way you've acted. I never see such an old ostrich for wanting to gobble everything —and I a-trusting you all the time, like you was my own father. You ought to been ashamed of yourself to stand by and hear it saddled on to a lot of poor niggers, and you never say a word for 'em. It makes me feel ridiculous to think I was soft enough to BELIEVE that rubbage. Cuss you, I can see now why you was so anxious to make up the deffisit—you wanted to get what money I'd got out of the Nonesuch and one thing or another, and scoop it ALL!"

The king says, timid, and still a-snuffling:

"Why, duke, it was you that said make up the deffisit; it warn't me."

"Dry up! I don't want to hear no more out of you!" says the duke. "And NOW you see what you GOT by it. They've got all their own money back, and all of OURN but a shekel or two BESIDES. G'long to bed, and don't you deffersit ME no more deffersits, long 's YOU live!"

So the king sneaked into the wigwam and took to his bottle for comfort, and before long the duke tackled HIS bottle; and so in about a half an hour they was as thick as thieves again, and the tighter they got the lovinger they got, and went off a-snoring in each other's arms. They both got powerful mellow, but I noticed the king didn't get mellow enough to forget to remember to not deny about hiding the money-bag again. That made me feel easy and satisfied. Of course when they got to snoring we had a long gabble, and I told Jim everything.

Chapter XXXI

We dasn't stop again at any town for days and days; kept right along down the river. We was down south in the warm weather now, and a mighty long ways from home. We begun to come to trees with Spanish moss on them, hanging down from the limbs like long, gray beards. It was the first I ever see it growing, and it made the woods look solemn and dismal. So now the frauds reckoned they was out of danger, and they begun to work the villages again.

First they done a lecture on temperance; but they didn't make enough for them both to get drunk on. Then in another village they started a dancing-school; but they didn't know no more how to dance than a kangaroo does; so the first prance they made the general public jumped in and pranced them out of town. Another time they tried to go at yellocution; but they didn't yellocute long till the audience got up and give them a solid good cussing, and made them skip out. They tackled missionarying, and mesmerizing, and doctoring, and telling fortunes, and a little of everything; but they couldn't seem to have no luck. So at last they got just about dead broke, and laid around the raft as she floated along, thinking and thinking, and never saying nothing, by the half a day at a time, and dreadful blue and desperate.

And at last they took a change and begun to lay their heads together in the wigwam and talk low and confidential two or three hours at a time. Jim and me got uneasy. We didn't like the look of it. We judged they was studying up some kind of worse deviltry than ever. We turned it over and over, and at last we made up our minds they was going to break into somebody's house or store, or was going into the counterfeit-money business, or something. So then we was pretty scared, and made up an agreement that we wouldn't have nothing in the world to do with such actions, and if we ever got the least show we would give them the cold shake and clear out and leave them behind. Well, early one morning we hid the raft in a good, safe place about two mile below a little bit of a shabby village named Pikesville, and the king he went ashore and told us all to stay hid whilst he went up to town and smelt around to see if anybody had got any wind of the Royal Nonesuch there yet. ("House to rob, you MEAN," says

I to myself; "and when you get through robbing it you'll come back here and wonder what has become of me and Jim and the raft—and you'll have to take it out in wondering.") And he said if he warn't back by midday the duke and me would know it was all right, and we was to come along.

So we stayed where we was. The duke he fretted and sweated around, and was in a mighty sour way. He scolded us for everything, and we couldn't seem to do nothing right; he found fault with every little thing. Something was a-brewing, sure. I was good and glad when midday come and no king; we could have a change, anyway—and maybe a chance for THE chance on top of it. So me and the duke went up to the village, and hunted around there for the king, and by and by we found him in the back room of a little low doggery, very tight, and a lot of loafers bullyragging him for sport, and he a-cussing and a-threatening with all his might, and so tight he couldn't walk, and couldn't do nothing to them. The duke he begun to abuse him for an old fool, and the king begun to sass back, and the minute they was fairly at it I lit out and shook the reefs out of my hind legs, and spun down the river road like a deer, for I see our chance; and I made up my mind that it would be a long day before they ever see me and Jim again. I got down there all out of breath but loaded up with joy, and sung out:

"Set her loose, Jim! we're all right now!"

But there warn't no answer, and nobody come out of the wigwam. Jim was gone! I set up a shout—and then another—and then another one; and run this way and that in the woods, whooping and screeching; but it warn't no use—old Jim was gone. Then I set down and cried; I couldn't help it. But I couldn't set still long. Pretty soon I went out on the road, trying to think what I better do, and I run across a boy walking, and asked him if he'd seen a strange nigger dressed so and so, and he says:

"Yes."

"Whereabouts?" says I.

"Down to Silas Phelps' place, two mile below here. He's a runaway nigger, and they've got him. Was you looking for him?"

"You bet I ain't! I run across him in the woods about an hour or two ago, and he said if I hollered he'd cut my livers out—and told me to lay down and stay where I was; and I done it. Been there ever since; afeard to come out."

"Well," he says, "you needn't be afeard no more, becuz they've got him. He run off f'm down South, som'ers."

"It's a good job they got him."

"Well, I RECKON! There's two hunderd dollars reward on him. It's like picking up money out'n the road."

"Yes, it is—and I could a had it if I'd been big enough; I see him FIRST. Who nailed him?"

"It was an old fellow—a stranger—and he sold out his chance in him for forty dollars, becuz he's got to go up the river and can't wait. Think o' that, now! You bet I'D wait, if it was seven year."

"That's me, every time," says I. "But maybe his chance ain't worth no more than that, if he'll sell it so cheap. Maybe there's something ain't straight about it."

"But it IS, though—straight as a string. I see the handbill myself. It tells all about him, to a dot—paints him like a picture, and tells the plantation he's frum, below Newrleans. No-sirree-bob, they ain't no trouble 'bout THAT speculation, you bet you. Say, gimme a chaw tobacker, won't ye?"

I didn't have none, so he left. I went to the raft, and set down in the wigwam to think. But I couldn't come to nothing. I thought till I wore my head sore, but I couldn't see no way out of the trouble. After all this long journey, and after all we'd done for them scoundrels, here it was all come to nothing, everything all busted up and ruined, because they could have the heart to serve Jim such a trick as that, and make him a slave again all his life, and amongst strangers, too, for forty dirty dollars.

Once I said to myself it would be a thousand times better for Jim to be a slave at home where his family was, as long as he'd GOT to be a slave, and so I'd better write a letter to Tom Sawyer and tell him to tell Miss Watson where he was. But I soon give up that notion for two things: she'd be mad and disgusted at his rascality and ungratefulness for leaving her, and so she'd sell him straight down the river again; and if she didn't, everybody naturally despises an ungrateful nigger, and they'd make Jim feel it all the time, and so he'd feel ornery and disgraced. And then think of ME! It would get all around that Huck Finn helped a nigger to get his freedom; and if I was ever to see anybody from that town again I'd be ready to get down and lick his boots for shame. That's just the way: a person does a low-down thing, and then he don't want to take no consequences of it. Thinks as long as he can hide, it ain't no disgrace. That was my fix exactly. The more I studied about this the more my conscience went to grinding me, and the more wicked and low-down and ornery I got to feeling. And at last, when it hit me all of a sudden that here was the plain hand of Providence slapping me in the face and letting me know my wickedness was being watched all the time from up there in heaven, whilst I was stealing a poor old woman's nigger that hadn't ever done me no harm, and now was showing me there's One that's always on the lookout, and ain't a-going to allow no such miserable doings to go only just so fur and no further, I most dropped in my tracks I was so scared. Well, I tried the best I could to kinder soften it up somehow for myself by saying I was brung up wicked, and so I warn't so much to blame; but something inside of me kept saying, "There was the Sunday-school, you could a gone to it; and if you'd a done it they'd a learnt you there that people that acts as I'd been acting about that nigger goes to everlasting fire."

It made me shiver. And I about made up my mind to pray, and see if I couldn't try to quit being the kind of a boy I was and be better. So I kneeled down. But the words wouldn't come. Why wouldn't they? It warn't no use to try and hide it from Him. Nor from ME, neither. I knowed very well why they wouldn't come. It was because my heart warn't right; it was because I warn't square; it was because I was playing double. I was letting ON to give up sin, but away inside of me I was holding on to the biggest one of all. I was trying to make my mouth SAY I would do the right thing and the clean thing, and go and write to that nigger's owner and tell where he was; but deep down in me I knowed it was a lie, and He knowed it. You can't pray a lie—I found that out.

So I was full of trouble, full as I could be; and didn't know what to do. At last I had an idea; and I says, I'll go and write the letter—and then see if I can pray. Why, it was astonishing, the way I felt as light as a feather right straight off, and my troubles all gone. So I got a piece of paper and a pencil, all glad and excited, and set down and wrote:

Miss Watson, your runaway nigger Jim is down here two mile below Pikesville, and Mr. Phelps has got him and he will give him up for the reward if you send.
> *HUCK FINN*

I felt good and all washed clean of sin for the first time I had ever felt so in my life, and I knowed I could pray now. But I didn't do it straight off, but laid the paper down and set there thinking—thinking how good it was all this happened so, and how near I come to being lost and going to hell. And went on thinking. And got to thinking over our trip down the river; and I see Jim before me all the time: in the day and in the night-time, sometimes moonlight, sometimes storms, and we a-floating along, talking and singing and laughing. But somehow I couldn't seem to strike no places to harden me against him, but only the other kind. I'd see him standing my watch on top of his'n, 'stead of calling me, so I could go on sleeping; and see him how glad he was when I come back out of the fog; and when I come to him again in the swamp, up there where the feud was; and such-like times; and would always call me honey, and pet me and do everything he could think of for me, and how good he always was; and at last I struck the time I saved him by telling the men we had small-pox aboard, and he was so grateful, and said I was the best friend old Jim ever had in the world, and the ONLY one he's got now; and then I happened to look around and see that paper.

It was a close place. I took it up, and held it in my hand. I was a-trembling, because I'd got to decide, forever, betwixt two things, and I knowed it. I studied a minute, sort of holding my breath, and then says to myself:

"All right, then, I'll GO to hell"—and tore it up.

It was awful thoughts and awful words, but they was said. And I let them stay said; and never thought no more about reforming. I shoved the whole thing out of my head, and said I would take up wickedness again, which was in my line, being brung up to it, and the other warn't. And for a starter I would go to work and steal Jim out of slavery again; and if I could think up anything worse, I would do that, too; because as long as I was in, and in for good, I might as well go the whole hog.

Then I set to thinking over how to get at it, and turned over some considerable many ways in my mind; and at last fixed up a plan that suited me. So then I took the bearings of a woody island that was down the river a piece, and as soon as it was fairly dark I crept out with my raft and went for it, and hid it there, and then turned in. I slept the night through, and got up before it was light, and had my breakfast, and put on my store clothes, and tied up some others and one thing or another in a bundle, and took the canoe and cleared for shore. I landed below where I judged was Phelps's place, and hid my bundle in the woods, and then filled up the canoe with water, and loaded rocks into her and sunk her where I could find her again when I wanted her, about a quarter of a mile below a little steam sawmill that was on the bank.

Then I struck up the road, and when I passed the mill I see a sign on it, "Phelps's Sawmill," and when I come to the farm-houses, two or three hundred yards further along, I kept my eyes peeled, but didn't see nobody around, though it was good daylight now. But I didn't mind, because I didn't want to see nobody just yet—I only wanted to get the lay of the land. According to my plan, I was going to turn up there from the village, not from below. So I just took a look, and shoved along, straight for town. Well, the very first man I see when I got there was the duke. He was sticking up a bill for the Royal Nonesuch—three-night performance—like that other time. They had the cheek, them frauds! I was right on him before I could shirk. He looked astonished, and says:

"Hel-LO! Where'd YOU come from?" Then he says, kind of glad and eager, "Where's the raft?—got her in a good place?"

I says:

"Why, that's just what I was going to ask your grace."

Then he didn't look so joyful, and says:

"What was your idea for asking ME?" he says.

"Well," I says, "when I see the king in that doggery yesterday I says to myself, we can't get him home for hours, till he's soberer; so I went a-loafing around town to put in the time and wait. A man up and offered me ten cents to help him pull a skiff over the river and back to fetch a sheep, and so I went along; but when we was dragging him to the boat, and the man left me a-holt of the rope and went behind him to shove him along, he was too strong for me and jerked loose and run, and we after him. We didn't have no dog, and so we had to chase him all over the country till we tired him out. We never got him till dark; then we fetched him over, and I started down for the raft. When I got there and see it was gone, I says to myself, 'They've got into trouble and had to leave; and they've took my nigger, which is the only nigger I've got in the world, and now I'm in a strange country, and ain't got no property no more, nor nothing, and no way to make my living;' so I set down and cried. I slept in the woods all night. But what DID become of the raft, then?—and Jim—poor Jim!"

"Blamed if I know—that is, what's become of the raft. That old fool had made a trade and got forty dollars, and when we found him in the doggery the loafers had matched half-dollars with him and got every cent but what he'd spent for whisky; and when I got him home late last night and found the raft gone, we said, 'That little rascal has stole our raft and shook us, and run off down the river.'"

"I wouldn't shake my NIGGER, would I?—the only nigger I had in the world, and the only property."

"We never thought of that. Fact is, I reckon we'd come to consider him OUR nigger; yes, we did consider him so—goodness knows we had trouble enough for him. So when we see the raft was gone and we flat broke, there warn't anything for it but to try the Royal Nonesuch another shake. And I've pegged along ever since, dry as a powder-horn. Where's that ten cents? Give it here."

I had considerable money, so I give him ten cents, but begged him to spend it for something to eat, and give me some, because it was all the money I had, and I hadn't had nothing to eat since yesterday. He never said nothing. The next minute he whirls on me and says:

"Do you reckon that nigger would blow on us? We'd skin him if he done that!"

"How can he blow? Hain't he run off?"

"No! That old fool sold him, and never divided with me, and the money's gone."

"SOLD him?" I says, and begun to cry; "why, he was MY nigger, and that was my money. Where is he?—I want my nigger."

"Well, you can't GET your nigger, that's all—so dry up your blubbering. Looky here—do you think YOU'D venture to blow on us? Blamed if I think I'd trust you. Why, if you WAS to blow on us—"

He stopped, but I never see the duke look so ugly out of his eyes before. I went on a-whimpering, and says:

"I don't want to blow on nobody; and I ain't got no time to blow, nohow. I got to turn out and find my nigger."

He looked kinder bothered, and stood there with his bills fluttering on his arm, thinking, and wrinkling up his forehead. At last he says:

"I'll tell you something. We got to be here three days. If you'll promise you won't blow, and won't let the nigger blow, I'll tell you where to find him."

So I promised, and he says:

"A farmer by the name of Silas Ph—" and then he stopped. You see, he started to tell me the truth; but when he stopped that way, and begun to study and think again, I reckoned he was changing his mind. And so he was. He wouldn't trust me; he wanted to make sure of having me out of the way the whole three days. So pretty soon he says:

"The man that bought him is named Abram Foster—Abram G. Foster—and he lives forty mile back here in the country, on the road to Lafayette."

"All right," I says, "I can walk it in three days. And I'll start this very afternoon."

"No you wont, you'll start NOW; and don't you lose any time about it, neither, nor do any gabbling by the way. Just keep a tight tongue in your head and move right along, and then you won't get into trouble with US, d'ye hear?"

That was the order I wanted, and that was the one I played for. I wanted to be left free to work my plans.

"So clear out," he says; "and you can tell Mr. Foster whatever you want to. Maybe you can get him to believe that Jim IS your nigger—some idiots don't require docu-ments—leastways I've heard there's such down South here. And when you tell him the handbill and the reward's bogus, maybe he'll believe you when you explain to him what the idea was for getting 'em out. Go 'long now, and tell him anything you want to; but mind you don't work your jaw any BETWEEN here and there."

So I left, and struck for the back country. I didn't look around, but I kinder felt like he was watching me. But I knowed I could tire him out at that. I went straight out in the country as much as a mile before I stopped; then I doubled back through the woods towards Phelps'. I reckoned I better start in on my plan straight off without fooling around, because I wanted to stop Jim's mouth till these fellows could get away. I didn't want no trouble with their kind. I'd seen all I wanted to of them, and wanted to get entirely shut of them.

Chapter XXXII

When I got there it was all still and Sunday-like, and hot and sunshiny; the hands was gone to the fields; and there was them kind of faint dronings of bugs and flies in the air that makes it seem so lonesome and like everybody's dead and gone; and if a breeze fans along and quivers the leaves it makes you feel mournful, because you feel like it's spirits whispering—spirits that's been dead ever so many years—and you always think they're talking about YOU. As a general thing it makes a body wish HE was dead, too, and done with it all.

Phelps' was one of these little one-horse cotton plantations, and they all look alike. A rail fence round a two-acre yard; a stile made out of logs sawed off and up-ended in steps, like barrels of a different length, to climb over the fence with, and or the women to stand on when they are going to jump on to a horse; some sickly grass-patches in the big yard, but mostly it was bare and smooth, like an old hat with the nap rubbed off; big double log-house for the white folks—hewed logs, with the chinks stopped up with mud or mortar, and these mud-stripes been whitewashed some time or another; round-log kitchen, with a big broad, open but roofed passage joining it to the house; log smoke-house back of the kitchen; three little log nigger-cabins in a row t'other side the smoke-house; one little hut all by itself away down against the back fence, and some outbuildings down a piece the other side; ash-hopper and big kettle to bile soap in by the little hut; bench by the kitchen door, with bucket of water and a gourd; hound asleep there in the sun; more hounds asleep round about; about three shade trees away off in a corner; some currant bushes and gooseberry bushes in one place by the fence; outside of the fence a garden and a watermelon patch; then the cotton fields begins, and after the fields the woods.

I went around and clumb over the back stile by the ash- hopper, and started for the kitchen. When I got a little ways I heard the dim hum of a spinning-wheel wailing along up and sinking along down again; and then I knowed for certain I wished I was dead—for that IS the lonesomest sound in the whole world.

I went right along, not fixing up any particular plan, but just trusting to Providence to put the right words in my mouth when the time come; for I'd noticed that Providence always did put the right words in my mouth if I left it alone.

When I got half-way, first one hound and then another got up and went for me, and of course I stopped and faced them, and kept still. And such another powwow as they made! In a quarter of a minute I was a kind of a hub of a wheel, as you may say—spokes made out of dogs—circle of fifteen of them packed together around me, with their necks and noses stretched up towards me, a-barking and howling; and more a-coming; you could see them sailing over fences and around corners from everywheres.

A nigger woman come tearing out of the kitchen with a rolling-pin in her hand, singing out, "Begone YOU Tige! you Spot! begone sah!" and she fetched first one and then another of them a clip and sent them howling, and then the rest followed; and the next second half of them come back, wagging their tails around me, and making friends with me. There ain't no harm in a hound, nohow.

And behind the woman comes a little nigger girl and two little nigger boys without anything on but tow-linen shirts, and they hung on to their mother's gown, and peeped out from behind her at me, bashful, the way they always do. And here comes the white woman running from the house, about forty-five or fifty year old, bare-headed, and her spinning-stick in her hand; and behind her comes her little white children, acting the same way the little niggers was going. She was smiling all over so she could hardly stand—and says:

"It's YOU, at last!—AIN'T it?"

I out with a "Yes'm" before I thought.

She grabbed me and hugged me tight; and then gripped me by both hands and shook and shook; and the tears come in her eyes, and run down over; and she couldn't seem to hug and shake enough, and kept saying, "You don't look as much like your mother as I reckoned you would; but law sakes, I don't care for that, I'm so glad to see you! Dear, dear, it does seem like I could eat you up! Children, it's your cousin Tom!—tell him howdy."

But they ducked their heads, and put their fingers in their mouths, and hid behind her. So she run on:

"Lize, hurry up and get him a hot breakfast right away—or did you get your breakfast on the boat?"

I said I had got it on the boat. So then she started for the house, leading me by the hand, and the children tagging after. When we got there she set me down in a split-bottomed chair, and set herself down on a little low stool in front of me, holding both of my hands, and says:

"Now I can have a GOOD look at you; and, laws-a-me, I've been hungry for it a many and a many a time, all these long years, and it's come at last! We been expecting you a couple of days and more. What kep' you?—boat get aground?"

"Yes'm—she—"

"Don't say yes'm—say Aunt Sally. Where'd she get aground?"

I didn't rightly know what to say, because I didn't know whether the boat would be coming up the river or down. But I go a good deal on instinct; and my instinct said she would be coming up—from down towards Orleans. That didn't help me much, though; for I didn't know the names of bars down that way. I see I'd got to invent a bar, or forget the name of the one we got aground on—or—Now I struck an idea, and fetched it out:

"It warn't the grounding—that didn't keep us back but a little. We blowed out a cylinder-head."

"Good gracious! anybody hurt?"

"No'm. Killed a nigger."

"Well, it's lucky; because sometimes people do get hurt. Two years ago last Christmas your uncle Silas was coming up from Newrleans on the old Lally Rook, and she blowed out a cylinder-head and crippled a man. And I think he died afterwards. He was a Baptist. Your uncle Silas knowed a family in Baton Rouge that knowed his people very well. Yes, I remember now, he DID die. Mortification set in, and they had to amputate him. But it didn't save him. Yes, it was mortification—that was it. He turned blue all over, and died in the hope of a glorious resurrection. They say he was a sight to look at. Your uncle's been up to the town every day to fetch you. And he's gone again, not more'n an hour ago; he'll be back any minute now. You must a met him on the road, didn't you?—oldish man, with a—"

"No, I didn't see nobody, Aunt Sally. The boat landed just at daylight, and I left my baggage on the wharf-boat and went looking around the town and out a piece in the country, to put in the time and not get here too soon; and so I come down the back way."

"Who'd you give the baggage to?"

"Nobody."

"Why, child, it 'll be stole!"

"Not where I hid it I reckon it won't," I says.

"How'd you get your breakfast so early on the boat?"

It was kinder thin ice, but I says:

"The captain see me standing around, and told me I better have something to eat before I went ashore; so he took me in the texas to the officers' lunch, and give me all I wanted."

I was getting so uneasy I couldn't listen good. I had my mind on the children all the time; I wanted to get them out to one side and pump them a little, and find out who I was. But I couldn't get no show, Mrs. Phelps kept it up and run on so. Pretty soon she made the cold chills streak all down my back, because she says:

"But here we're a-running on this way, and you hain't told me a word about Sis, nor any of them. Now I'll rest my works a little, and you start up yourn; just tell me EVERYTHING—tell me all about 'm all every one of 'm; and how they are, and what they're doing, and what they told you to tell me; and every last thing you can think of."

Well, I see I was up a stump—and up it good. Providence had stood by me this fur all right, but I was hard and tight aground now. I see it warn't a bit of use to try to go ahead—I'd got to throw up my hand. So I says to myself, here's another place where I got to resk the truth. I opened my mouth to begin; but she grabbed me and hustled me in behind the bed, and says:

"Here he comes! Stick your head down lower—there, that'll do; you can't be seen now. Don't you let on you're here. I'll play a joke on him. Children, don't you say a word."

I see I was in a fix now. But it warn't no use to worry; there warn't nothing to do but just hold still, and try and be ready to stand from under when the lightning struck.

I had just one little glimpse of the old gentleman when he come in; then the bed hid him. Mrs. Phelps she jumps for him, and says:

"Has he come?"

"No," says her husband.

"Good-NESS gracious!" she says, "what in the warld can have become of him?"

"I can't imagine," says the old gentleman; "and I must say it makes me dreadful uneasy."

"Uneasy!" she says; "I'm ready to go distracted! He MUST a come; and you've missed him along the road. I KNOW it's so—something tells me so."

"Why, Sally, I COULDN'T miss him along the road—YOU know that."

"But oh, dear, dear, what WILL Sis say! He must a come! You must a missed him. He—"

"Oh, don't distress me any more'n I'm already distressed. I don't know what in the world to make of it. I'm at my wit's end, and I don't mind acknowledging 't I'm right down scared. But there's no hope that he's come; for he COULDN'T come and me miss him. Sally, it's terrible—just terrible—something's happened to the boat, sure!"

"Why, Silas! Look yonder!—up the road!—ain't that somebody coming?"

He sprung to the window at the head of the bed, and that give Mrs. Phelps the chance she wanted. She stooped down quick at the foot of the bed and give me a pull, and out I come; and when he turned back from the window there she stood, a-beaming and a-smiling like a house afire, and I standing pretty meek and sweaty alongside. The old gentleman stared, and says:

"Why, who's that?"

"Who do you reckon 't is?"

"I hain't no idea. Who IS it?"

"It's TOM SAWYER!"

By jings, I most slumped through the floor! But there warn't no time to swap knives; the old man grabbed me by the hand and shook, and kept on shaking; and all the time how the woman did dance around and laugh and cry; and then how they both did fire off questions about Sid, and Mary, and the rest of the tribe.

But if they was joyful, it warn't nothing to what I was; for it was like being born again, I was so glad to find out who I was. Well, they froze to me for two hours; and at last, when my chin was so tired it couldn't hardly go any more, I had told them more about my family—I mean the Sawyer family—than ever happened to any six Sawyer families. And I explained all about how we blowed out a cylinder-head at the mouth of White River, and it took us three days to fix it. Which was all right, and worked first-rate; because THEY didn't know but what it would take three days to fix it. If I'd a called it a bolthead it would a done just as well.

Now I was feeling pretty comfortable all down one side, and pretty uncomfortable all up the other. Being Tom Sawyer was easy and comfortable, and it stayed easy and comfortable till by and by I hear a steamboat coughing along down the river. Then I says to myself, s'pose Tom Sawyer comes down on that boat? And s'pose he steps in here any minute, and sings out my name before I can throw him a wink to keep quiet?

Well, I couldn't HAVE it that way; it wouldn't do at all. I must go up the road and waylay him. So I told the folks I reckoned I would go up to the town and fetch down my baggage. The old gentleman was for going along with me, but I said no, I could drive the horse myself, and I druther he wouldn't take no trouble about me.

Chapter XXXIII

So I started for town in the wagon, and when I was half-way I see a wagon coming, and sure enough it was Tom Sawyer, and I stopped and waited till he come along. I says "Hold on!" and it stopped alongside, and his mouth opened up like a trunk, and stayed so; and he swallowed two or three times like a person that's got a dry throat, and then says:

"I hain't ever done you no harm. You know that. So, then, what you want to come back and ha'nt ME for?"

I says:

"I hain't come back—I hain't been GONE."

When he heard my voice it righted him up some, but he warn't quite satisfied yet. He says:

"Don't you play nothing on me, because I wouldn't on you. Honest injun, you ain't a ghost?"

"Honest injun, I ain't," I says.

"Well—I—I—well, that ought to settle it, of course; but I can't somehow seem to understand it no way. Looky here, warn't you ever murdered AT ALL?"

"No. I warn't ever murdered at all—I played it on them. You come in here and feel of me if you don't believe me."

So he done it; and it satisfied him; and he was that glad to see me again he didn't know what to do. And he wanted to know all about it right off, because it was a grand adventure, and mysterious, and so it hit him where he lived. But I said, leave it alone till by and by; and told his driver to wait, and we drove off a little piece, and I told him the kind of a fix I was in, and what did he reckon we better do? He said, let him alone a minute, and don't disturb him. So he thought and thought, and pretty soon he says:

"It's all right; I've got it. Take my trunk in your wagon, and let on it's your'n; and you turn back and fool along slow, so as to get to the house about the time you ought to; and I'll go towards town a piece, and take a fresh start, and get there a quarter or a half an hour after you; and you needn't let on to know me at first."

I says:

"All right; but wait a minute. There's one more thing—a thing that NOBODY don't know but me. And that is, there's a nigger here that I'm a-trying to steal out of slavery, and his name is JIM—old Miss Watson's Jim."

He says:

"What! Why, Jim is—"

He stopped and went to studying. I says:

"I know what you'll say. You'll say it's dirty, low-down business; but what if it is? I'm low down; and I'm a-going to steal him, and I want you keep mum and not let on. Will you?"

His eye lit up, and he says:

"I'll HELP you steal him!"

Well, I let go all holts then, like I was shot. It was the most astonishing speech I ever heard—and I'm bound to say Tom Sawyer fell considerable in my estimation. Only I couldn't believe it. Tom Sawyer a NIGGER-STEALER!

"Oh, shucks!" I says; "you're joking."

"I ain't joking, either."

"Well, then," I says, "joking or no joking, if you hear anything said about a runaway nigger, don't forget to remember that YOU don't know nothing about him, and I don't know nothing about him."

Then we took the trunk and put it in my wagon, and he drove off his way and I drove mine. But of course I forgot all about driving slow on accounts of being glad and full of thinking; so I got home a heap too quick for that length of a trip. The old gentleman was at the door, and he says:

"Why, this is wonderful! Whoever would a thought it was in that mare to do it? I wish we'd a timed her. And she hain't sweated a hair—not a hair. It's wonderful.

Why, I wouldn't take a hundred dollars for that horse now—I wouldn't, honest; and yet I'd a sold her for fifteen before, and thought 'twas all she was worth."

That's all he said. He was the innocentest, best old soul I ever see. But it warn't surprising; because he warn't only just a farmer, he was a preacher, too, and had a little one-horse log church down back of the plantation, which he built it himself at his own expense, for a church and schoolhouse, and never charged nothing for his preaching, and it was worth it, too. There was plenty other farmer-preachers like that, and done the same way, down South.

In about half an hour Tom's wagon drove up to the front stile, and Aunt Sally she see it through the window, because it was only about fifty yards, and says:

"Why, there's somebody come! I wonder who 'tis? Why, I do believe it's a stranger. Jimmy" (that's one of the children) "run and tell Lize to put on another plate for dinner."

Everybody made a rush for the front door, because, of course, a stranger don't come EVERY year, and so he lays over the yaller-fever, for interest, when he does come. Tom was over the stile and starting for the house; the wagon was spinning up the road for the village, and we was all bunched in the front door. Tom had his store clothes on, and an audience—and that was always nuts for Tom Sawyer. In them circumstances it warn't no trouble to him to throw in an amount of style that was suitable. He warn't a boy to meeky along up that yard like a sheep; no, he come ca'm and important, like the ram. When he got a-front of us he lifts his hat ever so gracious and dainty, like it was the lid of a box that had butterflies asleep in it and he didn't want to disturb them, and says:

"Mr. Archibald Nichols, I presume?"

"No, my boy," says the old gentleman, "I'm sorry to say 't your driver has deceived you; Nichols's place is down a matter of three mile more. Come in, come in."

Tom he took a look back over his shoulder, and says, "Too late—he's out of sight."

"Yes, he's gone, my son, and you must come in and eat your dinner with us; and then we'll hitch up and take you down to Nichols's."

"Oh, I CAN'T make you so much trouble; I couldn't think of it. I'll walk —I don't mind the distance."

"But we won't LET you walk—it wouldn't be Southern hospitality to do it. Come right in."

"Oh, DO," says Aunt Sally; "it ain't a bit of trouble to us, not a bit in the world. You must stay. It's a long, dusty three mile, and we can't let you walk. And, besides, I've already told 'em to put on another plate when I see you coming; so you mustn't disappoint us. Come right in and make yourself at home."

So Tom he thanked them very hearty and handsome, and let himself be persuaded, and come in; and when he was in he said he was a stranger from Hicksville, Ohio, and his name was William Thompson—and he made another bow.

Well, he run on, and on, and on, making up stuff about Hicksville and everybody in it he could invent, and I getting a little nervous, and wondering how this was going to help me out of my scrape; and at last, still talking along, he reached over and kissed Aunt Sally right on the mouth, and then settled back again in his chair comfortable, and was going on talking; but she jumped up and wiped it off with the back of her hand, and says:

"You owdacious puppy!"

He looked kind of hurt, and says:

"I'm surprised at you, m'am."

"You're s'rp—Why, what do you reckon I am? I've a good notion to take and— Say, what do you mean by kissing me?"

He looked kind of humble, and says:

"I didn't mean nothing, m'am. I didn't mean no harm. I—I—thought you'd like it."

"Why, you born fool!" She took up the spinning stick, and it looked like it was all she could do to keep from giving him a crack with it. "What made you think I'd like it?"

"Well, I don't know. Only, they—they—told me you would."

"THEY told you I would. Whoever told you's ANOTHER lunatic. I never heard the beat of it. Who's THEY?"

"Why, everybody. They all said so, m'am."

It was all she could do to hold in; and her eyes snapped, and her fingers worked like she wanted to scratch him; and she says:

"Who's 'everybody'? Out with their names, or ther'll be an idiot short."

He got up and looked distressed, and fumbled his hat, and says:

"I'm sorry, and I warn't expecting it. They told me to. They all told me to. They all said, kiss her; and said she'd like it. They all said it—every one of them. But I'm sorry, m'am, and I won't do it no more —I won't, honest.

"You won't, won't you? Well, I sh'd RECKON you won't!"

"No'm, I'm honest about it; I won't ever do it again—till you ask me."

"Till I ASK you! Well, I never see the beat of it in my born days! I lay you'll be the Methusalem-numskull of creation before ever I ask you —or the likes of you."

"Well," he says, "it does surprise me so. I can't make it out, somehow. They said you would, and I thought you would. But—" He stopped and looked around slow, like he wished he could run across a friendly eye somewheres, and fetched up on the old gentleman's, and says, "Didn't YOU think she'd like me to kiss her, sir?"

"Why, no; I—I—well, no, I b'lieve I didn't."

Then he looks on around the same way to me, and says:

"Tom, didn't YOU think Aunt Sally 'd open her arms and say, 'Sid Sawyer—'"

"My land!" she says, breaking in and jumping for him, "you impudent young rascal, to fool a body so—" and was going to hug him, but he fended her off, and says:

't till you've asked me first."

idn't lose no time, but asked him; and hugged him and kissed him over
⌐ again, and then turned him over to the old man, and he took what was left.
And after they got a little quiet again she says:

"Why, dear me, I never see such a surprise. We warn't looking for YOU at all, but
only Tom. Sis never wrote to me about anybody coming but him."

"It's because it warn't INTENDED for any of us to come but Tom," he says; "but
I begged and begged, and at the last minute she let me come, too; so, coming down the
river, me and Tom thought it would be a first-rate surprise for him to come here to the
house first, and for me to by and by tag along and drop in, and let on to be a stranger.
But it was a mistake, Aunt Sally. This ain't no healthy place for a stranger to come."

"No—not impudent whelps, Sid. You ought to had your jaws boxed; I hain't been
so put out since I don't know when. But I don't care, I don't mind the terms—I'd be
willing to stand a thousand such jokes to have you here. Well, to think of that performance! I don't deny it, I was most putrified with astonishment when you give me that
smack."

We had dinner out in that broad open passage betwixt the house and the kitchen;
and there was things enough on that table for seven families —and all hot, too; none
of your flabby, tough meat that's laid in a cupboard in a damp cellar all night and tastes
like a hunk of old cold cannibal in the morning. Uncle Silas he asked a pretty long
blessing over it, but it was worth it; and it didn't cool it a bit, neither, the way I've seen
them kind of interruptions do lots of times. There was a considerable good deal of
talk all the afternoon, and me and Tom was on the lookout all the time; but it warn't no
use, they didn't happen to say nothing about any runaway nigger, and we was afraid to
try to work up to it. But at supper, at night, one of the little boys says:

"Pa, mayn't Tom and Sid and me go to the show?"

"No," says the old man, "I reckon there ain't going to be any; and you couldn't go
if there was; because the runaway nigger told Burton and me all about that scandalous
show, and Burton said he would tell the people; so I reckon they've drove the owdacious
loafers out of town before this time."

So there it was!—but I couldn't help it. Tom and me was to sleep in the same
room and bed; so, being tired, we bid good-night and went up to bed right after supper, and clumb out of the window and down the lightning-rod, and shoved for the
town; for I didn't believe anybody was going to give the king and the duke a hint, and
so if I didn't hurry up and give them one they'd get into trouble sure.

On the road Tom he told me all about how it was reckoned I was murdered, and
how pap disappeared pretty soon, and didn't come back no more, and what a stir there
was when Jim run away; and I told Tom all about our Royal Nonesuch rapscallions,
and as much of the raft voyage as I had time to; and as we struck into the town and up
through the—here comes a raging rush of people with torches, and an awful whooping and yelling, and banging tin pans and blowing horns; and we jumped to one side to

let them go by; and as they went by I see they had the king and the duke astraddle of a rail—that is, I knowed it WAS the king and the duke, though they was all over tar and feathers, and didn't look like nothing in the world that was human—just looked like a couple of monstrous big soldier-plumes. Well, it made me sick to see it; and I was sorry for them poor pitiful rascals, it seemed like I couldn't ever feel any hardness against them any more in the world. It was a dreadful thing to see. Human beings CAN be awful cruel to one another.

We see we was too late—couldn't do no good. We asked some stragglers about it, and they said everybody went to the show looking very innocent; and laid low and kept dark till the poor old king was in the middle of his cavortings on the stage; then somebody give a signal, and the house rose up and went for them.

So we poked along back home, and I warn't feeling so brash as I was before, but kind of ornery, and humble, and to blame, somehow—though I hadn't done nothing. But that's always the way; it don't make no difference whether you do right or wrong, a person's conscience ain't got no sense, and just goes for him anyway. If I had a yaller dog that didn't know no more than a person's conscience does I would pison him. It takes up more room than all the rest of a person's insides, and yet ain't no good, nohow. Tom Sawyer he says the same.

Chapter XXXIV

We stopped talking, and got to thinking. By and by Tom says: "Looky here, Huck, what fools we are to not think of it before! I bet I know where Jim is."

"No! Where?"

"In that hut down by the ash-hopper. Why, looky here. When we was at dinner, didn't you see a nigger man go in there with some vittles?"

"Yes."

"What did you think the vittles was for?"

"For a dog."

"So 'd I. Well, it wasn't for a dog."

"Why?"

"Because part of it was watermelon."

"So it was—I noticed it. Well, it does beat all that I never thought about a dog not eating watermelon. It shows how a body can see and don't see at the same time."

"Well, the nigger unlocked the padlock when he went in, and he locked it again when he came out. He fetched uncle a key about the time we got up from table—same key, I bet. Watermelon shows man, lock shows prisoner; and it ain't likely there's two prisoners on such a little plantation, and where the people's all so kind and good. Jim's the prisoner. All right—I'm glad we found it out detective fashion; I wouldn't give shucks for any other way. Now you work your mind, and study out a plan to steal Jim, and I will study out one, too; and we'll take the one we like the best."

What a head for just a boy to have! If I had Tom Sawyer's head I wouldn't trade it off to be a duke, nor mate of a steamboat, nor clown in a circus, nor nothing I can think of. I went to thinking out a plan, but only just to be doing something; I knowed very well where the right plan was going to come from. Pretty soon Tom says:

"Ready?"

"Yes," I says.

"All right—bring it out."

"My plan is this," I says. "We can easy find out if it's Jim in there.

Then get up my canoe to-morrow night, and fetch my raft over from the island. Then the first dark night that comes steal the key out of the old man's britches after he goes to bed, and shove off down the river on the raft with Jim, hiding daytimes and running nights, the way me and Jim used to do before. Wouldn't that plan work?"

"WORK? Why, cert'nly it would work, like rats a-fighting. But it's too blame' simple; there ain't nothing TO it. What's the good of a plan that ain't no more trouble than that? It's as mild as goose-milk. Why, Huck, it wouldn't make no more talk than breaking into a soap factory."

I never said nothing, because I warn't expecting nothing different; but I knowed mighty well that whenever he got HIS plan ready it wouldn't have none of them objections to it.

And it didn't. He told me what it was, and I see in a minute it was worth fifteen of mine for style, and would make Jim just as free a man as mine would, and maybe get us all killed besides. So I was satisfied, and said we would waltz in on it. I needn't tell what it was here, because I knowed it wouldn't stay the way, it was. I knowed he would be changing it around every which way as we went along, and heaving in new bullinesses wherever he got a chance. And that is what he done.

Well, one thing was dead sure, and that was that Tom Sawyer was in earnest, and was actuly going to help steal that nigger out of slavery. That was the thing that was too many for me. Here was a boy that was respectable and well brung up; and had a character to lose; and folks at home that had characters; and he was bright and not leather-headed; and knowing and not ignorant; and not mean, but kind; and yet here he was, without any more pride, or rightness, or feeling, than to stoop to this business, and make himself a shame, and his family a shame, before everybody. I COULDN'T understand it no way at all. It was outrageous, and I knowed I ought to just up and tell him so; and so be his true friend, and let him quit the thing right where he was and save himself. And I DID start to tell him; but he shut me up, and says:

"Don't you reckon I know what I'm about? Don't I generly know what I'm about?"

"Yes."

"Didn't I SAY I was going to help steal the nigger?"

"Yes."

"WELL, then."

That's all he said, and that's all I said. It warn't no use to say any more; because when he said he'd do a thing, he always done it. But I couldn't make out how he was willing to go into this thing; so I just let it go, and never bothered no more about it. If he was bound to have it so, I couldn't help it.

When we got home the house was all dark and still; so we went on down to the hut by the ash-hopper for to examine it. We went through the yard so as to see what the hounds would do. They knowed us, and didn't make no more noise than country dogs is always doing when anything comes by in the night. When we got to the cabin we took a look at the front and the two sides; and on the side I warn't acquainted with—which was the north side—we found a square window-hole, up tolerable high, with just one stout board nailed across it. I says:

"Here's the ticket. This hole's big enough for Jim to get through if we wrench off the board."

Tom says:

"It's as simple as tit-tat-toe, three-in-a-row, and as easy as playing hooky. I should HOPE we can find a way that's a little more complicated than THAT, Huck Finn."

"Well, then," I says, "how 'll it do to saw him out, the way I done before I was murdered that time?"

"That's more LIKE," he says. "It's real mysterious, and troublesome, and good," he says; "but I bet we can find a way that's twice as long. There ain't no hurry; le's keep on looking around."

Betwixt the hut and the fence, on the back side, was a lean-to that joined the hut at the eaves, and was made out of plank. It was as long as the hut, but narrow—only about six foot wide. The door to it was at the south end, and was padlocked. Tom he went to the soap-kettle and searched around, and fetched back the iron thing they lift the lid with; so he took it and prized out one of the staples. The chain fell down, and we opened the door and went in, and shut it, and struck a match, and see the shed was only built against a cabin and hadn't no connection with it; and there warn't no floor to the shed, nor nothing in it but some old rusty played-out hoes and spades and picks and a crippled plow. The match went out, and so did we, and shoved in the staple again, and the door was locked as good as ever. Tom was joyful. He says;

"Now we're all right. We'll DIG him out. It 'll take about a week!"

Then we started for the house, and I went in the back door—you only have to pull a buckskin latch-string, they don't fasten the doors—but that warn't romantical enough for Tom Sawyer; no way would do him but he must climb up the lightning-rod. But after he got up half way about three times, and missed fire and fell every time, and the last time most busted his brains out, he thought he'd got to give it up; but after he was rested he allowed he would give her one more turn for luck, and this time he made the trip.

In the morning we was up at break of day, and down to the nigger cabins to pet the dogs and make friends with the nigger that fed Jim—if it WAS Jim that was being fed. The niggers was just getting through breakfast and starting for the fields; and Jim's nigger was piling up a tin pan with bread and meat and things; and whilst the others was leaving, the key come from the house.

This nigger had a good-natured, chuckle-headed face, and his wool was all tied up in little bunches with thread. That was to keep witches off. He said the witches was pestering him awful these nights, and making him see all kinds of strange things, and hear all kinds of strange words and noises, and he didn't believe he was ever witched so long before in his life. He got so worked up, and got to running on so about his troubles, he forgot all about what he'd been a-going to do. So Tom says:

"What's the vittles for? Going to feed the dogs?"

The nigger kind of smiled around gradually over his face, like when you heave a brickbat in a mud-puddle, and he says:

"Yes, Mars Sid, A dog. Cur'us dog, too. Does you want to go en look at 'im?"

"Yes."

I hunched Tom, and whispers:

"You going, right here in the daybreak? THAT warn't the plan."

"No, it warn't; but it's the plan NOW."

So, drat him, we went along, but I didn't like it much. When we got in we couldn't hardly see anything, it was so dark; but Jim was there, sure enough, and could see us; and he sings out:

"Why, HUCK! En good LAN'! ain' dat Misto Tom?"

I just knowed how it would be; I just expected it. I didn't know nothing to do; and if I had I couldn't a done it, because that nigger busted in and says:

"Why, de gracious sakes! do he know you genlmen?"

We could see pretty well now. Tom he looked at the nigger, steady and kind of wondering, and says:

"Does WHO know us?"

"Why, dis-yer runaway nigger."

"I don't reckon he does; but what put that into your head?"

"What PUT it dar? Didn' he jis' dis minute sing out like he knowed you?"

Tom says, in a puzzled-up kind of way:

"Well, that's mighty curious. WHO sung out? WHEN did he sing out? WHAT did he sing out?" And turns to me, perfectly ca'm, and says, "Did YOU hear anybody sing out?"

Of course there warn't nothing to be said but the one thing; so I says:

"No; I ain't heard nobody say nothing."

Then he turns to Jim, and looks him over like he never see him before, and says:

"Did you sing out?"

"No, sah," says Jim; "I hain't said nothing, sah."

"Not a word?"

"No, sah, I hain't said a word."

"Did you ever see us before?"

"No, sah; not as I knows on."

So Tom turns to the nigger, which was looking wild and distressed, and says, kind of severe:

"What do you reckon's the matter with you, anyway? What made you think somebody sung out?"

"Oh, it's de dad-blame' witches, sah, en I wisht I was dead, I do. Dey's awluz at it, sah, en dey do mos' kill me, dey sk'yers me so. Please to don't tell nobody 'bout it sah, er ole Mars Silas he'll scole me; 'kase he say dey AIN'T no witches. I jis' wish to goodness he was heah now —DEN what would he say! I jis' bet he couldn' fine no way to git aroun' it DIS time. But it's awluz jis' so; people dat's SOT, stays sot; dey won't look into noth'n'en fine it out f'r deyselves, en when YOU fine it out en tell um 'bout it, dey doan' b'lieve you."

Tom give him a dime, and said we wouldn't tell nobody; and told him to buy some more thread to tie up his wool with; and then looks at Jim, and says:

"I wonder if Uncle Silas is going to hang this nigger. If I was to catch a nigger that was ungrateful enough to run away, I wouldn't give him up, I'd hang him." And whilst the nigger stepped to the door to look at the dime and bite it to see if it was good, he whispers to Jim and says:

"Don't ever let on to know us. And if you hear any digging going on nights, it's us; we're going to set you free."

Jim only had time to grab us by the hand and squeeze it; then the nigger come back, and we said we'd come again some time if the nigger wanted us to; and he said he would, more particular if it was dark, because the witches went for him mostly in the dark, and it was good to have folks around then.

Chapter XXXV

It would be most an hour yet till breakfast, so we left and struck down into the woods; because Tom said we got to have SOME light to see how to dig by, and a lantern makes too much, and might get us into trouble; what we must have was a lot of them rotten chunks that's called fox-fire, and just makes a soft kind of a glow when you lay them in a dark place. We fetched an armful and hid it in the weeds, and set down to rest, and Tom says, kind of dissatisfied:

"Blame it, this whole thing is just as easy and awkward as it can be. And so it makes it so rotten difficult to get up a difficult plan. There ain't no watchman to be drugged—now there OUGHT to be a watchman. There ain't even a dog to give a sleeping-mixture to. And there's Jim chained by one leg, with a ten-foot chain, to the leg of his bed: why, all you got to do is to lift up the bedstead and slip off the chain. And Uncle Silas he trusts everybody; sends the key to the punkin-headed nigger, and don't send nobody to watch the nigger. Jim could a got out of that window-hole before this, only there wouldn't be no use trying to travel with a ten-foot chain on his leg. Why, drat it, Huck, it's the stupidest arrangement I ever see. You got to invent ALL the difficulties. Well, we can't help it; we got to do the best we can with the materials we've got. Anyhow, there's one thing—there's more honor in getting him out through a lot of difficulties and dangers, where there warn't one of them furnished to you by the people who it was their duty to furnish them, and you had to contrive them all out of your own head. Now look at just that one thing of the lantern. When you come down to the cold facts, we simply got to LET ON that a lantern's resky. Why, we could work with a torchlight procession if we wanted to, I believe. Now, whilst I think of it, we got to hunt up something to make a saw out of the first chance we get."

"What do we want of a saw?"

"What do we WANT of a saw? Hain't we got to saw the leg of Jim's bed off, so as to get the chain loose?"

"Why, you just said a body could lift up the bedstead and slip the chain off."

"Well, if that ain't just like you, Huck Finn. You CAN get up the infant-schooliest ways of going at a thing. Why, hain't you ever read any books at all?—Baron Trenck, nor Casanova, nor Benvenuto Chelleeny, nor Henri IV., nor none of them heroes? Who ever heard of getting a prisoner loose in such an old-maidy way as that? No; the way all the best authorities does is to saw the bed-leg in two, and leave it just so, and swallow the sawdust, so it can't be found, and put some dirt and grease around the sawed place so the very keenest seneskal can't see no sign of it's being sawed, and thinks the bed-leg is perfectly sound. Then, the night you're ready, fetch the leg a kick, down she goes; slip off your chain, and there you are. Nothing to do but hitch your rope ladder to the battlements, shin down it, break your leg in the moat —because a rope ladder is nineteen foot too short, you know—and there's your horses and your trusty vassles, and they scoop you up and fling you across a saddle, and away you go to your native Langudoc, or Navarre, or wherever it is. It's gaudy, Huck. I wish there was a moat to this cabin. If we get time, the night of the escape, we'll dig one."

I says:

"What do we want of a moat when we're going to snake him out from under the cabin?"

But he never heard me. He had forgot me and everything else. He had his chin in his hand, thinking. Pretty soon he sighs and shakes his head; then sighs again, and says:

"No, it wouldn't do—there ain't necessity enough for it."

"For what?" I says.

"Why, to saw Jim's leg off," he says.

"Good land!" I says; "why, there ain't NO necessity for it. And what would you want to saw his leg off for, anyway?"

"Well, some of the best authorities has done it. They couldn't get the chain off, so they just cut their hand off and shoved. And a leg would be better still. But we got to let that go. There ain't necessity enough in this case; and, besides, Jim's a nigger, and wouldn't understand the reasons for it, and how it's the custom in Europe; so we'll let it go. But there's one thing—he can have a rope ladder; we can tear up our sheets and make him a rope ladder easy enough. And we can send it to him in a pie; it's mostly done that way. And I've et worse pies."

"Why, Tom Sawyer, how you talk," I says; "Jim ain't got no use for a rope ladder."

"He HAS got use for it. How YOU talk, you better say; you don't know nothing about it. He's GOT to have a rope ladder; they all do."

"What in the nation can he DO with it?"

"DO with it? He can hide it in his bed, can't he? That's what they all do; and HE'S got to, too. Huck, you don't ever seem to want to do anything that's regular; you want to be starting something fresh all the time. S'pose he DON'T do nothing with it? ain't it there in his bed, for a clew, after he's gone? and don't you reckon they'll want clews? Of course they will. And you wouldn't leave them any? That would be a PRETTY howdy-do, WOULDN'T it! I never heard of such a thing."

"Well," I says, "if it's in the regulations, and he's got to have it, all right, let him have it; because I don't wish to go back on no regulations; but there's one thing, Tom Sawyer—if we go to tearing up our sheets to make Jim a rope ladder, we're going to get into trouble with Aunt Sally, just as sure as you're born. Now, the way I look at it, a hickry-bark ladder don't cost nothing, and don't waste nothing, and is just as good to load up a pie with, and hide in a straw tick, as any rag ladder you can start; and as for Jim, he ain't had no experience, and so he don't care what kind of a—"

"Oh, shucks, Huck Finn, if I was as ignorant as you I'd keep still —that's what I'D do. Who ever heard of a state prisoner escaping by a hickry-bark ladder? Why, it's perfectly ridiculous."

"Well, all right, Tom, fix it your own way; but if you'll take my advice, you'll let me borrow a sheet off of the clothesline."

He said that would do. And that gave him another idea, and he says:

"Borrow a shirt, too."

"What do we want of a shirt, Tom?"

"Want it for Jim to keep a journal on."

"Journal your granny—JIM can't write."

"S'pose he CAN'T write—he can make marks on the shirt, can't he, if we make him a pen out of an old pewter spoon or a piece of an old iron barrel-hoop?"

"Why, Tom, we can pull a feather out of a goose and make him a better one; and quicker, too."

"PRISONERS don't have geese running around the donjon-keep to pull pens out of, you muggins. They ALWAYS make their pens out of the hardest, toughest, troublesomest piece of old brass candlestick or something like that they can get their hands on; and it takes them weeks and weeks and months and months to file it out, too, because they've got to do it by rubbing it on the wall. THEY wouldn't use a goose-quill if they had it. It ain't regular."

"Well, then, what'll we make him the ink out of?"

"Many makes it out of iron-rust and tears; but that's the common sort and women; the best authorities uses their own blood. Jim can do that; and when he wants to send any little common ordinary mysterious message to let the world know where he's captivated, he can write it on the bottom of a tin plate with a fork and throw it out of the window. The Iron Mask always done that, and it's a blame' good way, too."

"Jim ain't got no tin plates. They feed him in a pan."

"That ain't nothing; we can get him some."

"Can't nobody READ his plates."

"That ain't got anything to DO with it, Huck Finn. All HE'S got to do is to write on the plate and throw it out. You don't HAVE to be able to read it. Why, half the time you can't read anything a prisoner writes on a tin plate, or anywhere else."

"Well, then, what's the sense in wasting the plates?"

"Why, blame it all, it ain't the PRISONER'S plates."

"But it's SOMEBODY'S plates, ain't it?"

"Well, spos'n it is? What does the PRISONER care whose—"

He broke off there, because we heard the breakfast-horn blowing. So we cleared out for the house.

Along during the morning I borrowed a sheet and a white shirt off of the clothes-line; and I found an old sack and put them in it, and we went down and got the fox-fire, and put that in too. I called it borrowing, because that was what pap always called it; but Tom said it warn't borrowing, it was stealing. He said we was representing prisoners; and prisoners don't care how they get a thing so they get it, and nobody don't blame them for it, either. It ain't no crime in a prisoner to steal the thing he needs to get away with, Tom said; it's his right; and so, as long as we was representing a prisoner, we had a perfect right to steal anything on this place we had the least use for to get ourselves out of prison with. He said if we warn't prisoners it would be a very different thing, and nobody but a mean, ornery person would steal when he warn't a prisoner. So we allowed we would steal everything there was that come handy. And yet he made a mighty fuss, one day, after that, when I stole a watermelon out of the nigger-patch and eat it; and he made me go and give the niggers a dime without telling them what it was for. Tom said that what he meant was, we could steal anything we NEEDED. Well, I says, I needed the watermelon. But he said I didn't need it to get out of prison with; there's where the difference was. He said if I'd a wanted it to hide a knife in, and smuggle it to Jim to kill the seneskal with, it would a been all right. So I let it go at that, though I couldn't see no advantage in my representing a prisoner if I got to set down and chaw over a lot of gold-leaf distinctions like that every time I see a chance to hog a watermelon.

Well, as I was saying, we waited that morning till everybody was settled down to business, and nobody in sight around the yard; then Tom he carried the sack into the lean-to whilst I stood off a piece to keep watch. By and by he come out, and we went and set down on the woodpile to talk. He says:

"Everything's all right now except tools; and that's easy fixed."

"Tools?" I says.

"Yes."

"Tools for what?"

"Why, to dig with. We ain't a-going to GNAW him out, are we?"

"Ain't them old crippled picks and things in there good enough to dig a nigger out with?" I says.

He turns on me, looking pitying enough to make a body cry, and says:

"Huck Finn, did you EVER hear of a prisoner having picks and shovels, and all the modern conveniences in his wardrobe to dig himself out with? Now I want to ask you—if you got any reasonableness in you at all—what kind of a show would THAT give him to be a hero? Why, they might as well lend him the key and done with it. Picks and shovels—why, they wouldn't furnish 'em to a king."

"Well, then," I says, "if we don't want the picks and shovels, what do we want?"

"A couple of case-knives."

"To dig the foundations out from under that cabin with?"

"Yes."

"Confound it, it's foolish, Tom."

"It don't make no difference how foolish it is, it's the RIGHT way—and it's the regular way. And there ain't no OTHER way, that ever I heard of, and I've read all the books that gives any information about these things. They always dig out with a case-knife—and not through dirt, mind you; generly it's through solid rock. And it takes them weeks and weeks and weeks, and for ever and ever. Why, look at one of them prisoners in the bottom dungeon of the Castle Deef, in the harbor of Marseilles, that dug himself out that way; how long was HE at it, you reckon?"

"I don't know."

"Well, guess."

"I don't know. A month and a half."

"THIRTY-SEVEN YEAR—and he come out in China. THAT'S the kind. I wish the bottom of THIS fortress was solid rock."

"JIM don't know nobody in China."

"What's THAT got to do with it? Neither did that other fellow. But you're always a-wandering off on a side issue. Why can't you stick to the main point?"

"All right—I don't care where he comes out, so he COMES out; and Jim don't, either, I reckon. But there's one thing, anyway—Jim's too old to be dug out with a case-knife. He won't last."

"Yes he will LAST, too. You don't reckon it's going to take thirty-seven years to dig out through a DIRT foundation, do you?"

"How long will it take, Tom?"

"Well, we can't resk being as long as we ought to, because it mayn't take very long for Uncle Silas to hear from down there by New Orleans. He'll hear Jim ain't from there. Then his next move will be to advertise Jim, or something like that. So we can't resk being as long digging him out as we ought to. By rights I reckon we ought to be a couple of years; but we can't. Things being so uncertain, what I recommend is this: that we really dig right in, as quick as we can; and after that, we can LET ON, to ourselves, that we was at it thirty-seven years. Then we can snatch him out and rush him away the first time there's an alarm. Yes, I reckon that 'll be the best way."

"Now, there's SENSE in that," I says. "Letting on don't cost nothing; letting on ain't no trouble; and if it's any object, I don't mind letting on we was at it a hundred and fifty year. It wouldn't strain me none, after I got my hand in. So I'll mosey along now, and smouch a couple of case-knives."

"Smouch three," he says; "we want one to make a saw out of."

"Tom, if it ain't unregular and irreligious to sejest it," I says, "there's an old rusty saw-blade around yonder sticking under the weather-boarding behind the smoke-house."

He looked kind of weary and discouraged-like, and says:

"It ain't no use to try to learn you nothing, Huck. Run along and smouch the knives—three of them." So I done it.

Chapter XXXVI

As soon as we reckoned everybody was asleep that night we went down the lightning-rod, and shut ourselves up in the lean-to, and got out our pile of fox-fire, and went to work. We cleared everything out of the way, about four or five foot along the middle of the bottom log. Tom said we was right behind Jim's bed now, and we'd dig in under it, and when we got through there couldn't nobody in the cabin ever know there was any hole there, because Jim's counter-pin hung down most to the ground, and you'd have to raise it up and look under to see the hole. So we dug and dug with the case-knives till most midnight; and then we was dog-tired, and our hands was blistered, and yet you couldn't see we'd done anything hardly. At last I says:

"This ain't no thirty-seven year job; this is a thirty-eight year job, Tom Sawyer."

He never said nothing. But he sighed, and pretty soon he stopped digging, and then for a good little while I knowed that he was thinking. Then he says:

"It ain't no use, Huck, it ain't a-going to work. If we was prisoners it would, because then we'd have as many years as we wanted, and no hurry; and we wouldn't get but a few minutes to dig, every day, while they was changing watches, and so our hands wouldn't get blistered, and we could keep it up right along, year in and year out, and do it right, and the way it ought to be done. But WE can't fool along; we got to rush; we ain't got no time to spare. If we was to put in another night this way we'd have to knock off for a week to let our hands get well—couldn't touch a case-knife with them sooner."

"Well, then, what we going to do, Tom?"

"I'll tell you. It ain't right, and it ain't moral, and I wouldn't like it to get out; but there ain't only just the one way: we got to dig him out with the picks, and LET ON it's case-knives."

"NOW you're TALKING!" I says; "your head gets leveler and leveler all the time, Tom Sawyer," I says. "Picks is the thing, moral or no moral; and as for me, I don't care shucks for the morality of it, nohow. When I start in to steal a nigger, or a watermelon, or a Sunday-school book, I ain't no ways particular how it's done so it's done. What I want is my nigger; or what I want is my watermelon; or what I want is my Sunday-school book; and if a pick's the handiest thing, that's the thing I'm a-going to dig that nigger or that watermelon or that Sunday-school book out with; and I don't give a dead rat what the authorities thinks about it nuther."

"Well," he says, "there's excuse for picks and letting-on in a case like this; if it warn't so, I wouldn't approve of it, nor I wouldn't stand by and see the rules broke— because right is right, and wrong is wrong, and a body ain't got no business doing wrong when he ain't ignorant and knows better. It might answer for YOU to dig Jim out with a pick, WITHOUT any letting on, because you don't know no better; but it wouldn't for me, because I do know better. Gimme a case-knife."

He had his own by him, but I handed him mine. He flung it down, and says:

"Gimme a CASE-KNIFE."

I didn't know just what to do—but then I thought. I scratched around amongst the old tools, and got a pickaxe and give it to him, and he took it and went to work, and never said a word.

He was always just that particular. Full of principle.

So then I got a shovel, and then we picked and shoveled, turn about, and made the fur fly. We stuck to it about a half an hour, which was as long as we could stand up; but we had a good deal of a hole to show for it. When I got up stairs I looked out at the window and see Tom doing his level best with the lightning-rod, but he couldn't come it, his hands was so sore. At last he says:

"It ain't no use, it can't be done. What you reckon I better do? Can't you think of no way?"

"Yes," I says, "but I reckon it ain't regular. Come up the stairs, and let on it's a lightning-rod."

So he done it.

Next day Tom stole a pewter spoon and a brass candlestick in the house, for to make some pens for Jim out of, and six tallow candles; and I hung around the nigger cabins and laid for a chance, and stole three tin plates. Tom says it wasn't enough; but I said nobody wouldn't ever see the plates that Jim throwed ut, because they'd fall in the dog-fennel and jimpson weeds under the window-hole—then we could tote them back and he could use them over again. So Tom was satisfied. Then he says:

"Now, the thing to study out is, how to get the things to Jim."

"Take them in through the hole," I says, "when we get it done."

He only just looked scornful, and said something about nobody ever heard of such an idiotic idea, and then he went to studying. By and by he said he had ciphered out two or three ways, but there warn't no need to decide on any of them yet. Said we'd got to post Jim first.

That night we went down the lightning-rod a little after ten, and took one of the candles along, and listened under the window-hole, and heard Jim snoring; so we pitched it in, and it didn't wake him. Then we whirled in with the pick and shovel, and in about two hours and a half the job was done. We crept in under Jim's bed and into the cabin, and pawed around and found the candle and lit it, and stood over Jim awhile, and found him looking hearty and healthy, and then we woke him up gentle and gradual. He was so glad to see us he most cried; and called us honey, and all the pet names he could think of; and was for having us hunt up a cold-chisel to cut the chain off of his leg with right away, and clearing out without losing any time. But Tom he showed him how unregular it would be, and set down and told him all about our plans, and how we could alter them in a minute any time there was an alarm; and not to be the least afraid, because we would see he got away, SURE. So Jim he said it was all right, and we set there and talked over old times awhile, and then Tom asked a lot of questions, and when Jim told him Uncle Silas come in every day or two to pray with him, and Aunt Sally come in to see if he was comfortable and had plenty to eat, and both of them was kind as they could be, Tom says:

"NOW I know how to fix it. We'll send you some things by them."

I said, "Don't do nothing of the kind; it's one of the most jackass ideas I ever struck;" but he never paid no attention to me; went right on. It was his way when he'd got his plans set.

So he told Jim how we'd have to smuggle in the rope-ladder pie and other large things by Nat, the nigger that fed him, and he must be on the lookout, and not be surprised, and not let Nat see him open them; and we would put small things in uncle's coat-pockets and he must steal them out; and we would tie things to aunt's apron-strings or put them in her apron-pocket, if we got a chance; and told him what they would be and what they was for. And told him how to keep a journal on the shirt with his blood, and all that. He told him everything. Jim he couldn't see no sense in the most of it, but he allowed we was white folks and knowed better than him; so he was satisfied, and said he would do it all just as Tom said.

Jim had plenty corn-cob pipes and tobacco; so we had a right down good sociable time; then we crawled out through the hole, and so home to bed, with hands that looked like they'd been chawed. Tom was in high spirits. He said it was the best fun he ever had in his life, and the most intellectural; and said if he only could see his way to it we would keep it up all the rest of our lives and leave Jim to our children to get out; for he believed Jim would come to like it better and better the more he got used to it. He said that in that way it could be strung out to as much as eighty year, and would be the best time on record. And he said it would make us all celebrated that had a hand in it.

In the morning we went out to the woodpile and chopped up the brass candlestick into handy sizes, and Tom put them and the pewter spoon in his pocket. Then we went to the nigger cabins, and while I got Nat's notice off, Tom shoved a piece of candlestick into the middle of a corn-pone that was in Jim's pan, and we went along with Nat to see how it would work, and it just worked noble; when Jim bit into it it most mashed all his teeth out; and there warn't ever anything could a worked better. Tom said so himself. Jim he never let on but what it was only just a piece of rock or something like that that's always getting into bread, you know; but after that he never bit into nothing but what he jabbed his fork into it in three or four places first.

And whilst we was a-standing there in the dimmish light, here comes a couple of the hounds bulging in from under Jim's bed; and they kept on piling in till there was eleven of them, and there warn't hardly room in there to get your breath. By jings, we forgot to fasten that lean-to door! The nigger Nat he only just hollered "Witches" once, and keeled over on to the floor amongst the dogs, and begun to groan like he was dying. Tom jerked the door open and flung out a slab of Jim's meat, and the dogs went for it, and in two seconds he was out himself and back again and shut the door, and I knowed he'd fixed the other door too. Then he went to work on the nigger, coaxing him and petting him, and asking him if he'd been imagining he saw something again. He raised up, and blinked his eyes around, and says:

"Mars Sid, you'll say I's a fool, but if I didn't b'lieve I see most a million dogs, er devils, er some'n, I wisht I may die right heah in dese tracks. I did, mos' sholy. Mars Sid, I FELT um—I FELT um, sah; dey was all over me. Dad fetch it, I jis' wisht I could git my han's on one er dem witches jis' wunst—on'y jis' wunst—it's all I'd ast. But mos'ly I wisht dey'd lemme 'lone, I does."

Tom says:

"Well, I tell you what I think. What makes them come here just at this runaway nigger's breakfast-time? It's because they're hungry; that's the reason. You make them a witch pie; that's the thing for YOU to do."

"But my lan', Mars Sid, how's I gwyne to make 'm a witch pie? I doan' know how to make it. I hain't ever hearn er sich a thing b'fo'."

"Well, then, I'll have to make it myself."

"Will you do it, honey?—will you? I'll wusshup de groun' und' yo' foot, I will!"

"All right, I'll do it, seeing it's you, and you've been good to us and showed us the runaway nigger. But you got to be mighty careful. When we come around, you turn your back; and then whatever we've put in the pan, don't you let on you see it at all. And don't you look when Jim unloads the pan—something might happen, I don't know what. And above all, don't you HANDLE the witch-things."

"HANNEL 'm, Mars Sid? What IS you a-talkin' 'bout? I wouldn' lay de weight er my finger on um, not f 'r ten hund'd thous'n billion dollars, I wouldn't."

Chapter XXXVII

That was all fixed. So then we went away and went to the rubbage-pile in the back yard, where they keep the old boots, and rags, and pieces of bottles, and wore-out tin things, and all such truck, and scratched around and found an old tin washpan, and stopped up the holes as well as we could, to bake the pie in, and took it down cellar and stole it full of flour and started for breakfast, and found a couple of shingle-nails that Tom said would be handy for a prisoner to scrabble his name and sorrows on the dungeon walls with, and dropped one of them in Aunt Sally's apron-pocket which was hanging on a chair, and t'other we stuck in the band of Uncle Silas's hat, which was on the bureau, because we heard the children say their pa and ma was going to the runaway nigger's house this morning, and then went to breakfast, and Tom dropped the pewter spoon in Uncle Silas's coat-pocket, and Aunt Sally wasn't come yet, so we had to wait a little while.

And when she come she was hot and red and cross, and couldn't hardly wait for the blessing; and then she went to sluicing out coffee with one hand and cracking the handiest child's head with her thimble with the other, and says:

"I've hunted high and I've hunted low, and it does beat all what HAS become of your other shirt."

My heart fell down amongst my lungs and livers and things, and a hard piece of corn-crust started down my throat after it and got met on the road with a cough, and was shot across the table, and took one of the children in the eye and curled him up like a fishing-worm, and let a cry out of him the size of a warwhoop, and Tom he turned kinder blue around the gills, and it all amounted to a considerable state of things for about a quarter of a minute or as much as that, and I would a sold out for half price if there was a bidder. But after that we was all right again—it was the sudden surprise of it that knocked us so kind of cold.

Uncle Silas he says:

"It's most uncommon curious, I can't understand it. I know perfectly well I took it OFF, because—"

"Because you hain't got but one ON. Just LISTEN at the man! I know you took it off, and know it by a better way than your wool-gethering memory, too, because it was on the clo's-line yesterday—I see it there myself. But it's gone, that's the long and the short of it, and you'll just have to change to a red flann'l one till I can get time to make a new one. And it 'll be the third I've made in two years. It just keeps a body on the jump to keep you in shirts; and whatever you do manage to DO with 'm all is more 'n I can make out. A body 'd think you WOULD learn to take some sort of care of 'em at your time of life."

"I know it, Sally, and I do try all I can. But it oughtn't to be altogether my fault, because, you know, I don't see them nor have nothing to do with them except when they're on me; and I don't believe I've ever lost one of them OFF of me."

"Well, it ain't YOUR fault if you haven't, Silas; you'd a done it if you could, I reckon. And the shirt ain't all that's gone, nuther. Ther's a spoon gone; and THAT ain't all. There was ten, and now ther's only nine. The calf got the shirt, I reckon, but the calf never took the spoon, THAT'S certain."

"Why, what else is gone, Sally?"

"Ther's six CANDLES gone—that's what. The rats could a got the candles, and I reckon they did; I wonder they don't walk off with the whole place, the way you're always going to stop their holes and don't do it; and if they warn't fools they'd sleep in your hair, Silas—YOU'D never find it out; but you can't lay the SPOON on the rats, and that I know."

"Well, Sally, I'm in fault, and I acknowledge it; I've been remiss; but I won't let to-morrow go by without stopping up them holes."

"Oh, I wouldn't hurry; next year 'll do. Matilda Angelina Araminta PHELPS!"

Whack comes the thimble, and the child snatches her claws out of the sugar-bowl without fooling around any. Just then the nigger woman steps on to the passage, and says:

"Missus, dey's a sheet gone."

"A SHEET gone! Well, for the land's sake!"

"I'll stop up them holes to-day," says Uncle Silas, looking sorrowful.

"Oh, DO shet up!—s'pose the rats took the SHEET? WHERE'S it gone, Lize?"

"Clah to goodness I hain't no notion, Miss' Sally. She wuz on de clo'sline yistiddy, but she done gone: she ain' dah no mo' now."

"I reckon the world IS coming to an end. I NEVER see the beat of it in all my born days. A shirt, and a sheet, and a spoon, and six can—"

"Missus," comes a young yaller wench, "dey's a brass cannelstick miss'n."

"Cler out from here, you hussy, er I'll take a skillet to ye!"

Well, she was just a-biling. I begun to lay for a chance; I reckoned I would sneak out and go for the woods till the weather moderated. She kept a-raging right along, running her insurrection all by herself, and everybody else mighty meek and quiet; and at last Uncle Silas, looking kind of foolish, fishes up that spoon out of his pocket.

She stopped, with her mouth open and her hands up; and as for me, I wished I was in Jeruslem or somewheres. But not long, because she says:

"It's JUST as I expected. So you had it in your pocket all the time; and like as not you've got the other things there, too. How'd it get there?"

"I reely don't know, Sally," he says, kind of apologizing, "or you know I would tell. I was a-studying over my text in Acts Seventeen before breakfast, and I reckon I put it in there, not noticing, meaning to put my Testament in, and it must be so, because my Testament ain't in; but I'll go and see; and if the Testament is where I had it, I'll know I didn't put it in, and that will show that I laid the Testament down and took up the spoon, and—"

"Oh, for the land's sake! Give a body a rest! Go 'long now, the whole kit and biling of ye; and don't come nigh me again till I've got back my peace of mind."

I'd a heard her if she'd a said it to herself, let alone speaking it out; and I'd a got up and obeyed her if I'd a been dead. As we was passing through the setting-room the old man he took up his hat, and the shingle-nail fell out on the floor, and he just merely picked it up and laid it on the mantel-shelf, and never said nothing, and went out. Tom see him do it, and remembered about the spoon, and says:

"Well, it ain't no use to send things by HIM no more, he ain't reliable." Then he says: "But he done us a good turn with the spoon, anyway, without knowing it, and so we'll go and do him one without HIM knowing it—stop up his rat-holes."

There was a noble good lot of them down cellar, and it took us a whole hour, but we done the job tight and good and shipshape. Then we heard steps on the stairs, and blowed out our light and hid; and here comes the old man, with a candle in one hand and a bundle of stuff in t'other, looking as absent-minded as year before last. He went a mooning around, first to one rat-hole and then another, till he'd been to them all. Then he stood about five minutes, picking tallow-drip off of his candle and thinking. Then he turns off slow and dreamy towards the stairs, saying:

"Well, for the life of me I can't remember when I done it. I could show her now that I warn't to blame on account of the rats. But never mind —let it go. I reckon it wouldn't do no good."

And so he went on a-mumbling up stairs, and then we left. He was a mighty nice old man. And always is.

Tom was a good deal bothered about what to do for a spoon, but he said we'd got to have it; so he took a think. When he had ciphered it out he told me how we was to do; then we went and waited around the spoon-basket till we see Aunt Sally coming, and then Tom went to counting the spoons and laying them out to one side, and I slid one of them up my sleeve, and Tom says:

"Why, Aunt Sally, there ain't but nine spoons YET."

She says:

"Go 'long to your play, and don't bother me. I know better, I counted 'm myself."

"Well, I've counted them twice, Aunty, and I can't make but nine."

She looked out of all patience, but of course she come to count—anybody would.

"I declare to gracious ther' AIN'T but nine!" she says. "Why, what in the world—plague TAKE the things, I'll count 'm again."

So I slipped back the one I had, and when she got done counting, she says:

"Hang the troublesome rubbage, ther's TEN now!" and she looked huffy and bothered both. But Tom says:

"Why, Aunty, I don't think there's ten."

"You numskull, didn't you see me COUNT 'm?"

"I know, but—"

"Well, I'll count 'm AGAIN."

So I smouched one, and they come out nine, same as the other time. Well, she WAS in a tearing way—just a-trembling all over, she was so mad. But she counted and counted till she got that addled she'd start to count in the basket for a spoon sometimes; and so, three times they come out right, and three times they come out wrong. Then she grabbed up the basket and slammed it across the house and knocked the cat galley-west; and she said cle'r out and let her have some peace, and if we come bothering around her again betwixt that and dinner she'd skin us. So we had the odd spoon, and dropped it in her apron-pocket whilst she was a-giving us our sailing orders, and Jim got it all right, along with her shingle nail, before noon. We was very well satisfied with this business, and Tom allowed it was worth twice the trouble it took, because he said NOW she couldn't ever count them spoons twice alike again to save her life; and wouldn't believe she'd counted them right if she DID; and said that after she'd about counted her head off for the next three days he judged she'd give it up and offer to kill anybody that wanted her to ever count them any more.

So we put the sheet back on the line that night, and stole one out of her closet; and kept on putting it back and stealing it again for a couple of days till she didn't know how many sheets she had any more, and she didn't CARE, and warn't a-going to bullyrag the rest of her soul out about it, and wouldn't count them again not to save her life; she druther die first.

So we was all right now, as to the shirt and the sheet and the spoon and the candles, by the help of the calf and the rats and the mixed-up counting; and as to the candlestick, it warn't no consequence, it would blow over by and by.

But that pie was a job; we had no end of trouble with that pie. We fixed it up away down in the woods, and cooked it there; and we got it done at last, and very satisfactory, too; but not all in one day; and we had to use up three wash-pans full of flour before we got through, and we got burnt pretty much all over, in places, and eyes put out with the smoke; because, you see, we didn't want nothing but a crust, and we couldn't prop it up right, and she would always cave in. But of course we thought of the right way at last—which was to cook the ladder, too, in the pie. So then we laid in with Jim the second night, and tore up the sheet all in little strings and twisted them together, and long before daylight we had a lovely rope that you could a hung a person with. We let on it took nine months to make it.

And in the forenoon we took it down to the woods, but it wouldn't go into the pie. Being made of a whole sheet, that way, there was rope enough for forty pies if we'd a wanted them, and plenty left over for soup, or sausage, or anything you choose. We could a had a whole dinner.

But we didn't need it. All we needed was just enough for the pie, and so we throwed the rest away. We didn't cook none of the pies in the wash-pan—afraid the solder would melt; but Uncle Silas he had a noble brass warming-pan which he thought considerable of, because it belonged to one of his ancesters with a long wooden handle that come over from England with William the Conqueror in the Mayflower or one of them early ships and was hid away up garret with a lot of other old pots and things that was valuable, not on account of being any account, because they warn't, but on account of them being relicts, you know, and we snaked her out, private, and took her down there, but she failed on the first pies, because we didn't know how, but she come up smiling on the last one. We took and lined her with dough, and set her in the coals, and loaded her up with rag rope, and put on a dough roof, and shut down the lid, and put hot embers on top, and stood off five foot, with the long handle, cool and comfortable, and in fifteen minutes she turned out a pie that was a satisfaction to look at. But the person that et it would want to fetch a couple of kags of toothpicks along, for if that rope ladder wouldn't cramp him down to business I don't know nothing what I'm talking about, and lay him in enough stomach-ache to last him till next time, too.

Nat didn't look when we put the witch pie in Jim's pan; and we put the three tin plates in the bottom of the pan under the vittles; and so Jim got everything all right, and as soon as he was by himself he busted into the pie and hid the rope ladder inside of his straw tick, and scratched some marks on a tin plate and throwed it out of the window-hole.

Chapter XXXVIII

Making them pens was a distressid tough job, and so was the saw; and Jim allowed the inscription was going to be the toughest of all. That's the one which the prisoner has to scrabble on the wall. But he had to have it; Tom said he'd GOT to; there warn't no case of a state prisoner not scrabbling his inscription to leave behind, and his coat of arms.

"Look at Lady Jane Grey," he says; "look at Gilford Dudley; look at old Northumberland! Why, Huck, s'pose it IS considerble trouble?—what you going to do?—how you going to get around it? Jim's GOT to do his inscription and coat of arms. They all do."

Jim says:

"Why, Mars Tom, I hain't got no coat o' arm; I hain't got nuffn but dish yer ole shirt, en you knows I got to keep de journal on dat."

"Oh, you don't understand, Jim; a coat of arms is very different."

"Well," I says, "Jim's right, anyway, when he says he ain't got no coat of arms, because he hain't."

"I reckon I knowed that," Tom says, "but you bet he'll have one before he goes out of this—because he's going out RIGHT, and there ain't going to be no flaws in his record."

So whilst me and Jim filed away at the pens on a brickbat apiece, Jim a-making his'n out of the brass and I making mine out of the spoon, Tom set to work to think out the coat of arms. By and by he said he'd struck so many good ones he didn't hardly know which to take, but there was one which he reckoned he'd decide on. He says:

"On the scutcheon we'll have a bend OR in the dexter base, a saltire MURREY in the fess, with a dog, couchant, for common charge, and under his foot a chain embattled, for slavery, with a chevron VERT in a chief engrailed, and three invected lines on a field AZURE, with the nombril points rampant on a dancette indented; crest, a runaway nigger, SABLE, with his bundle over his shoulder on a bar sinister; and a couple of gules for supporters, which is you and me; motto, MAGGIORE FRETTA, MINORE OTTO. Got it out of a book—means the more haste the less speed."

"Geewhillikins," I says, "but what does the rest of it mean?"

"We ain't got no time to bother over that," he says; "we got to dig in like all git-out."

"Well, anyway," I says, "what's SOME of it? What's a fess?"

"A fess—a fess is—YOU don't need to know what a fess is. I'll show him how to make it when he gets to it."

"Shucks, Tom," I says, "I think you might tell a person. What's a bar sinister?"

"Oh, I don't know. But he's got to have it. All the nobility does."

That was just his way. If it didn't suit him to explain a thing to you, he wouldn't do it. You might pump at him a week, it wouldn't make no difference.

He'd got all that coat of arms business fixed, so now he started in to finish up the rest of that part of the work, which was to plan out a mournful inscription—said Jim got to have one, like they all done. He made up a lot, and wrote them out on a paper, and read them off, so:

1. Here a captive heart busted. 2. Here a poor prisoner, forsook by the world and friends, fretted his sorrowful life. 3. Here a lonely heart broke, and a worn spirit went to its rest, after thirty-seven years of solitary captivity. 4. Here, homeless and friendless, after thirty-seven years of bitter captivity, perished a noble stranger, natural son of Louis XIV.

Tom's voice trembled whilst he was reading them, and he most broke down. When he got done he couldn't no way make up his mind which one for Jim to scrabble on to the wall, they was all so good; but at last he allowed he would let him scrabble them all on. Jim said it would take him a year to scrabble such a lot of truck on to the logs with a nail, and he didn't know how to make letters, besides; but Tom said he would block them out for him, and then he wouldn't have nothing to do but just follow the lines. Then pretty soon he says:

"Come to think, the logs ain't a-going to do; they don't have log walls in a dungeon: we got to dig the inscriptions into a rock. We'll fetch a rock."

Jim said the rock was worse than the logs; he said it would take him such a pison long time to dig them into a rock he wouldn't ever get out. But Tom said he would let me help him do it. Then he took a look to see how me and Jim was getting along with the pens. It was most pesky tedious hard work and slow, and didn't give my hands no show to get well of the sores, and we didn't seem to make no headway, hardly; so Tom says:

"I know how to fix it. We got to have a rock for the coat of arms and mournful inscriptions, and we can kill two birds with that same rock. There's a gaudy big grindstone down at the mill, and we'll smouch it, and carve the things on it, and file out the pens and the saw on it, too."

It warn't no slouch of an idea; and it warn't no slouch of a grindstone nuther; but we allowed we'd tackle it. It warn't quite midnight yet, so we cleared out for the mill, leaving Jim at work. We smouched the grindstone, and set out to roll her home, but it was a most nation tough job. Sometimes, do what we could, we couldn't keep her from falling over, and she come mighty near mashing us every time. Tom said she was going to get one of us, sure, before we got through. We got her half way; and then we was plumb played out, and most drownded with sweat. We see it warn't no use; we got to go and fetch Jim So he raised up his bed and slid the chain off of the bed-leg, and wrapt it round and round his neck, and we crawled out through our hole and down there, and Jim and me laid into that grindstone and walked her along like nothing; and Tom superintended. He could out-superintend any boy I ever see. He knowed how to do everything.

Our hole was pretty big, but it warn't big enough to get the grindstone through; but Jim he took the pick and soon made it big enough. Then Tom marked out them things on it with the nail, and set Jim to work on them, with the nail for a chisel and an iron bolt from the rubbage in the lean-to for a hammer, and told him to work till the rest of his candle quit on him, and then he could go to bed, and hide the grindstone under his straw tick and sleep on it. Then we helped him fix his chain back on the bed-leg, and was ready for bed ourselves. But Tom thought of something, and says:

"You got any spiders in here, Jim?"

"No, sah, thanks to goodness I hain't, Mars Tom."

"All right, we'll get you some."

"But bless you, honey, I doan' WANT none. I's afeard un um. I jis' 's soon have rattlesnakes aroun'."

Tom thought a minute or two, and says:

"It's a good idea. And I reckon it's been done. It MUST a been done; it stands to reason. Yes, it's a prime good idea. Where could you keep it?"

"Keep what, Mars Tom?"

"Why, a rattlesnake."

"De goodness gracious alive, Mars Tom! Why, if dey was a rattlesnake to come in heah I'd take en bust right out thoo dat log wall, I would, wid my head."

"Why, Jim, you wouldn't be afraid of it after a little. You could tame it."

"TAME it!"

"Yes—easy enough. Every animal is grateful for kindness and petting, and they wouldn't THINK of hurting a person that pets them. Any book will tell you that. You try—that's all I ask; just try for two or three days. Why, you can get him so in a little while that he'll love you; and sleep with you; and won't stay away from you a minute; and will let you wrap him round your neck and put his head in your mouth."

"PLEASE, Mars Tom—DOAN' talk so! I can't STAN' it! He'd LET me shove his head in my mouf—fer a favor, hain't it? I lay he'd wait a pow'ful long time 'fo' I AST him. En mo' en dat, I doan' WANT him to sleep wid me."

"Jim, don't act so foolish. A prisoner's GOT to have some kind of a dumb pet, and if a rattlesnake hain't ever been tried, why, there's more glory to be gained in your being the first to ever try it than any other way you could ever think of to save your life."

"Why, Mars Tom, I doan' WANT no sich glory. Snake take 'n bite Jim's chin off, den WHAH is de glory? No, sah, I doan' want no sich doin's."

"Blame it, can't you TRY? I only WANT you to try—you needn't keep it up if it don't work."

"But de trouble all DONE ef de snake bite me while I's a tryin' him. Mars Tom, I's willin' to tackle mos' anything 'at ain't onreasonable, but ef you en Huck fetches a rattlesnake in heah for me to tame, I's gwyne to LEAVE, dat's SHORE."

"Well, then, let it go, let it go, if you're so bull-headed about it. We can get you some garter-snakes, and you can tie some buttons on their tails, and let on they're rattlesnakes, and I reckon that 'll have to do."

"I k'n stan' DEM, Mars Tom, but blame' 'f I couldn' get along widout um, I tell you dat. I never knowed b'fo' 't was so much bother and trouble to be a prisoner."

"Well, it ALWAYS is when it's done right. You got any rats around here?"

"No, sah, I hain't seed none."

"Well, we'll get you some rats."

"Why, Mars Tom, I doan' WANT no rats. Dey's de dadblamedest creturs to 'sturb a body, en rustle roun' over 'im, en bite his feet, when he's tryin' to sleep, I ever see. No, sah, gimme g'yarter-snakes, 'f I's got to have 'm, but doan' gimme no rats; I hain' got no use f'r um, skasely."

"But, Jim, you GOT to have 'em—they all do. So don't make no more fuss about it. Prisoners ain't ever without rats. There ain't no instance of it. And they train them, and pet them, and learn them tricks, and they get to be as sociable as flies. But you got to play music to them. You got anything to play music on?"

"I ain' got nuffn but a coase comb en a piece o' paper, en a juice-harp; but I reck'n dey wouldn' take no stock in a juice-harp."

"Yes they would. THEY don't care what kind of music 'tis. A jews-harp's plenty good enough for a rat. All animals like music—in a prison they dote on it. Specially, painful music; and you can't get no other kind out of a jews-harp. It always interests them; they come out to see what's the matter with you. Yes, you're all right; you're fixed very well. You want to set on your bed nights before you go to sleep, and early in the mornings, and play your jews-harp; play 'The Last Link is Broken'—that's the thing that 'll scoop a rat quicker 'n anything else; and when you've played about two minutes you'll see all the rats, and the snakes, and spiders, and things begin to feel worried about you, and come. And they'll just fairly swarm over you, and have a noble good time."

"Yes, DEY will, I reck'n, Mars Tom, but what kine er time is JIM havin'? Blest if I kin see de pint. But I'll do it ef I got to. I reck'n I better keep de animals satisfied, en not have no trouble in de house."

Tom waited to think it over, and see if there wasn't nothing else; and pretty soon he says:

"Oh, there's one thing I forgot. Could you raise a flower here, do you reckon?"

"I doan know but maybe I could, Mars Tom; but it's tolable dark in heah, en I ain' got no use f'r no flower, nohow, en she'd be a pow'ful sight o' trouble."

"Well, you try it, anyway. Some other prisoners has done it."

"One er dem big cat-tail-lookin' mullen-stalks would grow in heah, Mars Tom, I reck'n, but she wouldn't be wuth half de trouble she'd coss."

"Don't you believe it. We'll fetch you a little one and you plant it in the corner over there, and raise it. And don't call it mullen, call it Pitchiola—that's its right name when it's in a prison. And you want to water it with your tears."

"Why, I got plenty spring water, Mars Tom."

"You don't WANT spring water; you want to water it with your tears. It's the way they always do."

"Why, Mars Tom, I lay I kin raise one er dem mullen-stalks twyste wid spring water whiles another man's a START'N one wid tears."

"That ain't the idea. You GOT to do it with tears."

"She'll die on my han's, Mars Tom, she sholy will; kase I doan' skasely ever cry."

So Tom was stumped. But he studied it over, and then said Jim would have to worry along the best he could with an onion. He promised he would go to the nigger cabins and drop one, private, in Jim's coffee-pot, in the morning. Jim said he would "jis' 's soon have tobacker in his coffee;" and found so much fault with it, and with the work and bother of raising the mullen, and jews-harping the rats, and petting and flattering up the snakes and spiders and things, on top of all the other work he had to do on pens, and inscriptions, and journals, and things, which made it more trouble and worry and responsibility to be a prisoner than anything he ever undertook, that Tom most lost all patience with him; and said he was just loadened down with more gaudier chances than a prisoner ever had in the world to make a name for himself, and yet he didn't know enough to appreciate them, and they was just about wasted on him. So Jim he was sorry, and said he wouldn't behave so no more, and then me and Tom shoved for bed.

Chapter XXXIX

In the morning we went up to the village and bought a wire rat-trap and fetched it down, and unstopped the best rat-hole, and in about an hour we had fifteen of the bulliest kind of ones; and then we took it and put it in a safe place under Aunt Sally's bed. But while we was gone for spiders little Thomas Franklin Benjamin Jefferson Elexander Phelps found it there, and opened the door of it to see if the rats would come out, and they did; and Aunt Sally she come in, and when we got back she was a-standing on top of the bed raising Cain, and the rats was doing what they could to keep off the dull times for her. So she took and dusted us both with the hickry, and we was as much as two hours catching another fifteen or sixteen, drat that meddlesome cub, and they warn't the likeliest, nuther, because the first haul was the pick of the flock. I never see a likelier lot of rats than what that first haul was.

We got a splendid stock of sorted spiders, and bugs, and frogs, and caterpillars, and one thing or another; and we like to got a hornet's nest, but we didn't. The family was at home. We didn't give it right up, but stayed with them as long as we could; because we allowed we'd tire them out or they'd got to tire us out, and they done it. Then we got allycumpain and rubbed on the places, and was pretty near all right again, but couldn't set down convenient. And so we went for the snakes, and grabbed a couple of dozen garters and house-snakes, and put them in a bag, and put it in our room, and by that time it was supper-time, and a rattling good honest day's work: and hungry?—oh, no, I reckon not! And there warn't a blessed snake up there when we went back—we didn't half tie the sack, and they worked out somehow, and left. But it didn't matter much, because they was still on the premises somewheres. So we judged we could get some of them again. No, there warn't no real scarcity of snakes about the house for a considerable spell. You'd see them dripping from the rafters and places every now and then; and they generly landed in your plate, or down the back of your neck, and most of the time where you didn't want them. Well, they was handsome and striped, and there warn't no harm in a million of them; but that never made no difference to Aunt Sally; she despised snakes, be the breed what they might, and she couldn't stand them no way you could fix it; and every time one of them flopped down on her, it didn't make no difference what she was doing, she would just lay that work down and light out. I never see such a woman. And you could hear her whoop to Jericho. You couldn't get her to take a-holt of one of them with the tongs. And if she turned over and found one in bed she would scramble out and lift a howl that you would think the house was afire. She disturbed the old man so that he said he could most wish there hadn't ever been no snakes created. Why, after every last snake had been gone clear out of the house for as much as a week Aunt Sally warn't over it yet; she warn't near over it; when she was setting thinking about something you could touch her on the back of her neck with a feather and she would jump right out of her stockings. It was very curious. But Tom said all women was just so. He said they was made that way for some reason or other.

We got a licking every time one of our snakes come in her way, and she allowed these lickings warn't nothing to what she would do if we ever loaded up the place again with them. I didn't mind the lickings, because they didn't amount to nothing; but I minded the trouble we had to lay in another lot. But we got them laid in, and all the other things; and you never see a cabin as blithesome as Jim's was when they'd all swarm out for music and go for him. Jim didn't like the spiders, and the spiders didn't like Jim; and so they'd lay for him, and make it mighty warm for him. And he said that between the rats and the snakes and the grindstone there warn't no room in bed for him, skasely; and when there was, a body couldn't sleep, it was so lively, and it was always lively, he said, because THEY never all slept at one time, but took turn about, so when the snakes was asleep the rats was on deck, and when the rats turned in the snakes come on watch, so he always had one gang under him, in his way, and t'other gang having a circus over him, and if he got up to hunt a new place the spiders would take a chance at him as he crossed over. He said if he ever got out this time he wouldn't ever be a prisoner again, not for a salary.

Well, by the end of three weeks everything was in pretty good shape. The shirt was sent in early, in a pie, and every time a rat bit Jim he would get up and write a little in his journal whilst the ink was fresh; the pens was made, the inscriptions and so on was all carved on the grindstone; the bed-leg was sawed in two, and we had et up the sawdust, and it give us a most amazing stomach-ache. We reckoned we was all going to die, but didn't. It was the most undigestible sawdust I ever see; and Tom said the same. But as I was saying, we'd got all the work done now, at last; and we was all pretty much fagged out, too, but mainly Jim. The old man had wrote a couple of times to the plantation below Orleans to come and get their runaway nigger, but hadn't got no answer, because there warn't no such plantation; so he allowed he would advertise Jim in the St. Louis and New Orleans papers; and when he mentioned the St. Louis ones it give me the cold shivers, and I see we hadn't no time to lose. So Tom said, now for the nonnamous letters.

"What's them?" I says.

"Warnings to the people that something is up. Sometimes it's done one way, sometimes another. But there's always somebody spying around that gives notice to the governor of the castle. When Louis XVI was going to light out of the Tooleries a servant-girl done it. It's a very good way, and so is the nonnamous letters. We'll use them both. And it's usual for the prisoner's mother to change clothes with him, and she stays in, and he slides out in her clothes. We'll do that, too."

"But looky here, Tom, what do we want to WARN anybody for that something's up? Let them find it out for themselves—it's their lookout."

"Yes, I know; but you can't depend on them. It's the way they've acted from the very start—left us to do EVERYTHING. They're so confiding and mullet-headed they don't take notice of nothing at all. So if we don't GIVE them notice there won't be nobody nor nothing to interfere with us, and so after all our hard work and trouble this escape 'll go off perfectly flat; won't amount to nothing—won't be nothing TO it."

"Well, as for me, Tom, that's the way I'd like."

"Shucks!" he says, and looked disgusted. So I says:

"But I ain't going to make no complaint. Any way that suits you suits me. What you going to do about the servant-girl?"

"You'll be her. You slide in, in the middle of the night, and hook that yaller girl's frock."

"Why, Tom, that 'll make trouble next morning; because, of course, she prob'ly hain't got any but that one."

"I know; but you don't want it but fifteen minutes, to carry the nonnamous letter and shove it under the front door."

"All right, then, I'll do it; but I could carry it just as handy in my own togs."

"You wouldn't look like a servant-girl THEN, would you?"

"No, but there won't be nobody to see what I look like, ANYWAY."

"That ain't got nothing to do with it. The thing for us to do is just to do our DUTY, and not worry about whether anybody SEES us do it or not. Hain't you got no principle at all?"

"All right, I ain't saying nothing; I'm the servant-girl. Who's Jim's mother?"

"I'm his mother. I'll hook a gown from Aunt Sally."

"Well, then, you'll have to stay in the cabin when me and Jim leaves."

"Not much. I'll stuff Jim's clothes full of straw and lay it on his bed to represent his mother in disguise, and Jim 'll take the nigger woman's gown off of me and wear it, and we'll all evade together. When a prisoner of style escapes it's called an evasion. It's always called so when a king escapes, f'rinstance. And the same with a king's son; it don't make no difference whether he's a natural one or an unnatural one."

So Tom he wrote the nonnamous letter, and I smouched the yaller wench's frock that night, and put it on, and shoved it under the front door, the way Tom told me to. It said:

Beware. Trouble is brewing. Keep a sharp lookout. UNKNOWN FRIEND.

Next night we stuck a picture, which Tom drawed in blood, of a skull and crossbones on the front door; and next night another one of a coffin on the back door. I never see a family in such a sweat. They couldn't a been worse scared if the place had a been full of ghosts laying for them behind everything and under the beds and shivering through the air. If a door banged, Aunt Sally she jumped and said "ouch!" if anything fell, she jumped and said "ouch!" if you happened to touch her, when she warn't noticing, she done the same; she couldn't face noway and be satisfied, because she allowed there was something behind her every time—so she was always a-whirling around sudden, and saying "ouch," and before she'd got two-thirds around she'd whirl back again, and say it again; and she was afraid to go to bed, but she dasn't set up. So the thing was working very well, Tom said; he said he never see a thing work more satisfactory. He said it showed it was done right.

So he said, now for the grand bulge! So the very next morning at the streak of dawn we got another letter ready, and was wondering what we better do with it, because we heard them say at supper they was going to have a nigger on watch at both doors all night. Tom he went down the lightning-rod to spy around; and the nigger at the back door was asleep, and he stuck it in the back of his neck and come back. This letter said:

> *Don't betray me, I wish to be your friend. There is a desprate gang of cut-throats from over in the Indian Territory going to steal your runaway nigger to-night, and they have been trying to scare you so as you will stay in the house and not bother them. I am one of the gang, but have got relligion and wish to quit it and lead an honest life again, and will betray the helish design. They will sneak down from northards, along the fence, at midnight exact, with a false key, and go in the nigger's cabin to get him. I am to be off a piece and blow a tin horn if I see any danger; but stead of that I will BA like a sheep soon as they get in and not blow at all; then whilst they are getting his chains loose, you slip there and lock them in, and can kill them at your leasure. Don't do anything but just the way I am telling you; if you do they will suspicion something and raise whoop-jamboreehoo. I do not wish any reward but to know I have done the right thing.*
>
> *UNKNOWN FRIEND.*

Chapter XL

We was feeling pretty good after breakfast, and took my canoe and went over the river a-fishing, with a lunch, and had a good time, and took a look at the raft and found her all right, and got home late to supper, and found them in such a sweat and worry they didn't know which end they was standing on, and made us go right off to bed the minute we was done supper, and wouldn't tell us what the trouble was, and never let on a word about the new letter, but didn't need to, because we knowed as much about it as anybody did, and as soon as we was half up stairs and her back was turned we slid for the cellar cupboard and loaded up a good lunch and took it up to our room and went to bed, and got up about half-past eleven, and Tom put on Aunt Sally's dress that he stole and was going to start with the lunch, but says:

"Where's the butter?"

"I laid out a hunk of it," I says, "on a piece of a corn-pone."

"Well, you LEFT it laid out, then—it ain't here."

"We can get along without it," I says.

"We can get along WITH it, too," he says; "just you slide down cellar and fetch it. And then mosey right down the lightning-rod and come along. I'll go and stuff the straw into Jim's clothes to represent his mother in disguise, and be ready to BA like a sheep and shove soon as you get there."

So out he went, and down cellar went I. The hunk of butter, big as a person's fist, was where I had left it, so I took up the slab of corn-pone with it on, and blowed out my light, and started up stairs very stealthy, and got up to the main floor all right, but here comes Aunt Sally with a candle, and I clapped the truck in my hat, and clapped my hat on my head, and the next second she see me; and she says:

"You been down cellar?"

"Yes'm."

"What you been doing down there?"

"Noth'n."

"NOTH'N!"

"No'm."

"Well, then, what possessed you to go down there this time of night?"

"I don't know 'm."

"You don't KNOW? Don't answer me that way. Tom, I want to know what you been DOING down there."

"I hain't been doing a single thing, Aunt Sally, I hope to gracious if I have."

I reckoned she'd let me go now, and as a generl thing she would; but I s'pose there was so many strange things going on she was just in a sweat about every little thing that warn't yard-stick straight; so she says, very decided:

"You just march into that setting-room and stay there till I come. You been up to something you no business to, and I lay I'll find out what it is before I'M done with you."

So she went away as I opened the door and walked into the setting-room. My, but there was a crowd there! Fifteen farmers, and every one of them had a gun. I was most powerful sick, and slunk to a chair and set down. They was setting around, some of them talking a little, in a low voice, and all of them fidgety and uneasy, but trying to look like they warn't; but I knowed they was, because they was always taking off their hats, and putting them on, and scratching their heads, and changing their seats, and fumbling with their buttons. I warn't easy myself, but I didn't take my hat off, all the same.

I did wish Aunt Sally would come, and get done with me, and lick me, if she wanted to, and let me get away and tell Tom how we'd overdone this thing, and what a thundering hornet's-nest we'd got ourselves into, so we could stop fooling around straight off, and clear out with Jim before these rips got out of patience and come for us.

At last she come and begun to ask me questions, but I COULDN'T answer them straight, I didn't know which end of me was up; because these men was in such a fidget now that some was wanting to start right NOW and lay for them desperadoes, and saying it warn't but a few minutes to midnight; and others was trying to get them to hold on and wait for the sheep-signal; and here was Aunty pegging away at the questions, and me a-shaking all over and ready to sink down in my tracks I was that scared; and the place getting hotter and hotter, and the butter beginning to melt and run down my neck and behind my ears; and pretty soon, when one of them says, "I'M for going and getting in the cabin FIRST and right NOW, and catching them when they come," I most dropped; and a streak of butter come a-trickling down my forehead, and Aunt Sally she see it, and turns white as a sheet, and says:

"For the land's sake, what IS the matter with the child? He's got the brain-fever as shore as you're born, and they're oozing out!"

And everybody runs to see, and she snatches off my hat, and out comes the bread and what was left of the butter, and she grabbed me, and hugged me, and says:

"Oh, what a turn you did give me! and how glad and grateful I am it ain't no worse; for luck's against us, and it never rains but it pours, and when I see that truck I thought we'd lost you, for I knowed by the color and all it was just like your brains would be if—Dear, dear, whyd'nt you TELL me that was what you'd been down there for, I wouldn't a cared. Now cler out to bed, and don't lemme see no more of you till morning!"

I was up stairs in a second, and down the lightning-rod in another one, and shinning through the dark for the lean-to. I couldn't hardly get my words out, I was so anxious; but I told Tom as quick as I could we must jump for it now, and not a minute to lose—the house full of men, yonder, with guns!

His eyes just blazed; and he says:

"No!—is that so? AIN'T it bully! Why, Huck, if it was to do over again, I bet I could fetch two hundred! If we could put it off till—"

"Hurry! HURRY!" I says. "Where's Jim?"

"Right at your elbow; if you reach out your arm you can touch him. He's dressed, and everything's ready. Now we'll slide out and give the sheep-signal."

But then we heard the tramp of men coming to the door, and heard them begin to fumble with the pad-lock, and heard a man say:

"I TOLD you we'd be too soon; they haven't come—the door is locked. Here, I'll lock some of you into the cabin, and you lay for 'em in the dark and kill 'em when they come; and the rest scatter around a piece, and listen if you can hear 'em coming."

So in they come, but couldn't see us in the dark, and most trod on us whilst we was hustling to get under the bed. But we got under all right, and out through the hole, swift but soft—Jim first, me next, and Tom last, which was according to Tom's orders. Now we was in the lean-to, and heard trampings close by outside. So we crept to the door, and Tom stopped us there and put his eye to the crack, but couldn't make out nothing, it was so dark; and whispered and said he would listen for the steps to get further, and when he nudged us Jim must glide out first, and him last. So he set his ear to the crack and listened, and listened, and listened, and the steps a-scraping around out there all the time; and at last he nudged us, and we slid out, and stooped down, not breathing, and not making the least noise, and slipped stealthy towards the fence in Injun file, and got to it all right, and me and Jim over it; but Tom's britches catched fast on a splinter on the top rail, and then he hear the steps coming, so he had to pull loose, which snapped the splinter and made a noise; and as he dropped in our tracks and started somebody sings out:

"Who's that? Answer, or I'll shoot!"

But we didn't answer; we just unfurled our heels and shoved. Then there was a rush, and a BANG, BANG, BANG! and the bullets fairly whizzed around us! We heard them sing out:

"Here they are! They've broke for the river! After 'em, boys, and turn loose the dogs!"

So here they come, full tilt. We could hear them because they wore boots and yelled, but we didn't wear no boots and didn't yell. We was in the path to the mill; and when they got pretty close on to us we dodged into the bush and let them go by, and then dropped in behind them. They'd had all the dogs shut up, so they wouldn't scare off the robbers; but by this time somebody had let them loose, and here they come, making powwow enough for a million; but they was our dogs; so we stopped in our tracks till they catched up; and when they see it warn't nobody but us, and no excitement to offer them, they only just said howdy, and tore right ahead towards the shouting and clattering; and then we up-steam again, and whizzed along after them till we was nearly to the mill, and then struck up through the bush to where my canoe was tied, and hopped in and pulled for dear life towards the middle of the river, but didn't make no more noise than we was obleeged to. Then we struck out, easy and comfortable, for the island where my raft was; and we could hear them yelling and barking at each other all up and down the bank, till we was so far away the sounds got dim and died out. And when we stepped on to the raft I says:

"NOW, old Jim, you're a free man again, and I bet you won't ever be a slave no more."

"En a mighty good job it wuz, too, Huck. It 'uz planned beautiful, en it 'uz done beautiful; en dey ain't NOBODY kin git up a plan dat's mo' mixed-up en splendid den what dat one wuz."

We was all glad as we could be, but Tom was the gladdest of all because he had a bullet in the calf of his leg.

When me and Jim heard that we didn't feel so brash as what we did before. It was hurting him considerable, and bleeding; so we laid him in the wigwam and tore up one of the duke's shirts for to bandage him, but he says:

"Gimme the rags; I can do it myself. Don't stop now; don't fool around here, and the evasion booming along so handsome; man the sweeps, and set her loose! Boys, we done it elegant!—'deed we did. I wish WE'D a had the handling of Louis XVI., there wouldn't a been no 'Son of Saint Louis, ascend to heaven!' wrote down in HIS biography; no, sir, we'd a whooped him over the BORDER—that's what we'd a done with HIM—and done it just as slick as nothing at all, too. Man the sweeps—man the sweeps!"

But me and Jim was consulting—and thinking. And after we'd thought a minute, I says:

"Say it, Jim."

So he says:

"Well, den, dis is de way it look to me, Huck. Ef it wuz HIM dat 'uz bein' sot free, en one er de boys wuz to git shot, would he say, 'Go on en save me, nemmine 'bout a doctor f'r to save dis one?' Is dat like Mars Tom Sawyer? Would he say dat? You BET he wouldn't! WELL, den, is JIM gywne to say it? No, sah—I doan' budge a step out'n dis place 'dout a DOCTOR, not if it's forty year!"

I knowed he was white inside, and I reckoned he'd say what he did say—so it was all right now, and I told Tom I was a-going for a doctor. He raised considerable row about it, but me and Jim stuck to it and wouldn't budge; so he was for crawling out and setting the raft loose himself; but we wouldn't let him. Then he give us a piece of his mind, but it didn't do no good.

So when he sees me getting the canoe ready, he says:

"Well, then, if you re bound to go, I'll tell you the way to do when you get to the village. Shut the door and blindfold the doctor tight and fast, and make him swear to be silent as the grave, and put a purse full of gold in his hand, and then take and lead him all around the back alleys and everywheres in the dark, and then fetch him here in the canoe, in a roundabout way amongst the islands, and search him and take his chalk away from him, and don't give it back to him till you get him back to the village, or else he will chalk this raft so he can find it again. It's the way they all do."

So I said I would, and left, and Jim was to hide in the woods when he see the doctor coming till he was gone again.

Chapter XLI

The doctor was an old man; a very nice, kind-looking old man when I got him up. I told him me and my brother was over on Spanish Island hunting yesterday afternoon, and camped on a piece of a raft we found, and about midnight he must a kicked his gun in his dreams, for it went off and shot him in the leg, and we wanted him to go over there and fix it and not say nothing about it, nor let anybody know, because we wanted to come home this evening and surprise the folks.

"Who is your folks?" he says.

"The Phelpses, down yonder."

"Oh," he says. And after a minute, he says:

"How'd you say he got shot?"

"He had a dream," I says, "and it shot him."

"Singular dream," he says.

So he lit up his lantern, and got his saddle-bags, and we started. But when he sees the canoe he didn't like the look of her—said she was big enough for one, but didn't look pretty safe for two. I says:

"Oh, you needn't be afeard, sir, she carried the three of us easy enough."

"What three?"

"Why, me and Sid, and—and—and THE GUNS; that's what I mean."

"Oh," he says.

But he put his foot on the gunnel and rocked her, and shook his head, and said he reckoned he'd look around for a bigger one. But they was all locked and chained; so he took my canoe, and said for me to wait till he come back, or I could hunt around further, or maybe I better go down home and get them ready for the surprise if I wanted to. But I said I didn't; so I told him just how to find the raft, and then he started.

I struck an idea pretty soon. I says to myself, spos'n he can't fix that leg just in three shakes of a sheep's tail, as the saying is? spos'n it takes him three or four days? What are we going to do?—lay around there till he lets the cat out of the bag? No, sir; I know what I'LL do. I'll wait, and when he comes back if he says he's got to go any more I'll get down there, too, if I swim; and we'll take and tie him, and keep him, and shove out down the river; and when Tom's done with him we'll give him what it's worth, or all we got, and then let him get ashore.

So then I crept into a lumber-pile to get some sleep; and next time I waked up the sun was away up over my head! I shot out and went for the doctor's house, but they told me he'd gone away in the night some time or other, and warn't back yet. Well, thinks I, that looks powerful bad for Tom, and I'll dig out for the island right off. So away I shoved, and turned the corner, and nearly rammed my head into Uncle Silas's stomach!

He says:

"Why, TOM! Where you been all this time, you rascal?"

"I hain't been nowheres," I says, "only just hunting for the runaway nigger—me and Sid."

"Why, where ever did you go?" he says. "Your aunt's been mighty uneasy."

"She needn't," I says, "because we was all right. We followed the men and the dogs, but they outrun us, and we lost them; but we thought we heard them on the water, so we got a canoe and took out after them and crossed over, but couldn't find nothing of them; so we cruised along up-shore till we got kind of tired and beat out; and tied up the canoe and went to sleep, and never waked up till about an hour ago; then we paddled over here to hear the news, and Sid's at the post-office to see what he can hear, and I'm a-branching out to get something to eat for us, and then we're going home."

So then we went to the post-office to get "Sid"; but just as I suspicioned, he warn't there; so the old man he got a letter out of the office, and we waited awhile longer, but Sid didn't come; so the old man said, come along, let Sid foot it home, or canoe it, when he got done fooling around—but we would ride. I couldn't get him to let me stay and wait for Sid; and he said there warn't no use in it, and I must come along, and let Aunt Sally see we was all right.

When we got home Aunt Sally was that glad to see me she laughed and cried both, and hugged me, and give me one of them lickings of hern that don't amount to shucks, and said she'd serve Sid the same when he come.

And the place was plum full of farmers and farmers' wives, to dinner; and such another clack a body never heard. Old Mrs. Hotchkiss was the worst; her tongue was a-going all the time. She says:

"Well, Sister Phelps, I've ransacked that-air cabin over, an' I b'lieve the nigger was crazy. I says to Sister Damrell—didn't I, Sister Damrell?—s'I, he's crazy, s'I—them's the very words I said. You all hearn me: he's crazy, s'I; everything shows it, s'I. Look at that-air grindstone, s'I; want to tell ME 't any cretur 't's in his right mind 's a goin' to scrabble all them crazy things onto a grindstone, s'I? Here sich 'n' sich a person busted his heart; 'n' here so 'n' so pegged along for thirty-seven year, 'n' all that—natcherl son o' Louis somebody, 'n' sich everlast'n rubbage. He's plumb crazy, s'I; it's what I says in the fust place, it's what I says in the middle, 'n' it's what I says last 'n' all the time—the nigger's crazy—crazy 's Nebokoodneezer, s'I."

"An' look at that-air ladder made out'n rags, Sister Hotchkiss," says old Mrs. Damrell; "what in the name o' goodness COULD he ever want of—"

"The very words I was a-sayin' no longer ago th'n this minute to Sister Utterback, 'n' she'll tell you so herself. Sh-she, look at that-air rag ladder, sh-she; 'n' s'I, yes, LOOK at it, s'I—what COULD he a-wanted of it, s'I. Sh-she, Sister Hotchkiss, sh-she—"

"But how in the nation'd they ever GIT that grindstone IN there, ANYWAY? 'n' who dug that-air HOLE? 'n' who—"

"My very WORDS, Brer Penrod! I was a-sayin'—pass that-air sasser o' m'lasses, won't ye?—I was a-sayin' to Sister Dunlap, jist this minute, how DID they git that grindstone in there, s'I. Without HELP, mind you —'thout HELP! THAT'S wher 'tis. Don't tell ME, s'I; there WUZ help, s'I; 'n' ther' wuz a PLENTY help, too, s'I; ther's ben a DOZEN a-helpin' that nigger, 'n' I lay I'd skin every last nigger on this place but I'D find out who done it, s'I; 'n' moreover, s'I—"

"A DOZEN says you!—FORTY couldn't a done every thing that's been done. Look at them case-knife saws and things, how tedious they've been made; look at that bed-leg sawed off with 'm, a week's work for six men; look at that nigger made out'n straw on the bed; and look at—"

"You may WELL say it, Brer Hightower! It's jist as I was a-sayin' to Brer Phelps, his own self. S'e, what do YOU think of it, Sister Hotchkiss, s'e? Think o' what, Brer Phelps, s'I? Think o' that bed-leg sawed off that a way, s'e? THINK of it, s'I? I lay it never sawed ITSELF off, s'I—somebody SAWED it, s'I; that's my opinion, take it or leave it, it mayn't be no 'count, s'I, but sich as 't is, it's my opinion, s'I, 'n' if any body k'n start a better one, s'I, let him DO it, s'I, that's all. I says to Sister Dunlap, s'I—"

"Why, dog my cats, they must a ben a house-full o' niggers in there every night for four weeks to a done all that work, Sister Phelps. Look at that shirt—every last inch of it kivered over with secret African writ'n done with blood! Must a ben a raft uv 'm at it right along, all the time, amost. Why, I'd give two dollars to have it read to me; 'n' as for the niggers that wrote it, I 'low I'd take 'n' lash 'm t'll—"

"People to HELP him, Brother Marples! Well, I reckon you'd THINK so if you'd a been in this house for a while back. Why, they've stole everything they could lay their hands on—and we a-watching all the time, mind you. They stole that shirt right off o' the line! and as for that sheet they made the rag ladder out of, ther' ain't no telling how many times they DIDN'T steal that; and flour, and candles, and candle-sticks, and spoons, and the old warming-pan, and most a thousand things that I disremember now, and my new calico dress; and me and Silas and my Sid and Tom on the constant watch day AND night, as I was a-telling you, and not a one of us could catch hide nor hair nor sight nor sound of them; and here at the last minute, lo and behold you, they slides right in under our noses and fools us, and not only fools US but the Injun Territory robbers too, and actuly gets AWAY with that nigger safe and sound, and that with sixteen men and twenty-two dogs right on their very heels at that very time! I tell you, it just bangs anything I ever HEARD of. Why, SPERITS couldn't a done better and been no smarter. And I reckon they must a BEEN sperits—because, YOU know our dogs, and ther' ain't no better; well, them dogs never even got on the TRACK of 'm once! You explain THAT to me if you can!—ANY of you!"

"Well, it does beat—"

"Laws alive, I never—"

"So help me, I wouldn't a be—"

"HOUSE-thieves as well as—"

"Goodnessgracioussakes, I'd a ben afeard to live in sich a—"

"'Fraid to LIVE!—why, I was that scared I dasn't hardly go to bed, or get up, or lay down, or SET down, Sister Ridgeway. Why, they'd steal the very—why, goodness sakes, you can guess what kind of a fluster I was in by the time midnight come last night. I hope to gracious if I warn't afraid they'd steal some o' the family! I was just to that pass I didn't have no reasoning faculties no more. It looks foolish enough NOW, in the daytime; but I says to myself, there's my two poor boys asleep, 'way up stairs in that lonesome room, and I declare to goodness I was that uneasy 't I crep' up there and locked 'em in! I DID. And anybody would. Because, you know, when you get scared that way, and it keeps running on, and getting worse and worse all the time, and your wits gets to addling, and you get to doing all sorts o' wild things, and by and by you think to yourself, spos'n I was a boy, and was away up there, and the door ain't locked, and you—" She stopped, looking kind of wondering, and then she turned her head around slow, and when her eye lit on me—I got up and took a walk.

Says I to myself, I can explain better how we come to not be in that room this morning if I go out to one side and study over it a little. So I done it. But I dasn't go fur, or she'd a sent for me. And when it was late in the day the people all went, and then I come in and told her the noise and shooting waked up me and "Sid," and the door was locked, and we wanted to see the fun, so we went down the lightning-rod, and both of us got hurt a little, and we didn't never want to try THAT no more. And then I went on and told her all what I told Uncle Silas before; and then she said she'd forgive us, and maybe it was all right enough anyway, and about what a body might expect of boys, for all boys was a pretty harum-scarum lot as fur as she could see; and so, as long as no harm hadn't come of it, she judged she better put in her time being grateful we was alive and well and she had us still, stead of fretting over what was past and done. So then she kissed me, and patted me on the head, and dropped into a kind of a brown study; and pretty soon jumps up, and says:

"Why, lawsamercy, it's most night, and Sid not come yet! What HAS become of that boy?"

I see my chance; so I skips up and says:

"I'll run right up to town and get him," I says.

"No you won't," she says. "You'll stay right wher' you are; ONE'S enough to be lost at a time. If he ain't here to supper, your uncle 'll go."

Well, he warn't there to supper; so right after supper uncle went.

He come back about ten a little bit uneasy; hadn't run across Tom's track. Aunt Sally was a good DEAL uneasy; but Uncle Silas he said there warn't no ccasion to be—boys will be boys, he said, and you'll see this one turn up in the morning all sound and right. So she had to be satisfied. But she said she'd set up for him a while anyway, and keep a light burning so he could see it.

And then when I went up to bed she come up with me and fetched her candle, and tucked me in, and mothered me so good I felt mean, and like I couldn't look her in the face; and she set down on the bed and talked with me a long time, and said what a splendid boy Sid was, and didn't seem to want to ever stop talking about him; and kept asking me every now and then if I reckoned he could a got lost, or hurt, or maybe drownded, and might be laying at this minute somewheres suffering or dead, and she not by him to help him, and so the tears would drip down silent, and I would tell her that Sid was all right, and would be home in the morning, sure; and she would squeeze my hand, or maybe kiss me, and tell me to say it again, and keep on saying it, because it done her good, and she was in so much trouble. And when she was going away she looked down in my eyes so steady and gentle, and says:

"The door ain't going to be locked, Tom, and there's the window and the rod; but you'll be good, WON'T you? And you won't go? For MY sake."

Laws knows I WANTED to go bad enough to see about Tom, and was all intending to go; but after that I wouldn't a went, not for kingdoms.

But she was on my mind and Tom was on my mind, so I slept very restless. And twice I went down the rod away in the night, and slipped around front, and see her setting there by her candle in the window with her eyes towards the road and the tears in them; and I wished I could do something for her, but I couldn't, only to swear that I wouldn't never do nothing to grieve her any more. And the third time I waked up at dawn, and slid down, and she was there yet, and her candle was most out, and her old gray head was resting on her hand, and she was asleep.

Chapter XLII

The old man was uptown again before breakfast, but couldn't get no track of Tom; and both of them set at the table thinking, and not saying nothing, and looking mournful, and their coffee getting cold, and not eating anything. And by and by the old man says:

"Did I give you the letter?"

"What letter?"

"The one I got yesterday out of the post-office."

"No, you didn't give me no letter."

"Well, I must a forgot it."

So he rummaged his pockets, and then went off somewheres where he had laid it down, and fetched it, and give it to her. She says:

"Why, it's from St. Petersburg—it's from Sis."

I allowed another walk would do me good; but I couldn't stir. But before she could break it open she dropped it and run—for she see something. And so did I. It was Tom Sawyer on a mattress; and that old doctor; and Jim, in HER calico dress, with his hands tied behind him; and a lot of people. I hid the letter behind the first thing that come handy, and rushed. She flung herself at Tom, crying, and says:

"Oh, he's dead, he's dead, I know he's dead!"

And Tom he turned his head a little, and muttered something or other, which showed he warn't in his right mind; then she flung up her hands, and says:

"He's alive, thank God! And that's enough!" and she snatched a kiss of him, and flew for the house to get the bed ready, and scattering orders right and left at the niggers and everybody else, as fast as her tongue could go, every jump of the way.

I followed the men to see what they was going to do with Jim; and the old doctor and Uncle Silas followed after Tom into the house. The men was very huffy, and some of them wanted to hang Jim for an example to all the other niggers around there, so they wouldn't be trying to run away like Jim done, and making such a raft of trouble, and keeping a whole family scared most to death for days and nights. But the others said, don't do it, it wouldn't answer at all; he ain't our nigger, and his owner would turn up and make us pay for him, sure. So that cooled them down a little, because the people that's always the most anxious for to hang a nigger that hain't done just right is always the very ones that ain't the most anxious to pay for him when they've got their satisfaction out of him.

They cussed Jim considerble, though, and give him a cuff or two side the head once in a while, but Jim never said nothing, and he never let on to know me, and they took him to the same cabin, and put his own clothes on him, and chained him again, and not to no bed-leg this time, but to a big staple drove into the bottom log, and chained his hands, too, and both legs, and said he warn't to have nothing but bread and water to eat after this till his owner come, or he was sold at auction because he didn't come in a certain length of time, and filled up our hole, and said a couple of farmers with guns must stand watch around about the cabin every night, and a bulldog tied to the door in the daytime; and about this time they was through with the job and was tapering off with a kind of generl good-bye cussing, and then the old doctor comes and takes a look, and says:

"Don't be no rougher on him than you're obleeged to, because he ain't a bad nigger. When I got to where I found the boy I see I couldn't cut the bullet out without some help, and he warn't in no condition for me to leave to go and get help; and he got a little worse and a little worse, and after a long time he went out of his head, and wouldn't let me come a-nigh him any more, and said if I chalked his raft he'd kill me, and no end of wild foolishness like that, and I see I couldn't do anything at all with him; so I says, I got to have HELP somehow; and the minute I says it out crawls this nigger from somewheres and says he'll help, and he done it, too, and done it very well. Of course I judged he must be a runaway nigger, and there I WAS! and there I had to stick right straight along all the rest of the day and all night. It was a fix, I tell you! I had a couple of patients with the chills, and of course I'd of liked to run up to town and see them, but I dasn't, because the nigger might get away, and then I'd be to blame; and yet never a skiff come close enough for me to hail. So there I had to stick plumb until daylight this morning; and I never see a nigger that was a better nuss or faithfuller, and yet he was risking his freedom to do it, and was all tired out, too, and I see plain enough he'd been worked main hard lately. I liked the nigger for that; I tell you, gentlemen, a nigger like that is worth a thousand dollars—and kind treatment, too. I had everything I needed, and the boy was doing as well there as he would a done at home— better, maybe, because it was so quiet; but there I WAS, with both of 'm on my hands, and there I had to stick till about dawn this morning; then some men in a skiff come by, and as good luck would have it the nigger was setting by the pallet with his head propped on his knees sound asleep; so I motioned them in quiet, and they slipped up on him and grabbed him and tied him before he knowed what he was about, and we never had no trouble. And the boy being in a kind of a flighty sleep, too, we muffled the oars and hitched the raft on, and towed her over very nice and quiet, and the nigger never made the least row nor said a word from the start. He ain't no bad nigger, gentlemen; that's what I think about him."

Somebody says:

"Well, it sounds very good, doctor, I'm obleeged to say."

Then the others softened up a little, too, and I was mighty thankful to that old doctor for doing Jim that good turn; and I was glad it was according to my judgment of him, too; because I thought he had a good heart in him and was a good man the first time I see him. Then they all agreed that Jim had acted very well, and was deserving to have some notice took of it, and reward. So every one of them promised, right out and hearty, that they wouldn't cuss him no more.

Then they come out and locked him up. I hoped they was going to say he could have one or two of the chains took off, because they was rotten heavy, or could have meat and greens with his bread and water; but they didn't think of it, and I reckoned it warn't best for me to mix in, but I judged I'd get the doctor's yarn to Aunt Sally somehow or other as soon as I'd got through the breakers that was laying just ahead of me —explanations, I mean, of how I forgot to mention about Sid being shot when I was telling how him and me put in that dratted night paddling around hunting the runaway nigger.

But I had plenty time. Aunt Sally she stuck to the sick-room all day and all night, and every time I see Uncle Silas mooning around I dodged him.

Next morning I heard Tom was a good deal better, and they said Aunt Sally was gone to get a nap. So I slips to the sick-room, and if I found him awake I reckoned we could put up a yarn for the family that would wash. But he was sleeping, and sleeping very peaceful, too; and pale, not fire-faced the way he was when he come. So I set down and laid for him to wake. In about half an hour Aunt Sally comes gliding in, and there I was, up a stump again! She motioned me to be still, and set down by me, and begun to whisper, and said we could all be joyful now, because all the symptoms was first-rate, and he'd been sleeping like that for ever so long, and looking better and peacefuller all the time, and ten to one he'd wake up in his right mind.

So we set there watching, and by and by he stirs a bit, and opened his eyes very natural, and takes a look, and says:

"Hello!—why, I'm at HOME! How's that? Where's the raft?"

"It's all right," I says.

"And JIM?"

"The same," I says, but couldn't say it pretty brash. But he never noticed, but says:

"Good! Splendid! NOW we're all right and safe! Did you tell Aunty?"

I was going to say yes; but she chipped in and says: "About what, Sid?"

"Why, about the way the whole thing was done."

"What whole thing?"

"Why, THE whole thing. There ain't but one; how we set the runaway nigger free—me and Tom."

"Good land! Set the run—What IS the child talking about! Dear, dear, out of his head again!"

"NO, I ain't out of my HEAD; I know all what I'm talking about. We DID set him free—me and Tom. We laid out to do it, and we DONE it. And we done it elegant, too." He'd got a start, and she never checked him up, just set and stared and stared, and let him clip along, and I see it warn't no use for ME to put in. "Why, Aunty, it cost us a power of work —weeks of it—hours and hours, every night, whilst you was all asleep. And we had to steal candles, and the sheet, and the shirt, and your dress, and spoons, and tin plates, and case-knives, and the warming-pan, and the grindstone, and flour, and just no end of things, and you can't think what work it was to make the saws, and pens, and inscriptions, and one thing or another, and you can't think HALF the fun it was. And we had to make up the pictures of coffins and things, and nonnamous letters from the robbers, and get up and down the lightning-rod, and dig the hole into the cabin, and made the rope ladder and send it in cooked up in a pie, and send in spoons and things to work with in your apron pocket—"

"Mercy sakes!"

"—and load up the cabin with rats and snakes and so on, for company for Jim; and then you kept Tom here so long with the butter in his hat that you come near spiling the whole business, because the men come before we was out of the cabin, and we had to rush, and they heard us and let drive at us, and I got my share, and we dodged out of the path and let them go by, and when the dogs come they warn't interested in us, but went for the most noise, and we got our canoe, and made for the raft, and was all safe, and Jim was a free man, and we done it all by ourselves, and WASN'T it bully, Aunty!"

"Well, I never heard the likes of it in all my born days! So it was YOU, you little rapscallions, that's been making all this trouble, and turned everybody's wits clean inside out and scared us all most to death. I've as good a notion as ever I had in my life to take it out o' you this very minute. To think, here I've been, night after night, a—YOU just get well once, you young scamp, and I lay I'll tan the Old Harry out o' both o' ye!"

But Tom, he WAS so proud and joyful, he just COULDN'T hold in, and his tongue just WENT it—she a-chipping in, and spitting fire all along, and both of them going it at once, like a cat convention; and she says:

"WELL, you get all the enjoyment you can out of it NOW, for mind I tell you if I catch you meddling with him again—"

"Meddling with WHO?" Tom says, dropping his smile and looking surprised.

"With WHO? Why, the runaway nigger, of course. Who'd you reckon?"

Tom looks at me very grave, and says:

"Tom, didn't you just tell me he was all right? Hasn't he got away?"

"HIM?" says Aunt Sally; "the runaway nigger? 'Deed he hasn't. They've got him back, safe and sound, and he's in that cabin again, on bread and water, and loaded down with chains, till he's claimed or sold!"

Tom rose square up in bed, with his eye hot, and his nostrils opening and shutting like gills, and sings out to me:

"They hain't no RIGHT to shut him up! SHOVE!—and don't you lose a minute. Turn him loose! he ain't no slave; he's as free as any cretur that walks this earth!"

"What DOES the child mean?"

"I mean every word I SAY, Aunt Sally, and if somebody don't go, I'LL go. I've knowed him all his life, and so has Tom, there. Old Miss Watson died two months ago, and she was ashamed she ever was going to sell him down the river, and SAID so; and she set him free in her will."

"Then what on earth did YOU want to set him free for, seeing he was already free?"

"Well, that IS a question, I must say; and just like women! Why, I wanted the ADVENTURE of it; and I'd a waded neck-deep in blood to —goodness alive, AUNT POLLY!"

If she warn't standing right there, just inside the door, looking as sweet and contented as an angel half full of pie, I wish I may never!

Aunt Sally jumped for her, and most hugged the head off of her, and cried over her, and I found a good enough place for me under the bed, for it was getting pretty sultry for us, seemed to me. And I peeped out, and in a little while Tom's Aunt Polly shook herself loose and stood there looking across at Tom over her spectacles—kind of grinding him into the earth, you know. And then she says:

"Yes, you BETTER turn y'r head away—I would if I was you, Tom."

"Oh, deary me!" says Aunt Sally; "IS he changed so? Why, that ain't TOM, it's Sid; Tom's—Tom's—why, where is Tom? He was here a minute ago."

"You mean where's Huck FINN—that's what you mean! I reckon I hain't raised such a scamp as my Tom all these years not to know him when I SEE him. That WOULD be a pretty howdy-do. Come out from under that bed, Huck Finn."

So I done it. But not feeling brash.

Aunt Sally she was one of the mixed-upest-looking persons I ever see —except one, and that was Uncle Silas, when he come in and they told it all to him. It kind of made him drunk, as you may say, and he didn't know nothing at all the rest of the day, and preached a prayer-meeting sermon that night that gave him a rattling ruputation, because the oldest man in the world couldn't a understood it. So Tom's Aunt Polly, she told all about who I was, and what; and I had to up and tell how I was in such a tight place that when Mrs. Phelps took me for Tom Sawyer—she chipped in and says, "Oh, go on and call me Aunt Sally, I'm used to it now, and 'tain't no need to change"—that when Aunt Sally took me for Tom Sawyer I had to stand it—there warn't no other way, and I knowed he wouldn't mind, because it would be nuts for him, being a mystery, and he'd make an adventure out of it, and be perfectly satisfied. And so it turned out, and he let on to be Sid, and made things as soft as he could for me.

And his Aunt Polly she said Tom was right about old Miss Watson setting

Jim free in her will; and so, sure enough, Tom Sawyer had gone and took all that trouble and bother to set a free nigger free! and I couldn't ever understand before, until that minute and that talk, how he COULD help a body set a nigger free with his bringing-up.

Well, Aunt Polly she said that when Aunt Sally wrote to her that Tom and SID had come all right and safe, she says to herself:

"Look at that, now! I might have expected it, letting him go off that way without anybody to watch him. So now I got to go and trapse all the way down the river, eleven hundred mile, and find out what that creetur's up to THIS time, as long as I couldn't seem to get any answer out of you about it."

"Why, I never heard nothing from you," says Aunt Sally.

"Well, I wonder! Why, I wrote you twice to ask you what you could mean by Sid being here."

"Well, I never got 'em, Sis."

Aunt Polly she turns around slow and severe, and says:

"You, Tom!"

"Well—WHAT?" he says, kind of pettish.

"Don t you what ME, you impudent thing—hand out them letters."

"What letters?"

"THEM letters. I be bound, if I have to take a-holt of you I'll—"

"They're in the trunk. There, now. And they're just the same as they was when I got them out of the office. I hain't looked into them, I hain't touched them. But I knowed they'd make trouble, and I thought if you warn't in no hurry, I'd—"

"Well, you DO need skinning, there ain't no mistake about it. And I wrote another one to tell you I was coming; and I s'pose he—"

"No, it come yesterday; I hain't read it yet, but IT'S all right, I've got that one."

I wanted to offer to bet two dollars she hadn't, but I reckoned maybe it was just as safe to not to. So I never said nothing.

Chapter the Last

The first time I catched Tom private I asked him what was his idea, time of the evasion?—what it was he'd planned to do if the evasion worked all right and he managed to set a nigger free that was already free before? And he said, what he had planned in his head from the start, if we got Jim out all safe, was for us to run him down the river on the raft, and have adventures plumb to the mouth of the river, and then tell him about his being free, and take him back up home on a steamboat, in style, and pay him for his lost time, and write word ahead and get out all the niggers around, and have them waltz him into town with a torchlight procession and a brass-band, and then he would be a hero, and so would we. But I reckoned it was about as well the way it was.

We had Jim out of the chains in no time, and when Aunt Polly and Uncle Silas and Aunt Sally found out how good he helped the doctor nurse Tom, they made a heap of fuss over him, and fixed him up prime, and give him all he wanted to eat, and a good time, and nothing to do. And we had him up to the sick-room, and had a high talk; and Tom give Jim forty dollars for being prisoner for us so patient, and doing it up so good, and Jim was pleased most to death, and busted out, and says:

"DAH, now, Huck, what I tell you?—what I tell you up dah on Jackson islan'? I TOLE you I got a hairy breas', en what's de sign un it; en I TOLE you I ben rich wunst, en gwineter to be rich AGIN; en it's come true; en heah she is! DAH, now! doan' talk to ME—signs is SIGNS, mine I tell you; en I knowed jis' 's well 'at I 'uz gwineter be rich agin as I's a-stannin' heah dis minute!"

And then Tom he talked along and talked along, and says, le's all three slide out of here one of these nights and get an outfit, and go for howling adventures amongst the Injuns, over in the Territory, for a couple of weeks or two; and I says, all right, that suits me, but I ain't got no money for to buy the outfit, and I reckon I couldn't get none from home, because it's likely pap's been back before now, and got it all away from Judge Thatcher and drunk it up.

"No, he hain't," Tom says; "it's all there yet—six thousand dollars and more; and your pap hain't ever been back since. Hadn't when I come away, anyhow."

Jim says, kind of solemn:

"He ain't a-comin' back no mo', Huck."

I says:

"Why, Jim?"

"Nemmine why, Huck—but he ain't comin' back no mo."

But I kept at him; so at last he says:

"Doan' you 'member de house dat was float'n down de river, en dey wuz a man in dah, kivered up, en I went in en unkivered him and didn' let you come in? Well, den, you kin git yo' money when you wants it, kase dat wuz him."

Tom's most well now, and got his bullet around his neck on a watch-guard for a watch, and is always seeing what time it is, and so there ain't nothing more to write about, and I am rotten glad of it, because if I'd a knowed what a trouble it was to make a book I wouldn't a tackled it, and ain't a-going to no more. But I reckon I got to light out for the Territory ahead of the rest, because Aunt Sally she's going to adopt me and sivilize me, and I can't stand it. I been there before.

The End

Made in the USA
San Bernardino, CA
05 August 2016